Recommended Reference Books
for Small and Medium-Sized Libraries
and Media Centers

American Reference Books Annual
Advisory Board

RECOMMENDED REFERENCE BOOKS

for Small and Medium-Sized Libraries
and Media Centers

Volume 36

2016 Edition

Juneal M. Chenoweth, Associate Editor

LIBRARIES
UNLIMITED™

An Imprint of ABC-CLIO, LLC
Santa Barbara, California • Denver, Colorado

LIBRARIES UNLIMITED
An Imprint of ABC-CLIO, LLC
130 Cremona Drive
P.O. Box 1911
Santa Barbara, California 93116-1911
www.abc-clio.com

Library of Congress Cataloging-in-Publication Data

Main entry under title:

Recommended reference books for small and medium-sized
libraries and media centers.

"Selected from the 2016 edition of American
reference books annual."
  Includes index.
  I. Reference books--Bibliography. 2. Reference
services (Library)--Handbooks, manuals, etc.
3. Instructional materials centers--Handbooks,
manuals, etc. I. Chenoweth, Juneal M.
II. American reference books annual.
Z1035.1.R435 011'.02 81-12394
ISBN 978-1-4408-4702-8
ISSN 0277-5948

Contents

Preface

Here is the interesting and challenging landscape for reference resources today. On the one hand, we clearly see the reference book diminished in the work of students, and the priorities of libraries. Going or gone are the vast collections of bound volumes in designated reference reading rooms. The disruptive element of course is technology: instantaneous access to online information. And reference seems to be the loser.

On the other hand, technology makes reference activity a winner too, but so seamlessly that the connection to old-fashioned reference work can be overlooked. All of us enjoy and use online tools to find airline ticket prices and flight schedules, weather forecasts and current conditions, currency exchange rates, stock prices, hotel and restaurant reviews, street maps, and foreign language translators. In the past we turned to print tools to meet these needs, with less convenience and less currency. Thanks to technology, we now have alternatives that match, and often surpass, yesterday's print reference works: timetables, weather almanacs, financial reports, tourist guidebooks, atlases, and bilingual dictionaries. So if reference is alive and well, but living under another name, where is the crisis? Which is to say, where is the change taking place?

Scholars have defined reference works in administrative, descriptive, and functional terms. The administration definition was something like this: "a reference book is a book located in a non-circulating reference collection." Today, we no longer focus on printed books (though we may work with their e-book descendants), and resource access is no longer confined to a specific place. The descriptive definition has been more durable: a reference work incorporates elements of organization and presentation that reflect and promote its intended use … consultation as quickly and easily as possible. Hence subject indexes, alphabetical order for entries, or numerical coding, as well as newer features like cross-reference hot links. The functional definition perhaps has held up the best: while many sources can conceivably be used to answer a "reference question," a reference work is created for that purpose, and its form (those elements in the descriptive definition) follows that function. As long as readers seek information, that function has value.

Nor have the characteristics of "good" reference tools changed: when we want information, we want information that is accurate, objective, authoritative, current, and complete, as well as reliably accessible, clearly presented, and easily understood. Online reference sources meet these requirements just as thoroughly as do print-format classics like the *Oxford English Dictionary*, the *World Book*, the *National Geographic World Atlas*, or the *Statistical Abstract of the United States* (all of which have expanded to online versions).

One final element makes modern life tough for reference: the general discounting of authority. Reference tools rely on the notion that important information is stable and therefore can be discovered, described, and evaluated. Behind the pursuit of "facts" to answer a reference query is an assumption that "facts" exist, that one answer is true and "best," that the "right" answer is available to us, and that reasonable people will agree about the "correct" answer when they see it. We may expect to argue about the best 10 American novels, but we expect to agree about the melting temperature of copper. In a world of relativism, conspiracy theories, and Heisenberg's uncertainty principle, not only are authorities in doubt, but even the facts themselves. And without the concept of correct facts, reference has no leg to stand on.

It is encouraging to see this aphorism widely quoted: "Everyone is entitled to his own opinion, but not to his own facts." When most of us can agree about facts, reference can thrive. Incidentally, this quotation itself illustrates the reference value of truth-seeking and fact-checking. Generally attributed to Daniel Patrick Moynihan, the *Dictionary of Modern Proverbs* (Yale, 2012) also documents similar statements extending back to Bernard Baruch in 1946.

If there are four participants in the ecology of reference—readers, authors, publishers, and librarians—then perhaps it is fair to say that two are leading and two are catching up. Readers still have plenty of questions to answer, and authors still eagerly turn out resources to meet that need. The challenges seem greatest for publishers and librarians, as value-added contributions shift from presentation in print to presentation in online form.

Steven W. Sowards, Michigan State University Libraries

Introduction

We are pleased to provide you with volume 36 of *Recommended Reference Books for Small and Medium-Sized Libraries and Media Centers* (RRB), a far-reaching review service for reference books and electronic resources designed to assist smaller libraries in the systematic selection of suitable reference materials for their collections. As Steven Sowards points out in the preface, the reference landscape has changed considerably since the publication of RRB's first volume in 1981. Reference users no longer need to spend hours in a library consulting bound volumes, microfiche, or microfilm when much sought-after information is available online. As the preface also highlights, this easy accessibility does not eliminate the need for well-curated, professionally produced reference material and the guidance of trained librarians.

RRB reviews both subscription-based and free Websites, as well as dictionaries, encyclopedias, indexes, directories, bibliographies, guides, concordances, atlases, gazetteers, and other types of ready-reference tools. Generally, encyclopedias that are updated annually, yearbooks, almanacs, indexing and abstracting services, and other annuals or serials are reviewed at editorially determined intervals. Reviews of updated publications attempt to point out changes in scope or editorial policy and comparisons to older editions.

This volume of RRB contains unabridged reviews chosen from the current edition of *American Reference Books Annual* (ARBA) and ARBAonline. These have been written by scholars, practitioners, and library educators in all subject specialties at libraries and universities throughout the United States and Canada. All titles in this volume are coded with letters that provide suggested selection guidance for smaller college libraries (C), public libraries (P), or school media centers (S). Although all titles in RRB are recommended acquisitions, critical comments have not been deleted. Reviewers are asked to examine books and electronic resources and provide well-documented critical comments, both positive and negative. Coverage usually includes the usefulness of a given work; organization, execution, and pertinence of contents; prose style; format; availability of supplementary materials (e.g., indexes, appendixes); and similarity to other works and previous editions.

RRB 2016 consists of 37 chapters, an Author/Title index, and a Subject Index. It is divided into four alphabetically arranged parts: "General Reference Works," "Social Sciences," "Humanities," and "Science and Technology." "General Reference Works" is subdivided by form: almanacs, bibliography, biography, and so on. Within the remaining three parts, chapters are organized by topic. Thus, under "Social Sciences" the reader will find chapters titled "Economics and Business," "Education," "History," "Law," "Sociology," and so on.

Each chapter is subdivided to reflect the arrangement strategy of the entire volume. There is a section on general works followed by a topical breakdown. For example, in the chapter titled "Literature," "General Works" is followed by "Children's and Young Adult Literature" and "National Literature." Subsections are based on the amount of material available on a given topic and vary from year to year.

Users should keep in mind that many materials may fall under several different chapter topics. The comprehensive Author/Title and Subject indexes found at the end of the volume will assist users in finding specific works that could fall under several different chapters. Additionally, readers seeking out reviews of digital resources can find these quickly using the Website and Database Review Locator.

In closing, we wish to express our gratitude to the many talented contributors without whose support this volume of ARBA could not have been compiled. Many thanks also go out to our distinguished Advisory Board members whose contributions greatly enhance ARBA and ARBAonline. We would also like to thank the members of our staff who were instrumental in its preparation.

Contributors

Anthony J. Adam, Director, Institutional Assessment, Blinn College, Brenham, Tex.

January Adams, Asst. Director/Head of Adult Services, Franklin Township Public Library, Somerset, N.J.

Donald Altschiller, Librarian, Mugar Memorial Library, Boston Univ.

Mary Alice Anderson, Online Professional Development Instructor, Univ. of Wisconsin-Stout, Menomonie, Wis.

Adrienne Antink, Medical Group Management Association, Lakewood, Colo.

Thomas E. Baker, Assoc. Professor, Department of Criminal Justice, Univ. of Scranton, Pa.

Michael Francis Bemis, Asst. Librarian, Washington County Library, Woodbury, Minn.

Laura J. Bender, Librarian, Univ. of Arizona, Tucson.

Claire Berg, Information and Technology Literacy Specialist, Riverview Elementary School, Farmington, Minn.

Barbara M. Bibel, Reference Librarian, Science/Business/Sociology Dept., Main Library, Oakland Public Library, Calif.

Daniel K. Blewett, Reference Librarian, College of DuPage Library, College of DuPage, Glen Ellyn, Ill.

Alicia Brillon, Reference Librarian, James E. Faust Law Library, Univ. of Utah.

Georgia Briscoe, Assoc. Director and Head of Technical Services, Law Library, Univ. of Colorado, Boulder.

John R. Burch Jr., Dean of Distance Learning and Library Services, Campbellsville Univ., Ky.

Frederic F. Burchsted, Reference Librarian, Widener Library, Harvard Univ., Cambridge, Mass.

Joanna M. Burkhardt, Head Librarian, College of Continuing Education Library, Univ. of Rhode Island, Providence.

Vincent Burns, PhD, ABC-CLIO.

Diane M. Calabrese, Freelance Writer and Contributor, Silver Springs, Md.

Theresa Calcagno, IT & Engineering Librarian, George Mason Univ., Fairfax, Va.

Delilah R. Caldwell, Online Services Librarian and Adjunct Instructor, Southwestern College, Winfield, Kans.

Alice Chaffee, Freelance Editor, Carpinteria, Calif.

Bert Chapman, Government Publications Coordinator, Purdue Univ., West Lafayette, Ind.

Boyd Childress, Reference Librarian, Ralph B. Draughon Library, Auburn Univ., Ala.

Rosanne M. Cordell, (formerly) Head of Reference Services, Franklin D. Schurz Library, Indiana Univ., South Bend, Ind.

Gregory A. Crawford, Head of Public Services, Penn State Harrisburg, Middletown, Pa.

Gregory Curtis, Regional Federal Depository Librarian for Maine, New Hampshire, and Vermont, Fogler Library, Univ. of Maine, Presque Isle.

Norman Desmarais, Professor Emeritus, Providence (Rhode Island) College.

R. K. Dickson, Asst. Professor of Fine Arts, Wilson College, Chambersburg, Pa.

Scott R. DiMarco, Director of Library Services and Information Resources, Mansfield Univ., Mansfield, Pa.

Joe P. Dunn, Charles A. Dana Professor of History and Politics, Converse College, Spartanburg, S.C.

Bradford Lee Eden, Dean of Library Services, Valparaiso Univ., Valparaiso, Ind.

Sheri Edwards, Assistant Univ. Librarian, Florida Atlantic Univ.

Lorraine Evans, Social Science Research and Instruction Librarian, Univ. of Colorado, Denver.

Richard Fanning, Library Media Specialist, Spring Forest Middle School, Houston, Tex.

Autumn Faulkner, Asst Head of Cataloging and Metadata Services, Michigan State Univ. Libraries, East Lansing.

Judith J. Field, Senior Lecturer, Program for Library and Information Science, Wayne State Univ., Detroit.

Josh Eugene Finnell, Reference Librarian, Ohio.

Tracy A. Fitzwater, Teacher-Librarian, Crescent School District, Joyce, Wash.

Valerie Byrd Fort, Library Media Specialist, New Providence Elementary School, Lexington, S.C.

Julia Frankosky, Government Information Librarian, Michigan State Univ. Libraries, East Lansing.

Brian T. Gallagher, Access Services Librarian, Head of Access Services, Univ. of Rhode Island, Kingston.

Denise A. Garofalo, Systems and Catalog Services Librarian, Curtin Memorial Library, Mount Saint Mary College, Newburgh, N.Y.

John T. Gillespie, College Professor and Writer, N.Y.

Caroline L. Gilson, Coordinator, Prevo Science Library, DePauw Univ., Greencastle, Ind.

Ralph Hartsock, Senior Music Catalog Librarian, Univ. of North Texas, Denton.

Muhammed Hassanali, Independent Consultant, Shaker Heights, Ohio.

David Hawksworth, Wildlife Biologist, Albuquerque, N.Mex.

Lucy Heckman, Reference Librarian (Business-Economics), St. John's Univ. Library, Jamaica, N.Y.

Laura Herrell, Writer/editor, Santa Barbara, Calif.

Mark Y. Herring, Dean of Library Services, Winthrop Univ., Dacus Library, Rock Hill, S.C.

Ladyjane Hickey, Reference Librarian, Austin College, Tex.

Jennifer Brooks Huffman, Serials/ILL Librarian, Univ. of Wisconsin - Stevens Point, Wis.

Jonathan F. Husband, Program Chair of the Library/Reader Services Librarian, Henry Whittemore Library, Framingham State College, Mass.

Amanda Izenstark, Asst. Professor, Reference and Instructional Design Librarian, Univ. of Rhode Island, Kingston.

Andrea C Kepsel, Health Sciences Educational Technology Librarian, Michigan State Univ. Libraries, East Lansing.

Sue Ellen Knowlton, Branch Manager, Hudson Regional Library, Pasco County Library System, Hudson, Fla.

Amy Koehler, Support Services Librarian, Moody Bible Institute, Chicago, Ill.

Lori D. Kranz, Freelance Editor, Chambersburg, Pa.

Natalie Kupferberg, Biological Sciences/Pharmacy Library, Ohio State Univ., Columbus.

Robert V. Labaree, Reference/Public Services Librarian, Von KleinSmid Library, Univ. of Southern California, Los Angeles.

Shireen Lalla, Coordinator, Academic Affairs, Florida Atlantic Univ., Davie.

Rob Laurich, Acting Chief of Technical Services, Collection Department, Cohen Library, The City College of the City Univ. of New York.

Martha Lawler, Assoc. Librarian, Louisiana State Univ., Shreveport.

Kristin Kay Leeman, Adjunct Faculty Instructor, Univ. of Maryland, Univ. College, Largo, Md.

Robert M. Lindsey, Instruction and Reference Librarian, Pittsburg State Univ., Pittsburg, Kans.

Megan W. Lowe, Reference/Instruction Librarian, Univ. Library, Univ. of Louisiana at Monroe.

Tyler Manolovitz, Digital Resources Coordinator, Newton Gresham Library, Sam Houston State Univ., Huntsville, Tex.

Sara Marcus, Asst. Professor of Education, Touro Univ. International, N.Y.

Michelle Martinez, Librarian, Newton Gresham Library, Sam Houston State Univ., Huntsville, Tex.

Judith Matthews, physics-astronomy subject librarian, Michigan State Univ., East Lansing.

Melinda F. Matthews, Interlibrary Loan/Reference Librarian, Univ. of Louisiana at Monroe.

Kevin McDonough, Reference and Electronic Resources Librarian, Northern Michigan Univ., Olson Library, Marquette.

Jessica Crossfield McIntosh, Reference Services Coordinator, Asst. Professor, Otterbein Univ., Westerville, Ohio.

Lawrence Joseph Mello, Asst. Reference and Instruction Librarian, Florida Atlantic Univ., Boca Raton.

Rachel Meredith Minkin, Head of Reference Services, Michigan State Univ. Libraries, East Lansing.

Janis Minshull, Library Consultant, Phippsburg, Maine.

Sara Mofford, Youth Services Librarian, Catawba County Library System, Newton, N.C.

Alda Moore, Head Librarian, Matoaca High School, Chesterfield, Va.

Lisa Morgan, Branch Manager, Pasco County Library System, Hudson, Fla.

Kat Landry Mueller, Electronic Resources Librarian, Sam Houston State Univ., Huntsville, Tex.

Paul M. Murphy III, Director of Marketing, PMX Medical, Denver, Colo.

Madeleine Nash, Reference/Instruction Librarian, Molloy College, Rockville Center, N.Y.

Mary Northrup, Reference Librarian, Metropolitan Community College-Maple Woods, Kansas City, Mo.

Herbert W. Ockerman, Professor, Ohio State Univ., Columbus.

Lawrence Olszewski, Director, OCLC Library and Information Center, Dublin, Ohio.

Cynthia Ortiz, School Librarian, Hackensack (New Jersey) High School.

Amy B. Parsons, Metadata Librarian/Assoc. Professor, Courtright Memorial Library, Otterbein College, Westerville, Ohio.

Leslie Greaves Radloff, Licensed Library Media Specialist, The Heights Community School, St. Paul, Minn.

Ellen Range, Media Specialist, Harding Senior High School. St. Paul, Minn.

Jack Ray, Asst. Director, Loyola/Notre Dame Library, Baltimore, Md.

Allen Reichert, Electronic Access Librarian, Courtright Memorial Library, Otterbein College, Westerville, Ohio.

Richard Salvucci, Professor, Economics, Trinity Univ., San Antonio, Tex.

Lisa Schultz, Instructional Services Research Librarian, Univ. of Colorado School of Law, Boulder.

Mark Schumacher, Art and Humanities Librarian, UNC Greensboro, Greensboro, N.C.

Ralph Lee Scott, Professor, Assistant Head of Special Collections for Public Services, and Curator of Printed Books and Maps, East Carolina Univ. Library, Greenville, N.C.

Susan E. Searing, Professor Emerita, Univ. of Illinois, Urbana-Champaign.

William Shakalis, Assistant Librarian, Worcester State Univ., Worcester, Mass.

Ravindra Nath Sharma, Dean of Library, Monmouth Univ. Library, West Long Branch, N.J.

Stephen J. Shaw, Library Director, Antioch Univ. Midwest, Yellow Springs, Ohio.

Brian J. Sherman, Head of Access Services and Systems, Noel Memorial Library, Louisiana State Univ., Shreveport.

Breezy Silver, Collection Coordinator and Business Reference Librarian, Michigan State Univ. Libraries, East Lansing.

Todd Simpson, Assistant Professor/Catalog Librarian, York College, CUNY, Jamaica, N.Y.

Kay Stebbins Slattery, Coordinator Librarian, Louisiana State Univ., Shreveport.

Mary Ellen Snodgrass, Freelance Writer, Charlotte, N.C.

Lee Sochay, Head of Acquisitions, Michigan State Univ. Libraries, East Lansing.

Steven W. Sowards, Asst. Director for Collections, Michigan State Univ. Libraries, East Lansing.

Eric Tans, Environmental Sciences Librarian, Michigan State Univ. Libraries, East Lansing.

Joseph E. Taylor III, Professor of History, Simon Fraser Univ., Burnaby, BC, Canada.

David Tipton, managing editor, ABC-CLIO, Santa Barbara, Calif.

Diane J. Turner, Science/Engineering Liaison, Auraria Library, Univ. of Colorado, Denver.

Linda M. Turney, E-Resources Cataloging Librarian, Walker Library, Middle Tennessee State Univ., Murfreesboro.

Catherine Vinson, Instructional Strategist, L G Alleman Middle School, Lafayette, La.

Karen T. Wei, Head, Asian Library, Univ. of Illinois, Urbana.

Holly Whitt, Librarian, Walnut Grove Elementary, New Market, Ala.

W. Cole Williamson, Instruction Librarian, Sam Houston State Univ., Huntsville, Tex.

Julienne L. Wood, Head, Research Services, Noel Memorial Library, Louisiana State Univ., Shreveport.

Susan Yutzey, School Library Media Specialist, Upper Arlington High School, Columbus, Ohio.

Website and Database Review Locator

Reference is to entry number.

Part I

GENERAL
REFERENCE
WORKS

1 General Reference Works

Almanacs

P, S

1.   **The American Book of Days.** 5th ed. Bronx, N.Y., H. W. Wilson, 2015. 1062p. illus. index. $195.00. ISBN 13: 978-1-61925-469-5.

This is the fifth edition of the *American Book of Days,* first published in 1937 under the editorship of George W. Douglas. This new edition updates and revises entries from the fourth edition and includes approximately 200 new essays, including pieces on the 9/11 terrorist attacks, the assassination of Osama bin-Laden, the Patient Protection and Affordable Care Act, the Boston Marathon bombing, the wars in Afghanistan and Iraq, and the 2008 financial crisis.

The book begins with a list of days and events; each day of the year (including February 29th) has at least one entry. These entries are accompanied by page numbers, so users can skip to the page directly. Months and dates serve as guide words at the top of every page for those who want to browse the entire volume. To accommodate moveable events such as Thanksgiving and Passover, the *American Book of Days* uses the date the event occurred in either the 1970 or 1997 editions. Each moveable event is so indicated. Entries range in length from about half a column on May 10th for Fort Ticonderoga Falls to nearly eight pages containing the text of George Washington's Farewell Address, which he delivered on September 19th. Altogether, the entries cover American history and culture from the colonial period to the present. Black-and-white photographs sprinkled throughout add interest.

The end of the book is packed with nine appendixes: The Calendar, The Era, The Days of the Week, The Signs of the Zodiac, the United States Constitution, the Articles of Confederation, the Mayflower Compact of 1620, and Important Public Holidays and Events. An index rounds out the work, which is recommended for school and public libraries.—**ARBA Staff Reviewer**

C, P, S

2.   **The World Almanac and Book of Facts 2016.** New York, Infobase Publishing, 2016. 1008p. illus. maps. index. $34.95. ISBN 13: 978-1-60057-199-2.

Having begun publication in 1868, *The World Almanac and Book of Facts* remains a staple of reference collections in almost all libraries. The 2016 edition continues the excellence of the series. Of added interest are the special features and year in review for 2015. This section includes the top 10 news topics for the year, notable quotes, U.S.

Supreme Court decisions, obituaries of famous and infamous individuals who died during the year, and the year in pictures among other topics. Two special features are also included. The first focuses on the 2016 election and provides information such as the dates for presidential primaries and caucuses and the dates of the nominating conventions. The second is entitled, "Coming to America: Immigration in History and Today," and provides good background information for the ongoing debate about immigration and its impact on the United States. The volume also includes the standard statistical data found in earlier editions such as sections on the economy, crime, science and technology, U.S. facts and history, world maps and flags, world history and culture, and sports. As a ready reference tool, *The World Almanac and Book of Facts* is indispensable and should be on the reference shelves of every school, public, and academic library.—**Gregory A. Crawford**

Biography

P

3.   **Current Biography Yearbook, 2015.** Bronx, N.Y., H. W. Wilson, 2015. 723p. illus. $199.00. ISBN 13: 978-1-61925-707-8.

Current Biography Yearbook 2015 is the 76th annual reference offering a select collection of over 200 biographical sketches of contemporary newsmakers from a variety of professions. It also includes a number of compact obituaries marking the passing of other notable persons between the later months of 2014 and into the publication year.

The collection emphasizes true diversity in choosing its subjects, who hold a range of professions such as, among many others, ecologist, actor, king, fashion designer, philosopher, mixed martial artist, and chef. Each biography lists the birth date and occupation of its subject before its main essay which touches on their early life, career trajectory, notable achievements, and personal life. The biographies also include a list of suggested reading about the subject and selected works as appropriate. Many, but not all, biographies come with a black-and-white photograph of their subject. Readers up on current events will recognize names such as writer and musician Carrie Brownstein, baseball player Madison Bumgarner, journalist Ta-Nahisi Coates, and U.S. Navy Admiral Michelle Howard.

The obituaries section lists birth date, death date and profession; it then offers a brief memorial including details of the death if known. They also include a reference to the subject's particular volume of *Current Biography* in which they are included.

All biography and obituary subjects are listed at the beginning of the volume and biographies are classified by profession at the volume's end.—**ARBA Staff Reviewer**

P

4.   Davis, Anita Price, and Marla J. Selvidge. **Women Nobel Peace Prize Winners.** Jefferson, N.C., McFarland, 2015. 238p. illus. index. $45.00pa. ISBN 13: 978-0-7264-9917-5; 978-1-4766-2212-5 (e-book).

Living through many of the regional conflicts that would lay the groundwork for the First World War, Bertha von Suttner was fervent in her work as a pacifist and novelist and is thought to be the inspiration behind Alfred Nobel's Peace Prize. In fact, Bertha won the prestigious award herself in 1905. This second edition of *Women Nobel Peace Prize*

Winners (see ARBA 2007, entry 11) collects efficient but satisfying biographies of all female Peace Prize winners in one enlightening book.

With the addition of the three latest female winners, this edition now presents 15 total entries and covers such dignitaries as Emily Green Balch, Mother Teresa, Aung San Suu Kyi and the award's youngest female recipient, Malala Yousafzai. Each biography includes a black-and-white photograph, as well as excellent background focusing on interesting details of its subject's lives, a bit of historical context, and each woman's award-winning work. For example, we read how the senseless deaths of Mairead Maguire's young niece and nephews propelled her and a fed-up Betty Williams to create the Community of Peace People, which fought to address the violence raging in 1970s Northern Ireland.

Including a list of all Nobel Peace Prize winners by year, a bibliography for each entry, and a piece on Alfred Nobel himself, this book provides an important way for readers to connect with these determined figures devoted to the idea of a peaceful world.—**Laura Herrell**

Dictionaries and Encyclopedias

P, S

5.   **Famous First Facts: A Record of First Happenings, Discoveries, and Inventions in American History.** 7th ed. Bronx, N.Y., H. W. Wilson, 2015. 1425p. illus. index. $195.00. ISBN 13: 978-1-61925-468-8.

Famous First Facts, now in its seventh edition, was first published by editor Joseph Kane for H.W. Wilson in 1933. The sixth edition appeared in 2006 (see ARBA 2008, entry 26). The current edition has almost 8,000 entries, more than 100 illustrations, 4 indexes, and 16 chapters covering firsts in several arenas—scientific, medical, technological, political, legal, social, and financial—from the colonial period to the present. Entries can be as short as a sentence, but most are several sentences in length.

The book begins with a preface, notes on how to use the book, and "Expanded Contents." Chapters are organized into alphabetized subsections; "firsts" in these subsections are presented in chronological order. The chapters are as follows: Arts and Entertainment, Business and Industry, Daily Life, Education, Engineering, Media and Communications, Medicine and Health, Military and War, Nature and Environment, Population and Settlement, Religion, Science and Technology, Society, Sports and Recreation, and Transportation. Four indexes—subject, index by years, index to personal names, and a geographical index—facilitate searches.

This book of first facts would be a welcome addition to a public or school library.—**ARBA Staff Reviewer**

Directories

P

6.   **AllAreaCodes.com. http://www.allareacodes.com/.** [Website] Free. Date reviewed: 2016.

AllAreaCodes.com is a freely available, easily searchable, and regularly updated resource of area code information within the North American Numbering Plan.

There is a prominent search screen in the middle of the home page that allows searches by number, area code, city, or state—this serves the function of a basic search screen for the entire site. Users can also use an area code search box or a city search box. On the right side of the screen, there is a list of area codes (from the 200s to the 900s) next to the name of the city with which the area code is associated. For example, 505 is listed with Albuquerque, New Mexico. Clicking on Albuquerque takes users to another page with a map of the region associated with the area code (this is printable), the names of other cities and towns in the area code, a full-number search screen, and time zone information.

The newest feature of the site is a reverse phone lookup. Simply typing in a number will produce (if available) the name of the person associated with the number along with city and zip code information. The site provides information about for-fee services that can find information about unknown numbers. For those who want to protect their privacy, there is a form that allows users to remove their personal information from this site. Other site offerings include a list of international dialing codes plus basic instructions on placing an international call, as well as an infographics and articles section.—**ARBA Staff Reviewer**

P

7.   **Associations Canada, 2016.** 37th ed. Amenia, N.Y., Grey House Publishing, 2016. 2026p. index. $449.00pa. ISBN 13: 978-1-61925-957-7; 978-1-61925-958-4 (e-book).

This edition of *Associations Canada* provides the most current directory of nonprofit associations. It includes over 20,000 associations which are either headquartered in Canada, headquartered elsewhere but house a branch in Canada, or entirely foreign but of potential interest to Canadians. All entries have been meticulously verified in terms of providing the most up-to-date information as of publication, including association name change, event dates, etc. Introductory information is conveyed in both English and French. Individual listings may be conveyed in either or both languages.

Opening pages provide a wealth of insightful information: a page on how to read an entry; a list of abbreviations and translations; "Canadian Associations at a Glance"; historical and organizational association information; several essays regarding timely and applicable topics (e.g., social media usage); and a comprehensive subject index.

Canadian associations, ranging from the Abbeyfield Houses Society of Canada to the Zurich & District Chamber of Commerce are profiled first, followed by foreign associations. Entries are alphabetized within each section and may include an association's current and former names and acronyms; address and other contact information; social media; overview; mission; affiliation; executives; membership; conferences; awards, grants or scholarship information; and more.

Entries are followed by a number of supplemental indexes which are necessary and helpful in regard to the great volume of information. All indexes are arranged alphabetically. There is an acronym index, providing a listing of acronyms and their corresponding associations; a budget index, organizing associations within eight budget categories; a conferences and conventions index, covering dates scheduled between 2016 and 2023; an executive name index; a geographic index; a mailing list index; and, finally, a registered charitable organization index.

This essential and well-curated source will prove a valuable addition to libraries.—**ARBA Staff Reviewer**

Quotation Books

P

8.   **Oxford Dictionary of Quotations.** 8th ed. Elizabeth Knowles, ed. New York, Oxford University Press, 2014. 1126p. index. $50.00. ISBN 13: 978-0-19-966870-0.

Surely with the Internet now so firmly ensconced in every inch and fiber of our lives, we no longer need bulky, tree-killing tomes like this one? Moreover, even this text is on the godalmighty Internet. Coming in at over five pounds and more than 1,100 pages, what could possibly possess any publisher, especially one as reputable as Oxford, to undertake such an expensive and laborious undertaking for what we might call a publishing *paralipomenon*?

Accuracy of phrase, ease of use, and profound assurance of source are just three reasons that come to mind, any one of which justifies the existence of the volume but all three make it *a fortiori,* or QED, as the philosophers might say. Yet apart from these reasons, the inclusion in this edition of the history of the volume and the introduction to the first edition by Berenard Darwin should make the matter incontestable even for tree-huggers. Well, okay, for everyone but them. Begins Darwin, "Quotation brings to many people one of the intensest [sic] joys of living." He goes on to point out that some will be disappointed at what is both included *and* what is left out, and he even points out one of his favorites that did not make that first edition cut. To which he muses, "Can it be, I ask myself, that this is due to the fact an Oxford scholar put several of the Master's [William Hepworth Thompson] sayings into his Greek exercise book and attributed them to one Talirantes? Down, base thought! I only mention this momentary and unworthy suspicion to show other readers the sort of thing they should avoid as they would the very devil." Alas, no one writes like this anymore but it is so charming to be reminded once again that elocution and felicitous expression used to be not only taught and practiced, but also admired.

The *Oxford Dictionary of Quotations* brings together thousands (and thousands) of quotations with their sources matched and their phrasing parsed as pluperfectly as possible. As with all other editions the arrangement is by author with birth and death dates, when applicable, in place. The author's nationality and occupation is noted and the original language of the quotation given. Cross-references, when appropriate, are given. A most expansive keyword index is included. What makes this edition so important is that many contemporaries, for better or for worse, are given their place in the sun. Thus, Frank Zappa, Joan Baez, Bob Marley, John Lennon, and Paul McCartney are all included as well as scores of others one has never heard of.

While it may not always be true that the Internet will give you several million answers in a few nanoseconds but a librarian the right one, when it is true, it is because of books such as this one are still published and still used. *Lauditor temporis acti.*—**Mark Y. Herring**

P

9.   **The Quotable Amelia Earhart.** Michele Wehrwein Albion, ed. Albuquerque, N.Mex., University of New Mexico Press, 2015. 255p. illus. index. $24.95. ISBN 13: 978-0-8263-4562-2; 978-0-8263-4563-9 (e-book).

A remarkable, dense little tome, *The Quotable Amelia Earhart,* edited by author,

Michele Wehrwein Albion, who is known for similar collections of other historical notables like Eleanor Roosevelt and Henry Ford, is a thematic arrangement of quotations by the celebrated aviatrix. Albion's preface/acknowledgement provides a brief biography of the famous lady but stresses that the book has no intentions of exploring Earhart's disappearance. In addition to the fascinating collection of wise and witty words, Albion includes a chronology of major events in Earhart's life. This title would be an excellent fit for a public library and fans of the amazing female pilot. Highly recommended.—**Megan W. Lowe**

Websites and Databases

C

10. **Academic Video Online: Premium. http://alexanderstreet.com/products/ academic-video-online-premium.** [Website] Alexandria, Va. Alexander Street Press. Price negotiated by site. Date reviewed: 2016.

Academic Video Online: Premium provides a vast database of film and video clips from documentary, newsreel, entertainment, and television sources. The range of material is deep and broad, organized into eight "disciplines" more appropriately understood as general themes that range from history to arts, literature, social science, and science and engineering but also the idiosyncratic categories of "diversity" and "personal interest." The oldest clips are 1894 footage of Sioux Indians performing "ghost dances." Much of the oldest footage comes from the Edison Company and Library of Congress. As of this review the newest videos date from late 2015.

The collection will appeal to researchers for several reasons. Users can browse generally or through discipline folders. Browsing the health science category produced a number of public service announcements and interviews with scientists and doctors, while personal interest videos included many railroad aficionado films. Keyword searches can quickly identify useful resources if the terms are selective enough, but the user must take care and be lucky to avoid a vast data dump, most of which is not useful. The advanced search function enables much more targeted queries by author, title, date, subject, and other typical categories singly or in combination. These searches were much more successful for ferreting out specific items and themes.

The materials are useful for teaching high school and college-level courses. The thematic range and temporal span make the collection relevant to many disciplines, courses, and student levels. Subjects and events can be teased out easily using the search functions, making the clips accessible for students conducting assignments or for accentuating lectures. Teaching with these clips is trickier. Large items load slowly, and lecturers will want to boot up the material ahead of time to avoid awkward delays while presenting material in the classroom because none of the items can be downloaded to a computer desktop. Older films are also grainy, making them poor choices for projection.

Many of the older clips are in the public domain and accessible through the Library of Congress or *Internet Archive,* but some older items are not easily available and most of the newer material is still copyright protected, including feature film and television shows such as several Ken Burns documentaries. Silent films sometimes have little documentation about the context of footage, but sound-era clips are better documented and usually include searchable transcripts. This feature is particularly notable and useful.— **Joseph E. Taylor III**

C, P, S

11.   **Canada In Context http://solutions.cengage.com/InContext/Canada/.** [Website] Farmington Hills, Mich., Gale/Cengage Learning. Price negotiated by site. Date reviewed: 2016.

Canada In Context is an online research resource dedicated to Canada. It pulls together reference information, academic journals, news, videos, maps, critical essays, and primary documents from a variety of sources to help researchers learn more about Canadian people, history, and contemporary issues from a Canadian perspective. It spans a range of subjects from technology to literature and sports to business. The database includes video and audio from CBC, NPR, and other authoritative sources. Articles from more than 370 Canadian publications including *Maclean's, The Toronto Star,* and Globe and Mail are continually added to the site.

Samples of topics include Lucy Maude Montgomery (author of *Anne of Green Gables*), Canada under British Rule, and Hockey. There are many topics that do not appear to be germane to Canada (e.g., Leonardo DaVinci, Nigeria, and the American Civil War), but these are included because study of or reference to them is made in a Canadian publication or by a Canadian author or politician. This is useful for examining the Canadian perspective on the world.

The resource can be searched by keyword or browsed by topic. There are so many topics to browse, that a helpful filter for category (e.g,. geography, government, sports, social issues, etc.) is also included. An advanced keyword search option allows users to combine keywords with title and/or publication title. Users can also limit their search to full-text or peer-reviewed journals or specify a desired document type or content type. Teachers will appreciate the ability to search by content level (beginner to advanced) and Lexile level. Educators will also appreciate the curriculum standards provided in the site which include Canadian standards among those from other English-speaking countries.

The database integrates with Google apps including Google Drive and Google Classroom. This makes it easy for both students and teachers to save documents to their own Google Drive. The ability to save to a central location is very useful. Any highlights and notes made in the database can be retained when the document is saved to Google Drive. Teachers have the added ability to save a document to their Google Classroom as an announcement or an assignment.

This dynamic resource is recommended for school and public libraries in Canada or to libraries that serve large populations with Canadian research interests. It provides an engaging way to study Canada with a wide variety of resources including multimedia.—**Kristin Kay Leeman**

C, P, S

12.   **Internet Archive. https://archive.org/.** [Website] Free. Date reviewed: 2016.

Internet Archive is a 501(c)(3) nonprofit Website that stores millions of books, movies, and music that can be downloaded for free. They provide "universal access to all knowledge" and offer a variety of genres for each type of media provided on the site. From animation and cartoons to spirituality and religion, *Internet Archive* is truly comprehensive.

Because this Website was founded to build an Internet library, the creators of this site have librarians, historians, scholars, and researchers in mind when broadening their collection of literature and media. *Internet Archive* creators are in charge of overseeing one of the world's largest book digitization projects and are based in three Californian cities.

These digitally formatted files, of which there are more than 15 petabytes worth, can be both uploaded and downloaded directly.

Students in particular will find the clean layout welcoming and easy to use. Tabs at the top of the page allow users to choose the form of media they would like to browse and, upon selecting a form, they can choose a specific category. A search tab is beneficial for users looking for information on a particular subject. Users can hover over the *Internet Archive* symbol to find information about the organization, browse blog posts, contact the library with questions, and discover what new projects *Internet Archive* is investing in. Users can access information in multiple languages and though the site may seem advanced for those new to the internet, the intuitive design will appeal to novice and expert alike.

Librarians, students, and the general public will find this site useful. Both academic and entertainment sources can be accessed, and there is likely information on any subject users can think of. This resource is relevant and highly recommended for all.—**ARBA Staff Reviewer**

C, P

13.   **Very Short Introductions. http://www.veryshortintroductions.com/.** [Website] New York, Oxford University Press. Price negotiated by site. Date reviewed: 2015.

This online assemblage of over 400 books from Oxford's Very Short Introductions (VSI) series covers topics in the arts and humanities, law, medicine and health, science and mathematics, and social sciences. The material is easy to navigate from the home page via a quick search or a browse by subfield of all available books. For example, clicking on Human Geography under Social Sciences returns a list of five books. This search can be narrowed further by the use of a buildable search query on the left side of the screen. For example, once a book like *Modern Ireland: A Very Short Introduction* is selected, researchers will see an abstract of the book, clickable keywords that link to other publications in the VSI database, and bibliographic information including the ISBN, a digital object identifier, and online and print publication dates. A clickable table of contents below this allows users to move around in the book, while the left-hand side of the results page has links to quick reference terms like Orange Order and land tenure. Once the full text of a chapter or a book is accessed, users can take advantage of tools that enable the creation of a personal profile or citations. Citations are provided in the MLA, APA, Chicago, or AMA formats and are exportable to EndNote, ProCite, RefWorks, and more. Use of the Oxford Index Underbar allows users to find related Oxford University Press content.

The VSI database comes equipped with other special features. Under the About tab on the main page, librarians will find a variety of resources, including online support for K-12 librarians in using VSI material to meet Common Core Standards. Thirty-nine author videos and 98 author-written reading guides are also offered under the About tab, along with links to the OUPblog and VSI Facebook page. Institutional subscribers can purchase access to all or part of the VSI content, depending on library needs. This comprehensive, easily navigable collection of products is recommended for academic libraries, especially for those that do not already own print copies of the sources included in the database.— **ARBA Staff Reviewer**

Part II
SOCIAL SCIENCES

2 Social Sciences in General

General Works

Dictionaries and Encyclopedias

C, P, S

14. **The SAGE Encyclopedia of Alcohol: Social, Cultural, and Historical Perspectives.** Scott C. Martin, ed. Thousand Oaks, Calif., Sage, 2015. 3v. index. $475.00/ set. ISBN 13: 978-1-4833-2525-5.

The *SAGE Encyclopedia of Alcohol: Social, Cultural, and Historical Perspectives* is a unique documentation of the uses of alcohol in human societies. Taking a sociocultural approach rather than a medical stance warning against the use and abuse alcohol consumption, this title examines various cultures and their affinities for certain types of alcohol. Because alcohol has strongly impacted societies for millennia, there is much to explore in the social, cultural, historical, economic, and political realms of human history.

Included in the text is a lengthy glossary and detailed subject index for quick reference. A chronology traces the use of alcohol back to 5400 B.C.E. and the appendixes include social trends of toasting and a per capita alcohol consumption study. There are 550 entries that are organized alphabetically and are authored and signed by academics with cross-references and further readings, in addition to a helpful resource guide that highlights classic books, journals, and Websites for more specialized study.—**ARBA Staff Reviewer**

Handbooks and Yearbooks

C

15. Cumo, Christopher. **The Ongoing Columbian Exchange: Stories of Biological and Economic Transfer in World History.** Santa Barbara, Calif., ABC-CLIO, 2015. 393p. illus. index. $89.00. ISBN 13: 978-1-61069-795-; 978-1-61069-796-5 (e-book).

This book (8-by-10-inch hard cover with 395 pages) covers stories of biological and economic transfer in world history. The author is well qualified. The book starts with an alphabetical list of approximately 100 entries that covers animals, plants and their derivatives, insects, and diseases. A topical list of entries is followed by the 12 primary documents utilized in writing this book. Next, the book presents a preface, introduction, and then a timeline of events from 1492 to 1943. The major portion of the book is an alphabetical discussion that explains the historical importance of each entry; discussions range from a short paragraph to several pages. A further reading of primary documents follows the discussions. The book concludes with a bibliography, index, and brief author biography.

The book is an interesting read, and it explains many of the historical events that have shaped where we are today. A few photographs illustrate the written material. The binding and paper is average, but the font is a little small for long-term reading. I would recommend this book for any agricultural, food, or history library.—**Herbert W. Ockerman**

C, P

16.   **The Gallup Poll: Public Opinion** 2013. Frank Newport, ed. Lanham, Md., Rowman & Littlefield, 2015. 524p. index. $135.00; $134.99 (e-book). ISBN 13: 978-1-4422-4132-9; 978-1-4422-4133-6 (e-book).

Here is a complete gathering of more than 500 Gallup Poll reports for the year 2013. A seminal reference, it is home to an abundance of interesting data covering topics such as patriotism, personal wealth, foreign sympathies, optimism, job engagement, presidential approval, and much more.

Reports are presented chronologically, and may include a number of charts in addition to narrative summaries providing context for the data, drawing conclusions and noting survey methods. Furthermore, reports can reflect general information gleaned from the surveys, such as how stressed Americans felt, or very specific information, such as how depression increased in areas hit the hardest by 2012's Superstorm Sandy.

As the entirety of the Gallup Poll reports date back to 1935, it would be fascinating to compare this volume with prior volumes. Users would be able to discern the trends and sharp detours in public opinion throughout the decades.

Supplementary information includes a 2013 chronology, explanations of Gallup economic indexes, and a volume index particularly relevant in terms of identifying the many topics broached by the polls. Recommended for academic and public libraries.—**Laura Herrell**

C, P, S

17.   **Human Rights Studies Online. http://alexanderstreet.com/products/human-rights-studies-online.** [Website] Alexandria, Va. Alexander Street Press. Price negotiated by site. Date reviewed: 2016.

Developed by an editorial board at Alexander Street Press, *Human Rights Studies Online* is a collection of research and learning databases. With a diverse assemblage of content types including multimedia formats, options for human rights studies are plentiful.

The worldwide database covers a broad array of human rights violations and atrocities between 1900 and 2010. The expanse of more than a century will prove useful for students seeking historical perspective. Overall, the comparative documentation, analysis, and interpretation are rich with human rights information. The databases include: 137 hours of visual media on 272 videos and 3,992 documents and books as well as related Web sources which are easily assessed. Information can be found as both primary and secondary sources.

The online collection is organized with a sidebar which will provide access from four different entryways; Browse, Discipline Perspectives, Human Rights Themes, and Featured Playlists will provide paths to human rights data. Each area segues to other topics—for example, under the heading of Discipline Perspectives, subtopics are many and incorporate areas of diplomacy, law, and sociology, just to name a few. For those who want to narrow their search and already know their topic, search and advanced search options will give a more direct route. Filtering is key to using these online resources, and the organization is a clear advantage. A very comprehensive list of organizations is another superb option as is the Human Rights Events Content. References are easily garnered by clicking the citing tab.

Grueling subject matter, *Human Rights Studies Online* offers insight into the human struggle and horrors of the twentieth century. The multiplicity of human suffering and the personal stories bring the greatest meaning to this collection. For example, authentic documentation (UNAMIR Evening Sitrep: June 12, 1994) on a daily basis from the Rwandan civil war and genocide (1994) bring not only real life data, but also the harsh realities of such atrocities. Titles such as *What We Knew: Terror, Mass Murder, and Everyday Life in Nazi Germany, An Oral History* repeatedly expose the tragedy of each individual experience and the larger implications. High quality of content is very consistent though there were instances of inferior work; *Threat of the Faithful* has dynamic information about Orthodox Jews in Israel but the double layering of subtitles is distracting.

Unfortunately, there is a vast amount of human rights tragedy in this world and this collection provides plentiful documentation of that tragedy and also the resilience of the human spirit. *Human Rights Studies Online* is a very solid online resource for high school and undergraduate students, as well as for general research. Areas of study might include: human rights, social sciences, history, or global politics.

Highly Recommended.—**Janis Minshull**

C, S
18.   **Issues in U.S. Immigration.** 2d ed. Carl L. Bankston, III and Danielle Antoinette Hidalgo, eds. Hackensack, N.J., Salem Press, 2015. 2v. illus. index. $195.00/set. ISBN 13: 978-1-61925-708-5.

This hefty, retitled, second edition of *Immigration in U.S. History* (see ARBA 2007, entry 735) contains 215 essays, all signed by the contributors and arranged alphabetically, on "the many issues surrounding immigration—from the earliest settlement of British North America in the seventeenth century to the latest twenty-first century legislation," (p. xiv) including 75 new articles and rich supplementary material such as recent state and federal immigration statistics. Each article includes a title, brief definition, list of issues covered, dates and places if relevant, a note on significance, explanatory text, annotated "Further Reading" list and *see also* cross-references to related articles. Volume one contains a complete list of contents and of all contributors as well as a publisher's note. This volume presents 114 articles ranging from "Affordable Care Act and Undocumented Immigrants" to "Alien and Sedition Acts," "Federal Riot of 1799," "Hull House," and "Indentured Servitude." Volume two yields 101 additional articles such as "International Adoptions," "Ku Klux Klan," "Little Havana," "Sikh Immigrants," and "War Brides Act," plus "U.S. State briefs," individual essays on all 50 states together with New York City, and Washington, D.C. These state and city essays each present a profile table showing number and percentage of immigrants in each area's population and the largest immigrant groups, based on 2013 U.S. census data, an analysis of the area's significance, and an annotated book list for "Further Reading." Together, the two volumes offer more than 200 black-and-white illustrations.

The appendixes consist of an annotated bibliography (books only) and a "Time Line of U.S. Immigration History" through 2014 and are followed by the new, 100-page "Immigration Statistics" (1820-2012) section with 41 detailed tables of U.S. Department of Homeland Security, Office of Immigration Statistics data current as of 2012. Finally, the category index of topics groups related articles into 37 broader categories while the more traditional alphabetical subject index provides page numbers for specific keywords including names, events, laws, places, groups, and organizations.

Readers may quarrel over specific topic selections or omissions, but this well-designed set is broad in scope and content and deserves a place in high school, public, community college, and many university libraries. Given the great current interest in U.S. immigration issues, these two volumes should help stimulate and support additional research on many, diverse, immigration-related topics.—**Julienne L. Wood**

C, P, S

19.   **Procon.org. http://www.procon.org/.** [Website] Free. Date reviewed: 2016.

Procon.org is a Website that provides comprehensive information about controversial topics popular in contemporary discourse. The homepage has links to discussions about each issue clearly divided into topics such as health and medicine, education, politics, science and technology, and more, including a section featuring the most popular issues. When a link is selected, a wealth of information about each issue becomes available to view, including an introduction, a "did you know" set of facts, ample arguments in favor of and opposed to arguments, a thorough background essay about the issue, and videos featuring news clips and speeches. Additional features include a teacher's corner, reader comments, in-the-news articles, and access to the bulletin board of the procon.org office. Overall, the site provides a wealth of information to teenagers and adults interested in educating themselves about hot-button issues and polarizing topics.

This resource is especially useful to students who are writing persuasive essays, as well as individuals who want to learn as much as possible about an issue before casting a vote for a candidate or a ballot measure. This is due to the accessible nature of the writing, and the visual layout of the Website, which enables the researcher to easily access any relevant and accurate information. There is some variation in format between topics, in that some issues have a straightforward and color-coded pro/con layout, and other topics have links to essays that explore the topic but do not include the color-coded visual graphic. There is also the issue of providing false balance to topics such as vaccines, though the treatment on the Website remains overwhelmingly unbiased.

Procon.org is easy to navigate, filled with a near-overwhelming amount of content, and curated in a manner that makes information easy to access and cite. It is highly recommended to public and academic libraries, individual users, and schools.—**ARBA Staff Reviewer**

C, P, S

20.   **The Statesman's Yearbook 2015: The Politics, Cultures and Economies of the World.** Barry Turner, ed. New York, Palgrave Macmillan, 2014. 1588p. illus. maps. index. $350.00. ISBN 13: 978-1-13732-324-8.

This long-standing title, begun during the American Civil War, remains extremely useful today for its political, economic, and sociocultural information. Its organization is straightforward, presenting information first on scores of international organizations (both worldwide like the United Nations and regional like the Organization of American States), then entries on the 194 countries of the world, with geographical subdivisions for the United Kingdom, India, Canada, and the United States, among others. From biographies of the current political leaders (e.g., the president and prime minister of France) to population tables by region within a country and summaries of social institutions, this volume provides concise but accurate details about many aspects of the world's nations. A brief "Further Reading" section provides other resources, and occasionally Internet sites. Highly recommended to those libraries who can afford to purchase it. It is also available in an online format at http://www.statesmansyearbook.com/.—**Mark Schumacher**

3 Area Studies

General Works

Handbooks and Yearbooks

P

21. **Nations of the World, 2015: A Political, Economic, and Business Handbook.** 14th ed. Amenia, N.Y., Grey House Publishing, 2015. 2153p. maps. $180.00pa. ISBN 13: 978-1-61925-288-2.

This comprehensive handbook profiles every country and self-governing territory in the world from Afghanistan to Zimbabwe with the goal of providing readers with a clear view of the country's political, economic, and business situations. The book provides an abundance of useful details in an easy to follow format. This 14th edition has been updated with new information relative to changing political climates.

Each country's entry opens with an overview of the current political environment, covering nation-specific topics such as corruption in Bosnia and Herzegovina, Hong Kong's strained relationship with mainland China, or the strong demand for fishing licenses in Kiribati, for example. A Country Profile section presents a general timeline of significant political events followed by a breakdown of a country's governing and civil structures, such as form of state, legal system, political parties, education, ethnicities, media, agriculture, tourism, and banking. Information is ample and the directory employs many headings and subheadings for clarity. Some country profiles include a category new to this edition—People to Watch—which highlights individual newsmakers. Each country's entry concludes with a business directory listing contact information for a number of ministries, chambers, organizations, news agencies, and more.

Shaded sidebars house key facts where readers can find data and statistics fast, like land area, head of state, official language, etc., as well as economic data like exchange rate, GDP, and unemployment rate. Most every profile has a country map and two tables reflecting risk assessment and key economic indicators.

The work concludes with the essay "The World in 2014," which provides a generalized, global, and rather "gloomy" outlook, then moves on to five regional profiles providing summaries, a regional map, and two tables displaying currency values against the U.S. dollar and key indicators.

An invaluable reference for business travelers, government officials, researchers, and more.—**ARBA Staff Reviewer**

United States

General Works

C, P

22.　**Worldmark Encyclopedia of the States.** 8th ed. Farmington Hills, Mich., Gale/ Cengage Learning, 2016. 2v. index. $370.00/set. ISBN 13: 978-1-4144-3396-7; 978-1- 4103-3344-5 (e-book).

A familiar component of undergraduate reference, Gale's latest edition of the *Worldmark Enyclopedia of the States* continues to provide a detailed overview of each state as well as the District of Columbia, Puerto Rico, and the U.S. dependencies in the Caribbean and the Pacific Ocean.

The information one would expect to find about each state is available in this text: maps, flags, state seals, etc. However, this set is more than just an almanac of ready reference facts. This set also provides information on a range of topics from mining to securities, health to social welfare, from press to tourism. Each entry also contains its own bibliography, a hallmark of all encyclopedias published by Gale/Cengage. Most helpful, though, is the way both the print and online versions are arranged within each entry. Each entry has the same 50 subheadings, always arranged in the same order. These subheadings have a small number next to them so that patrons can quickly skim multiple entries for the same subject. As an example, number 43 always refers to Libraries and Museums and so readers can quickly find just that specific information.

A compact two volumes in print, this set is a good addition to any undergraduate, community college, and public library reference collection, providing a lot of information but not taking up too much shelf space. Overall, whether in print or online, the *Worldmark Encyclopedia of the States* is useful for ready reference and for readers at the beginning of their research.—**Rachel Meredith Minkin**

California

C, P, S

23.　**Compare 50. http://compare50.org/.** [Website] Free. Date reviewed: 2015.

Compare 50 is a Next 10 Project, which is "focused on innovation and the intersection between the economy, the environment, and quality of life issues for all Californians." It is a data tool that allows users to compare all 50 states and gauge differences in the topics of Economy, Innovation, Jobs, Income & Equity, and Demographics. Users simply select a topic and the states they wish to compare, then click the "submit" button for a graph chart that displays the information. It is also possible to select states to compare to the national average. All graphs can be downloaded in PNG, JPEG, and SVG image forms as well as in a PDF document, a useful feature for students who need visuals for presentations.

Overall, the site is simple and does not overwhelm the user. Apart from the bar at the top of the page including the main categories for search, there is not much else to click on. An index page provides shortcuts to all searchable subcategories and applicable data series, but this feature is best used for users who don't have a specific search in mind and are simply curious about the variety of information available on the Website. Otherwise, the topics on the bar at the top of the page contain the same information and would be more useful for users who want to carry out a specific search. To provide clarification, there is a technical notes tab below each graph that users can click on to obtain more information about statistical measurements and terminology, as well as general clarification for users who are less familiar with statistics.

While this site contains visually appealing and easy-to-read statistics and graphs, it unfortunately only includes data from 1990 to 2011, making it outdated enough to hinder users. Those who require updated information beyond 2011 will have to find another source. Another drawback is the format of the information, which is limited to the graph. Students who need to compare multiple states or record multiple numbers will have to hover the mouse directly over the state and the year on the graph in order to obtain the number they want, and then record it independently. This is time consuming, and it would therefore be helpful to have the numbers and any other relevant chart information recorded in document form somewhere else on the page, perhaps directly under the chart.

Compare 50 is a free Website and may be useful for students, academics, and researchers who need comparative reference sources.—**ARBA Staff Reviewer**

Puerto Rico

P, S

24.   Méndez-Méndez, Serafín, and Ronald Fernández. **Puerto Rico Past and Present: An Encyclopedia.** 2d ed. Santa Barbara, Calif., Greenwood Press/ABC-CLIO, 2015. 449p. illus. index. $100.00. ISBN 13: 978-1-4408-2831-7; 978-1-4408-2832-4 (e-book).

The first edition of this work (see ARBA 2009, entry 93) was one of the earliest reference works to exclusively focus on Puerto Rico. This edition, which contains more than 185 entries, provides an overview of the island's history and culture from the twentieth century to the present. The depth of coverage within each of the essays varies widely. Educational topics, for example, are extremely detailed. Others, like "Economy," provide the bare essentials. Although the economy article does not paint a pretty picture, it does not address the depths of Puerto Rico's economic calamities which have its leadership exploring legal means to declare bankruptcy. Another significant weakness is its lack of attention to Puerto Rico's history prior to it becoming a possession of the United States. For instance, there is no entry for the Spanish American War. That conflict saw Puerto Rico invaded by the United States military. Important economic engines from the past, like the coffee industry, are likewise forgotten. Despite these shortcomings, this work is appropriate for public and school libraries.—**John R. Burch Jr.**

Africa

General Works

C, P, S

25.   **Africa: An Encyclopedia of Culture and Society.** Toyin Falola and Daniel Jean-Jacques, eds. Santa Barbara, Calif., ABC-CLIO, 2015. 3v. index. $294.00/set. ISBN 13: 978-1-59884-665-2; 978-1-59884-666-9 (e-book).

African culture and society is as rich and diverse as the African continent itself, from its indigenous development to the internal and external forces that have permanently shaped its varied sociocultural landscape. While many of those transformations have been at great cost to human life and treasure, the achievements of African socioculture continue to evolve at a pace that is unbridled in both stride and form. It is fortuitous, then, that this three-volume encyclopedia is geared specifically toward students and nonscholars who are just beginning to learn about African society and its corresponding culture.

The three volumes total 54 entries written by scholars who are from institutions spanning three continents and who are either African themselves or who have lived in Africa. Each entry describes an African country and any associated islands and includes a corresponding black-and-white map (with major cities plotted). The entries are ordered alphabetically, beginning with Algeria and ending with Zimbabwe, and include brief snippets of factual information (capital cities, types of government, and the like). Each entry is divided into 15 culturally relevant subtopics, ranging from the typical (religion, social customs, and literary and oral traditions) to the specialized (cuisine and accompanying recipes, sports and games, and media). Included with each entry is a brief introduction of its respective country's geography, ethnic communities, and language(s). On that note, the first volume includes a comprehensive introduction in which Africa's geographical and historical background is explicated according to its five regional divisions (North, East, West, Central, and Southern); a comprehensive but concise chronology of African history (40,000 B.C.E. to 2014); and one map each of the continent's topography and geography, although, as with the other maps throughout the encyclopedia, both are in black and white and thus rather one-dimensional. Duly, the third volume includes an extensive index and complete bibliography.

Given the editors' stated purpose of placidly introducing students and readers to the scope and essence of African socioculture, a useful addition to the front matter in the first volume could be a small section that explains how to use and interpret the encyclopedia beyond its A to Z arrangement. Moreover, a wider selection of photos might lend the encyclopedia a more dynamic tone than do the current black-and-white photos, of which there are a modest amount. Nonetheless, the encyclopedia is all-inclusive, well-organized, informative, and expressed in a straightforward and easy-to-digest writing style.—**Sheri Edwards**

P, S

26.   **Countries, Peoples & Cultures: Eastern & Southern Africa.** Michael Shally-Jensen, ed. Hackensack, N.J., Salem Press, 2015. 586p. illus. maps. index. (Countries, Peoples & Cultures, Volume 6). $125.00. ISBN 13: 978-1-61925-782-5.

This sixth volume in the nine-volume Countries, Peoples & Cultures series focuses on 23 distinct countries in eastern and southern Africa, including Botswana, Djibouti, Kenya, Rwanda, Somalia, Tanzania, and Zimbabwe to name a few, aiming to provide readers with a sound understanding of a large amount of material.

An introduction provides a good overview which helps readers grasp the scale of the information concerning economics, politics, cultures, and more in the very different countries described in this volume. The material for each country is well organized into several categories: General Information, Environment and Geography, Customs and Courtesies, Lifestyle, Cultural History, Culture, Society, Social Development, Government, and Economy. These categories are further subdivided. For example, the Cultural History section discusses art, architecture, drama, music, and literature.

Readers will also find the country's flag, as well as fast facts, statistics, and maps depicting major cities, landmarks, and regional location. Color photographs sprinkled throughout the volume add interest. Country essays, at approximately 15 pages each, provide current details about youth culture, food, women's issues, and language, among other things.

Two extensive appendixes, World Governments and World Religions, close out the volume (the same appendixes appear in each volume of the series). World Governments describes 21 different forms of government and includes a list of current examples and a bibliography. The second appendix provides information about faiths like Islam and Christianity, explaining basic tenets, religious leaders, and religious philosophy. These essays also include bibliographies. An index rounds out the work.—**ARBA Staff Reviewer**

Asia

General Works

P, S

27.   **Countries, Peoples & Cultures: East Asia & the Pacific.** Michael Shally-Jensen, ed. Hackensack, N.J., Salem Press, 2015. 534p. illus. maps. index. (Countries, Peoples & Cultures, Volume 9). $125.00. ISBN 13: 978-1-61925-790-0.

This book is part of a new nine-volume series exploring the social, cultural, historical, religious, and economic story of most every country in the world. This ninth volume focuses on six distinct countries in East Asia (China, Japan, Mongolia, Taiwan, and the Koreas), in addition to the large country of Australia and 13 island countries (New Zealand, Samoa, Fiji, etc.) spread throughout the waters of the Pacific. Overall, the volume conveys the stories of 20 countries within the area.

The introduction provides a good overview which helps readers grasp the scale of the information concerning the very different countries described in this volume. The book then presents the essays on the East Asian nations, followed by the essays covering Australia and the island nations. Within each country's essay, readers will find a variety of umbrella ideas which do well to organize the material: General Information, Environment and Geography, Customs and Courtesies, Lifestyle, Cultural History, Culture, Society, Social Development, Government, and Economy. Particular topics then fill in the narrative under each umbrella idea. For example, the Economy section begins with an overview, followed by discussions on industry, labor, energy, agriculture, and tourism, among other topics. Readers will also find the country's flag, as well as fast facts, statistics, and maps depicting major cities, landmarks, and regional location. Color photographs are used sparingly throughout the volume. Each country's essay concludes with a thorough bibliography. Essays average about 15 pages long, and truly provide an informative snapshot of each country, filled with current details about youth culture, food, women's issues, language, and much more.

Two rather lengthy appendixes close out the volume (and are the same in all volumes of the series). World Governments describes 21 types of governments employed throughout all regions of the world today, including parliamentary monarch, communist, and so forth. Each description exposes the guiding premise behind the government, its typical structure, and the role of the citizen. Each essay also includes a list of current examples and a bibliography. The second appendix, World Religions, presents essays on 10 of the world's most-practiced faiths like Islam, Christianity, and Jainism. Each essay offers a general description of the faith in addition to a number of topics like basic tenets, major figures, and philosophical basis. These essays also include bibliographies.

The structure and scope of this series makes it ideal for secondary school students across several disciplines, including history and geography.—**ARBA Staff Reviewer**

Afghanistan

P, S

28.   **Afghanistan   Online: http://www.afghan-web.com/.**   [Website]   Free.   Date reviewed: 2015.

Afghanistan Online is a privately owned Website that provides news and information about everything Afghanistan. It was launched in 1997 and claims to be the most-used Afghan Website on the Internet today. It provides information on numerous topics and is updated frequently to stay relevant.

While the Website offers access to a variety of information, advertisements clutter the look and make navigation difficult; ads are usually pertinent to the Website content, forcing users to question whether or not clickables will lead to spam or relevant external pages. Users can look to the left side of the homepage to find dozens of links to locate legitimate informational pages about entertainment, culture, history, education, travel, health, Islam, and much more. Each link provides something different and exciting. The weather link informs the reader about current weather in various locations throughout Afghanistan, while the food link provides access to dozens of delicious recipes. Though there is no glossary, a search tab allows users to type in inquiries and subjects of interest, and questions can be directed to the Website host via email under the "contact us" tab.

The Website has received many awards of excellence since its launch and continues to provide comprehensive information about Afghanistan, which is its main appeal. Though it will undoubtedly appeal to those interested in the culture, it is not recommended for use as an academic resource.—**ARBA Staff Reviewer**

China

C, P, S

29.   Li, Xiaobing. **Modern China.** Santa Barbara, Calif., ABC-CLIO, 2015. 419p. illus. maps. index. (Understanding Modern Nations). $89.00. ISBN 13: 978-1-61069-625-8; 978-1-56720-761-3 (e-book).

This interdisciplinary work focuses mainly on China's rise to become the second largest economy in the world during the 1980s through the 2010s. The author closely examines China's transformation from a third-world country to a modernized nation, taking into consideration Chinese values and attitudes towards social transition and economic growth, as well as identifying key elements behind China's modernization. Following a brief introduction, the book is organized into 16 chapters addressing topics ranging from history, politics, and government to economy, media, and popular culture. Each chapter contains an overview, followed by entries on important events, major issues of contemporary relevance, biographies pertaining to the chapter's theme, and ending with cross-references and further readings. The volume concludes with a selected bibliography, an alphabetical index, and four appendixes, consisting of a day in the life, a glossary of key terms, facts and figures, and a holidays chart. By exhibiting a Chinese perspective, this well-researched and well-presented book has attained its goal of introducing the complex nature of the tremendous changes in China that have occurred during the past 30 years to a wide audience. This comprehensive work is particularly suitable for high school and undergraduate students and the general public who are interested in understanding the incredible transformation of modern China.—**Karen T. Wei**

Canada

C, P, S
30. **The Encyclopedia of Saskatchewan. http://esask.uregina.ca.** [Website] Free. Date reviewed: 2016.

The *Encyclopedia of Saskatchewan* published by the Canadian Plains Research Center at the University of Regina, launched online in 2007. The encyclopedia contains approximately 2,300 entries arranged alphabetically and over 1,000 charts, graphs, maps, tables, and photographs. The entries vary in length and some have suggestions for further readings. Cross-references within entries are highlighted. The site offers several search options: browsing by subject, an A-Z entry list, an image list, and a contributor index. A "related subjects" link on the left-hand side of the page takes users to related entries. The names of contributors appear with each entry, and a list of the editorial board and encyclopedia sponsors is available. This freely accessible encyclopedia is easy to use and will serve as a source of basic information or a starting point for further research.—**ARBA Staff Reviewer**

Europe

General Works

P, S
31. **Countries, Peoples & Cultures: Eastern Europe.** Michael Shally-Jensen, ed. Amenia, N.Y., Salem Press, 2015. 652p. illus. maps. index. (Countries, Peoples & Cultures, Volume 4). $125.00. ISBN 13: 978-1-61925-794-8.

This is the fourth volume of a projected nine-volume series. The volume provides 20-page profiles of the 25 countries that comprise Eastern Europe. Each begins with a colorful map of the country's location in the world, the country itself that highlights major cities and natural landmarks, and the nation's flag. The common format includes General Information, Environment & Geography, Customs & Courtesies, Lifestyle, Cultural History, Culture, Society, Social Development, Government, and Economy, each with several topical subdivisions. Full-color photographs, tables of information that include important statistics and useful facts, "Do You Know" fun facts, and a bibliography augment the profiles. Two lengthy appendixes, that I assume are included in each volume, address the 21 types of governments found in the world and extensive introductions to 10 of the world's religions.

This is an exceptionally beautiful and useful source, but as with all such volumes, online sources are readily available and much less expensive for libraries.—**Joe P. Dunn**

P, S

32.   Thompson, Wayne C. **The World Today Series, 2015-2016: Western Europe.** 34th ed. Lanham, Md., Rowman & Littlefield, 2015. 454p. illus. maps. (World Today series). $21.00 pa.; $19.99 (e-book). ISBN 13: 978-1-4758-1884-0; 978-1-4758-1884-0 (e-book).

Since 1982, the World Today Series has provided an annually updated, comprehensive snapshot of countries within the context of their national and regional milieu. This particular volume in the series surveys seven major regions in Western Europe: the United Kingdom and the Republic of Ireland, Benelux, The French Republic, The Eastern Mediterranean, The Alpine Democracies, The Italian Peninsula, and the Iberian Peninsula. Note that "western" is used in this series in a geographic sense rather than a political one.

Whether tiny like San Marino, or possessing longstanding regional power like the United Kingdom, the book presents each entity's essay respectfully and informatively. Each entry opens with a map(s) and a number of quick facts for easy reference, such as GDP per capita, capital city, official language, etc. All entries are then subdivided into a number of standard topics, such as history, economy, culture, and education. The narrative does well to emphasize significant characteristics of a nation's story, giving broad space to subjects like tolerance in the Netherlands or the tensions rendered by the competing Turkish and Greek ethnic groups on the small island of Cyprus. Readers may also delight in the random odd facts peppered throughout, such as the fact that the Industrial Revolution began in Belgium earlier than almost anywhere else in Europe. Preceding the national entries is a section introducing the region in general terms, which provides good insight into the ways and means of governing apparatus like NATO and the European Union.

Complete with many black-and-white photos and an extensive Website directory and English language bibliography, this volume does an excellent job of surveying a region both immensely diverse, yet inextricably linked.—**Laura Herrell**

Spain

C, P

33.   López, Enrique Ávila. **Modern Spain.** Santa Barbara, Calif., ABC-CLIO, 2016. 427p. illus. index. (Understanding Modern Nations). $89.00. ISBN 13: 978-1-61069-600-5; 978-1-61069-601-2 (e-book).

The series, Understanding Modern Nations, furnishes titles written about countries around the world. Questions about cultures, societies, and customs in the twenty-first century are answered. In this book, Enrique Ávila López, professor of humanities and general studies at Mount Royal University in Calgary, Canada, focuses on modern Spain.

This book is available as an e-book or in hardcover and contains 450 pages. The collaged cover photo is inviting and exotic in feel. A table of contents is functional as are the references, appendixes, and index. Tables and figures support the text throughout and Appendix C (Facts and Figures) will be useful for those solely seeking data. Sourcing information follows charts but tends to be from the same sources, time and time again.

Sixteen chapters structure the text and chapters begin with a very useful overview for those looking for brief information. Black-and-white photos throughout are not engaging though they are well captioned. For deeper learning, chapters are well organized into subtopics. These key entries are followed by "cross-references" for easy access to related information elsewhere in the book and further reading suggestions, both print and digital. Chapters end with references.

In a few instances, paragraphs seem misplaced. For example, a paragraph in the geography chapter discusses fish and food production which could have been more easily accessed in chapter four under the topic section about agriculture and the fishing industry.

Modern Spain provides detailed data on contemporary culture and issues. López does well to intertwine facts with the multifaceted history and rich diversity of Spain. This book represents a fusion of many elements and in researching present-day Spain; López does well to expose the country and its issues while giving a succinct picture of what life looks like for Spaniards. Spain as part of the global community is introduced, but the focus is weightier on culture and modern life. This book is a solid overview of Spain today and will give readers a greater appreciation of the country. This book will be useful to high school and undergraduate students, and most practical to those who intend to travel to Spain. Not a travel guide, but a worthy tool for access to modern Spain.

Recommended.—**Janis Minshull**

Latin America and the Caribbean

General Works

P, S

34.   **Countries, Peoples & Cultures: Central & South America.** Michael Shally-Jensen, ed. Hackensack, N.J., Salem Press, 2015. 532p. illus. maps. index. (Countries, Peoples & Cultures, Volume 1). $125.00. ISBN 13: 978-1-61925-788-7; 978-1-61925-789-4 (e-book).

This reference explores the countries of Central and South America, showing us similarities and differences. For each nation we are given general demographics as well as brief descriptions of its geography; customs; lifestyle; culture; the economy; social development to include standard of living, education, women's rights, and health care; government to include structure and foreign policy; as well as a bibliography for further reading. As an example of what we learn, Sao Paulo, Brazil, is the largest city in the Americas, surpassing Mexico City and New York City. Landlocked Bolivia is a plurinational state in which the constitution requires each "nation" or region to be recognized and respected. The Quechua and the Aymara, indigenous Amerindian peoples, represent 55 percent of the population. At least 39 official languages are spoken in Bolivia. The University of San

Francisco Xavier in Sucre, Bolivia, is considered the oldest university in the Americas. It was established two years prior to the founding of Harvard. The appendixes include essays on the world's different forms of government and religions. This survey introduces the secondary student to this vibrant and diverse part of our globe.—**Adrienne Antink**

4 Economics and Business

General Works

Dictionaries and Encyclopedias

C, P

35. **Encyclopedia of Business Information Sources.** 31st ed. Farmington Hills, Mich., Gale/Cengage Learning, 2014. 2v. index. $687.00/set. ISBN 13: 978-1-4144-7814-2.

The *Encyclopedia of Business Information Sources* is designed to assist researchers "in locating material relevant to today's rapidly changing business environment." The *Encyclopedia* contains nearly 25,000 citations covering over 1,100 business, financial, and industrial topics including accounting, personnel management, specific industries, foreign trade, and information industry topics. Types of sources listed and annotated include: abstracts and indexes; almanacs and yearbooks; bibliographies; e-books; financial ratios; online databases; periodicals and newsletters; handbooks and manuals; encyclopedias and dictionaries; trade and professional associations; and research centers and institutes. The *Encyclopedia* contains an outline of contents with listings of topics and cross-references; the entries for each topic, including cross-references; and a list of sources cited. The *Encyclopedia* covers a diverse range of topics among which are: directories of corporations in the United States and overseas; economic research; economic indicators, business history, mass media; marketing; telecommunications; and specific industries (e.g., cosmetics, fitness, and banks and banking). For each topic, items are arranged within categories including online databases, directories, handbooks and manuals, and trade/professional associations. For example the topic Savings and Loan Associations contains a *see also* reference to Savings Banks and information resources grouped under types of sources categories: bibliographies, CD-ROM databases, directories, Internet databases, online database, other sources, periodicals and newsletters, and statistics sources. Each entry includes name of publisher, cost, frequency of publication, and a brief description of content. Addresses of publishers are located in the sources cited section. Each entry in sources cited includes name and address of publisher, Website, contact information, and a description of resource. The *Encyclopedia of Business Information* is a good starting point to research in various topics in business and economics. It is recommended to public, academic, and special libraries. Students and faculty researching specific industries will find a wide range of resources available. Highly recommended.—**Lucy Heckman**

C, P, S

36.   **Gale Encyclopedia of U.S. Economic History.** 2d ed. Thomas Riggs, ed. Farmington Hills, Mich., Gale/Cengage Learning, 2015. 3v. illus. maps. index. $532.00/set. ISBN 13: 978-1-57302-753-3; 978-1-57302-757-1 (e-book).

I have contributed to or reviewed approximately two dozen encyclopedias. This is the most interesting that I have seen. This second edition added 257 entirely new topics from the first edition. The 987 alphabetically arranged entries are lengthy, substantive, and well written. Most items have a bibliography that is more than merely token entries. Even more impressive are the 200 sidebars, 60 text excerpts, and more than 450 images and drawings, most in color. It constitutes an impressive visual display. Possibly the most valuable features are the lengthy "think pieces" that treat socioeconomic issues of import in American history. An example is "The History of Economic Inequality in the United States." The volumes are full of statistical information presented in a very readable fashion. Among my favorite inclusions are essays on the economic history of each state, complete with a color map that incorporates the Interstate highways and all the national and state parks, forests, and wildlife areas. Standard encyclopedia features include a list of articles, a thematic outline of contents, a quite extensive chronology, and the list of contributors.

I am not a specialist on economic history and I found myself spending hours reading various topics at random through the volumes because the material was so interesting and informative. Printed encyclopedias are at a great disadvantage against the ready access of online reference sources, but this may be one printed source whose merits allow it to compete for users.—**Joe P. Dunn**

C, S

37.   **Government and the Economy: An Encyclopedia.** Dieterle, David A. and Kathleen C. Simmons, eds. Santa Barbara, Calif., Greenwood Press/ABC-CLIO, 2014. 552p. index. $100.00. ISBN 13: 978-1-4408-2903-1; 978-1-4408-2904-8 (e-book).

This textbook provides an in-depth examination of the American government and how it is affected by the United States economy and the global economies. Twenty-five economic scholars have contributed to this collection of essays that describe important Supreme Court cases that have impacted the economic infrastructure, the biographies of famous economists, and the seven key economic systems—socialism, democratic socialism, fascism, market capitalism, state capitalism, transitional, and welfare state. The alphabetic entries are in alignment with the 20 National Content Standards in Economics and the United States History Content Standards.

There are four appendixes. They cover the Constitution of the United States, the Supreme Court and its opinions, legislative acts with economic impact, and online resources for educators and researchers. A glossary of terms used in the text, a bibliography, and an index are provided.

I would recommend this book for the business and economic collections of high school and academic libraries. It provides a very insightful study of the world government and how the economy affects them.—**Kay Stebbins Slattery**

Directories

P

38.   **The Directory of Business Information Resources, 2016.** 23d ed. Amenia, N.Y., Grey House Publishing, 2015. 2013p. index. $195.00pa.; $495.00 (online database). ISBN 13: 978-61925-900-3.

This substantial volume offers a comprehensive collection of industry-specific resources that make for a one-stop business reference. This 23d edition has enhanced a number of industry categories with nearly 300 new listings, predominantly in the alternative energy, environment and conservation, food and beverage and health care sectors, although other sectors have been enhanced, as well.

One hundred and one industries are efficiently segmented into categories of affiliated associations, directories, databases, trade shows, magazines, journals, newsletters, and Websites. The number of listings within each category will vary with industry. Listings under each of the prior categories include key names, contact information, and a brief description. Social media (Facebook, Twitter, etc.) availability is also noted if applicable. Industries and listings within the industries are presented alphabetically.

Supplementary material helps make this resource extremely navigable, such as the user guide, a content summary of chapter listings (further segmenting industry categories into more specific businesses), the NAICS and SIC (industry classification systems) reference tables, and two indexes.

Whether desiring to research an industry from a scholarly or a commercial point of view, this book and its trove of well-organized information is an indispensable starting point.—**ARBA Staff Reviewer**

Handbooks and Yearbooks

C

39.   **Business Statistics of the United States, 2014: Patterns of Economic Change.** 19th ed. Cornelia J. Strawser, ed. Lanham, Md., Bernan Press, 2015. 573p. $165.00. ISBN 13: 978-1-59888-732-7.

Business Statistics of the United States is "a basic desk reference for anyone requiring statistics on the U.S. economy. It contains over 3,000 economic time series portraying the period from World War II to December 2013 in industry, product, and demographic detail." Also, in 200 time series, the period from 1925 through 1948 is presented. New features for the 2014 edition are: a comprehensive revision of data back to 1925 on private and government fixed assets; comprehensive revision of the International Transactions Accounts and the international investment position; and expanded producer price indexes covering services as well as goods. *Business Statistics of the United States* is arranged as follows: Preface; an essay on cycle and growth perspectives; an essay with graphs on the U.S. economy, 1929-1948; general notes, including a list of data sources; and the following chapters which contain tables of data, sources of data, and definitions: "National Income and Product," "Industrial Production and Capacity Utilization," "Income Distribution and Poverty," "Consumer Income and Spending," "Savings and Investment," "Government," "U.S. Foreign Trade and Finance," "Price," "Employment

Costs, Productivity, and Profits," "Employment, Hours, and Earnings," "Energy," "Money, Interest, Assets, Liabilities and Asset Prices," "International Comparisons," "Product and Income by Industry," "Employment, Hours, and Earnings by NAICS Industry," "Key Sector Statistics," and "Index." In addition to the data, there are essays analyzing historical economic events (e.g., what was the Great Depression?) and URLs for U.S. government statistics sources. *Business Statistics of the United States* is a valuable, thorough source of data and recommended for researchers, as well as business school faculty and students. This is an essential source for research and larger academic library business and economics collections.—**Lucy Heckman**

C, P, S
40.   **Econ Lowdown. https://www.stlouisfed.org/education.** [Website] Free. Date reviewed: 2016.

Econ Lowdown is a free online resource published by the Federal Reserve Bank of St. Louis for educators, parents, and consumers who want to learn about economics, personal finance, money and banking, and the Federal Reserve. Resources are conveniently organized by educational level: elementary, middle school, high school, college, and consumer. Within the elementary category, there are lessons appropriate for various ages. For example, K-Grade 1 learns about spending vs. saving, while Grades 5-8 are taught that money was an invention. Middle school lessons get into everything from debit cards to choosing a college, and high school students are warned about predatory lending and "alternative financial services" like pawn shops and payday loans, instructed in the basics of car buying, and introduced to capital markets and the characteristics of entrepreneurs. Consumers, by which they do not mean "adults," as one might have expected, are actually given lesson plans for all ages, including podcasts and videos. This category appears to include many (all?) of the lessons available in the other categories.

In each category, lessons are arranged alphabetically and a brief summary is provided. Some are available in Spanish. Users can also perform a keyword search, so it is not necessary to guess which categories contain which lesson plans. Pinned to the top of each list is "10 FRED Activities in 10 Minutes." FRED is the Federal Reserve Economic Data free online database, and the activities range from finding and graphing GDP data to creating custom graphs. There are videos and other online tutorials to help along the way.

By far the most interesting lesson plan to this reviewer is Barbie® in the Labor Force, intended for a high school audience. The goal is to teach students about changing career options for women in the past half century by encouraging a dialog about what careers were available to Barbie® as indicated by her outfits. (If you were unaware that Barbie® had any career options at all, other than the first one, fashion model (1959), you are not alone). Notwithstanding questions about whether popular culture reflects reality, or influences it, or lags far behind it, this lesson plan asks thought-provoking questions about women's choices in different eras in thoroughly engaging ways. It also provides suggested answers, saving teachers hours of Googling. It is no wonder that the developers of *Econ Lowdown* were awarded the 2015 Abbejean Kehler Technology Award by the National Association of Economic Educators and the Council for Economic Education. The variety and depth of the lesson plans and activities are highly recommended for students of all ages, their teachers and professors, school libraries as well as public libraries looking for materials for public workshops in financial and economic literacy.—**ARBA Staff Reviewer**

S

41.   Garbus, Julia. Corridor, Shawn, ed. **U*X*L Money: Making Sense of Economics and Personal Finance.** Farmington Hills, Mich., Gale/Cengage Learning, 2015. 3v. illus. maps. index. ISBN 13: 978-1-57302-979-7; 978-1-57302-983-4 (e-book).

Connections between macroeconomics and the importance of establishing a good credit history can seem tenuous, but this excellent three-volume set makes the case that understanding economic theory, from international trade to the workings of the stock market, relates to being a savvy consumer. Each volume includes the complete index and table of contents for the set. Chapters include brief summaries of main ideas, study questions, glossaries, and recommended print and online sources for additional reading. Well-written entries interweave explanations of economic concepts such as Smith's invisible hand and the prisoner's dilemma with current events such as the Great Recession. The third volume will be of especial importance to many high school students because it focuses on the basics of personal finance, providing concrete examples to help young people understand such topics as the implications of various types of student loans and the basics of investing in stocks and bonds.—**Delilah R. Caldwell**

C

42.   **Worldmark Global Business and Economy Issues.** Farmington Hills, Mich., Gale/Cengage Learning, 2015. 2v. $310.00/set. ISBN 13: 978-1-4109-1756-8; 978-1-4103-1759-9 (e-book).

International business knowledge is growing with importance as globalization continues to make the world a smaller place. *Worldmark Global Business and Economy Issues* covers a wide range of relevant topics that include marketing, human resource management, finance/accounting, and development economics. Intended to reach the needs of students focusing on global studies, this collection provides users with an in-depth look at issues surrounding international business. This new collection is split into two volumes; volume one being Business and volume two being Economy. There are a variety of sections that include resources for more information, a list of key organizations, and an index, as well as thematic outlines for both volumes. Brief sidebars highlight additional relevant information, such as extended text on certain topics, biographical information, and pop culture topics. Graphics and images support the relevant information throughout the text and help keep the content engaging.

One of the more unique aspects of this collection is the inclusion of primary source information shared by way of subheadings in the main chapters. There is a Using Primary Sources section in volume one that discusses how and why to use primary sources. These additions help provide context and history for the reader. A glossary of terms is located in the beginning of each volume and both sections have a chronology of events, which are very useful for a newcomer to international business. These sections help put historical and current development into perspective. *Worldmark Global Business and Economy Issues* is an effective text for teaching relevant international business issues. It covers topics that affect consumers and business owners worldwide, and provides context for readers to analyze, understand, and apply important topics in the discipline. It can be used in the classroom or as a resource text. This set is a valuable addition to any academic or business-oriented library.—**Jessica Crossfield McIntosh**

Accounting

C, P

43.   Shim, Jae K., Joel G. Siegel, Nick Dauber, and Anique A. Qureshi. **Accounting Handbook.** 6th ed. Hauppauge, N.Y., Barron's Educational Series, 2014. 1062p. index. $39.99pa. ISBN 13: 978-0-7641-6657-0.

Since accounting is a detail-oriented field, it is helpful to both students and professionals to have access to a desk reference to look up quick information. This handbook is from Barron's, a publisher known for their guides. The authors are professors, a former professor, and a lecturer at universities so they should have a strong understanding of the academic area and its needs.

The handbook is a large single volume which makes it handier than multiple volume competitors even if less detailed. The handbook is a combined encyclopedia and dictionary in one. It is organized by topic with descriptions and examples, and includes a section for a dictionary of accounting terms. It includes chapters on financial statements and analysis, financial reporting requirements, management accounting, individual income taxation, information technology, quantitative methods for accounting, auditing and internal control, personal financial planning, governmental and nonprofit accounting, international accounting and financial reporting standards, and forensic accounting. It also includes appendixes on a summary of the Sarbanes-Oxley Act of 2002 and a Sarbanes-Oxley Compliance Practice Aid.

This is not a handbook for beginners or people with no accounting or business experience. There are terms and concepts that they may not be familiar enough with to be able to understand this handbook fully. For example, there is not a good explanation of accounting standards and the types of standards. In addition, the organization of the handbook is not clear. For example, the accounting terms are stuck in the middle of the handbook. The table of contents and index are very helpful in navigating the book. It also has cross-references to be able to find additional information. The individual entries are concise and easily readable. While the content may be confusing to beginners, it could be a valuable resource for accounting or business students and some professionals needing a refresher or to look up something quickly.—**Breezy Silver**

Consumer Guides

C

44.   **Real-World Decision Making: An Encyclopedia of Behavioral Economics.** Morris Altman, ed. Santa Barbara, Calif., Greenwood Press/ABC-CLIO, 2015. 499p. index. $100.00. ISBN 13: 978-1-4408-2815-7; 978-1-4408-2816-4 (e-book).

Economics is a multifaceted discipline which regularly subdivides into more specialized research areas. This book has been compiled as an attempt to provide the reader with a comprehensive set of definitions and explanations of key concepts used by researchers in the area of behavioral economics. The definitions have been written to be useful to the scholars doing research in this multidisciplinary area as well as providing insight for students, public policy experts, and journalists. Over 240 concepts are defined and over a dozen well-known experts in the field are profiled. A list of the contributors who provided the definitions for this encyclopedia has been included. Just reviewing the lists of terms shows the reader how diverse the field has become and the types of methodological tools that are used in developing their premises. The reader will find that each term includes a short, appended reading list.

This book will be useful in academic institutions that have economic departments.—**Judith J. Field**

Finance and Banking

C, P

45. **The Directory of Venture Capital & Private Equity Firms: Domestic & International.** 19th ed. Amenia, N.Y., Grey House Publishing, 2015. 1352p. index. $395.00pa. ISBN 13: 978-1-61925-550-0.

Now in its 19th edition, *The Directory of Venture Capital & Private Equity Firms* provides information on over 3,000 firms, more than 1,000 branches, and more than 12,000 partners. This edition includes approximately 300 new firms and 1,000 new partners.

Like the other editions, this one is logically organized and easy to use. The information is divided into four major sections: Domestic Firms, Canadian Firms, Domestic Associations, and International Firms; information in each section is listed alphabetically.

The firm profiles include such necessary pieces of information as mission statements, geographic preferences, contact information, and investment criteria. Users will also find career and education information on partners. Each firm profile is assigned a number, which is referenced in the indexes.

The five indexes enhance the usability of this resource. The college/university index lists approximately 800 schools and the executives who attended them. The executive index lists the key partners (more than 12,000). For those who want to search by area, the geographic index organizes firms by state in the case of domestic listings and by country for international listings. These three finding aids are followed by the industry reference index—this lists more than 200 industry segments alphabetically along with the names of the firms that invest. The final index, the portfolio companies index, lists in alphabetical order more than 15,000 companies that receive venture capital from a firm listed in the directory.

Those buyers interested in purchasing this as an online database should consult http://gold.greyhouse.com. Public libraries and academic libraries will want a copy of this valuable reference resource.—**ARBA Staff Reviewer**

C, P

46. Downes, John, and Jordan E. Goodman. **Finance & Investment Handbook.** 9th ed. Hauppauge, N.Y., Barron's Educational Series, 2014. 1152p. index. $39.99. ISBN 13: 978-0-7641-6751-5.

The purpose of this *Finance & Investment Handbook* is not to advise, but to "join in one volume the different elements" that together make up the world of finance and investment. This one-volume handbook provides a comprehensive presentation of terms and concepts of financial and investment terms that will enable the investor to talk knowledgeably with their broker, or as a broker, to be a better source of advice.

The handbook is divided into five parts: how to invest your money, which defines 30 key personal investment opportunities; how to read annual and quarterly reports; how to understand the financial news; the dictionary of finance and investment terms; and a finance and investment reference that provides a listing of organizations and government agencies, financial institutions, mutual funds, historical data, and publicly traded companies.

The definitions are concise and are accompanied by graphs and sidebars of additional information. Cross-references are minimal. The finance and investment ready reference lists provide names and contact information for financial sources. There is an appendix that provides a bibliography of financial and economic books, currencies of the world, and abbreviations and acronyms used in the book.

I would recommend this handbook to public and academic libraries business sections.—**Kay Stebbins Slattery**

C, P

47.   **Encyclopedia of Education Economics & Finance.** Dominic J. Brewer and Lawrence O. Picus, eds. Thousand Oaks, Calif., Sage, 2014. 2v. index. $375.00/set. ISBN 13: 978-1-4522-8185-8.

The Encyclopedia of Education Economics & Finance is edited by Dominic J. Brewer, Gale and Ira Drukier Dean of New York University's Steinhardt School of Culture, Education, and Human Development and Lawrence O. Picus, professor of education finance and policy at the Rossier School of Education at the University of Southern California. These two, along with an editorial board of leading academics in the field of education policy and economics, solicited the more than 300 scholarly entries that comprise this two-volume work.

The entries are arranged alphabetically; however, a reader's guide at the beginning of each volume organizes topics thematically under such categories as "Accountability and Education Policy," "Production and Costs of Schooling," "Revenue and Aid for Schools," and "Teacher Labor Markets." Entries are several pages in length and each concludes with suggestions for further reading and *see also* references. The second volume includes three appendixes: a resource guide, an education chronology, and a glossary, followed by a subject index that contains *see* and *see also* references. The electronic version of the encyclopedia combines the index, reader's guide, and cross-references for easy searching.

A brief entry list is enough to indicate the scope of this encyclopedia in which users can find information on the Common Core, the benefits of higher education, *Brown* v. *Board of Education,* early childhood education, education technology, for-profit higher education, general obligation bonds, property taxes, private contributions to schools, professional development, and much more. Public and academic libraries will want to own a copy of this well-researched, inclusive, and highly recommended title.—**ARBA Staff Reviewer**

C, P

48.   Lehu, Pierre A. **Living on Your Own: The Complete Guide to Setting up Your Money, Your Space, and Your Life.** Sanger, Calif., Quill Driver, 2014. 232p. index. $18.95pa. ISBN 13: 978-1-61035-212-3.

Perhaps you've recently graduated from college. You've landed your first real job and mom is eyeing your bedroom for a new yoga studio. You're geared up to move out and move on, but where do you start and what should you expect? This book provides much of what you need to know in terms of planning, financing, and maintaining a life away from the nest.

The book is divided into sections covering home, personal, and financial aspects of life on one's own. Initial chapters help determine budgets and moving and living expenses, followed by the brass tacks of day-to-day life such as home furnishings, house cleaning, and utilities. The latter half of the book gets personal regarding issues of medical care, diet, and relationships. The book concludes with basic but important financial and legal advice.

Chapters are brief with generous headings, bulleted lists, and sidebars which make the information highly engaging and accessible. The author includes an ample supply of personal anecdotes, money-saving tips, and helpful community resources as well. From advice on air-drying laundry (saves money and smells nice) to the contemporary issues surrounding managing one's life via smart phone, *Living on Your Own* is the book for any adult taking their first baby steps out into the real world.—**Laura Herrell**

C, P, S

49.   **Personal Finance: An Encyclopedia of Modern Money Management.** Barbara Friedberg, ed. Santa Barbara, Calif., Greenwood Press/ABC-CLIO, 2015. 403p. index. $89.00. ISBN 13: 978-1-4408-3031-0; 978-1-4408-3032-7 (e-book).

Personal Finance: An Encyclopedia of Modern Money Management is a complete source that reports research and trends on sound financial decisions for the average person. Designed for researchers, scholars, and novices *Personal Finance* fills the need for personal financial education reference resources. Author Barbara Friedberg has previously published books on financial education and also has experience as an educator, chief financial officer, chief information officer, and chief executive officer. The book includes supplementary items such as an index, glossary, and suggested further reading on topics mentioned in the book.

The book is formatted akin to an encyclopedia but does differ in some aspects. The book is divided into three sections concerning personal finance—Ideas and Concepts, Events, and People. Within those three sections, topics are arranged alphabetically as one would find in an encyclopedia. Entries under those sections are neatly organized and typically include a general introduction followed by writings on specific topics. As an example Alimony is filed under the Ideas and Concepts section and has further sections on the history of alimony, alimony and gender, and more. This type of format is great for neophytes to the financial world because it provides a broad understanding of a subject as well as the option to dig deeper into the subject. The contents of this book, devoid of personal commentary from Friedman, provide the reader with a more research-driven and fact-driven reporting style. The reader will not necessarily be guided into making decisions about their own finances but will be educated in the process and history of the financial world. This book would be a solid addition to any academic or high school library and would correlate with the curriculum of any economics class. That said, the same lack of personal finance resources coupled with the general lack of knowledge surrounding personal finances also make this a great addition to a public library.

Personal Finance: An Encyclopedia of Modern Money Management is recommended for high school, academic, and public libraries.—**Sara Mofford**

Insurance

C, P

50.   Heckman, Lucy. **The ALA Guide to Information Sources in Insurance, Risk Management and Actuarial Science.** Chicago, American Library Association, 2016. 213p. index. $70.00pa.; $63.00pa. (ALA members). ISBN 13: 978-0-8389-1275-1.

Lucy Heckman (Head of Reference, St. John's University Library and author of several business-related guides to information sources) has focused her expertise on the insurance industry, creating a detailed bibliography covering all aspects of insurance and actuarial science. Written for a wider audience than librarians, this book is organized intuitively, with materials for general insurance information, and textbooks comprising the first two chapters, and then delving deeper into the many subspecialties of insurance, risk management, and actuarial science. Within those chapters, sources are broken out by format, allowing readers the option to locate materials most conducive to their reading preferences. Heckman finishes her bibliography with chapters dedicated to information sources geared towards education and finding careers in insurance and then a chapter of miscellaneous sources. Particularly helpful for librarians in smaller institutions, or in institutions without dedicated reference for business and related disciplines, Heckman provides several appendixes, covering an alphabet soup of abbreviations and acronyms, lists of associations and agencies with their Websites, select journals with ISSN numbers, school and university departments supporting insurance, risk management and/or actuarial science, and selected major libraries (academic and public) supporting business and management. A small but detailed reference work, this paperback could function as the one insurance, risk management, and actuarial science resource for academic libraries with smaller collections or for public libraries with a strong business focus. For larger institutions, this text would provide a handy quick guide in a reference collection.—**Rachel Meredith Minkin**

Labor

Career Guides

P, S

51.   **Careers in Building Construction.** Michael Shally-Jensen, ed. Hackensack, N.J., Salem Press, 2015. 351p. illus. index. $95.00. ISBN 13: 978-1-61925-862-4; 978-1-61925-863-1 (e-book).

This book provides a compact resource for examining the many career possibilities in building construction. Readers will learn general information about this growing and changing sector, as well as more targeted information regarding specific jobs. Particular mention is made of "green" construction and its emphasis on sustainability, energy efficiency, and environmental awareness.

Alphabetically arranged chapters guide readers through 26 diverse jobs, such as brickmason, electrician, plumber, surveyor, and landscape architect. Within each chapter, readers will find ample and varied information detailing specific work duties, the expected work environment, occupation specialties (a heavy-equipment operator may specialize in a particular vehicle, e.g., a crawler-tractor, scraper, or fine-grade bulldozer), educational requirements, earnings and advancement potential, and much more. The use of bullet points, shaded sidebars, tables, and photographs make the material easy to navigate. Some special features include "Fun Facts," "Famous Firsts," projected employment trends, interviews with professionals, and a listing of applicable organizations readers can consult for further information.

Appendixes explain the Holland Code, which provides a useful tool to help potential job seekers match their personalities with career possibilities, and provide a bibliography.

Compiled in a positive, straightforward manner, this book will appeal to young readers just beginning to considering their career path or even older readers mulling a shift into this job sector. An index makes for quick searching for those interested in a particular career.—**ARBA Staff Reviewer**

P, S

52.　**Careers in Human Services.** Michael Shally-Jensen, ed. Hackensack, N.J., Salem Press, 2015. 357p. illus. index. $95.00. ISBN 13: 978-1-61925-778-8; 978-1-61925-779-5 (e-book).

Human Services is a broad career category that includes many compelling and surprisingly diverse jobs that call for attention and study. This well-organized, easy-to-use reference can help job seekers learn general information about Human Services and perhaps narrow their choices within the field.

Alphabetically arranged chapters guide readers through 25 different specialties, ranging from activities therapist to vocational rehabilitation counselor. Within each chapter, readers will find ample and encouraging information detailing specific job duties, the expected work environment, occupation specialties, educational requirements, earnings and advancement potential, and much more. The use of such devices as bullet points, shaded sidebars, and tables makes the material easy to navigate. Some special features include a brief history of a particular job, a typical day in the life on the job, interviews with professionals, a "snapshot" of the job, and a listing of applicable organizations readers can consult for more information.

The book also includes a helpful overview providing a general sense of the types of people who might pursue a career in Human Services, the types of people who might benefit from these jobs (e.g., the elderly, military veterans, immigrants, etc.), the types of professional Human Services organizations available, and more. In addition, an appendix provides a useful tool to help potential job seekers match their personalities with career possibilities, followed by a bibliography and an index.

Compiled in a positive, comprehensive manner, this book will appeal to those embarking on their first job search as well as those considering a shift into this fulfilling job sector. Recommended for students at the high school and undergraduate level.—**Laura Herrell**

P, S

53.　**Careers in Technical Services & Equipment Repair.** Michael Shally-Jensen, ed. Amenia, N.Y., Grey House Publishing, 2015. 326p. illus. index. $95.00. ISBN 13: 978-1-61925-780-1; 978-1-61925-781-8 (e-book).

This guidebook is a go-to source for those considering entering the broad field of technical services and equipment repair. It not only educates readers as to what types of jobs are available, but also provides ample information regarding the greater job environment in an engaging way.

Alphabetically arranged chapters guide readers through 25 different jobs, ranging from aircraft mechanic to vending machine repair. Within each chapter, readers will take a straightforward and thorough look at specific job duties, elements of the work environment, occupation specialties, educational and training requirements, earnings and advancement potential, and much more. The use of bullet points, shaded sidebars, tables and more makes the material easy to follow. Some special features include "Famous Firsts," a typical day in the life on the job, conversations with professionals, a "snapshot" of the job, and a listing of applicable organizations readers can consult for more information.

The book also includes a helpful overview providing a general sense of the types of people who might pursue a technical career, an employment outlook, and information about training, skills, and certifications. In addition, an appendix provides a useful tool based on the Holland Code to help potential job seekers match their personalities with career possibilities.

Compiled in a positive, comprehensive manner, this book will appeal to those embarking on their first job search as well as those considering a shift into this fulfilling job sector.—**Laura Herrell**

P, S

54.   **Encyclopedia of Careers and Vocational Guidance.** 16th ed. New York, Infobase Publishing, 2015. 5v. $249.95/set. ISBN 13: 978-0-8160-8503-3.

The Encyclopedia of Careers and Vocational Guidance has been in print for more than 45 years and is now in its 16th edition. This edition includes more than 50 new job articles, over 15 new career field and industry articles, hundreds of new photographs, and updated career information about 820 jobs in 120 fields in five volumes. This edition also includes such new sections as Career Ladders and Tips for Entry.

The first volume's Career Guidance section provides chapters on preparing for a career, finding a job, applying for a job, and what job seekers need to know once hired. In each of these chapters, users will find an annotated list of related Websites. Career Guidance is followed by Career Fields and Industries, which has overviews of 120 career fields or industries such as book publishing, computer and video game design, insurance, railroads, trucking, and waste management. The first volume concludes with two appendixes, the first of which, "Career Resources and Associations for Individuals with Disabilities," supplies Web and physical addresses, phone numbers, and other information. The second, "Internships, Apprenticeships, and Training Programs," has been completely updated for this edition and gives names, physical and Web addresses, and phone numbers for government and other organizations. Four indexes conclude the first volume.

The career articles are arrayed in four alphabetically organized volumes; each starts with a list of the career articles it contains and concludes with a job index that pertains to the whole set. Black-and-white photographs and sidebars with quick facts enhance these entries. Individual job descriptions convey a wealth of information about earnings potential, required education and training, advancement prospects, and much more.

This reference makes accessible a large amount of career-related information and is recommended to public and school libraries.—**ARBA Staff Reviewer**

Handbooks and Yearbooks

C, P

55. **Employment, Hours, and Earnings 2015.** 10th ed. Ryan, Mary Meghan, ed. Lanham, Md., Bernan Press, 2014. 726p. $105.00; $104.99 (e-book). ISBN 13: 978-1-59888-787-7; 978-1-59888-788-4 (e-book).

   Employment Hours, and Earnings: States and Areas 2015, a special addition to Bernan Press's *Handbook of U.S. Labor Statistics: Employment, Earnings, Prices, Productivity, and Other Labor Data* "is a consolidated wealth of employment information, providing monthly and annual data on hours worked and earnings made by industry across America for the years 2005 through 2014." This resource covers the 50 states, the District of Columbia, and America's 75 largest metropolitan statistical areas (MSAs). *Employment, Hours and Earnings* is divided into sections: Part A, State Data, and Part B, Metropolitan Statistical Area (MSA) Data. Part A contains data for individual states; coverage includes: population (2005 estimate, 2010 census, and 2014 estimate); percent change in population for 2005-2014 and 2010-2014; percent change in total nonfarm employment; industry with the largest growth in employment, 2005-2014; industry with the largest decline or smallest growth in employment, 2005-2014; civilian labor force for 2005, 2010, and 2014; unemployment rate and rank among states for 2005, 2010, 2014; over-the-year change in employment rates 2011-2012, 2012-2013, 2013-2014; employment by industry (pie chart); and tables for employment by industry, 2005-2014 and average hourly earnings by selected industry, 2010-2014. Part B contains MSA data including employment by industry 2005-2014. Additionally the book includes a table of 75 MSAs ranked by population; in the overall rankings list, each MSA provides employment and unemployment rates. Specific MSAs covered include: New York-Newark-Jersey City, NY-NJ-PA; Los Angeles-Long Beach-Anaheim, CA; Denver-Auroroa-Lakewood, CO; and Raleigh, NC. The appendix contains the 75 largest MSAs and components (as defined February 2013). Each MSA entry includes core based statistical area; state/county FIPS code; and a list of counties included within each MSA. This reference resource fills a need for employment data by state and MSA and provides approximately 300 tables. An explanation of concepts and terms is included in the Overview section. Recommended to larger public and academic libraries.—**Lucy Heckman**

Management

P

56. Alexander, Geoff. **The Nonprofit Survival Guide: A Strategy for Sustainability.** Jefferson, N.C., McFarland, 2015. 212p. index. $29.95pa. ISBN 13: 978-0-7864-9844-4; 978-1-4766-2050-3 (e-book).

   The big picture challenges of the nonprofit organization are many. How do you attract funding from limited pockets? How does your cause stand out above the crowd of equally worthy organizations? And how do you and your mission stay afloat during tough economic times? This book helps readers gain control of the smaller challenges behind running a nonprofit so that they can keep their focus on the big picture and keep their nonprofit running smoothly.

Short but informative chapters organize a variety of topics geared around the overall theme of success. Information details how to set up an office, how to create and maintain an online presence, the importance of volunteers, pursuing sponsorships and nontraditional modes of income, managing publicity, and thinking alternatively, among other things. Prevalent use of subheadings, checklists, real-life examples, and more helps make the material memorable and actionable.

There are two appendixes. The first provides case studies of three successful nonprofits and the second a sample checklist that organizes a nonprofit's inventory (down to software particulars) and important access information. There are also extensive notes, a good bibliography, and an index.

Written in an experienced and encouraging tone, this book is the right choice for those interested in running or working within the growing nonprofit sector.—**ARBA Staff Reviewer**

P

57.   Bolton, Robert, and Dorothy Grover Bolton. **What Great Trainers Do: The Ultimate Guide to Delivering Engaging and Effective Learning.** New York, AMACOM/ American Management Association, 2015. 304p. index. $45.00pa. ISBN 13: 978-0-8144-2006-5; 978-0-8144-2007-2 (e-book).

Even the best job trainers need training, and this book offers a warehouse full of the latest, most effective tips and tools for helping readers become the best corporate trainers they can.

The book addresses the many elements of successful training in a way that allows readers to comprehend the importance of utilizing these elements together. Key sections highlight the overall importance of fusing solid content with active training, with particular emphasis on developing a dynamic workshop, the trainer as facilitator, and maturing as a trainer.

Singular topics under these umbrella concepts include how to best use flip charts and PowerPoint slides, how to actively engage workshop participants, how to keep training positive, and how to improve things in training that don't work well.

Material is broken down into small, headed sections for ease of reference, and the authors use lists, bullet points, charts, and other devices as well. Appendixes offer worksheets to help trainers prepare a course, tips on how to adapt workshops to their audience, and advice on how to "install" one's training program.

With its positive tone and solid selection of best practices, the book will set readers off on the right path to enhance job training to the point of vastly improved corporate result.—**Laura Herrell**

Marketing and Trade

C, P

58.   VanAuken, Brad. **Brand Aid: A Quick Reference Guide to Solving your Branding Problems and Strengthening Your Market Position.** 2d ed. New York, AMACOM/ American Management Association, 2014. 352p. index. $29.95. ISBN 13: 978-0-8144-3473-4.

In the ultracompetitive world of business, it is your brand that sets you apart. And a brand, of course, is much more than a simple logo. *Brand Aid* is a perfect book for marketing novices or business veterans who are looking to strengthen their grasp of the elements behind building, sustaining, and maximizing a brand.

The author has condensed his many years of experience in the marketing and brand management world into this information-packed resource. He begins with the essentials by establishing the importance of brand management, a common branding vocabulary, and an overview of the total brand management process. The book then concisely explores numerous topics related to designing, building, and leveraging a brand. Chapters explore the need to understand consumers and competition, the effectiveness of nontraditional marketing approaches like contests or sponsorships, the ideas behind a "total brand experience," the ability to brand globally, and much more. The book further explores related topics such as legal issues and common brand problems.

This second edition includes expanded coverage of many of these topics, as well as more up-to-date brand examples throughout. It has also been updated with information related to how branding can be maximized online via multiple social media formats and blogs. The new edition further incorporates the latest ideas appealing to marketers and consumers, such as sustainability, neuromarketing, and brand storytelling.

The book incorporates case studies, charts, best practices, and detailed checklists. It includes three appendixes: Brand Audits, Online Brand Management and Advertising Resources, and References/Further Reading. Notes and an index round out the work. The book's ease of use and thorough coverage will satisfy readers from all aspects of the branding process—marketers, advertisers, and seasoned executives alike. Recommended for academic, business, and public libraries.—**Laura Herrell**

Service Industries

P
59. Miziker, Ron. **Miziker's Complete Event Planner's Handbook.** Albuquerque, N.Mex., University of New Mexico Press, 2015. 459p. illus. index. $34.95pa. ISBN 13: 978-0-8263-5551-5.

Written by the founder and director of the Miziker Entertainment Group in Los Angeles, this book packs an enormous amount of valuable information into more than 450 pages in a title compact enough to be truly portable.

There are approximately 300 pages of terminology entries arranged alphabetically for ease of use. The entries also contain cross-references; some entries are followed by further tips and suggestions. Throughout the terms section of the book users will find sidebars related to the author's event planning experiences. The definitions themselves are useful for all planners, from the novice to the experienced professional. The terminology section is followed by more than 150 pages of "Tables and Techniques," which detail beverage consumption per person, the temperature at which to serve different types of wine, a sample event budget, the proper flowers for theme dinners, flag protocol, food quantities, invitations, linens, napkin folding, wedding seating arrangements, room setup, and more. A list of Websites and a bibliography complete this offering.

This excellent and extensive guide will be useful to event planners, students studying hospitality or related fields, or anyone planning an event. Highly recommended.—**ARBA Staff Reviewer**

5 Education

General Works

Almanacs

C, P

60. **The Almanac of American Education 2014-2015.** 8th ed. Deirdre A. Gaquin and Gwenavere W. Dunn, eds. Lanham, Md., Bernan Press, 2015. 563p. index. $79.00pa. ISBN 13: 978-1-59888-736-5; 978-1-59888-737-2 (e-book).

The Almanac of American Education is a useful print compilation of statistics from the U.S. Census Bureau, the National Center for Education Statistics, and other sources. The book is broken down into three education statistics sections; national, region and state, and county. Each part opens with informative graphs and analysis followed by numerous tables of current and historical data. Each section ends with notes and definitions about the data. The statistics focus on enrollment, both current and historical, educational attainment, and county by county comparisons on a number of differing variables. Numbers can be found on per student expenditures, free or reduced lunch programs, unemployment rates based on educational attainment, dropout rates, and more. The almanac has a very useful appendix providing a guide to educational resources on the Internet for further research. This almanac is a must have in any educational research setting, and would be a good addition to any public or academic library collection. The scope of the almanac, stated clearly in the preface, makes it essential for anyone doing comparative research.—**Sue Ellen Knowlton**

Dictionaries and Encyclopedias

C, P

61. **Encyclopedia of Christian Education.** George Thomas Kurian and Mark A. Lamport, eds. Lanham, Md., Rowman & Littlefield, 2015. 3v. index. $340.00/set; $329.99 (e-book). ISBN 13: 978-0-8108-8492-2; 978-0-8108-8493-9 (e-book).

Libraries that serve students of the Christian faith, whether in the context of a seminary, undergraduate institution, or public library, are well advised to purchase a copy of the landmark, three-volume *Encyclopedia of Christian Education.* As attested to by each of the forewords, prologue, preface, and introduction (all written with pathos by leading theologians and practitioners), *Christian Education* aims to enrich the mind and faith of believers in the Christian gospel using the tools of all available disciplines and knowledge of how and what residents of the Christian world have learned over the millennia. In it, well-credentialed scholars from all over the globe describe the 2,000-year history of Christian education and its contemporary, global state in 1,200 articles. Entries detailing biographies, institutions, philosophies, praxis, and more fill a sizeable gap in reference literature, while most denominations that adhere to the orthodox, Trinitarian doctrine and most nations that feature some level of Christian education receive treatment. Naturally, we read much about the philosophies, pedagogies, curricula, and administration of education itself. We also learn about the settings of education, from institutions of higher learning to those of the Church and its organizations, or even the home. While the editors have included articles about the Christian faith and its doctrines, these are introductory compared to the length and breadth of the articles dealing with education itself (compare the length of "Jesus Christ" to "Learning and the Rise of Vernacular Languages").

In terms of accessibility, librarians might determine that effective use of the encyclopedia will require some assistance given some of its unique features. For example, the A-Z list of 1,200 entries corresponds to 19 lead-in introductions that are found after the last Z article. Articles dealing with Christian pedagogy, then, have a five-page introduction in the third volume, though the articles themselves can be found throughout the whole alphabet. For optimal searching, the user would wish to have all of the volumes present. Secondly, some of the entries are titled in ways that may confuse novice readers. "Diversity," for example, refers narrowly to ethnic diversity rather than multiculturalism, while "Special Needs" refers to special education or entries related to disability. "Deaf" and "Blind" receive their own entries. One could easily overlook some of these related articles because of the dearth of *see also* references in the articles themselves.

Yet these unique features detract only little from the value of this important addition. I found the set a treasure, from the front matter described above to the A-Z entries, the 17-page bibliography, and the appendixes with statistics on the global Christian community, its populations, and universities. The set closes with an index of names and entries and short biographies of the contributors. Highly recommended.—**Amy Koehler**

Directories

C, P, S

62. **Educators Resource Directory 2015/2016.** 11th ed. Amenia, N.Y., Grey House Publishing, 2015. 765p. index. $145.00pa. ISBN 13: 978-1-61925-549-4.

Designed to allow busy education professionals easy and well-curated access to associations, publications, trade shows, workshops, and training programs, as well as educational resources for their students and schools, *Educators Resource Directory 2015/2016* is organized into three sections. Of the 6,408 entries in section one, 140 are new to this edition. Here users will find key contact names, fax numbers, e-mail addresses, and Websites arranged into 13 chapters: "Associations & Organizations"; "Conferences & Trade Shows"; "Consultants; Teaching Opportunities Abroad"; "Financial Resources; Government Agencies"; "Professional Development"; "Publications, Publishers"; "Research Centers"; "School Supplies"; "Testing Resources"; "Software"; and "Hardware & Internet Resources." Section two presents ample information on national and state statistics. Valuably, this section also includes international and Canadian data. The indexes—publisher, geographic, and subject—and a glossary comprise section three. This incomparable source is recommended for every school, public, and academic library.— **Melinda F. Matthews**

Handbooks and Yearbooks

C, P, S

63. **Causation or Correlation? http://jfmueller.faculty.noctrl.edu/100/correlation_ or_causation.htm.** [Website] Free. Date reviewed: 2016

This Website was created by a teacher in order to help his upper-grade students identify the differences between causal relationships and correlations. The Web page has a simple design and features two columns. The left column contains headlines of public press articles and clickable links that lead to external pages. If the articles are based on academic studies, those are also included. At the bottom of the column, "Related Resources" includes cartoons, graphs, and blogs that will better equip students to use and identify correlation and causal language. The right column is text-heavy and describes the purpose of this Website to users. A few links are included that lead to student activities most helpful for teachers to download and use in class. Teachers should be aware that the Website seems to be in an early stage of development and does not contain much content apart from the columns and is not comprehensive.

This resource is recommended for both high school students and teachers. Students will benefit most from the left column and the dozens of interesting articles that will teach them about correlations and causations. The activities would be helpful for middle school students as well, though some of the article content is mature; BBC's "Higher Beer Prices 'Cut Gonorrhea Rates'" is an informative read, but may be inappropriate for a younger audience. The right column will be useful for any teachers, especially those instructing a statistics course.—**ARBA Staff Reviewer**

C, P, S

64. **Digital Public Library of America: Primary Source Sets. http://dp.la/primary-source-sets/sets?tags[]=law-government.** [Website] Free. Date reviewed: 2016.

Provides a wide selection (100 as of this review) of primary source sets designed to help educators promote critical thinking skills with their students. The sets, created by the Digital Public Library of America (DPLA)'s Educational Advisory Board, address a variety of topics related to American history, art, and literature including *Beloved, The Scarlet Letter,* the internment of Japanese Americans, the Underground Railroad, the 1878 yellow fever epidemic, school desegregation in Boston, the invention of the telephone, and the populist movement. Each set begins with a brief overview and a link to a teaching guide, followed by digital reproductions of 10 to 15 sources from the DPLA, and links to authoritative online sources on the topic for further research. The sets have all been assigned one or two subjects and a time period allowing users to easily narrow the array or find related source sets. Each source suggests that students consider the author's point of view, the author's purpose, the historical context, and audience, and includes a citation and links to the content record both at DPLA and the item's home institution. The digital scans are good quality and can be enlarged, but not always enough to read the fine print on some items. The teaching guides present discussion questions and classroom activities linked to individual primary sources. General suggestions for primary source analysis and links to information on using primary sources from the National Archives and the Library of Congress are also included. Overall this will be a useful and intriguing collection for educators in history and literature.—**ARBA Staff Reviewer**

C, S

65. **InfoSci-Educational Science and Technology. http://www.igi-global.com/e-resources /infosci-subject-databases/infosci-education/.** [Website] Hershey, Pa., Information Science Reference/IGI Global. Price negotiated by site. Date reviewed: 2016.

The *InfoSci-Educational Science and Technology* database provides full-text access to over 430 e-books on education and educational technology research. This academic reference collection also includes some teaching cases and appears to also be adding some video resources.

The collection represents the work of education and technology researchers on a wide range of topics from blended and mobile learning to gaming trends in education, and from educational administration and leadership to special education. These topics are covered from all perspectives from K-12 to higher education.

The search interface provides three different search options: basic, advanced, and "expert." The advanced search option allows full-text keyword searching as well as title, author, DOI, and publication date. The "expert" search option allows you to exclude and weight search terms. This is very interesting and the option is appreciated while not anticipated to see much use. The books are indexed and searchable at the chapter level.

The database delivers the e-books in a very usable manner. Each book has an annotated table of contents and a search box to search within the book. The text of each book is provided by chapter and available as both an HTML file and a PDF for easy download. The viewing pane also gives options for citing the book.

Teachers, education administrators, education policy-makers, researchers, and librarians will find this a rich resource. It is a trove of reputable and timely research on everything concerning the intersection of technology and education—a subject that will be of great importance for the foreseeable future. IGI provides these titles in both print and electronic format, but database subscribers receive the digital versions much faster.— **Kristin Kay Leeman**

C, S

66. Kwon, Samuel M., Daniel R. Tomal, and Aram S. Agajanian. **Technology for Classroom and Online Learning: An Educator's Guide to Bits, Bytes, and Teaching.** Lanham, Md., Rowman & Littlefield, 2015. 187p. index. $38.00pa.; $37.99 (e-book). ISBN 13: 978-1-4758-1544-3; 978-1-4758-1545-0 (e-book).;

In *Technology for Classroom and Online Learning* the authors provide a succinct overview of hardware, software, and computer networks for the classroom teacher. Chapter one starts out with brief histories of electricity, electronic devices, and computer technologies, before defining key hardware and software components. Chapter two discusses the fundamentals of electricity and electronics. Chapter three covers computer peripherals (e.g., printers, scanners, external hard drives), connection hardware, supporting software, and troubleshooting. The remaining chapters focus more on traditional educational technology concepts such as computing platforms for schools, teaching and learning with technology, and online and blended learning. Finally there is a chapter on security and maintenance. Each chapter starts out with stated objectives and concludes with a case study, exercises, and discussion questions, thereby serving as both a textbook and reference work. There are also four short appendixes that include a list of Websites for school technology resources, common technology acronyms, technology standards for educators, and trademark sources for products mentioned in the book. Upon initial review it appeared this was going to be an academic text and hard to understand. On the contrary, although one of the authors is an engineer, the text was clearly written, making the concepts very accessible. That said, there are not many images, and some of the concepts discussed, such as electronics and electricity are hard to understand, even when simplified. As a whole, the appendixes don't offer much value. Even with these shortcomings this short book (187 pages) is an important introductory text for future classroom technology professionals or as a succinct reference source for practicing educators.—**Kevin McDonough**

Elementary and Secondary Education

Handbooks and Yearbooks

P, S

67.   Brooks-Young, Susan J. **Creating Content with Your Tablet.** Thousand Oaks, Calif., Corwin Press, 2015. 121p. index. $26.95pa. ISBN 13: 978-1-4522-7183-5.

This book is a perfect guide to using iPads and tablets in the classroom. The book begins with a tutorial on choosing the right apps for the classroom and moves to taking photographs and videos for student publishing. Each of the chapters includes strategies for classroom use and suggested activities to get things started. The text is easy to follow and well-organized. For teachers who are looking for a way to start using hand-held technology, this book is a wonderful place to begin. A bibliography and index round out the work.—**Catherine Vinson**

S

68.   Haven, Kendall. **Writing Workouts to Develop Common Core Writing Skills: Step-by-Step Exercises, Activities, and Tips for Student Success, Grades 7-12.** Santa Barbara, Calif., Libraries Unlimited/ABC-CLIO, 2015. 121p. index. $42.00pa. ISBN 13: 978-1-61069-868-9; 978-1-61069-869-6 (e-book).

This book is a collection of tips and activities intended to help teachers build basic writing skills and confidence in their students. Activities support core curriculum and state language arts standards. The focus is on the content of student writing rather than mechanics. The 30 workout topics are student-friendly. It would be helpful to have more about overall goals and requirements of the Common Core Writing Standards as a reference. Examples of specific standards each activity most specifically supports would also be helpful. These missing elements aside, the book is easy to use and very practical. An index rounds out the work.—**Mary Alice Anderson**

S

69.   Haven, Kendall. **Writing Workouts to Develop Common Core Writing Skills: Step-by-Step Exercises, Activities, and Tips for Student Success, Grades 2-6.** Santa Barbara, Calif., Libraries Unlimited/ABC-CLIO, 2014. 133p. index. $21.00pa. ISBN 13: 978-1-61069-866-5; 978-1-61069-867-2 (e-book).

Effective communication is the goal of writing. Like any other skill, success at writing requires practice. This book provides ample suggestions, and ways to engender enthusiasm, all geared toward supporting writing skills required by Common Core. The workouts focus mainly on the content skills rather than the mechanical skills. Engaging activities include building a scene, story starters, sequencing, revising and editing, persuasive writing, and varying point of view. The skills and activities presented could also be adapted for older students. A purpose, directions, and review and discussion for each workout are included. For some there is also evaluation and postdiscussion. The book contains a list of other sources of writing games and activities. An index rounds out the work.—**Cynthia Ortiz**

P, S

70.   **Research   In   Context.   http://solutions.cengage.com/incontext/research/.** [Website] Farmington Hills, Mich., Gale/Cengage Learning. Price negotiated by site. Date reviewed: 2016.

Research In Context is an online database designed to support the learning and research needs of middle school students. It provides them access to a wide range of information in a variety of formats to address nearly every subject studied by students in grades 6-8. The homepage and navigation are dominated by images and encourage browsing and discovery in the following topics: Culture, Geography, Government, Literature, People, Science, Social Issues, and History.

Information on the topics in the collection is presented in a diverse array of formats including videos, audio, newspapers, books, and images. Content is drawn from *National Geographic,* NPR, NASA, and Gale's own products. All of these sources are integrated on one page for a holistic view of the topic. This presentation approach creates a sort of information "command center" that has the potential to inspire and empower students to draw connections with the content.

Though the database is designed for browsing, it can be searched by keyword, and there is an advanced search option to allow searchers to combine keywords and limit searches to full-text or images. The advanced search menu is simplified for the intended audience. Educators will appreciate the curriculum standards provided in the site. State and national standards are included as is Common Core.

The database integrates with Google Drive and Google Classroom making it easy for both students and teachers to save documents to their own Google drive. The ability to save research to a central location is a very useful feature. Any highlights and notes made in the database can be retained when the document is saved to Google Drive. Teachers have the added ability to save a document to their Google Classroom as an announcement or an assignment.

This is a fantastic resource to engage younger students in the habits of responsible, academic research at an early age. It is an excellent tool for encouraging information literacy especially as there are many different content formats and sources. It is highly recommended for school and public libraries.—**Kristin Kay Leeman**

S

71.   Sheninger, Eric. **Digital Leadership: Changing Paradigms for Changing Times.**
Thousand Oaks, Calif., Corwin Press, 2015. 227p. $27.95pa. ISBN 13: 978-1-4522-7661-
8; 978-1-4833-3996-2 (e-book).

This is a book for those people who are leading other teachers in how to use technology
to enrich their instruction. It would be a great college text as well. The book is well-
organized and easy to read. One of the most useful chapters is about the importance of
PLNs, Professional Learning Networks. These networks provide support and the sharing
that is necessary to quickly learn how to manage changing technology. As a book for
leaders, there is also a chapter on coaching the reluctant teacher on how to use technology
efficiently. An index completes the work.—**Catherine Vinson**

P, S

72.   **Student Resources In Context. http://solutions.cengage.com/InContext/Student-
Resources/.** [Website] Farmington Hills, Mich., Gale/Cengage Learning. Price negotiated
by site. Date reviewed: 2016.

Student Resources In Context is a multidisciplinary database that integrates a wide
variety of content types from academic journal articles to interactive maps to inform on
topics ranging from John Adams to Mark Zuckerberg.

Content is sourced from Gale publications and its partners. In addition to these
reference sources, the database includes full-text access to many respected newspapers
(e.g., *Newsweek, The Economist,* and the *New York Times*), images, videos, and audio clips
from the BBC and NPR, among others. The content is aligned to curricular standards at
state and national levels including Common Core.

All of the sources related to a topic are presented together, curated on one page for
a holistic view of the topic in question—from news commentary to academic research.
This approach creates an information "command center" experience and gives teachers
and librarians a compelling argument to students on why they should never use Wikipedia
again. There are also tools to highlight, bookmark, share, and cite resources.

The resource can be searched by keyword or browsed by topic. There are so many
topics to browse that a helpful filter for category (e.g., Social Issues, Sports, Government,
New and Updated, etc.) is also included. An advanced keyword search option allows
users to combine keywords with article and/or publication title. Users can also limit their
search to full-text or peer-reviewed journals, specify a desired document type (e.g., map,
cover story, pamphlet, or video among many options), or content type (book, journal,
experiments, Websites, etc.). Teachers will especially appreciate the ability to search by
content level (beginner to advanced) and Lexile level. Educators will also appreciate the
curriculum standards provided in the site. Curriculum standards for not only the United
States (both national and state) are provided, but so are the standards for other English-
speaking countries like Canada, Australia, New Zealand, Ireland, and the countries of
Great Britain.

This Gale resource integrates with Google apps including Google Drive and Google
Classroom. This makes it easy for both students and teachers to save documents to their
own Google Drive. The ability to save to a central location is very useful. Any highlights
and notes made in the database can be retained when the document is saved to Google
Drive. Teachers have the added ability to save a document to their Google Classroom as

an announcement or an assignment.

This is a fantastic resource, and it is highly recommended for school and public libraries. It brings a fresh and engaging perspective to research and breathes fresh air into the research process with engaging, multimedia resources. Students and teachers alike will find this a "go-to" resource for research on anything from Steve Jobs to steampunk. By including additional database tools (save and share search results, citation tools, etc.) this becomes a tool everyone will want to use. Rather than going to many different places to find this information, it is all now available in one powerful, user-friendly dashboard.—**Kristin Kay Leeman**

P, S

73.   **TeachUNICEF. http://teachunicef.org/.** [Website] Free. Date reviewed: 2016.

TeachUNICEF—an initiative of the United Nations Children's Fund (UNICEF)—is a free online resource for teachers and K–12 students that aims to foster global citizenship and intercultural awareness through education, advocacy, and leadership. Drawing from a "rights-based framework," *TeachUNICEF* doubles as both a reference and support site that can be easily navigated by teachers and students alike. Its offering of a wide range of support materials for students is useful for helping teachers approach often difficult topics of global concern through dynamic and engaging lessons and activities.

Armed conflict, children with disabilities, gender equality, and sustainable development are a just a few of among the more than 15 "global education" topics included on the site. For each topic, teachers can easily download units and lesson plans for their particular grade levels (PK-2, 3–5, 6–8, and 9–12). Each of these clearly states the objectives of the lesson, outline the relevant standards being touched upon, and include different ideas for activities (complete with handouts). These are all presented in a graphic, visually appealing, and easy-to-follow format.

Additional support-related materials include photos of the month, which provide questions for class discussion and background on a featured photograph; UNICEF's *ACT: Action for Children Today* student magazine (available in both a diplomat edition for students in grades 3–5 and an ambassador edition for students in grades 6–8); and global maps. Furthermore, each of *TeachUNICEF's* lessons has been crafted to align to both national and state education standards.

A separate component of *TeachUNICEF's* site includes workshops and information on making a change through action and leadership. Details on how to get involved in UNICEF's advocacy and volunteer programs (UNICEF LIVE, UNICEF global action, UNICEF kid power, and UNICEF Tap Project) is readily available on the site, as is information on how to get involved in fundraising and other campus initiatives. Additionally, the "Get Involved" section of the site offers links to social media, where students can share projects that they have undertaken, teachers can share lesson plans, and where interested parties can sign up for *TeachUNICEF's* monthly newsletter.

With its engaging lessons and wealth of interactive, multimedia material, *TeachUNICEF* is a highly useful resource for guiding educators through teaching difficult global issues in a wide variety of formats across the K–12 spectrum. It is also a great resource for inspiring action, community building, global awareness, and leadership in students.—**ARBA Staff Reviewer**

P, S

74.   Thornburg, David, Norma Thornburg, and Sara Armstrong. **The Invent to Learn Guide to 3D Printing in the Classroom: Recipes for Success.** Torrance, Calif., Constructing Modern Knowledge Press, 2014. 178p. $24.95pa. ISBN 13: 978-0-9891511-4-6.

For anyone setting up a makerspace or adding a 3D printer to their engineering or technology classes, this book is essential. The authors have logically laid out what one needs to know before setting up the space. The book covers the basics necessary for safety, how consumer 3D printers work, and what features to look for when purchasing a 3D printer. They explore three pathways for creating designs and examples of programs and platforms. Finally, there is a wide variety of beginner to intermediate project ideas. Each project includes background information, Next Generation Science Standards, Common Core Math Standards, and connections associated with the project, a materials list, and construction details. This book will be a favorite with educators!—**Claire Berg**

Higher Education

Handbooks and Yearbooks

P, S

75.   Brooks, F. Erik, and Glenn L. Starks. **African American Students Guide to College Success.** Santa Barbara, Calif., Greenwood Press/ABC-CLIO, 2015. 232p. index. $37.00. ISBN 13: 978-1-4408-2929-1; 978-1-4408-2930-7 (e-book).

Higher education professionals understand that the transition for many students from high school to college is difficult—hence the proliferation of first-year experience and "student success" programs at many colleges. Editors Brooks and Starks, both public policy specialists, have a general grasp of the difficulties faced by African American students as they begin their college careers and have sought to guide this population from the application process through integration into the network. Although the guide is informative, the intended audience itself is unclear—is the work written more for the parents/guardians of potential students or for the students themselves? Some of the information does not apply to all higher education institutions in all states—community colleges rarely require written essays and are often open admissions, for example—and some information seems almost quaint, such as "Appropriate Student Attire in Class" (how many male students wear single-breasted suits to class?). Roughly half of the book includes such advice, much of it good, but the volume is filled out with 87 pages of tables and another 32 of "How We Did It," success stories related by former African American students. Despite these issues, Brooks and Starks is a welcome update to earlier similar works, including Kunjufu's *Black College Student Survival Guide* (African American Images, 1998) and Black's *African American Student's College Guide* (Wiley, 2000). Recommended for all undergraduate and high school collections.—**Anthony J. Adam**

C, P

76.   **Coursera. https://www.coursera.org/.** [Website] Free. Date reviewed: 2015.

Coursera is an educational platform that has partnered with universities across the country to offer students free access to online courses. While it claims to provide "universal access to the world's best education," it is not a college and there is no way to obtain a degree. Students can, however, receive formal recognition for course completion and course certificates may be provided upon request. Students can study from anywhere as long as they have Internet connection, and will find their classes to be exciting and interactive. The Website layout is simple and intuitive, and users should have no trouble navigating it to select their courses and access material.

Each class includes online video instructions and lectures, quizzes, peer-graded assignments, and the opportunity to connect with others and delve deeper into the course material through online forums. Students can choose their schedules, making this platform perfect for working students, parents, teachers, and those interested in gaining skills and knowledge in a particular subject matter without the stress of enrolling at a formal academic institution. Still, students are required to put in the work to pass these classes and will find the material as challenging as it is enriching. Because *Coursera* partners with top universities, such as Yale, Stanford, and Northwestern, and offers classes taught by professors at these schools, students can expect top-notch instruction.

Coursera offers nearly 1,500 courses in the following subjects: Arts and Humanities, Business, Computer Science, Data Science, Life Sciences, Math and Logic, Personal Development, Physical Science and Engineering, and Social Sciences. It is a highly recommended source for busy scholars, curious intellectuals, and those who simply want to learn something new.—**ARBA Staff Reviewer**

C, P, S

77.   **History Departments Around the World: http://chnm.gmu.edu/history-departments-around-the-world/departments/.** [Website] Free. Date reviewed: 2016.

This is an interesting site that allows users to search for history departments from among thousands of U.S. and hundreds of non-U.S. universities and colleges. It has a simple, clean layout that contains only a search tab on the home page that allows users to narrow their search by university, city, state, and U.S. or non-U.S departments. The page states that it can help users "find ideas for creating departmental Web pages, let you look in on or locate colleagues, conduct historical research, or help out with a graduate or undergraduate application." The latter seems to be the most appropriate way to use this site, and therefore it should prove useful for high school juniors and seniors interested in history, as well as former history majors scouting graduate schools for a potential fit. There does not seem to be a way to search for individuals; therefore, locating colleagues would be difficult.

Conducting historical research would also be difficult to do with this Website because it simply links to department Web pages, which contain more information about the history programs offered and less historical and academic information. Users would benefit from this site most as a tool for gauging what kinds of specializations and tracks are available at various universities and colleges. It is highly recommended for upper grade high school students and graduate applicants to get a feel for prospective schools.—**ARBA Staff Reviewer**

6 Ethnic Studies and Anthropology

Anthropology

Archaeology

C, P

78.   Springate, Megan E. **Coffin Hardware in Nineteenth-Century America.** Walnut Creek, Calif., Left Coast Press, Inc., 2015. 116p. illus. index. (Guides to Historical Artifacts). $29.95pa. ISBN 13: 978-1-59874-135-3; 978-1-62958-053-1 (e-book).

There is an amazing interest among people in old coffin hardware. Coffin hardware appears to have become an inspiration point for a new generation of artists. This volume explores nineteenth-century coffin hardware from a historical artifact perspective. The introduction of mass-produced coffin hardware in the nineteenth century provides insight into how individuals living in the period felt about themselves and the afterlife. Based on a British coffin hardware antecedent, the American hardware incorporated a unique new world vision of the afterlife. Through a series of topical chapters the book explores concepts such as: coffin typology, children's hardware, coffins as artifacts, safety and security (in case the person was buried alive), the coffin industry in America, and themes of design and social factors (status, religion, gender, ethnicity) in coffins. Appendixes included are: a list of coffin catalogs in public repositories, an excellent bibliography, and an index. The blurb on the back cover states that the book is "extensively illustrated" but this reviewer would rather say that it has some illustrations of coffin hardware and burial practices in the nineteenth century. Most reference collections will find this volume useful, especially around Halloween time. The book covers a topic about which not much is written in an excellent and informative manner.—**Ralph Lee Scott**

Ethnic Studies

General Works

Dictionaries and Encyclopedias

C, P

79.   **Ethnic Dress in the United States: A Cultural Encyclopedia.** Annette Lynch and Mitchell D. Strauss, eds. Lanham, Md., Rowman & Littlefield, 2015. 326p. illus. index. $75.00; $74.99 (e-book). ISBN 13: 978-0-7591-2148-5; 978-0-7591-2150-8 (e-book).

This concise examination of the impact of foreign cultures on the dress of the United States contains over 150 entries, ranging from lederhosen and djellaba to wingtips and polo shirt. Most entries have a short reading list for further exploration; many provide cross-references to related topics. The majority of the entries are comprised of three sections: a "history" section, which examines the origins of a type of clothing, hat, or footwear; a second section, the item "in the United States," which traces the evolution and development of the item within the American context; and a third section, "influence and impact," which looks at the current state of the garment, its customer base, and other contemporary aspects.

This volume would be most appropriate for interested readers in public libraries and for undergraduates seeking an introduction to the subject. From more well-known items, like muumuus, oxford shirts, and espadrilles to the more obscure jeogori and the Sibenik cap, this volume will provide the reader with intriguing information about their history.—**Mark Schumacher**

C, P

80.   **The SAGE Encyclopedia of African Cultural Heritage in North America.** Mwalimu J. Shujaa and Kenya J. Shujaa, eds. Thousand Oaks, Calif., Sage, 2015. 2v. illus. index. $375.00/set. ISBN 13: 978-1-4522-5821-8.

This set explores the numerous dimensions of Africa's cultural impact on North American society. Entries range from broad overviews (Education, Black Studies, Matriarchy and Patriarchy, Medicine) to narrower topics (Yoruba Symbolism, Bottle Trees, Quilts and Quilting, Pinkster Festival, Kwanzaa). Each entry includes cross-references to related entries and a brief bibliography. Some are very straightforward and easily understood, while others will require some background knowledge or consulting other related articles in this set. For example, the entry "Papa Legba," a spirit within the Vodu (voodoo) world, will probably attract specialists rather than casual readers.

Organized along the same clean lines as a number of other Sage encyclopedias published recently, and edited by a renowned scholar in the field of African and African-American Studies, these 250+ entries, from 140 authors around the world, present the multifaceted dimensions of African culture and how it has shaped lives in North America. Academic and public libraries will certainly benefit from this set.—**Mark Schumacher**

African Americans

C, S

81.   **Black Studies in Video. https://search.alexanderstreet.com/blsv.** [Website] Alexandria, Va., Alexander Street Press. Price negotiated by site. Date reviewed: 2016.

This collection of videos is an Alexander Street Press signature collection and contains award-winning documentaries, newsreels, interviews, and archival footage. California Newsreel has also allowed access to their African American Classics collection.

Black Studies in Video showcases 855 videos for a total of 55 hours of visual media on a spectrum of topics related to black culture in the United States. Video subject areas focus on black history, politics, art and culture, family structure, social and economic pressures, and gender relations. The films come in a variety of formats from drama and animation, to news clips and interviews. The majority of films would be classified as documentaries

(336); 50 contain speeches and 69 include a panel discussion on the challenges of being an African American.

The opening search tools include sidebars called Browse, People, and Specialized Areas of Interest. These tools will be useful for those who are not sure of the direction of their research. The search box provides direct searching for researchers with a specific time, person, keyword, or topic in mind. When a movie is selected, the landing page has another useful sidebar for further details. Information provided in this sidebar relates to the production of the film and contain: Content Type, Persons Discussed, Organizations Discussed, Topic/Theme, Director/Producer, and Speaker/Narrator. This page also provides options for correct citing of the film, email and sharing of this visual media.

The collection covers a broad array of major events and people important to the study of African Americans, but there is a lack of balance in subject areas at times. For example, in browsing "historical events," the query finds 140 entries under U.S. Civil Rights Movement and only 3 entries listed under Slavery and Abolition. More-well-known people who have contributed to black culture and the struggle for freedoms are well documented in this collection, but it also includes coverage of lesser-known personalities.

Diversity, challenge, and passion have been a mainstay of the African American experience. The collection of visual media gathered in *Black Studies in Video* brings this experience to life. In many instances, remarkable footage (i.e., *The Black Eagles, Part 1-Clipped Wings*) not only shows the challenging history of African Americans, but makes visceral this time period and its concomitant discrimination. Because of the breadth of information pertaining to black culture, the diversity of this collection will be useful to students in both high school and college. General researchers seeking engaging footage and a multiplicity of options will benefit from this video collection.

Recommended.—**Janis Minshull**

C, P

82. **Black Women of the Harlem Renaissance Era.** Lean'tin L. Bracks and Jessie Carney Smith, eds. Lanham, Md., Rowman & Littlefield, 2014. 304p. illus. index. $80.00; $79.99 (e-book). ISBN 13: 978-0-8108-8542-4; 978-0-8108-8543-1 (e-book).

The role of women in the Harlem Renaissance has been well-documented throughout the years, with biographies of both individuals and women as a whole. What distinguishes the current volume, edited under the direction of Fisk University's Bracks and Smith, is the inclusion of African American women other than poets and fiction writers active during the period 1919-1940. The reader should note that a number of these women were not directly associated with the Harlem Renaissance activities in New York City, hence the "Era" at the tag-end of the book's title. However, that broad scope is not to take away from the general usefulness and scholarship of the collection. The editors include roughly 200 one-to-three page signed biographies arranged alphabetically of women in the fields of community leadership and activism, the arts, education, journalism, and entrepreneurship, although the preponderance of entries are for literary and entertainment individuals. But for every familiar name such as Bessie Smith or Nella Larsen, the editors have rediscovered women such as anthropologist Caroline Day and activist Lugenia Burns Hope. A short bibliography is included at the end of the volume, but there are no bibliographic references appended to the entries themselves. Some of the entries also include black-and-white photos, but those are few and far between. In sum, the scope and utility make this volume an excellent addition to all African American Studies collections, along with Wall's *Women of the*

Harlem Renaissance (Indiana University Press, 1995) and Roses' and Randolph's *Harlem Renaissance and Beyond: Literary Biographies of One Hundred Black Women Writers, 1900-1945* (Harvard University Press, 1997).—**Anthony J. Adam**

C, P
83.   Drew, Bernard A. **Black Stereotypes in Popular Series Fiction, 1851-1955: Jim Crow Era Authors and Their Characters.** Jefferson, N.C., McFarland, 2015. 292p. illus. index. $55.00pa. ISBN 13: 978-0-7864-7410-3; 978-1-4766-1610-0 (e-book).

Drew, a prolific author of books delineating popular U.S. fiction, profiles 29 authors active between 1851 and 1955, both black and white, who featured stereotypical African American characters in their serialized short stories, newspaper columns, and other works. Although some of the authors are still remembered—Langston Hughes and Booth Tarkington, for example—many others such as Roark Bradford and Harris Dickson have become footnotes in American literature. Additionally, Drew supplements his work with brief single-paragraph biographies of another 72 authors such as Richard Wright and Zora Neale Hurston who used recurring black characters in their works. Black-and-white illustrations are scattered throughout (readers might find many of the period pieces offensive), and Drew is more than generous with providing examples of dialect conversation and humor from the cited authors. Drew's prose style takes some getting used to—he is a former newspaperman and retains the "short and sweet" style of that format—but his research is informative and extremely useful for those studying popular literary culture. Above all, readers will benefit greatly from Drew's primary and secondary bibliographies, which include lists of every serial appearance of the characters. Recommended for all popular culture collections and comprehensive collections of African-American studies and literature.—**Anthony J. Adam**

C, P, S
84.   **In Motion: The African-American Migration Experience. http://www.inmotionaame.org/home.cfm.** [Website] Free. Date reviewed: 2016.

This extensive and top-notch database from the Schomberg Center for Research in Black Culture presents the history of African American migration. The breadth of the site is immediately apparent. The African American migration narrative does not start in colonial Virginia but with migrations from Mexico and the Caribbean and includes everything in between up to contemporary African migrations. Taken altogether, *In Motion* shows the diversity of African Americans living in the United States and combines in one place all components of the African diaspora. Included in the approximately 35 million African Americans in the United States in the twenty-first century are African Americans, Africans, Afro-Caribbeans, Central Americans of African descent, and African and Afro-Cubans born in Europe. As the database demonstrates, all these groups are heirs to the migrations that have shaped U.S. history.

This well-curated site, written and organized by scholars and professionals, has 16,500 pages of text, 8,300 illustrations, and 60 maps arranged around 13 migrations: The Transatlantic Slave Trade (1450s-1867); Runaway Journeys (1630s-1865); The Domestic Slave Trade (1760s-1865); Colonization & Emigration (1783-1910s); Haitian Immigration: 18th and 19th Centuries (1791-1809); The Western Migration (1840s-1890); The Northern Migration (1840s-1890); The Great Migration (1916-1930); The Second

Great Migration (1940-1970); Caribbean Immigration (1900-Present); Return South Migration (1900-Present); Haitian Immigration: 20th Century (1970-Present); and African Immigration (1970-present). Each migration has a narrative; hundreds of illustrations, each with a caption, bibliographical indexing, and ordering information; 20-40 research resources (books, essays, book chapters, article, manuscripts, Websites); maps; and lesson plans. Searching could not be more intuitive. Users can browse by migrations, geography, or timeline and choose what to do from there. All migration texts have highlighted words that link to a glossary, which can also be accessed from a glossary box on the bottom of each page. Better still for students and teachers, the text is available in a printer-friendly format and all images are downloadable. As explained in the rights and usages link from the main page, these resources are intended for scholarly and personal use. For these purposes, the quality of the images is sufficient; however, high-resolution copies of images are available from the library.

In the opinion of this reviewer, the best way to gain a true appreciation of the information on this database is to search it by migration. The Western Migration, for example, opens with a sound clip and images on the top of the page. From there, a user can explore the image gallery; read "The Way West: Migration and the African-American Search for Freedom and Opportunity in the Western United States" by University of Washington professor Quintard Taylor; study maps created for the project by Rutgers University cartographer Michael Siegel; or jump straight to the educational materials. The bibliography and links in this essay alone are enough to launch dozens of research projects. For example, one link takes users to *African Americans and the Old West,* an extensive database of text, images, and further links created by Long Island University. The provided curriculum covers grades 6-12 and includes the necessary resources for such lesson plans as "OK in Oklahoma? All-Black Communities" for grades 9-12.

In Motion is a resource of the highest value and quality that will prove useful to students, researchers, and teachers.—**ARBA Staff Reviewer**

C, P, S

85.   **Smithsonian National Museum of African American History and Culture Online Collections. http://nmaahc.si.edu/.** [Website] Free. Date reviewed: 2016.

The Smithsonian National Museum of African American History and Culture Website provides an excellent and accessible online resource dedicated to the rich and diverse history and culture of the African American experience. This site includes information about exhibitions and programs, events, collections, and education workshops and is a companion for the physical gallery, currently located at the National Museum of American History. In September 2016, the five-acre museum will open to the public on the National Mall in Washington, D.C. The foundational collection of African American culture and history now includes 1,000 items, including photographs, artifacts, documents, and art that are searchable on the Website.

The site provides tabs with information about visiting the gallery and opportunities for getting involved through volunteering, membership, collaborations, and internships and fellowships. A "Connect" tab links visitors to the blog and social media, and the "Newsroom" shares chronological stories on the upcoming museum opening as well as articles related to African American culture and history. Visitors have ample opportunity to donate their time, money, or artifacts or become NMAAHC members.

While this comprehensive resource benefits virtual visitors, many of the resources like the exhibitions at the gallery and the museum itself are available only to physical visitors. A handful of activities suitable for K-6 classrooms are available for download, but nothing is offered for students at the secondary levels. The education section provides a link to request materials for Black History Month, but resources are currently unavailable as they "have reached capacity of requests" at this time. Overall, the Website is slick, polished, and provides access to multiple social media outlets, opportunities to become involved, and information about other activities. Recommended for all audiences.—**ARBA Staff Reviewer**

Asian Americans

C

86. **Asian American Religious Cultures.** Jonathan H.X. Lee, Fumitaka Matsuoka, Edmond Yee, and Ronald Nakasone, eds. Santa Barbara, Calif., ABC-CLIO, 2015. 2v. illus. index. $189.00/set. ISBN 13: 978-1-59884-330-9; 978-1-59884-331-6 (e-book).

This two-volume encyclopedia provides a comprehensive, accessible overview of Asian American religious cultures and social customs. The set provides a broad historical context for understanding the great diversity found within these cultures. Both volumes include a contents section, thematic guide to related topics, and alphabetical entries. Each entry concludes with *see also* references directing readers to related entries and essays and a bibliography of suggestions for further reading. Volume one contains an informative introduction highlighting the complex interplay of history, religion, and race in Asian American cultures as well as 19 essays covering a wide range of topics including politics, law, gender and sexuality, and LGBT issues. Volume two includes an up-to-date bibliography of print, online, and film resources, biographical information about the editors, and a list of contributors and their associated organizations. In addition, volume two contains a 42-page index with essays and main entries indicated by boldface page numbers. This is a user-friendly resource enhanced by clear writing and the inclusion of black-and-white photos. With more than 100 contributors including academics, religious leaders, and community elders, this encyclopedia covers a wide range of topics and serves as both a starting point for scholarly research and a general source for the casual reader. This encyclopedia is recommended for academic and large public libraries.—**Lisa Morgan**

C, P, S

87. **Asian American Society: An Encyclopedia.** Mary Yu Danico and Anthony C. Ocampo, eds. Thousand Oaks, Calif., Sage, 2014. 4v. index. $625.00/set. ISBN 13: 978-1-4522-8190-2.

This 2,000-page set explores many diverse topics relating to the Asian American experience. The first two volumes contain 320 alphabetically arranged entries. Topics include broad areas such as Japanese Americans, hate crimes, and families (overview), but also more focused entries such as Charlie Chan, Bollywood, Lunar New Year, and picture brides. Americans from Hawaii, Japan, Korea, China, Thailand, the Philippines, Bangladesh, Cambodia, Vietnam, and India are included in this comprehensive set.

Volumes three and four present primary documents covering the years 1849 to 2013. Earlier documents include court cases, articles in, and letters to, newspapers, and occasional legislation. Many of the recent items are government reports and congressional activities of various kinds, including declarations honoring Asian Americans and testimony before committees and subcommittees.

Any library with patrons investigating the Asian experience in America will find this reference work useful, although it may not fit, alas, into every budget. Copyediting needs work on occasion, but otherwise this is a very useful set.—**Mark Schumacher**

C, P, S

88.   **Chinese Americans: The History and Culture of a People.** Jonathan H. X. Lee, ed. Santa Barbara, Calif., ABC-CLIO, 2015. 498p. illus. index. $100.00. ISBN 13: 978-1-61069-549-7; 978-1-61069-550-3 (e-book).

This is a reference book devoted to all aspects of the Chinese American experience in North America. It is divided into four alphabetical (by subject) sections. Part one deals with Chinese American immigration. Part two delineates Chinese American political and economic life. Part three covers Chinese American cultural and religious life. Part four covers Chinese American contributions to literature, the arts, popular culture, and sports. There are many biographical articles. Each article contains a short bibliography. There is an additional bibliography of more than 100 books and articles and a chronology of Chinese American history from January 18, 1778, to February 11, 2015. Editor Jonathan H. X. Lee is an associate professor of Asian American studies at San Francisco State University. There is an editorial board of six academics and a list of consultants. A detailed index is included. A 20-page section of primary documents and numerous black-and-white illustrations are also included.

Many articles treat little-known or unknown aspects of Chinese American life. The ongoing history of the treatment of Chinese Americans (and other minority groups) is often a shameful one, but Chinese Americans have pressured and even prevailed in many areas of American life. There has been no lack of breathtakingly wrong-headed judicial decisions and laws. This is a book that should be in every secondary school, academic, and public library especially those libraries serving a Chinese American population.— **Jonathan F. Husband**

C, P, S

89.   **Smithsonian Asian Pacific American Center.** http://smithsonianapa.org/. [Website] Free. Date reviewed: 2016.

The Smithsonian Asian Pacific American Center, established in 1997, is a virtual space dedicated to highlighting and appreciating America's Asian Pacific culture and heritage through innovative digital and museum experiences. The splash page for the site highlights an exhibit on Japanese American civil rights activist Yuri Kochiyama in celebration of Women's History Month. The drop down menu in the upper left corner directs readers to information about the center, exhibitions, events calendar, blog, employment, and a page for donations. At the top of the page, visitors can connect with the site's social media pages.

The organization provides a "museum for the 21st century"—an interactive online entity that connects Asian American communities nationwide through partnerships, technology, and experiences both in person and online. These experiences are created through "Culture Labs" that provide participants with opportunities for critical inquiry and dialogue, guided by storytellers, through which to explore Asian Pacific American history, culture, and art. The "About Us" page provides a downloadable two-year "Blueprint," or strategic plan, for strengthening the organization and programs, developing a collection acquisitions strategy, and experimenting with new in-person and online programs. The page also provides their mission statement and information about board and staff members.

Although the site is slow to load and navigate (likely due to the extensive digital content) the strongest area is the "Exhibitions" page. Viewers can access information about traveling exhibits as well as view the entire content of four digital exhibitions. Each exhibit includes full color images, videos, artwork, and narratives. Recommended for all audiences.—**ARBA Staff Reviewer**

Indians of Central America

C, S

90. **Encyclopedia of the Ancient Maya.** Walter R.T. Witschey, ed. Lanham, Md., Rowman & Littlefield, 2016. 574p. illus. maps. index. $95.00; $94.99 (e-book). ISBN 13: 978-0-7591-2284-0; 978-0-7591-2286-4 (e-book).

The editor of this excellent reference work hopes to acquaint the reader with information regarding the ancient Maya, their architecture and writing, and the techniques used for gathering and analyzing archaeological information. The audience for this work is high school and college students.

The front matter begins with a table of contents and a thematic index containing 15 subject groupings such as Agriculture and Food, Ceramics, and Environment. This is followed by a list of maps, tables, and figures. The preface includes a brief history of Maya archaeology. It outlines the fascinating story of how Maya glyphs were deciphered and discusses the ongoing nature of discovery in Maya archaeology. A brief Note to Readers supplies helpful information about cross-referencing, orthography of Maya words, tips for understanding the complex Maya language, a list of Maya rulers, and definitions of abbreviations and units of measure used in the book. A chronology of the Mayan civilization from 14,000 B.C.E. to A.D. 2012 includes notes explaining a variety of dating methods used to anchor the Mayan civilization in time. Finally, the book explains the archaeological naming conventions for various time periods in the Maya civilization.

The introduction offers a very brief explanation of Maya civilization and the people who made prominent discoveries in that realm. It defines the geography of the Maya area and outlines the history of settlement and development of MesoAmerica and the Maya area. A list of recommended readings completes the Introduction.

Eight maps of different types precede the alphabetical entries for the encyclopedia. The entries include archaeological sites, brief biographies of people, cultural concepts (Craft Specialization, for example), and the roles played by individuals in Maya life. Each entry gives a definition of the term with a description. For archaeological sites geographic coordinates are included. Each entry has cross-references as appropriate, provides a brief bibliography for further reading, and may include a photo or drawing. Entries range from a single paragraph to six pages in length.

The alphabetical entries are followed by a glossary, an essay describing critical resources for information about the Maya, a list of selected Internet resources (often Websites for specific archaeological sites), a list of research institutes working on Maya topics, a list of series and journals relating to Maya topics, and an extensive bibliography.

The work is completed with an index to investigators and explorers, a general index to the entire encyclopedia, and very brief biographies of the 81 authors.

This work provides a wealth of information on the topic of the ancient Maya, couched in terms that can be understood by the layperson. It includes information on very recent discoveries as well as those of the distant past. This is an excellent introduction to the ancient Maya, the people who study them, and the techniques used in the process. This book should be in all high school and college libraries and in appropriate special libraries.—**Joanna M. Burkhardt**

Indians of North America

C, P, S
91.   **American Indian Culture: From Counting Coup to Wampum.** Bruce E. Johansen, ed. Santa Barbara, Calif., Greenwood Press/ABC-CLIO, 2015. 2v. illus. index. (Cultures of the American Mosaic). $189.00/set. ISBN 13: 978-1-4408-2873-7; 978-1-4408-2874-4 (e-book).

Edited by Bruce E. Johansen, Jacob J. Isaacson University Research Professor in Communication and Native American Studies at the University of Nebraska at Omaha and editor or coeditor of such works as *The Encyclopedia of Native American Legal Tradition* (see ARBA 1999, entry 388) and *Encyclopedia of the Haudenosaunee (Iroquois Confederacy)* (see ARBA 2001, entry 299), this is the most recent addition to Greenwood's Cultures of the American Mosaic series. It contains approximately 150 entries divided into 11 chapters: "Population and Demographics"; "Nations, Tribes, and Other Native Groups"; "General Historical Considerations"; "Arts"; "Family, Education, and Community Overview"; "Food"; "Language and Literature"; "Media, Popular Culture, Sports, and Gaming"; "Spirituality"; and "Transportation and Housing." Each of the entries contains bibliographic citation. Some include "Spotlights," which are utilized like sidebars, and cross-references to related articles. Sprinkled throughout the two volumes are black-and-white illustrations and reproductions of photographs. Concluding the reference are a 24-page "Selected Bibliography" and a general index. Written in language accessible to high school students, this work is recommended for high school, public, and undergraduate libraries.—**John R. Burch Jr.**

P, S
92.   Dennis, Yvonne Wakim, Arlene Hirschfelder, and Shannon Rothenberger Flynn. **Native American Almanac: More Than 50,000 Years of the Cutlures and Histories of Indigenous Peoples.** Canton, Mich., Visible Ink Press, 2016. 643p. illus. maps. index. $24.95pa. ISBN 13: 978-1-57859-507-5; 978-1-57859-608-9 (e-book).

Once pushed to the side by the Eurocentric version of new world events, Native Americans and their story have been lifted by dogged scholarship and patient dissemination. This story is, of course, a long one, beginning prehistorically and continuing through today even as cultures have blended. In this almanac, readers will find abundant and enlightening details of Native American life and history which fill in the account of many great and diverse tribes spread throughout the United States.

Three sections organize the material, following a historical overview of Indian-white relations in the United States in the opening pages. The essay here is generally chronological and touches on many of the events, treaties, and acts which have determined the course of relations since the Europeans began colonization. It mentions everything from the Doctrine of Discovery, adopted into U.S. law in 1823 and giving Christian people dominion of non-Christian, "heathen" people; federal assimilation policies enacted throughout the decades; and the 2010 Congressional Resolution of Apology which marked the U.S. government's remorse for centuries of neglect, manipulation, and violence towards the Native American peoples.

The second and largest section groups tribes geographically (e.g., Northeast, Southwest, etc.), and presents many topics within broader ideas of tribal history, cultural signifiers, and political struggles. Some examples of topics covered in this section include Art Traditions, Native Languages, and The Struggle for Citizenship and Land Rights. Select biographies chronologically profile tribal leaders, politicians, artists, and others of note.

A generous use of headings and subheadings helps readers navigate all the material throughout the two main sections. It is important to point out that topics within each regional section may differ from tribe to tribe and from region to region.

A final section carries numerous appendixes, including condensed native histories for Canada, Mexico, the Caribbean, and Greenland; a regional listing of all indigenous nations and groups throughout North America (alphabetized within regions); Indian Lands: Definitions and Explanations; a glossary of Indigenized English; Indigeneity From Sea to Sea, listing sacred sites throughout the United States; Selected Indigenous Firsts: People, Places and Things; Native Owned and Operated Museums; The Indigeneity of the Powwow; and finally Indigenous Ancestry Affiliation of Some Notable People.

While offering new and abundant information, the book is not meant to be comprehensive or encyclopedic, nor is it meant to be considered scholarly. The book also includes suggestions for further reading and an index. Recommended.—**ARBA Staff Reviewer**

C, P, S

93.   **Smithsonian National Museum of the American Indian Collections. http:// nmai.si.edu/explore/collections/.** [Website] Free. Date reviewed: 2016.

The Smithsonian's National Museum of the American Indian has two locations. The main museum, located in Washington, D.C., on the National Mall, houses one of the world's largest collections of some 825,000 items related to Native America. The second location is in New York City in the Alexander Hamilton U.S. Custom House. The "Visit" tab on the Website provides virtual visitors with information about both locations of the museum including hours, admission, parking, and directions for public transportation and driving. The "Explore" tab provides detailed descriptions about the current, upcoming, and past exhibitions at both locations, as well as details about traveling exhibits. This section also includes extensive information about the history, significance, conservation, repatriation, and use of the collections as well as an online search tool. The top of the collections page provides a "featured item" along with other collection highlights. The site offers a variety of ways for visitors to search by people, individuals, places, and objects.

In the "Education" section, educators and students will find information about programs and resources as well as past and present education e-newsletters. The museum hosts Native American film screenings and festivals and provides a searchable film and media catalog, blog, and live Webcasts. Other tabs on the Website give details about how visitors can connect to and support the museum through memberships, donations, internships, events, and programs for both American Indians and non-American Indians. The "Shop" tab allows visitors to view and purchase a wide range of books for all readers, children's books, Spanish language books, and CDs and DVDs. One drawback is that items can only be purchased by calling and ordering over the phone (available 24-hours) or downloading and faxing the order form.

Visitors can hover over a tab to see the available links. Upon clicking on one of the links, it not only opens to that page but also lists all of the available links for that tab on the left-hand side of the page for easy navigation. A "Share" link in the upper right hand corner links visitors with a variety of social media for the site. Overall, the Website is well-organized and filled with engaging, full-color images. Recommended for all audiences.— **ARBA Staff Reviewer**

Indians of South America

C, P, S

94.   **Encyclopedia of the Incas.** Urton, Gary and Adriana Von Hagen, eds. Lanham, Md., Rowman & Littlefield, 2015. 324p. illus. maps. index. $75.00; $74.99 (e-book). ISBN 13: 978-0-7591-2362-5; 978-0-7591-2363-2 (e-book).

At the peak of its influence the Inca Empire extended from Columbia to Chile, and from the Pacific Ocean into the Amazon rainforest. The empire covered a wide variety of terrain, including mountains, deserts, and tropical jungles. Keeping control over the many and diverse people in this far-flung empire relied on a fascinating mixture of cultural overlay and actual conquest. The workings of the empire were interrupted and eventually destroyed with the arrival of Spanish explorers in the sixteenth century.

The editors of this volume are well-known experts in Pre-Columbian Inca studies. Entries were written by the editors and by 35 other Inca experts from fields such as anthropology, archaeology, geography, and ethnohistory. The purpose of the work is to provide newcomers with an introduction to the Inca civilization and to place each of the subjects covered in the 128 entries into its larger cultural context.

The volume begins with a table of contents listing the individual entries in alphabetical order. This is followed by a thematic contents listing subjects and the individual entries that pertain to those subjects. The introduction that follows gives a brief description of the geographic boundaries of the Inca Empire. It goes on to explain the sources of information available concerning this nonliterate people and describes the pros and cons associated with the use of those sources. A very brief description of the history of the Incas and their rise to power is followed by an explicit rationale for the creation of this encyclopedia. The introduction ends with a note about the orthography of the Quechua language and the spellings used in this book. A map of the Inca Empire, its road system, its political boundaries, and the location of modern cities and capitals completes the introductory materials. The entries follow in alphabetical order. A comprehensive index allows an additional means of access. A brief section about the editors and the authors completes the volume.

A typical entry is two to three pages long. It explains the term, gives its history, and describes its cultural context. Many entries contain a photograph or a classic drawing relating to the subject of the entry. Entries contain cross-references to other entries in the encyclopedia, as appropriate. Each entry ends with suggestions for further reading. All entries are signed.

While the entries are relatively short and the total number of entries is limited, this volume will serve the stated purposes of providing an introduction to the Inca civilization and placing the entries in their cultural context. This volume will be useful to high school, public, and undergraduate libraries.—**Joanna M. Burkhardt**

Latin Americans

C, P, S

95.   **Leaders of the Mexican American Generation: Biographical Sketches.** Anthony Quiroz, ed. Boulder, Colo., University Press of Colorado, 2015. 368p. illus. index. $35.95; $19.95 (e-book). ISBN 13: 978-1-60732-336-5; 978-1-60732-336-5 (e-book).

This timely and important book shares the stories of the people who carved out the long road taken by millions of Mexican Americans on their journey towards social, political, and economic acceptance in the United States. Focusing on the years between 1920 and 1965, the book presents interesting biographical sketches of the prominent thinkers and doers of the "Mexican American Generation."

The book divides its essays into two sections. The first section, Intellectuals and Ethnic Consciousness, shines a spotlight on the prime movers behind the Mexican American identity, such as José de la Luz Sáenz, World War I veteran and cofounder of LULAC (League of United Latin American Citizens), and Alice Dickerson Montemayor, who came to inject a feminist angle into LULAC's mission by working to advance women's issues. The second section focuses on Legal, Political and Labor Activists; identifying those who took the reins from the early thinkers and pushed Mexican American issues into the greater civil rights conversation. Chapters here feature biographies on John J. Herrera, Ralph Estrada, and others, including Dr. Héctor P. García, considered by his essay's author a "giant of the twentieth century." Detailed notes follow up each biography. Black-and-white illustrations enhance the book, which is rounded out by an index.

At a time when the topic of immigration has become a hot-button political issue, this book can acquaint readers with the trailblazers who helped their people surmount significant hurdles and establish themselves as a proud component of the American ideal.—**ARBA Staff Reviewer**

C, P, S

96.   **Smithsonian Latino Center. http://latino.si.edu/.** [Website] Free. Date reviewed: 2016.

The Smithsonian Latino Center, created in 1997, promotes Latino culture through research, public programs, exhibitions, education programs, leadership and professional development programs, and Web-based content. The center is not housed in a physical building but exists on a virtual platform in which participants collaborate with communities, institutions, and individuals around the country. This colorful site opens with engaging and constantly changing images of Latino culture and artifacts. Under the "About Us" tab, visitors will find contact information, social media links, an interactive events calendar, and at the center of the page, their Twitter feed. Visitors can hover over events to get additional information or click on the event title for even more detail. Most of the events are in various locations at Smithsonian institutions in Washington, D.C., and New York City. The overall feel is one of active engagement. Bold headings tell visitors that the mission of the center is to engage, inspire, and support Latino heritage.

Other tabs provide visitors with links to current, upcoming, and past exhibitions, public programs, education opportunities, press, resources, and ways to support the center. One of the most striking parts of the Website is found under the Virtual Museum tab that includes 2-D and 3-D collections, educational activities, and other simulations in the virtual world related to Latino culture and heritage. Visitors can click on the Virtual Museum tab and be transported to a virtual world where they'll find a simulated town square. Viewers can hover over parts of the town to find pop up images linked to a variety of exhibits, podcasts, galleries, and archived performances. Overall, this is an engaging and lively site with excellent virtual information on Latino culture and heritage. Recommended for all audiences.—**ARBA Staff Reviewer**

7   Genealogy and Heraldry

Genealogy

P
97.   Carangelo, Lori. **The Ultimate Search Book: U.S. Adoption, Genealogy & Other Search Secrets.** Baltimore, Md., Genealogical Publishing, 2015. 85p. illus. $19.95pa. ISBN 13: 978-0-8063-5729-4.

A small volume that carries significant and specialized material, *The Ultimate Search Book* provides tips and resources designed to assist readers in their search for missing people. Adults who have been adopted as children, families seeking missing children, and many more may all find this material useful.

In chapters that are brief and to the point, the book does very well to take what may be an overwhelming endeavor and break it down into manageable bits. After listing 50 clear and actionable search tips (e.g., how to read a birth certificate, how to use Facebook, etc.), the book then targets its material to specific groups: families separated by adoption or divorce, missing or runaway children, missing adults, novice genealogists, and more. This 2015 edition conveys information on many of the most up-to-date organizations, Websites, databases and other sources that readers can turn to in their searches.

A chapter providing tips on how to start one's own search business is an added bonus, as are the list of resources and Websites and samples of birth certificates and other documents useful to searches.—**ARBA Staff Reviewer**

P
98.   Jacobson, Judy. **History for Genealogists: Using Chronological Time Lines to Find and Understand Your Ancestors.** Baltimore, Md., Genealogical Publishing, 2016. 310p. $37.50pa. ISBN 13: 978-0-8063-5768-3.

The field of genealogy can be so much more than dusty archives and lists of names and places. Rather, the study of genealogy is like a black-and-white line drawing, and it is the accompanying history which fills in the colors between the lines. This book helps genealogists understand the need to incorporate historical research into their work to create a more contextualized and colorful picture of the people of the past. In particular, it points to the use of chronological timelines to help readers understand the times their ancestors were living in, in addition to pinpointing particular events or things which may have affected them.

Chapters mark information which may help users to organize and understand their searches. For example, they emphasize a large number of reasons for migration (e.g., wars, politics, religion, disease, etc.), how ancestors may have traveled, where certain groups of people went, and more. The author also touches on issues which readers may not have thought of in their genealogical searches, such as name changes of people and places, slaves, orphans, and shifting territorial boundaries. In addition, the book lists many ideas for focusing one's search such as historical books and diaries, or historical group affiliations, societies, and unions.

Dotted throughout all this information are specific timelines readers can use to hone and "color" their research. For example, there is a religion timeline which tracks global religious events which sparked migration and settlement. There is also a timeline marking the rise of labor unions which helps readers see the assembling of various groups (textile workers, railroad workers). And perhaps most importantly, there are state timelines covering settlement and major events such as natural disasters and military involvement.

In addition to the plentiful timelines, the author uses bullet points, quotes, lists, charts, an extensive timeline bibliography, and an index of people and places and wars and battles to make the information easy to navigate. This revised edition has been updated with an addendum reflecting editorial corrections to the 2009 edition, which appear to be the addition of an early-twentieth-century "hardship" timeline and a fashion and leisure timeline.—**ARBA Staff Reviewer**

Heraldry

P, S
99.   **Coats of Arms. http://www.heraldry.ws/.** [Website] Free. Date reviewed: 2016.

This free-to-browse Website offers images of coats of arms for over 10,000 surnames, focusing on Ireland. The site is easy to search by an alphabetical index on the left side of the page. The site also offers a featured coat of arms. At the time of this review, the coats of arms were for the surnames (O) Healy, Hely, Haly, and Heeley, with a note on McHale. Besides images of the different coats of arms, there is a significant amount of genealogical research on the families. An additional link takes users to a history of heraldry that explains the parts, patterns, and colors used for coats of arms.

The information on the site is created and maintained by an individual. While there is a general bibliography of the sources he consulted to create the coats of arms, citations do not accompany the individual images. This for-profit Website has some nonintrusive advertising and offers high-quality graphics for sale. However, users can download images in GIF/JPG format; these images are smaller and at a lower resolution. Clearly this is not a place for advanced research, but it would be sufficient for a class project or for the casual user interested in coats of arms.—**ARBA Staff Reviewer**

P, S
100.   **European Heraldry. http://www.europeanheraldry.org/.** [Website] Free. Date reviewed: 2016.

European Heraldry is an online collection of hundreds of coats of arms from the early years of the seventeenth century to the present. The site is free to use, easy to navigate, and regularly updated (updates are clearly listed on the home page).

A series of tabs runs across the top of the home page: France, Iberian Peninsula, Italy, Germany, United Kingdom, Scandinavia, Eastern Europe, Central Europe, and Benelux.

There is also a simple search link. These main categories are further subdivided, so a click on France pops up links to Royal, Maison du Roi, Great Officers of the Crown of France, Colonel Généraux, Duc-Paris, and Families. Spain and Portugal have separate links under the Iberian Peninsula. Italy has sublinks for Naples and Sicily, Modena, Masserano, Savoy, Parma, Tuscany, and Mantua. Coats of arms in Germany can be searched by clicking on Holy Roman Empire 1745, House of Hapsburg, House of Lorraine, Electoral Houses, Mediatised States, and Ecclesiastical States of the Empire. A search for coats of arms in the United Kingdom can be further refined by clicking on England, Scotland, Ireland, Great Britain, the United Kingdom of Great Britain and Ireland, and Families. Scandinavia includes links for Sweden and Denmark. Eastern Europe includes links for Russia, Poland and Courland; Central Europe has sublinks for Austria, Bohemia, and Hungary. A click on the last tab, Benelux, produces links to the Netherlands, Belgium, Luxembourg, and Hapsburg Netherlands.

The images of the coats of arms are clear, but not downloadable. Additionally, the site does not provide much in the way of context. Nevertheless, it is extensive and sufficient for someone looking to find a particular coat of arms or as a place to start further research.—**ARBA Staff Reviewer**

Personal Names

P

101.   Shane, Neala. **Inspired Baby Names from Around the World: 6,000 International Names and the Meaning behind Them.** Novato, Calif., New World Library, 2015. 712p. $21.95pa. ISBN 13: 978-1-60868-320-8.

This compilation of baby names from around the world provides information on name meanings, name origin, and pronunciation, but it also gives readers a spiritual affirmation for each name or variation of a name. For example, the description for the name Justina gives its meaning as just, judicious, and fair, its usage as English, and a quote from Proverbs. The spiritual affirmations are drawn from a large variety of such sources as the Bible (22 different versions), Buddhist sutras, and proverbs from Japan, Hawaii, and Africa. The book's introduction is followed by sections on naming customs from around the world, how to choose a name, and name changes; it concludes with lists of most popular names by decade from the 1910s, grandparent names (nana, memaw, papa, zaide, etc), the most popular names of kittens and puppies, an index of names by meaning, and a list of sources. This fun and informative book would be a welcome addition to public libraries.—**ARBA Staff Reviewer**

8 Geography and Travel Guides

Geography

General Works

Atlases

C, P, S

102.   **Atlases, Gazetteers, Guidebooks, and Other Books. http://digitalcollections. nypl.org/collections/atlases-gazetteers-guidebooks-and-other-books#/?tab=about.** [Website] Free. Date reviewed: 2016.

This collection from the New York Public Library contains atlases, gazetteers, guidebooks, and more from John H. Levine estate, received by the library in 1990. The easy-to-navigate site offers hundreds of clickable images from places worldwide from the seventeenth-nineteenth centuries. On the left-hand side of the page users will find a navigation tab which allows searches by region or type. Users will find a seventeenth-century map of Brazil, eighteenth-century maps of the coast of Norway, an eighteenth-century map of the solar system, an eighteenth-century map of Barbary (including Fez, Algiers, Tunis & Tripoli, and adjacent countries), and a nineteenth-century map of England and Wales (including principal roads), among so much more.

Each still image provides the user with the following information: type of resource, genre, date issued, division, publisher, cartographer, notes, identifiers, citations (in MLA, APA, Chicago, and Wikipedia), as well as additional descriptive information. A timeline shows when the creator of the image was born and died, when the image was issued, and when it was digitized. Users can also download the images in a variety of sizes and resolutions.—**ARBA Staff Reviewer**

C, P, S

103.   **Atlases of New York City. http://digitalcollections.nypl.org/collections/atlases-of-new-york-city#/?tab=navigation.** [Website] Free. Date reviewed: 2016.

The *Atlases of New York City* page in The New York Public Library Digital Collections is a compilation of real estate maps from William Perris who, during the mid-1800s, mapped the city building by building in order to help fire insurance companies appropriately price their customers' policies. The maps depict Manhattan and Brooklyn, and show streets, blocks, tax lots, and current use classifications. They also show streams and other natural features, earlier roads, lot lines, and more. Other items in this collection include aerial maps of New York City from 1924, topographical surveys of Central Park, and atlases that show surrounding regions such as Long Island and Queens.

Because these maps are extremely specific to one region, they would be most useful for professionals, including historians, architects, archeologists, and urban planners. According to the site, they can use the maps to research the history of particular buildings and neighborhoods, for social history and design, and also for ecological and engineering purposes. Though these maps are attractive, students who are not specifically studying New York City in the 1800s and early 1900s would not get much context.—**ARBA Staff Reviewer**

C, P, S

104. **Atlases of the United States. http://digitalcollections.nypl.org/collections/atlases-of-the-united-states#/?tab=navigation.** [Website] Free. Date reviewed: 2016.

This collection from the New York Public Library contains nearly four thousand historical atlases from many different states and regions in the United States. Most are atlases of New York, New Jersey, and other east-coast states. Upper-grade students in geography classes may benefit from viewing these maps to see how the regions have changed over time. Like many of the other online collections in the New York Public Library, this one would be most appropriate for professional historians, architects, engineers, and archeologists who would better understand these maps and be able to use them for professional study.

This page is recommended for students as an additional resource to geography studies, and highly recommended for professionals who could use these maps as tools to aid their work.—**ARBA Staff Reviewer**

P, S

105. **World Atlas. http://www.worldatlas.com/aatlas/world.htm.** [Website] Free. Date reviewed: 2016.

World Atlas is a great resource for elementary and middle grade students. On the home page, a clickable world map allows users to search for information about all seven continents and the Middle East. Users simply hover the mouse over the region of their choosing and click the highlighted area, which leads to a separate page that provides a historical account of the countries and territories that comprise it. This site also includes a search bar at the top of the page for users to find famous natives, flags, fast facts, maps, symbols, and more. The layout is slightly cluttered with ads, but it is fairly easy to distinguish them from the page content. Filled with pictures and other clickables, this Website would be a perfect option for students new to the study of geography who need to gain experience with maps and general research.

Older students who are conducting research may not find this particular Website useful, as it provides a general overview of various regions, but does not contain a search tab for those looking for specialized information. On the home page, students can scroll down to find additional links to help them locate bodies of water, latitude and longitude, currency conversion, and populations. Still, this information will be more useful for younger students conducting beginner-level research.—**ARBA Staff Reviewer**

Dictionaries and Encyclopedias

C, S

106.   Quinn, Joyce A., and Susan L. Woodward. **Earth's Landscape: An Encyclopedia of the World's Geographic Features.** Santa Barbara, Calif., ABC-CLIO, 2015. 2v. illus. index. $205.00/set. ISBN 13: 978-1-61069-445-2; 978-1-61069-446-9 (e-book).

Earth's Landscape: An Encyclopedia of the World's Geographic Features is a two-volume encyclopedia that provides 460 articles that define the diversity of the world's continents and oceans. This geography encyclopedia discusses lesser-known, as well as, prominent geologic features of our planet Earth. The articles are alphabetically arranged. The format for each of the entries are an overview, the geographic coordinates, a description, its geologic history, the circulation and major currents (in entries for oceans and seas only), the biota, which is the animal and plant life of the region, protected areas, environmental issues, and a bibliography for further reading. There is a list of the entries by geologic location, and a list of abbreviations used in the text. Supplemental tables and black-and-white photographs are interspersed through the text. There is a table of contents for both volumes in volume one, but the index and glossary are only available in volume two. There are three appendixes at the end of volume two, entitled "The Highest, Lowest, Biggest, Deepest Places: 'Top Tens' and Other Global Comparisons," "Opposing Viewpoints: Issues Related to Natural Features," and "Activities and Discussion Questions."

I believe this work would be a great purchase for the geology collections of high school and undergraduate libraries.—**Kay Stebbins Slattery**

Handbooks and Yearbooks

C, P, S

107.   **GeoBeats. http://www.geobeats.com/.** [Website] Free. Date reviewed: 2016.

GeoBeats is a fantastic free video Website, perfect for students of all ages and travelers. According to the About Us page, *GeoBeats* is essentially a video production company that produces and distributes professional content. Filmmakers for the company are located around the world. The site features close to 1,000 videos from approximately 80 countries, featuring specific tourist destinations, cultural sites, etiquette, restaurants, iconic foods, traditional performances, and much more. Videos range from around 1 minute 30 seconds to 3 minutes. The homepage of *GeoBeats* includes a section called "Hot Topics," which allows users to link directly to city-specific videos. There are also videos grouped into "Recently Popular," "Editors' Choices," and "New Releases." A feature video—on Balinese Dance—is also front and center on the homepage. Users can Browse All Videos, or can select a Category (the only available category is Travel), Sub-Category (a specific country and city), and Video (on a specific topic in a specific city).

GeoBeats would appeal to students of all ages, in particular middle and high school users. Travelers would also find the videos helpful. Due to their brevity, the videos are easy to watch and are presented in an accessible, engaging way, offering an alternative for students who benefit from more interactive ways of learning. Some—but not all—of the videos include a transcript, which users will find helpful. References and further readings are not listed, but some videos provide links to more information. For instance, in the Italy-Florence-Gelato video, the contact information for Perche No, a gelateria featured in the video, is provided. Some narrators are American hosts, while others are locals of the areas being presented. The site is easy to navigate, although it could benefit from a general search engine and alphabetical listing of all videos (when looking at the Browse All Videos link, they don't seem to be in any specific order). However, users can easily find a video by using the drop down category menus. Sample videos include: Austria-Salzburg-Top 5 Travel Attractions; Azerbaijan-Baku-Baku Government House; Cuba-Havana-San Cristobal Cathedral; Italy-Florence-Gelato; Japan-Tokyo-Cherry Blossom; South Africa-Kruger-Kruger National Park; and Yemen-Socotra-Socotra Island. Some videos are live action, with the host actually in the city, and some videos are collages of images with a voiceover narration. While some videos skew more toward tourists, cultural and historical content can be found for student users. School, public, and college libraries should keep www.geobeats.com in mind when patrons are looking for information on specific countries.—**ARBA Staff Reviewer**

P, S

108.   **Geographia. http://geographia.com/.** [Website] Free. Date reviewed: 2016.

Produced by interKnowledge Corp, *Geographia* is a free Website that provides users with a mix of cultural and travel information. The homepage of *Geographia* is set up with world regions, called "Destinations," in the left margin, along with a column called "Contents," which links users directly to the most recently added destinations, and another column called "Features," which links users to articles on specific topics in select cities and countries. The world regions under "Destinations" include Africa, Asia, Caribbean, Europe, and Latin America, and these link to approximately 50 country and territory profiles. In general, the profiles include information broken down into two main sections: Location, Geography, and Climate; and History and People. A majority of the profiles have a similar look and feel, but many are set up differently, and some—such as those under the Caribbean—include different information that is geared more toward travel, such as listings of activities, accommodations, and travel tips. The readability of the profiles is consistent and looks to be geared toward middle school and high school students, as well as general readers interested in travel. The "Features" include articles such as "Magnificent Mulu" (about a rainforest in Borneo), "Nelson in Nevis" (about war hero Horatio Nelson in the Caribbean), "Pirates of the Bahamas," "Land of Fire & Ice" (about Iceland) and "A Journey to Moscow."

Geographia provides users with good introductory material on the culture, history, and people of various countries and world territories. However, student users should proceed with caution, as articles are not cited, and there are no listings for further reading or research. Users might be confused by the inconsistency of the country profiles, since many look different from country to country. Some profiles, such as Botswana, are accompanied by beautiful photos of the land, people, and animals. Other profiles, such as Burma (Myanmar), have only one to two small photos. Additionally, some very key countries are missing, such as China, Japan, and most of Europe (though there are links to tourism sites for missing European countries). The site is easy to navigate, with clearly labeled links that take users around from the country profiles, back to the regions, and back to the homepage. Users should be warned that since the site is free, there are many ads on every page. At the bottom of the homepage is a Google Search engine that allows users to search the Web or the www.geographia.com site. A search for the term "cheetah" pulls up the appropriate pages on the Kenya, Namibia, South Africa, and Zimbabwe country profiles. A search for "great wall," however, pulls up an odd listing of pages, since China is not included on the site. Overall, *Geographia* can be used as a supplementary Website that might help give users a starting point in researching culture and travel.—**ARBA Staff Reviewer**

C, P, S

109.   **Maps of North America. http://digitalcollections.nypl.org/collections/maps-of-north-america#/?tab=about.** [Website] Free. Date reviewed: 2016.

This collection from the New York Public Library contains hundreds of private maps that were once part of Lawrence H. Slaughter's private collection. Some others belonged to the John H. Levine estate. Most of these maps focus on the Middle Atlantic region and are a nice accompaniment to the NYPL collection "Atlases, Gazetteers, Guidebooks, and Other Books."

The attractive and organized site offers a variety of clickable images from the seventeenth-nineteenth centuries. Users will find maps of New France, Mexico, the Caribbean, the young United States and its territories, and so much more. Each still image provides the user with the following information: type of resource, genre, date issued, division, publisher, cartographer, notes, identifiers, citations (in MLA, APA, Chicago, and Wikipedia), as well as additional descriptive information. A timeline shows when the creator of the image was born and died, when the image was issued, and when it was digitized. Users can also download the images in a variety of sizes and resolutions.—**ARBA Staff Reviewer**

C, P, S

110.   **Old Maps Online. http://www.oldmapsonline.org/.** [Website] Free. Date reviewed: 2016.

Indexes over 400,000 maps that are available online from a variety of institutions including the New York Public Library, the USGS, the British Library, the Biblioteca Nacional de Colombia, and many others. Users of the site search by entering a place-name (Browse brings up maps for the user's location) to retrieve a window with a modern map of that location with a selection of older maps as search results to the right. Zooming the modern map or changing its focus will change the results accordingly. Users can also filter their results using a timeline or selecting specific attributes such as scale or keyword. Hovering over a map shows what portion of the modern map is included. The search results provide very basic information about each map (cartographer, date, scale, institution) and links to the map online at its home institution's Website. In some cases, users have the additional option of viewing the historic map as an overlay with a modern map of the same area.

This is a fascinating Website for finding, or just browsing, historic maps of regions throughout the world and will be useful for scholars, students, and the general public alike.—**ARBA Staff Reviewer**

Travel Guides

Handbooks and Yearbooks

C, P, S

111.   **Britannia. http://www.britannia.com/history/.** [Website] Free. Date reviewed: 2016.

Produced and maintained since 1996 by Britannia.com, LLC, a privately owned and operated American company, the *Britannia* Website is both a history and a travel resource. The site has no connection with *Britannia* Magazine, the British government, or any university or other organization. *Britannia* bills itself as a site run by Americans for Americans who are planning to travel to Britain, whether for formal study or for leisurely exploration. The site is currently funded by ad revenues, but plans are underway for creation of a "Reader Donation Program" to help finance future expansion. However, access to the site will remain free and open to all. Content is provided by contributors from around the world who are "experts in their field," and information is updated regularly, especially as regards the travel portion of the site. Many of the topic entries and biographies on the history side are drawn from older works—"Catherine of Aragon," for instance, comes from a 1909 publication by Emery Walker—and the larger overview pieces are signed by their contributors, though links allow readers to inquire about the author of any unsourced or unsigned piece.

Britannia covers the entire history of Britain, from the prehistoric period to the twenty-first century, with Arthurian Britain a particular emphasis. Besides King Arthur, major content sections include Monarchs of Britain, Church History, and Biographies of important Britons. Including about 200 individuals, from Caratacus to Margaret Thatcher, the biographies cover a good selection of political, military, and literary/cultural figures in essays averaging perhaps 200-300 words. Also provided are detailed narrative histories of England, Scotland, and Wales by Peter N. Williams, and of London by David Nash Ford. Timelines, narratives, topical essays of events and artifacts, bibliographies, and original sources—in many cases with relevant images—are offered for each broad period covered, i.e., Prehistoric Britain; Roman Britain; Anglo-Saxon Britain; Medieval Britain; Reformation and Restoration; Age of Empire; Modern Britain; and Myth, Legend, and Folklore. An Original Resources section offers further primary documents, timelines, and historical maps. The essays and biographies are generally well written and accurate and pitched to a level appropriate for high school and undergraduate students and interested general readers.

The travel side of the site allows users to search for hotels and lodging in London and across Britain and to find and book tours of all kinds. Links take the user to the site of the tour operator for full details and booking information. One can book tours of Arthurian sites; for Leeds Castle, Canterbury, and Dover in Kent, and for a tour of Downton Abbey sites in Oxfordshire. Would-be travelers can also obtain theatre tickets, attraction and event tickets, and airport transfers. The site also offers a series of virtual tours for such places as Hadrian's Wall, Northumberland's Battlefields, and Robin Hood's Yorkshire.

Britannia is highly recommended for anyone planning to travel to Britain, whether for study or for pleasure, who wishes to know more about the places he or she plans to see, and the best way to get to them.—**ARBA Staff Reviewer**

P

112.   Mitchell, Charles W. **Travels through American History in the Mid-Atlantic.** Baltimore, Md., Johns Hopkins University Press, 2014. 204p. maps. index. $24.95pa. ISBN 13: 978-1-4214-1514-7; 978-1-4214-1515-4 (e-book).

This book is both travel guide to historic sites and engaging historical narrative. It begins in the colonial period and moves through the Revolutionary era, Early Republic, antebellum period, and the Civil War. The 16 chapters cover, in order, Jamestown, Williamsburg, and Yorktown; St. Mary's City; Fort Frederick; Independence National Historical Park; Fort McHenry and the Star-Spangled Banner National Historic Trail; the Baltimore & Ohio Railroad Museum; the Chesapeake & Ohio Canal; Harper's Ferry;

Civil War Richmond; Antietam; Civil War Washington; Gettysburg; Fredericksburg, Chancellorsville, the Wilderness, and Spotsylvania; Cedar Creek and the Belle Grove National Historic Park; and Petersburg and the road to Appomattox. Chapters include detailed maps, suggestions for side trips, and further readings; in some cases, the author separates his further readings section into recommendations for adults and children.

The chapters create an interesting tapestry by interweaving historical context, suggestions for how to best enjoy a visit, vivid physical descriptions, and quotes from letters and diaries of those who witnessed and/or made history in the places described. For example, readers will find in the chapter on Valley Forge George Washington's opinion of Congress's inability to provision his soldiers during the Revolutionary War, what is on offer in the visitor center, hiking information, driving directions, and much more. The detailed map is a fine visual aid. Suggestions for further readings include three titles for adults and one for children, Jason Cooper's *Valley Forge* (2003).

Information is easily locatable within *Travels through American History* due to the table of contents and index, but the artful renderings of each place and its history will compel a cover-to-cover reading. Highly recommended.—**ARBA Staff Reviewer**

P

113.   Van Ellis, Mark D. **America and WWI: A Traveler's Guide.** Northampton, Mass., Interlink Books, 2015. 432p. illus. maps. index. $22.00pa. ISBN 13: 978-1-56656-975-0.

With time passing rapidly and memories fading, this thoughtful, well-researched book traces the path of American involvement in the Great War of 1914-1918. While primarily serving as a guide to both domestic and foreign locales, the book nonetheless conveys a reverent narrative that leaves no street corner bypassed when following American "Doughboys" through their first great international crisis.

The book sets the scene at the outbreak of the war as Americans consider their European sympathies then begin to prepare with the establishment of domestic military training camps throughout the homefront. From here we travel to ports of embarkation, major battle theaters (including naval and air), museums, memorials, and final resting places of American fallen.

Found along this journey are the stories that elevate these places beyond mere points on a map. We read of the famous exploits of Pvt. Alvin C. York, an uneducated sharpshooter who almost singlehandedly captured over 100 enemy troops in the Argonne Forest, of the tragic loss of the troopship *Tuscania* off the remote Scottish Isle of Islay, and of the needless death of Henry Gunther, shot just one minute before the Armistice ended the war. Each of these tales leaves behind gravestones, memorials, and other markers serving to preserve their place in history. It is worth commenting that while coming in at 400 pages, the paperback is relatively compact and would be an easy travel companion.

The book's four appendixes provide information on overseas cemeteries, country museums and historic sites, historical societies and tourism authorities, and books and Websites on the American experience in the Great War. These are followed by an index of place-names.—**Laura Herrell**

9 History

American History

Chronology

P
114.   Mickolus, Edward. **The Counterintelligence Chronology: Spying By and Against the United States from the 1700s through 2014.** Jefferson, N.C., McFarland, 2015. 240p. index. $75.00pa. ISBN 13: 978-1-4766-6251-0; 978-1-4766-2240-8 (e-book).

This is an exhaustively detailed and thoroughly researched resource on spying for and against the United States from the Revolutionary period to 2015. In addition to well-known cases of espionage, this book chronicles lesser-known instances of spying. *The Counterintelligence Chronology* includes several charts that detail the motivations of spies and would-be spies, the American targets of foreign intelligence services, and more. In addition, two appendixes provide the names of American spies and the countries for which they operated and the names of alleged foreign espionage agents and the countries for which they spied. Valuably, the book concludes with a 141-item annotated bibliography by Howard Peake, curator of the Historical Intelligence Collection of the Central Intelligence Agency, and an accurate index. A recommended title for anyone wanting to find information on espionage conducted by or against the United States.—**Melinda F. Matthews**

Dictionaries and Encyclopedias

C
115.   Grossman, Mark. **Encyclopedia of the Continental Congress.** Amenia, N.Y., Grey House Publishing, 2015. 2v. illus. index. $245.00/set. ISBN 13: 978-1-61925-175-5; 978-1-61925-176-2 (e-book).

The Encyclopedia of the Continental Congress offers an in-depth look into the first Continental Congress in 1774, the second Continental Congress, 1775-1789, and the first Federal Congress in 1789. It is written by Mark Grossman, author of *Encyclopedia of the United States Cabinet: 1789-2010* and *Speakers of the House of Representatives, 1789-2009,* both published by Grey House Publishing. This 1,746-page, two-volume set does not merely focus on the men who answered the call to serve as delegates to the Continental

Congress but also on those who did not serve during the days leading up to and during the American Revolution and creation of the U.S. Constitution. Mark Grossman also sheds light on and confronts issues dealing with the Native Americans as a people, the role of women in society, and our nation's ability to handle diplomacy to name a few. A small but interesting piece of information that exposes the depth and quality of research that went into creating this multivolume set is found in the preface under the heading The Story Behind the Story. While some may regard this small segment as trivial information, it opens the reader to the creational framework of the resource that lays before them, which was in fact 25 years in the making. Grossman shares how his conceived concept for the *Encyclopedia of the Continental Congress* was born out of the coverage the *Miami Herald* ran in 1987, tied to the 200th anniversary of the signing of the U.S. Constitution; the series was called "We the People": The Constitutional Convention of 1787. He noted that the newspaper only focused on daily happenings at the Constitutional Convention. After collecting and reading all the articles put out by the *Miami Herald,* he concluded there was no one single volume that discussed what other events and persons were influential during this period of America's history; moreover, there was no real definitive work that covered the Continental Congress as well. Through the course of the preface, the reader is provided with a very short and concise depiction of the events that transpired in 1774. This gives the reader enough insight to understand why the Continental Congresses were called into being. Grossman also explains his in-depth research methods and acknowledges the various institutes where he obtained the material used to see this work come to fruition.

The uniqueness of *The Encyclopedia of the Continental Congress* is evident on the very first page of the preface (xvii) where he introduces the reader to quotes from primary resources. "William Eddis, the Surveyor for Annapolis, who had a front row seat for the conflict that was about to reach a tipping point, wrote to a friend in England on 28 May 1774: 'All America is in a flame! I hear strange language every day. The colonists are ripe for any measure that will tend to the preservation of what they call natural liberty.'" Grossman's use of direct quotes from firsthand accounts sets the narrative hook if that is even possible for a reference book. The use of and placement of the quote on the very first page of the preface is shouting to the reader/researcher that they are in for a grandiose experience, more so than they may have come to expect based on their use of an ordinary encyclopedia regardless of the subject matter. We live in a digital age where Wikipedia and one's need for instant gratification in finding a quick but often bland tertiary encyclopedia entry on a particular topic has seemed to lessen the value of the encyclopedia as a true reference tool. *Encyclopedia of the Continental Congress* will help shatter the user's misconception of just what an encyclopedia can bring to the research process.

This nicely hardbound set presents detailed entries covering each delegate who served on either the first Continental Congress in 1774, the second Continental Congress from 1775 to 1789, or the first Federal Congress in 1789. Grossman focuses on both the more significant figures [historical household names] and those who may be lesser known or who were overshadowed by their more prominent counterparts. All of them regardless how large or small played a vital role in the Continental Congresses, and Grossman ensures the reader sees their importance. His focus shines light on all the delegates who attended these meetings, stressing the significant figures of the political social scene, as well as women and other figures involved at the time. In addition to these detailed biographies, this reference work includes comprehensive accounts of places, battles, laws, treaties, and court cases that were significant to the workings of the Continental Congresses.

The Encyclopedia of the Continental Congress is presented in a very straight-forward manner, regardless of whether the user is a novice first-year college student or ardent researcher. It offers a table of contents which lists the 509 entries from Andrew Adams to John Joachim Zubly. Grossman provides the reader not only a descriptive entry pertaining to the delegate's time as a member of the Continental Congress, but a comprehensive history of the men prior to and after their time served. The reader will not only be impressed by the extensive list of delegates presented to him, but will be astonished by the incredible collection of topics, including the Bank of the United States, Relations with France, Lexington and Concord, Nassau Hall, and the Olive Branch Petition. Nearly all entries include either an image or a state seal, italicized excerpts from relevant primary documents, and footnotes.

Since Grossman clearly understands that events in history just do not happen randomly or haphazardly in some spatial plane, he added a historical timeline right after the table of contents. This timeline will help the researcher who may not be as in tune with America's history during the years leading up to and during the American Revolution. He begins the timeline in 1764 with the passage of the Sugar Act and the Currency Act, both of which led to protests in the colonies. The timeline ends in 1789, when the U.S. Senate and House of Representatives met in New York City, marking the official end to the second Continental Congress. The timeline will provide the backstory to the formation of the Continental Congress and first Federal Congress.

There is some validity in the old cliché "When History Comes Alive!" Mark Grossman's use of 31 primary documents transports the reader into this period of American history. The use of the selected primary resources helps provide additional insight into this turbulent period of American history, promoting an understanding of the general and the detailed workings of the Continental Congresses. Here readers will find familiar documents, such as Patrick Henry's "Give Me Liberty or Give Me Death" speech, as well as more obscure texts like a letter from John Adams describing his journey to the first Continental Congress. One of the more interesting documents comes from *The Massachusetts Spy* newspaper, which provides one of the initial reports on the first salvos between colonial militiamen and British soldiers at Lexington and Concord, 1775. All documents include a brief but illuminating introductory note. Again, the use of primary sources will truly entice the reader to delve deeper into the history that is the Continental Congress and the delegates who shaped this key moment in America's history.

The true essence of any good secondary or tertiary resource will come in the way it is indexed and the quality of its appendixes. *The Encyclopedia of the Continental Congress* offers the researcher both. It offers a detailed subject index, which will help the readers to quickly find just what they are looking for, including individuals, places, battles, acts, and other items of interest related to the Continental Congresses. Grossman provides six appendixes which offer some very interesting details in a straightforward format: Delegates to the Continental Congress by State; Signers of the Declaration of Independence by Occupation; Signers of the Articles of Confederation by State; Presidents of the Continental Congress; Places and Times of Sessions of the Continental Congress; and Statistics on the Thirteen Colonies. Regardless of whether the researcher wants to leisurely browse the resource through the table of contents or knows exactly what he needs and heads straight for the indexes and appendixes, Grossman's style and format will ensure they find what they are looking for.

The Encyclopedia of the Continental Congress is not only a valuable resource on the subject matter but offers the researcher a comprehensive bibliography by type, including books and articles; unpublished dissertations, masters theses, and other works; newspapers and magazines used; Continental Congress and other federal colonial documents; U.S. government documents post-1789; colonial and state government documents; other U.S. government documents; British government documents; and manuscript collections. Such a bibliography will provide a reader with the means to dive headfirst into further research on the men, events, and actions of the Continental Congress as well as the American Revolution. It is a clear must have for any academic library's reference collection, let alone a historian who specializes in this era of American history.—**Lawrence Joseph Mello**

S

116.   **Ideas and Movements That Shaped America: From the Bill of Rights to "Occupy Wall Street".** Michael S. Green and Scott L. Stabler, eds. Santa Barbara, Calif., ABC-CLIO, 2015. 3v. illus. index. $294.00/set. ISBN 13: 978-1-60169-251-9; 978-1-61069-252-6 (e-book).

This exemplary three-volume set provides accompanying text from primary source documents, sometimes as many as four, for each entry. The historical documents, frequently edited for brevity and clarity, feature introductions providing context and historical information about the authors. In some cases, the text is complete, as in the case of several speeches. Material for the encyclopedia includes a wide variety of perspectives in order to fully showcase the intellectual foundation for the movements being discussed, from George Lincoln Rockwell's arguments in favor of white supremacy to Valerie Solanos' manifesto for the Society for Cutting Up Men.

Although each of the three volumes includes a full table of contents, only the third volume provides an index and bibliography. Readers will sometimes face a challenge in finding information since the entries are movements and concepts rather than more easily recognized names of persons and events. High school libraries should have this set.— **Delilah R. Caldwell**

C, P, S

117.   **Imperialism and Expansionism in American History: A Social, Political, and Cultural Encyclopedia and Document Collection.** Chris J. Magoc and David Bernstein, eds. Santa Barbara, Calif., ABC-CLIO, 2015. 4v. index. $415.00/set. ISBN 13: 978-1-61069-429-2; 978-1-61069-430-8 (e-book).

This encyclopedia developed as an opportunity to examine how the United States moved from a colony to a global military power. Imperialism and expansionism are defined broadly by this four-volume work. The editors argue that one of the key strengths of this book is how it includes social and cultural elements, such as music, film, and literature. The overall structure of this work divides each volume chronologically. Each volume is further subdivided into three different chronological sections. While this grouping does make narrative sense to show how topics relate, it does make it harder to use as a reference source. Fortunately, the table of contents and the index help clear up confusion. The addition of numerous primary sources is another benefit of this encyclopedia.

Overall, this is a fine addition to the body of reference sources about American history. Each section has a clear historic overview and the signed articles all have bibliographies to learn more about the topic. At times, the entries could have been more clearly tied to the organizing theme of this encyclopedia and a little more information about the authors could have been provided. Those minor concerns aside, this is a valuable work and is recommended for most collections.—**Allen Reichert**

S

118.   **Jim Crow: A Historical Encyclopedia of the American Mosaic.** Nikki L. M. Brown and Barry M. Stentiford, eds. Santa Barbara, Calif., Greenwood Press/ABC-CLIO, 2014. 471p. illus. index. $100.00. ISBN 13: 978-1-61069-663-0; 978-1-61069-664-7 (e-book).

Jim Crow (created in the mid-1880s and running through the mid-1960s), the laws and customs supporting legally sanctioned discrimination in the United States, is covered in-depth. The title not only provides a few primary documents, but also covers the history, events, and institutions involved, and describes the effects on politics, people, and culture. An alphabetical list of entries, a guide to related topics, a chronology, black-and-white photographs, and a select bibliography comprise the title. High school students and anyone with an interest in learning more about this racial segregation will find this title of interest.—**Denise A. Garofalo**

C, S

119.   **Reconstruction: A Historical Encyclopedia of the American Mosaic.** Richard Zuczek, ed. Santa Barbara, Calif., Greenwood Press/ABC-CLIO, 2015. 435p. illus. index. $100.00. ISBN 13: 978-1-61069-917-4; 978-1-61069-918-1 (e-book).

This is a handy guide to the American Reconstruction period that provides a series of brief essays written "for the high school student and lower-level college student." The essays are written by (for the most part, some are unsigned), "the most prominent historians in the field." These essays are well written and provide a concise treatment of topics such as: the Kirk-Holden War in Tennessee/North Carolina, Nathan Bedford Forrest, Edwin Stanton, and Joseph Hayne Rainey. In addition to the essay topics there are 11 primary source documents reprinted in the book. These documents include: the Emancipation Proclamation, the 14th and 15th Amendments to the Constitution, the Civil Rights Act of 1866, Articles of President Johnson's impeachment, Mississippi Black Codes, and the so-called Ku Klux Klan Act (Enforcement Act of 1871). The book has an index, a list of essay entries, a classed guide to inter-related topics, a chronology of Reconstruction, a list of Reconstruction governors, and a list of dates of readmission for former Confederate States, as well as a small bibliography. A quick check between the authors listed in the bibliography, and the "prominent historians in the field" who wrote the essays in this work produced no matches alas. This leads the reviewer to wonder exactly how "prominent" these folks are. A number of topics/persons mentioned in the chronology fail to appear in the book: Posse Comitatus Act, Wormley House "deal," Hamburg Massacre, Homestead Act, John McEnery, and Zebulon Vance. The brief "acknowledgements" section in the front of the book contains this odd statement in italics: "The views expressed herein… are not to be construed as official or reflecting views of the Commandant or of the U.S. Coast Guard." While the editor of the book teaches at the U.S. Coast Guard Academy and has previously written a two-volume Greenwood *Encyclopedia of the Reconstruction Era* (2006), one could hardly make the leap that the book is a statement of Coast Guard policy.

Overall this works does a good job of serving the audience for which is it was written.—
Ralph Lee Scott

C, S
120.   **The World of the American Revolution: A Daily Life Encyclopedia.** Merril D.
Smith, ed. Santa Barbara, Calif., Greenwood Press/ABC-CLIO, 2015. 2v. illus. index.
$198.00/set. ISBN 13: 978-1-4408-3027-3; 978-1-4408-3028-0 (e-book).

This Greenwood Press series, The Daily Life Encyclopedias, addresses a very
interesting concept—"What was life really like for ordinary people in different cultures
throughout history? What did they eat, wear, believe, think?" "By examining the social,
cultural, and material history topics—family life, political life, religious life, recreation and
social customs…we can examine their emotional life, interactions, intimate relationships,
opinions and beliefs, and the interactions between them and the greater world." Editor
Merril Smith presents us the two-volume *The World of the American Revolution* as part of
this series. The two volumes, Arts to Housing and Community and Politics and Warfare to
Science and Technology, respectively, contain primary documents, a selected bibliography,
and illustrations.

There are 265 individually authored, richly detailed entries that cover an eclectic
array of subjects grouped into 10 topical areas. Examples of entries indicate the breadth
of coverage: For the Arts: Books, Music, Intellectual Life, Oratory, and Political
Pamphlets; Economics and Work: Artisans, Debt, Fur Trade, and Printers; Family and
Gender: Breastfeeding, Celibacy, Fatherhood, Friendship, Old Age, and Orphans;
Fashion and Appearance: Cross-Dressing, Hats, Jewelry, and Textiles; Food and Drink:
Corn, Rum, Tea, and Wine; Housing and Community: Churches, Crime, Forts, Prisons,
and Slave Housing; Politics and Warfare: The Boston Massacre, Citizenship, Pacifists,
and Soldiers; Recreation and Social Customs: Duels, Etiquette, Libraries, Reading, and
Theater; Religion: Bible, Catholicism, Fast Days, Quakers, and Sermons; and Science and
Technology: Fires, Lightening, Mental Illness, and Ships.

Recommended for high school and undergraduate libraries.—**Scott R. DiMarco**

Handbooks and Yearbooks

C, S
121.   **American Eras: Primary Sources: Early American Civilizations and
Exploration to 1600.** Farmington Hills, Mich., Gale/Cengage Learning, 2015. 299p. illus.
index. $177.00. ISBN 13: 978-1-4144-9823-2; 978-1-4144-9840-9 (e-book).

The American Eras Primary Sources series packs a generous amount of information
into a compact, well-organized volume. This particular volume shares a plethora of primary
sources representing the era of early American civilizations and explorations to 1600.

Introductory information includes a thorough essay breaking down the presentation
of the primary sources and another essay discussing both benefits of and potential
limitations to using primary sources within one's research. This section also provides a
helpful general chronology of major world events within the era covered in this volume.
Over 75 primary sources cover a wide selection of artifacts, memoirs, charters, artwork,
maps, letters, and more. They are arranged into eight thematic chapters and presented

chronologically. Chapters include: "The Arts, Fashion and Leisure"; "Business and the Economy"; "Communications and Education"; "Government and Politics"; "Law and Justice""; Lifestyles and Social Trends"; "Religion;" and "Science, Medicine and Technology." Each chapter opens with an overview of its theme and then a chronology including events directly related to the theme and primary sources as well as more general events of note.

In presenting the primary source, the book first lists basic information such as who created it, when it was made, etc. An essay, accompanied by a photograph of the artifact, document, excerpt, etc., provides good contextual information and explains the significance of the primary source. Other photographs may accompany the essay as well. The entry concludes with a listing of resources for further study specific to the entry. Some of the primary sources featured in this book include the 1492 charter granting Christopher Columbus funding for his trip in search of a sea route to Asia, an illustration, *Florida Indians planting Maize,* and Martin Waldseemüller's 1513 *World Map.*

The volume concludes with additional generalized resources, a primary source type index (with headings such as Architecture, Charters, etc.), and a general index.

Recommended.—**ARBA Staff Reviewer**

C, S

122. **American Eras: Primary Sources: The Colonial Era, 1600-1754.** Farmington Hills, Mich., Gale/Cengage Learning, 2015. 438p. illus. index. $177.00. ISBN 13: 978-1-4144-9823-2; 978-1-4144-9839-3 (e-book).

The Colonial Era (1600-1754), is volume seven in the series American Eras: Primary Sources. Other titles in the series include the following: *Early American Civilization, Exploration to 1600; The Colonial Era (1600-1754); Revolutionary Era (1754-1783); Development of a Nation (1783-1815); Reform Era & Eastern U.S. Development (1815-1850); Westward Expansion (1800-1860); Civil War and Reconstruction (1860-1878)*; and *Development of the Industrial United States (1878-1899). The Colonial Era (1600-1754),* much like the other titles in the series, can be used as a stand-alone item when studying the colonial era, or it can be incorporated alongside the other volumes in the series when teaching, researching, and understanding American history on a broader scope instead of a singular era isolated in time and space. The volume can be purchased individually or as a set.

According to the Gale Publishing Website, this resource is written to allow the average student in ninth grade, college, and beyond to read and extrapolate the information from it. Regardless of whether the researcher is a novice or a seasoned veteran, this source will prove to be highly valuable to all who open its cover and begin the research process. This resource pulls from select primary sources encompassing a wide range of documents and images, from recipes and diary entries to cartoons and photos, to government legislation and court rulings. This varied mixture creates a diversity of perspectives that will provide the reader with a fresh insight into key events and figures of the colonial era. This volume, as well as the rest of the series, is designed to make the content as accessible as possible to the reader. Each entry is organized by standardized rubrics that allow the user to find information quickly within an entry and facilitate comparisons across entries. The introduction and significance sections are kept brief and focused. It covers the historical background and contributing factors, importance, and impact of the primary source, while it encourages the reader to begin to think critically about the source and how it played a role in history. Besides the key facts about the primary source and its creator, it offers a "Further Resources" section as the end of the entry. This will ignite the researcher to delve deeper into an event or person who shaped our history.

The Colonial Era (1600-1754) opens with an era overview, which will set the stage for the primary sources the reader is about to engage. The primary sources provide unique perspectives and a wealth of understanding through the use of oral histories, songs, speeches, advertisements, letters, laws, legal decisions, newspaper articles, cartoons, and recipes. History and the historical events are brought to life for the researcher largely because of the primary resources presented across the following categories: the arts, business and the economy, education, fashion and leisure, government and politics, law and justice, lifestyles and social trends, media, medicine and health, religion, and science and technology. Because of the varied categories offered to the reader, there is a little something for everyone who turns to this work to learn about the colonial era.

The print format is consistent across all the categories. Regardless of the topic, the user is presented with 10 primary sources relating to the subject heading. There is a topical overview that will set the stage for the section, and this will provide the researcher with a starting point to the particular subject and how it shaped the colonial era.

There is also a chronology list of key dates as it pertains to any particular section and this proves very advantageous for the user who needs a linear timeline to better understand how the particular topic shaped this era in history. Just as each section is structured in a similar format, so too is every entry within this book. The entry is presented in the following format: primary source type and title, author, date, source (from which the entry was taken from,) a short biography about the author, an introduction (to set the stage for the primary source,) and significance (of the entry to history). This wealth of background information not only aids the reader in learning about a particular "Primary Source Entry," but it just may become the spark that will light the fire to go beyond that particular entry and even this particular book in their quest to learn about the "Colonial Era." It is important to note that regardless of whether the reader is a beginner or a veteran doing research, this volume, like others in the series, lays before the reader a thorough explanation and gives them a detailed example of the format that every entry will look like and why it is formatted this way. *The Colonial Era (1600-1754)* offers up a couple of different indexes. The first one is a "Primary Source Type Index" which will provide the user a list of based on the type of resource. This will allow the user the unique ability to see all entries based on a particular type such as but not limited to artifacts, charters, or government documents. There is also a general index which is sorted word-by-word and the index offers bold page numbers as indicators to main essays and italic page locators which indicate images. Both types of indexes will allow them to hone into an area of interest when they are researching and under a time constraint. While the printed format and structure is very important to the reader or teacher in learning the topic, the physical structure while often overlooked is just as important. The physical version is well put together and the hardcover version can withstand the daily use that it will find in any respectable classroom or library reference department. The title is clearly presented on the spine as well as the cover of the book. The book's rear cover provides a quick synopsis of what this work will provide along with the 10 different perspectives offered up to the reader. *American Eras: Primary Sources: The Colonial Era (1600-1754)*, like the rest of the series, is a valued resource for the classroom and library alike.—**Lawrence Joseph Mello**

C, P, S

123.   **California Digital Newspaper Collection. http://cdnc.ucr.edu/cgi-bin/cdnc.** [Website] Free. Date reviewed: 2016.

The freely accessible *California Digital Newspaper Collection* (CDNC) has over 600,000 pages of newspapers, all of which are in the public domain and thus not subject to use restrictions. A selection of more recent newspapers is also available. The CDNC is produced and curated by the Center for Bibliographic Studies and Research (CBSR) at UC Riverside with support from the U.S. Institute of Museum and Library Services under the provisions of the Library Services and Technology Act. Funding was provided by grants from the National Endowment for the Humanities.

Four links on the right-hand side of the page—Browse by Title, Browse by Date, Browse by Tag, and Browse by County—make navigation a snap. Under Title, users will find links to papers from the *Amador Ledger* (Jackson, 1900-1911) to the *Wide West* (San Francisco, 1854-1858). Browsing by date starts in 1846 and runs through May, 2015. Clicking on a month and year will take users to a calendar which has links to different newspapers for each day of the month. On April 19, 1861, for example, there are links to the *California Farmer and Journal of the Useful Sciences,* the *Daily Alta California,* the *Red Bluff Independent,* and the *Sacramento Daily Union.* The tag for " Salt Lake City-Mormons deserting" links to an August 12, 1857, article from the *Sacramento Bee.* If someone wants to investigate happenings in Madera County, a click on the county name goes straight to the 1861-1922 issues of the *Mariposa Gazette.* A right click on articles accessed produces further options, like the ability to clip the article or create a PDF file.

For those hoping to use historic California newspapers, the highly recommended CDNC will truly amaze.—**ARBA Staff Reviewer**

C

124.   **Colonial America. Module 1: Settlement, Expansion and Rivalries. http:// www.amdigital.co.uk/m-collections/collection/colonial-america/.** [Website] Chicago, Adam Matthew Digital. Price negotiated by site. Date reviewed: 2016.

Colonial America is an extensive digital resource built using the Colonial Office document collection (mostly manuscripts) held by the National Archives in London. The collection includes original correspondence between the American colonial governments and the British government agencies responsible for administering them. This relationship dealt with all manner of subjects, and its archive documents a broad scope of issues encompassing political, economic, social, cultural, and military subjects. These topics are represented in both public and private documents ranging from letters and diaries to public notices, newspapers, and printed pamphlets. The collection also includes maps and some architectural drawings. All documents are available as high-resolution scanned images and can be downloaded, saved, and sent via email.

The full collection covers 1602-1822 and will be made available in five modules to be released over the next four years. (This review covers only Module 1 released in late 2015.) Module 1: Early Settlement, Expansion, and Rivalries focuses on the early development of and events in the American colonies including such major events as the 1688 Glorious Revolution and the French and Indian War of 1756-63.

Colonial America's primary navigation is organized by tabs, and the Document tab provides access to the manuscript collection. The collection has been scanned, indexed, and described at the document level allowing it to be searched and browsed by keyword, people or place-name, date, and theme. Dropdown menus at the top of the Document tab help users drill down to specific information and combine multiple search parameters. For example, a user can filter to show only diary entries on community organization in New York. The Popular Searches function provided by the editors highlights interesting topics in the collection.

Each document is described with a title, place-name, keyword, people, places, volume name, dates, and theme and is represented by a high-quality scan of the original. Users can zoom in several times without compromising the quality of the image. This is useful as some of the documents are faded or have difficult-to-read handwriting.

The Explore tab includes an interactive Government Chart, Essays, Biographies, Data Associations, and Popular Searches. The Government Structure Chart allows users to connect key information such as date, region, and office to key office-holders in time. This facilitates user's contextualization of the major players of this time period. Data Associations is a heatmap display illustrating the connections between people, places, and keywords.

The Map Gallery tab provides access to many interesting maps that can be filtered by image type, date, or keyword. Users can view full-size images of the maps, and images can be saved to a personalized collection (using "My Lightbox") or downloaded as a PDF.

Translating a manuscript archive of this size, scope, and historical importance into a usable online resource is an immense task. Great thought and care has gone into representing this body of material well. Emphasis has been placed on search, discovery, navigation, ease of access, and interpretation. Several different points of access have been provided and various methods have been employed to support specific searching and serendipitous browsing.

This resource is a treasure for scholars. It is immensely important for British and American history scholars, and any library or institution supporting this audience should consider this resource. It also has the potential to inspire young scholars by bringing them close to historical documents through digital media. This is a rich and extensive digital archive enhanced by thorough and thoughtful organization and judicious application of technology.—**Kristin Kay Leeman**

C, P

125.   **Defining Documents in American History: Postwar 1940s (1945-1950).** Michael Shally-Jensen, ed. Hackensack, N.J., Salem Press, 2015. 308p. index. $175.00. ISBN 13: 978-1-61925-739-9; 978-1-61925-740-5 (e-book).

This title is the latest in a series of books that examines discrete periods of American history through a close reading of the primary documents produced therein. Previous volumes by Salem Press include the Reconstruction Era (1865-1877) and the decade of the 1920s.

A standard format allows the user of any one work to be familiar with the entire set. An "Editor's Introduction" sets the scene by giving an objective overview of the period in question. Each chapter takes an in-depth look at a single speech, government report, legislative act, or other document, and uses this as a springboard to discuss not only the primary source itself, but also the social, cultural, and political ramifications.

A "Summary Overview" gives the researcher a snapshot of the contents of the document, while "Defining Moment" fleshes out the background that led up to its creation. This is followed by "Author Biography" (if appropriate, as some documents are created by committees or other groups, as opposed to an individual writer), "Document Analysis," which is self-explanatory, and "Essential Themes," which discusses the significance and historical import of the document. Lastly, a "Bibliography and Additional Reading" section lists resources helpful for further research. The core of each chapter, however, is a shaded box that contains the verbatim text of the primary source under examination. Shorter pieces appear in their entirety; more lengthy pieces are excerpted but can still run to several pages.

Editor Michael Shally-Jensen holds a doctorate in cultural anthropology from Princeton University. He has assembled a competent crew of academics whom likewise hold advanced degrees and that have contributed to the contents of this work.

As with previously published volumes in this series, *Postwar 1940s* is well written, exhibits solid scholarship, and presents an engaging read. As an understanding of our nation's past is central to becoming a well-rounded citizen, this volume is strongly recommended for purchase by all public and academic libraries.—**Michael Francis Bemis**

C, P

126.   **Defining Documents in American History: The Vietnam War (1956-1975).** Michael Shally-Jensen, ed. Hackensack, N.J., Salem Press, 2015. 288p. index. $175.00. ISBN 13: 978-1-61925-852-5; 978-1-61925-853-2 (e-book).

The Vietnam War continues playing a critical role in U.S. history and national security policy-making. References to its impact are regularly made by critics of proposed U.S. military interventions in other countries. This work covers various documents on this conflict between 1956 and 1975 representing a divergent spectrum of political views on why the United States should or should not participate in this war.

This compilation is broken up into the following sections: Kennedy's War, Johnson's War, The Antiwar Movement, Nixon's War, and Aftermath. Within these sections, overviews are provided of individual documents and the individual involved in creating them, the text of the document, analysis of the document's significance, and bibliographic references. Examples of documents in these sections include: a January 14, 1961, letter from John Kennedy to South Vietnamese ruler Ngo Dinh Diem; Lyndon Johnson's August 4, 1964, address on the Gulf of Tonkin incident; a July 21, 1965, meeting between LBJ and advisors such as Secretary of Defense Robert McNamara, Secretary of State Dean Rusk, and Undersecretary of State George Ball; a March 1965 call by the Students for a Democratic Society for a march on Washington, D.C., to oppose the Vietnam War; Robert Kennedy's February 8, 1968, speech "An Unwinnable War"; a September 1969 memorandum on Vietnamization from National Security Advisor Henry Kissinger to Richard Nixon; excerpts from the 1973 Paris Peace Treaty ending U.S. participation in the war; and Jimmy Carter's 1977 pardoning of draft evaders from this conflict.

This is a succinctly edited work which also features bibliographic references and Websites such as the State Department's Historians Office covering American diplomatic relations during the Vietnam War. It will serve as a useful introduction to undergraduate students beginning to study the complexities and controversies of the Vietnam War and their lingering impact in American foreign and national security policy.—**Bert Chapman**

C, P, S

127.   Derks, Scott. **Working Americans 1880-2015. Volume V: Americans at War.** 2d ed. Amenia, N.Y., Grey House Publishing, 2015. 685p. illus. index. $150.00. ISBN 13: 978-1-61925-743-6; 978-1-61925-744-3 (e-book).

Online sources have made many traditional printed reference volumes somewhat obsolete. However, that is not the case with this unique gem that cannot be captured electronically. The fifth contribution in a series that examines the lives of representative Americans, this volume addresses one of the occurrences in people's lives that affects them in the most dramatic ways—war. Beginning with the frontier conflicts of the 1880s, the volume extends through the present day. Organized by decades, the collection brings together personal stories, media excerpts, clippings, diaries, letters, cartoons, statistical information, and thousands of photographs, pictures, and other visuals. The inclusions are both traditional ones and segments of popular culture that include a wide range from song lyrics to mementoes of all kinds. The volume reminds me of both a truly excellent museum display and a Ken Burns documentary in printed rather than video medium.

Each of the 13 chapters begins with an overview of important events of the decade and contains personal profiles (a total of 38). The volume highlights individuals from a range of ethnicities and socio-economic levels to capture a snapshot of Americans from many perspectives. A common feature in each chapter is a chart of selected prices and average pay for jobs as one element that demonstrates statistical comparisons between the decades. The index is quite useful.

The volume is a tour de force, one that a reader can become absorbed in for hours on end. I recommend this compilation highly. It is an educational tool of impressive merit.—
Joe P. Dunn

C, P, S

128.   **The Gilder Lehrman Institute of American History. https://www.gilderlehrman. org/.** [Website] Free. Date reviewed: 2016.

New York's Gilder Lehrman Institute of American History is devoted to the improvement of history education. Its Website offers a unique Web resource ideal for students, teachers, and general readers.

The core of the site is the Institute's "History by Era" section, under the editorial aegis of historian Carol Berkin. Organized chronologically, "History by Era" tells the story of American history, divided into 10 distinct periods: Colonization & Settlement, 1585-1763; The American Revolution, 1763-1783; The New Nation, 1783-1815; National Expansion & Reform, 1815-1860; Civil War & Reconstruction, 1861-1877; Rise of Industrial America, 1877-1900; Progressive Era to New Era, 1900-1929; Great Depression & WWII, 1929-1945; and 1945 to the Present.

Each of the 10 eras covered includes an historical overview essay written by some of the most distinguished historians writing today, including John Demos, Pauline Maier, Alan Taylor, Eric Foner, Richard White, and David M. Kennedy, among others. Each of these overview essays are complemented with three additional thematic essays and a set of featured documents or primary sources, including letters, government and legal documents, paintings, photographs, and songs—all drawn from the extensive holdings of the Gilder Lehrman Collection. For those interested in exploring important topics across chronology and periodization, users can also search for content organized by various historical "themes"—African American History, American Indian History, Literature and Language Arts, etc.

The site's Multimedia section offers more than a dozen video series on subjects ranging from "Studying the Constitution" to "GIs, Generals, and American Wars." The "Historian's Now" video series features conversations with major historians of U.S.

history, including Gordon Wood, David Reynolds, Richard Brookhiser, and Julian Zelizer, among other luminaries.

Helpful lesson plans and other classroom resources from master teachers are also included in the site.

As Carol Berkin says in her introduction, the site "…is not an online textbook. From the beginning, we set ourselves the task of providing the reader with a far richer texture than a textbook can offer.… A collection of fifty individual essays written by some of the most distinguished scholars of our day…speaks to the reader not in one voice, but in fifty different, unique voices as each of these renowned scholars interprets the important developments, people, events, and ideas of a particular era." The Gilder Lehrman Institute's impressive Website is highly recommended for high school and college students, for teachers, and for American history buffs.—**ARBA Staff Reviewer**

C, P, S

129.   **The Great Chicago Fire and the Web of Memory. http://www.greatchicagofire. org/.** [Website] Free. Date reviewed: 2016.

A joint project of the Chicago History Museum and Northwestern University Information Technology Department of Academic and Research Technologies, the Website presents a documentary history-in-miniature of the Great Chicago Fire of 1871—one of the most infamous disasters in nineteenth-century U.S. history.

The site is divided into two main parts. "The Great Chicago Fire" includes background material on Chicago's growth in the decades before the fire, a brief narrative of the conflagration, as well as an essay on the rapid reconstruction of the city during the "Great Rebuilding" of 1871-73. "The Web of Memory" includes contemporaneous accounts of the fire from eyewitnesses and from the popular press, as well as a brief examination of how the fire was later commemorated in poetry, fiction, drama, song, and visual works. A rich variety of images are available, as well as fascinating audio and video clips.

Users interested in touring significant sites related to the fire can find interactive maps with 10 suggested tours of more than 50 landmarks, including the O'Leary's cottage, which miraculously survived the surrounding devastation. A minimal selected bibliography points users at a half-dozen print sources for further information on the subject.

The Website would be a logical place for students and history buffs to begin research on this infamous disaster.—**ARBA Staff Reviewer**

C, P, S

130.   **Hillstrom, Laurie Collier. Defining Moments: The Cuban Missile Crisis.** Detroit, Omnigraphics, 2015. 240p. illus. maps. index. (Defining Moments). $60.00. ISBN 13: 978-0-7808-1348-9.

This well-written and engaging work takes an in-depth look at the two-week period during October 1962, when the world stood on the brink of nuclear war. The bulk of the book is presented in a tripartite structure, as are other titles in this series. A "narrative overview" tells the story itself chronologically in six concise chapters, which are amply illustrated with black-and-white photographs of the period. Shaded text boxes provide amplifying information. A second section consists of two- to three-page biographical sketches of major actors involved in this drama. This compact tome is rounded out with a third section of excerpts from primary sources, such as President John F. Kennedy's televised announcement of the discovery of Soviet missiles on the island of Cuba. Special features include a glossary, timeline, and bibliography.

One of the outstanding features of this volume is the balanced, objective, and authoritative style of writing. Although no author background blurb is to be found, it is obvious that Laurie Collier Hillstrom has done her homework and has an obvious mastery of the subject matter at hand.

Produced with students in mind, this title would be especially appropriate for high school and academic libraries, although public libraries with strong American history collections may also wish to acquire this volume.—**Michael Francis Bemis**

C, P, S
131.   **Hillstrom, Laurie Collier. Defining Moments: The Lewis and Clark Expedition.** Detroit, Omnigraphics, 2016. 240p. illus. maps. index. $60.00. ISBN 13: 978-0-7808-1417-2.

This title in the Defining Moments series brings together the most essential information regarding the courageous Lewis and Clark Expedition and conveys it all in a variety of intelligent, focused ways. Arranging the book into three well-delineated sections provides readers with easy access to this rich and engaging history.

Chapters in the narrative overview chronologically establish the story of the fortuitous Louisiana Purchase, President Thomas Jefferson's long-held desire to explore far beyond his new nation's western border, the enlistment of the Corps of Discovery under the leadership of Meriwether Lewis and William Clark and ultimately the daring journey and its legacy. The next section, biographies, shines a spotlight on a number of prominent figures in the complex story. Aside from Lewis and Clark themselves, we read of Sacagawea, George Drouillard, Patrick Gass, and others. The primary sources section allows us then to examine some well-curated documents, such as excerpts from the Louisiana Purchase Treaty, Captain Lewis' "shopping list" of items he thought he would need for the journey, or Thomas Jefferson's address to representatives of several Native American nations residing in Louisiana Purchase territory.

Supplementary material includes a glossary of the main people, places, and terms, a detailed chronology, black-and-white illustrations and photographs, a list of references for further study, and, perhaps most helpful to readers, a generous list of potential research topics. All in all, this Defining Moments title is sure to engage readers in the fascinating historical topic at hand.—**ARBA Staff Reviewer**

P, S
132.   Hudson, David L., Jr. **The Handy American History Answer Book.** Canton, Mich., Visible Ink Press, 2016. 428p. illus. maps. index. $21.95pa. ISBN 13: 978-1-57859-471-9.

Condensing over 200 years of history is no easy task. While much information today may be only a computer click away, what is often lacking in many resources is context and connection. The success of the *Handy American History Answer Book* stems from its accessible and neatly organized chronological structure that melds the ease of a timeline with the satisfaction of significant research.

Three sections encompass the exciting eras and major events that shaped the United States into what it is today. The book begins with a chapter on pre-Revolutionary history followed by chronologically organized chapters that take readers into the early twenty-first century. This is followed by a chapter on sports history and a chapter on music and entertainment.

Uniquely, all information is presented as an answer to a question—a format both eye-catching and effective in terms of readability. Entries are generally brief, yet perfectly capture the essence of each topic. "What was the Teapot Dome Scandal?" is answered, for example, with the names, dates, and places relevant to this prime display of government corruption. Questions may be general ("What were the causes of the Civil War?") or intriguingly specific ("Who was Mrs. Catt?"), but all will encourage readers' curiosity and further their desire to learn more. Including nearly 1,000 entries exploring politics, social lives, literary contributions, military endeavors, and much more, this book is an excellent resource for history lovers, students, and others. The book includes a timeline of American history following the table of contents. The final chapter is followed by a short bibliography; a section that lists each state and its basic facts (date admitted to the Union, capital, largest city, state nickname, number of electoral votes, and population); a chronological list of U.S. presidents including life dates, office dates, political party, election opponent, home state, and vice president; the full text of the U.S. Constitution; and an index.—**Laura Herrell**

P, S

133.   **Memories of the Enslaved: Voices from the Slave Narratives.** Spencer R. Crew, Lonnie G. Bunch, III and Clement A. Price, eds. Santa Barbara, Calif., Praeger/ABC-CLIO, 2015. 303p. illus. index. $48.00. ISBN 13: 978-1-4408-3778-4; 978-1-4408-4179-1 (e-book).

Memories of the Enslaved is based upon the Library of Congress collection titled "Born in Slavery: Slave Narratives from the Federal Writer's Project, 1936-1938." The "Born in Slavery" collection includes over 2,300 first-person slavery accounts that *Memories of the Enslaved* used for the content of this book. Essentially, *Memories of the Enslaved* is an edited and curated collection of excerpts from those 2,300 accounts intended to provide easier accessibility to the content while highlighting larger themes and topics.

Memories of the Enslaved is divided into seven main chapters of approximately 650 excerpts discussing community culture, childhood recollections, the enslaved family, enslaved women, slave labor, punishments, and escape attempts. Each chapter includes a descriptive introduction, followed by excerpts ranging from a few lines to a few paragraphs that exemplify the topic at hand. The text also includes a chronology of slavery in the United States, an appendix explaining historians' views on slavery, recommended resources, and an index.

Memories of the Enslaved is a useful resource in acting as a gateway into these remarkable stories, while also providing some narrative context and understanding. The full text of these excerpts is available online, but this book is much more accessible and likely to be used by those being introduced to the history of slavery.—**Tyler Manolovitz**

C, P, S

134.   **Railroads and the Making of Modern America. http://railroads.unl.edu/.** [Website] Free. Date reviewed: 2016.

Railroads and the Making of Modern America is a digital, social history of railroads focused on the intersection of social history and technology. The principal editor of the project is William G. Thomas, III, the John and Catherine Angle Professor in the Humanities at the University of Nebraska-Lincoln. Links on the left-hand side of the home page will take the curious to information about other project directors and support personnel, partnerships, funding, and copyright.

The top of the page has links to Topics, Views, Data, Search, Student Projects, and Teaching Materials. The topics—Slavery and Southern Railways; Railroad Work and Workers; The Civil War and Strategy; The 1877 Railroad Strike; Politics and Corruption; Land Sales, Migration and Immigration; The Origins of Segregation; William Jennings Bryan's 1896 Presidential Campaign; Tourism and Mobility; and Representing the Railroad—incorporate personal letters, newspaper articles, images, business documents, and more. The Views tab takes users to assemblages of data and interpretations. The views are also comprised of original documents, maps, and more and are linked to relevant sources; views can be searched several ways—by topic, by category, and by a browsable list. Two of many such views are Passenger Mobility in the 1850s and Northern Expansion in the 1850s.

Following Topics and Views, the Data tab links researchers to the freely available data, for which there is download functionality. The Search feature allows users to access documents and databases by a variety of means—by type, by topic, etc. For those curious to see the sort of railroad-related research being conducted by graduate students at the University of Nebraska-Lincoln, there is a link to Student Projects. Lastly, the Teaching Materials link, all created with free, open-source material, is designed for teachers at all levels, elementary through college and university. This section has links to frequently asked questions for teaching *Railroads and the Making of Modern America,* connections to interviews with teachers, and access to the site's blog.—**ARBA Staff Reviewer**

C

135.   Teed, Paul E., and Melissa Ladd Teed. **Reconstruction: A Reference Guide.** Santa Barbara, Calif., ABC-CLIO, 2015. 281p. index. (Guides to Historic Events in America). $63.00. ISBN 13: 978-1-61069-532-9; 978-1-61069-533-6 (e-book).

In the latest entry in ABC-CLIO's Guides to Historical Events in America series, Saginaw Valley State history professors Paul and Melissa Teed attempt to provide students relatively unfamiliar with the details of the era with basic facts and documents which could direct their further research. The current volume follows the series pattern: chronology, historical overview, topical chapters, biographies of chief players, selected essential primary documents, and an annotated bibliography. The six topical chapters comprise roughly half of the volume, followed by four brief analytical essays. Twenty-three single-paragraph essays and 22 short primary documents support the essays, and students will find the short bibliography helpful. Because of the introductory nature of the work, readers will not find great depth in the presentation of the material, but undergraduate students in particular should benefit. Although a number of excellent reference books on Reconstruction are available, including *Reconstruction: A Historical Encyclopedia of the American Mosaic* edited by Richard Zuczek (Greenwood, 2015), the Teed volume is useful for its collection of primary documents and well-written topical chapters. Recommended for undergraduate U.S. history collections.—**Anthony J. Adam**

P, S

136.   **U.S. History In Context. http://solutions.cengage.com/InContext/US-History/.** [Website] Farmington Hills, Mich., Gale/Cengage Learning, 2016. Price negotiated by site. Date reviewed: 2016.

The *U.S. History In Context* database provides access to a broad range of resources spanning America's history from the arrival of Vikings to the 2008 financial crisis, from the Mayflower to Barack Obama. It even includes updated documentation on the 2016 presidential election.

The collection's scope encompasses many facets of U.S. history: political developments, social movements, Supreme Court rulings, conflicts, culture, etc. These topics are represented with reference entries, academic journal articles, videos, images, and audio files (e.g., NPR clips). Magazine and news articles and Websites are also included. The collection additionally contains a substantial amount of primary documents to serve the history researcher such as JFK's papers, excerpts from Thoreau's *Walden,* and the personal account of General Cornwallis's surrender at Yorktown.

For each topic in the collection, all of these different information formats are presented together on one page for a holistic view of the topic from a variety of viewpoints. This presentation approach creates information "command center." The authoritative data provided in the site. Teachers and librarians can use this database to make a compelling argument to students on why they should never use Wikipedia again. There are also tools to highlight, bookmark, share, and cite resources.

The resource can be searched by keyword or browsed by topic. There are so many topics to browse that a helpful filter for category is included (e.g., Government Documents; Political Constructs, Movements, and Organizations; Hispanic Americans, Economic, etc.). An advanced keyword search option allows users to combine keywords with article and/or publication title. Users can also limit their search to full-text or peer-reviewed journals, specify a desired document type (e.g., map, cover story, pamphlet, or video among many options), or content type (book, journal, experiments, Websites, etc.). Teachers will especially appreciate the ability to search by content level (beginner to advanced) and Lexile level. Educators will also appreciate the inclusion of curriculum standards.

The resource integrates with Google Drive and Google Classroom making it easy for both students and teachers to save documents to their own Google Drive. The ability to save to a central location is very useful. Any highlights and notes made in the database can be retained when the document is saved to Google Drive. Teachers have the added ability to save a document to their Google Classroom as an announcement or an assignment.

This is an excellent and fun resource. It is highly recommended for school and public libraries. It brings a fresh and engaging perspective to the study of American history and presents it in a way that is familiar and appealing to students. This will be a staple resource for both students and teachers.—**Kristin Kay Leeman**

C, P, S

137.   **WPA Posters. http://www.loc.gov/collections/works-progress-administration-posters/about-this-collection/.** [Website] Free. Date reviewed: 2016.

Under the New Deal beginning in 1936, thousands of out-of-work artists began creating posters for the Works Progress Administration; the WPA Posters Collection on the Library of Congress's Website includes more than 900 of these posters. The WPA posters were created for everything from theater productions, to national health campaigns, to travel and tourism ad campaigns. As a whole, the WPA posters provide a window into the 1930s-early 1940s United States, including the artistic styles of the time, what sorts of theater productions and recreational activities were popular (posters promoting reading and public libraries may be of particular interest to librarians), and what some of the major public health concerns were.

The site features a section of collection highlights (grouped into seven categories: Health and Safety, Cultural Programs, Travel and Tourism, Educational Programs, Community Activities, Federal Project Number One, and World War II); the Federal Art Project calendar, created to showcase the art being produced for the benefit of government officials; and an interview with Tony Velonis, a master silkscreen printer who worked on the posters.

The collection would benefit from the addition of essays discussing the WPA poster project or additional interviews with those involved in the project. However, even without additional context, the WPA posters are fascinating and often striking.

Each poster in the LOC collection is accompanied by basic information regarding the poster (where available; includes name of the artist, year the poster was produced, and program the poster was produced for), along with hi-resolution TIFFs and JPGs of the posters. Users can search the collection, and there are a number of filters for viewing subsets of the collection (e.g., Federal Theatre Project posters, posters from individual states).

The WPA poster collection is appropriate for all audiences, but those who are researching the 1930s or are interested in the history of the arts in the United States will find it particularly useful.—**ARBA Staff Reviewer**

Asian History

China

C, P
138.   Jian, Guo, Yongyi Song, and Yuan Zhou. **Historical Dictionary of the Chinese Cultural Revolution.** 2d ed. Lanham, Md., Rowman & Littlefield, 2015. 507p. illus. maps. (Historical Dictionaries of War, Revolution, and Civil Unrest). $130.00. ISBN 13: 978-1-4422-5171-7; 978-1-4422-5172-4 (e-book).

The Great Proletarian Cultural Revolution is a significant event in the history of the People's Republic of China. Lasting from 1966 to 1976 the movement severely disrupted millions of lives and radically changed the Chinese economy, society, and culture. It was a period of great confusion that necessitates the systematic collection and compilation of historical information such as the work under review. Armed with firsthand experience, the editors completed the first edition of the *Historical Dictionary* in 2006, followed by a paperback edition retitled *The A to Z of the Chinese Cultural Revolution* in 2009. The format of this new second edition follows the first edition closely, with main sections consisting of a chronology, an introduction, the dictionary, a glossary, and a bibliography. The excellent introduction highlights major events and includes an assessment of the legacy of the Cultural Revolution. The main body of the dictionary contains over 400 cross-referenced entries on key individuals, organizations, politics, economy, social issues, religion, and culture. A useful, bilingual glossary and an extensive 91-page bibliography complete the volume. There are no significant changes from the first edition except adding a couple dozen entries such as Xi Jinping and Bo Xilai, and making some corrections. As an alphabetically arranged dictionary, the book offers no index as a finding aid, which may present a challenge to users. The dictionary can be used alongside *The Cultural Revolution Database*. Recommended for reference collections.—**Karen T. Wei**

Canadian History

Handbooks and Yearbooks

C, P, S
139.   **Canadian National Digital Heritage Index. http://cndhi-ipnpc.ca/.** [Website] Free. Date reviewed: 2016.

Canadian National Digital Heritage Index (CNDHI) is an index of digitized collections from universities and provincial and territorial libraries across Canada. Produced by the Canadian Research Knowledge Network with funding from Library and Archives Canada's Documentary Heritage Community Program, the CNDHI seeks to provide a tool for librarians and members of the public for finding and accessing digitized collections, both to promote awareness and use of these collections among researchers and to foster collaborative digitization efforts among librarians and archivists.

The main page of the site allows the user to search for collections by keyword, collection title, hosting institution, collection description, original language, and media type. There is no browse option. Search results can be viewed in a list, on a map, or downloaded in .csv format. Each entry includes a URL linking to the collection, a brief description, and collection contact information. Hyperlinked media type, language, and keyword fields facilitate finding similar items in the index. The search function is not as intuitive as it could be and would benefit from more explanatory text; for example, "diaries" in the main search box retrieves one result while the same search under format retrieves seven (and keyword retrieves zero). Users will also want to be aware that not all of the collections indexed are publicly available. Overall, however, this is a useful resource for those interested in finding online collections related to Canada's history and heritage.—**ARBA Staff Reviewer**

European History

General Works

Dictionaries and Encyclopedias

C, S
140.   Ermatinger, James W. **The World of Ancient Rome: A Daily Life Encyclopedia.** Santa Barbara, Calif., Greenwood Press/ABC-CLIO, 2015. 2v. illus. index. $189.00/set. ISBN 13: 978-1-4408-2907-9; 978-1-4408-2908-6 (e-book).

James W. Ermatinger, Dean of the College of Liberal Arts and Sciences and professor of history at the University of Illinois, Springfield, has devoted his career to Ancient Rome, as evidenced in the detailed information in these encyclopedias.

The World of Ancient Rome: A Daily Life Encyclopedia is a two-volume set with 864 pages in total, available in hard copy or e-book format. Following a preface, the table of contents is extensive and reads somewhat like an index, albeit in order by chapters. A chronology placed near the beginning of the book illustrates the timeline of important events in Roman history; the early placement of this listing in volume one is logical for those wanting to understand the timing of ancient happenings. Found at the end of volume two, there is a helpful bibliography of print and nonprint information resources for further research, and a more-than-suitable index. The subject index (p. 765) is an excellent access point to topics whether a common topic like Cleopatra or an elusive subtopic, such as florists or naming children. Because of the great indexing, topics from the minor to those of a larger scope are easily found.

These volumes on life in Ancient Rome primarily cover the period of greatest transformation, the Republican period (509-31 B.C.E.), with some entries from the Monarchy and Empire periods. There are 10 chapters that begin with an introduction and then address areas of daily life in this ever-changing society. Organization of information is excellent with each chapter having subtopics in alphabetical order. There are 24-27 entries for each chapter and each includes *see also* references and further reading suggestions. Black-and-white photos are ineffective but break up the text and are well captioned.

There are 11 primary documents along with other literary sources and archaeological information to bring together evidence of how this society lived. Focusing on the lives of everyday people in Ancient Rome, these texts also examine life of all social orders: slaves, rural peasants, urban poor, middle-class merchants, and aristocratic leaders. Entries allow researchers to understand the influence these citizens had on modern society.

Ermatinger has done an exceptional job in pulling together valuable and interesting research on the culture of Ancient Rome. In true encyclopedia fashion, the volumes and topics are easily accessible and the *see also* segment and bibliography lead students to more information. *The World of Ancient Rome: A Daily Life Encyclopedia* is a superior reference tool for high school and college students studying world history, Roman civilization, or how the people of Rome influenced modern life. General readers who are interested in ancient history will also find these volumes very useful.

Highly Recommended.—**Janis Minshull**

Handbooks and Yearbooks

C, P, S

141. **United States Holocaust Memorial Museum. http://www.ushmm.org/.** [Website] Free. Date reviewed: 2015.

The United States Holocaust Memorial Museum offers a superb guide to scholars, students, teachers, genealogists, and the general public. This online resource fosters interest and understanding in the complex history of the Holocaust.

The clean and well-organized layout of the site allows for easy navigation and users can easily access hundreds of relevant articles with a simple search. The United States Holocaust Memorial Museum site is free to use and contains over 250,000 records in the Collections Search alone. Archival and primary source images are scanned and accessible to the public, providing information on people and historic events relating to the Holocaust.

At present, the site offers public access to over 35,000 images, a number that grows every year as the museum collects and publishes new information. Additional types of media available include art, audio and video interviews, three-dimensional objects, and works on paper. The *Holocaust Encyclopedia* resources are available in 14 different languages.

Videos from Holocaust survivors are particularly informative and provide a firsthand account of the Holocaust atrocities. To clarify or elaborate on information, users can view original documents written during World War II, access timelines, and even map the Holocaust via Google Earth to gain geographical knowledge of the concentration camps, battles, and important events. The museum provides documentation of events immediately following World War I through the closing of the displaced persons camps in the mid-1950s in order to maximize the historical context for the public.

This site is a perfect resource for students who are studying the Holocaust, and particularly for teachers who may struggle to find the best approach in teaching this complicated subject matter. An entire page is dedicated to resources for educators, providing worksheets, lesson plans, and tips on discussing the Holocaust with students.

Not only does the site offer a wealth of information for those seeking to learn more about World War II and the Holocaust, but the compelling stories and resources will undoubtedly encourage the public to visit the museum to witness artifacts and documents of the Holocaust in person.

The United States Holocaust Memorial Museum is a highly recommended reference source.—**ARBA Staff Reviewer**

C, P, S

142.   **Yad Vashem. http://www.yadvashem.org/.** [Website] Free. Date reviewed: 2016.

Yad Vashem (http://www.yadvashem.org/) has committed itself to the remembrance of the Holocaust through commemoration, documentation, research, and education. As part of this mission, they maintain a large collection of primary material, from oral histories to photo archives to primary document collections. In addition, they provide educational materials and exhibits to aid in interpreting the primary sources.

Whether trying to trace one person's story, or looking for an overview of the period, Yad Vashem's Website and digital archives can assist any student, researcher, or librarian. The collections include almost 180 million pages of documentation, including over 125,000 survivor testimonies (written, audiotaped, and videotaped), over 450,000 photographs, and over 2.7 million "pages of testimony" filled out by survivors, friends, and relatives of those who died. A section of the Website honors the "Righteous Among the Nations"—those who aided Jewish resistance.

The educational materials cover topics such as The Nazi Rise to Power, Jewish Resistance, and Antisemitism. The Website also provides a detailed chronology, glossary, and FAQs to aid in research. Teachers can access lesson plans, teacher's guides, sample ceremonies, and other educational resources.

Yad Vashem also offers conferences, seminars, online courses, publications, and other professional development materials. Use of this Website may inspire a trip to the Holocaust History Museum complex maintained in Jerusalem.

This site encourages users to delve into a wealth of information and witness the Holocaust through the eyes of historical and contemporary materials. Yad Vashem is a highly recommended reference source.—**ARBA Staff Reviewer**

Armenia

C, P

143.   **The Armenian Genocide: The Essential Reference Guide.** Alan Whitehorn, ed. Santa Barbara, Calif., ABC-CLIO, 2015. 425p. illus. maps. index. $89.00. ISBN 13: 978-1-61069-687-6; 978-1-61069-688-3 (e-book).

This is an extensive and valuable one-volume encyclopedia concerning the Armenian Genocide, published on the 100th anniversary of this atrocity. As noted in the preface, this is the first encyclopedia exclusively focused on this event. The overall structure of the book is concise and easy to follow. The editor Alan Whitehorn penned the seven introductory essays. These are two to four pages in length and look broadly at the genocide, featuring topics such as consequences, causes, and victims. They provide a helpful overarching view of the genocide. The main entries are all signed with short bibliographies. There are 23 primary sources, many of them coming from the British collection of documents *The Treatment of Armenians of Ottoman Empire, 1915-1916,* although there are also newspaper accounts and other letters. These documents serve as a useful gateway into studying the genocide. Of note is the relatively small, thought-provoking appendix that examines historical dilemmas surrounding the study of the Armenian Genocide, such as why it is not formally recognized by the United States, Israel, or the United Nations. A comprehensive bibliography and timeline round out this work. Well-sourced, concise, and clear, this is an immensely valuable work for understanding the Armenian Genocide. Highly recommended.—**Allen Reichert**

Great Britain

C

144.   **Churchill Archive. http://www.churchillarchive.com/.** [Website] New York, Bloomsbury Academic. Price negotiated by site. Date reviewed: 2016.

First published in 2012 in collaboration with the Churchill Archives Centre, this massive digital collection contains more than 800,000 pages of original documents produced between 1874 and 1965, including personal and official correspondence, speeches, photographs, telegrams, manuscripts, and government transcripts. This archive can be used by everyone from interested members of the general public to high school students to seasoned researchers in history, politics, international affairs, military affairs, public speaking, and more. The site includes a wealth of education resources including specially commissioned essays and overviews of key topics linked to the appropriate files and documents. For secondary students and teachers, the Churchill Archive has resources based on four themes: key developments in modern British and empire history; key developments in modern world history; Anglo-American relations in the twentieth century; and, Churchill: discussion, debate and controversy. Six to eight documents from the archive accompany these themes along with interpretive data designed to help students truly understand the topic. For teachers, there are additional resources and guidance and advice about such things as getting students to care about modern history. This schools section is available free of charge via registration on the Website through the end of December 2020.

Various search tools make for easy navigation: the catalog can be browsed by topic, place, period, or people. There is also a quick search on each page and a more advanced search function. Moreover, users can easily print articles, export citations, access reading lists and bibliographies, view online exhibitions, and take advantage of special features like Action this Day. Librarians can download for free MARC records and utilize the site's technical support.

To be sure, much Churchill-related material is available on the Web—for example, browsers can find some of what they are looking for at the Churchill Archives Centre (https://www.chu.cam.ac.uk/archives/), but the completeness, functionality, search capabilities, and resources offered through this site make it highly recommended for libraries that can afford the purchase price.—**ARBA Staff Reviewer**

C, P, S

145. **Richard III Society, American Branch. http://www.r3.org/).** [Website] Free. Date reviewed: 2016.

The Richard III Society was founded in England in 1924 as the Fellowship of the White Boar and took its current title in 1959. Today, branches of the Society are found in various countries worldwide, with the total membership of all branches put at about 4,000. The American Branch of the Society was founded in 1961 and today claims a membership of almost 400. The Society is dedicated to promoting study of the life and career of King Richard III, the history of the Wars of the Roses, and the history and culture of fifteenth-century England. The Society is also committed to securing a reassessment of the reputation of Richard III as he is portrayed in modern print and electronic media. Besides its primary audience of professional scholars and amateur enthusiasts who reject the traditional view of Richard III as a tyrant and child murderer, the site offers much to high school and college students and others interested in fifteenth-century English history.

The Website sponsored by the American Branch is maintained by volunteers. Portions of the site are password protected and restricted to members only, but the main links to news and information on Richard III and the Society itself are open to all. Links lead users to a wealth of current print and online scholarship regarding Richard III and life in fifteenth-century England. The Richard III link offers a detailed biography of the king and timeline of his life; a list of the 10 most common changes leveled at Richard and rebuttals for each; articles and bibliographies providing information on life in the fifteenth century; information on traveling to sites in England associated with Richard; and information on images of Richard. Of use to students and researchers is the Online Library Text and Essays link, which provides guidance for students on conducting research into the period and excerpts from various important primary documents (e.g., Crowland Chronicle, Cely Papers) and well-known modern studies (e.g., "The History of Richard III" from Richard Marius' 1984 biography of Thomas More). The Ricardian and Medieval Fiction link lists novels, movies, and television programs on Richard and late medieval England. Also available are recent issues of the Society newsletter, the "Ricardian Chronicle" and news and notes about recent Society events, free online classes provided by various universities, and important stories relating to Richard III, most spectacularly, the discovery of his remains in a Leicester car park in 2012.

The most useful aspect of the American Branch site is the many links it provides to other sources of information, such as Websites for archaeological survey projects at various Wars of the Roses battlefields, including Bosworth Field; Websites of various other related organizations, such as the Heraldry Society; and various medieval and renaissance studies organizations and primary document Websites, such as the Internet Medieval Sourcebook and the Centre for Medieval Studies at the University of York. Although users must always remember that the Richard III Society seeks to promote a particular view of the king, and should view the information provided on the king himself in this context, they will find much current and accurate information on this site covering the broader topics of the Wars of the Roses and life in late-fifteenth-century England. Probably because the site is maintained by volunteers, some links have not been updated—there were, for instance, still notices in early 2016 for trips and events that occurred in late 2015, though this problem relates mainly to Society and other events. More troubling is the occasional broken link, such as that for the Richard III and Yorkist History Trust, which prevents access to some of the information. A must for users who share the Society's view of Richard III, the American Brach site is also recommended for those studying or interested in the Wars of the Roses or the history and culture of late medieval England.—**ARBA Staff Reviewer**

C, P, S

146.   **Tudorhistory.org http://tudorhistory.org/.** [Website] Free. Date reviewed: 2016.

Residing at this domain name since 2000, *Tudorhistory.org* is produced and maintained by Laura E. Eakins; the site is not affiliated with any university, organization, or company. The site, which Eakins began in the 1990s under the name *Tudor England*, was originally intended simply as a vehicle for Eakins to share her passion for Tudor history with like-minded individuals. However, Eakins soon discovered that a growing portion of her audience was school children who turned to the site for help with classroom projects. As a result, *Tudorhistory.org* has in recent years become more focused on meeting the needs of student users, particularly elementary and junior high students. To this end, Eakins has kept the content basic and wide ranging, not focusing in-depth on any one aspect of the period, but providing a good introduction to Tudor history as a whole. For those interested in more in-depth information on Tudor fashion, food, music, literature, etc., Eakins supplies lists of useful sites on many such topics under Links to Other Sites of Interest.

The site is simple and straightforward, opening with 20 links to broad themes and topics and to useful features for research and study, such as Tudor Monarchs, The Six Wives of Henry VIII, Topics in Tudor History, Chronologies of People and Events, Texts and Documents, Glossaries of Words and Terms, Reference Maps, and Image Gallery. The biographies of the Tudor monarchs and of Henry VIII's queens provide life dates, accession and coronation dates, and burial dates and sites. The biographical information is very basic, averaging perhaps 300-500 words, and, in some cases (e.g., Henry VIII himself), provides information on only a portion of the individual's life, something that appears the understandable result of one person attempting to maintain a large site in her spare time. The Who's Who in Tudor History link leads to an impressive array of individuals, and, though most offer only very brief descriptions, e.g., "Physician of Henry VIII" for William Butts, most biographies also include images of the individual. Although often spare, the information in the biographical links is accurate and useful for the envisioned student audience.

The other research links also reflect the site's student audience. Texts and Documents contains about 20 items, which focus heavily on execution accounts and speeches, such as a description of Anne Boleyn's death and Edward Hall's version of her last words. The

Reference Maps link offers thumbnails of seven historical and modern maps, information on their source repositories, and, in some cases, links to high resolution versions. The Images Gallery provides thumbnails of known images of many individuals, including such unusual renderings as the wax figure of Anne of Cleves at Madame Tussaud's in London. This link could be useful for more advanced students seeking particular Tudor images and their source repositories. The Movies and Television link has an extensive list of movies and television programs with Tudor settings, from the 1913 French silent film *Anne de Boleyn* to the 2007-2010 Showtime series *The Tudors,* though each individual link only sends the user to the *Internet Movie Database* (http://www.imbd.com) description of the work. In short, though there is little here for advanced students or those undertaking more detailed research, the site's target audience—pre-high school students who are just seeking a sound basic introduction to the subject—will be well served by *Tudorhistory.org* and the site is recommended for their use.—**ARBA Staff Reviewer**

Russia

C, P, S

147.   **Gulag: Many Days, Many Lives. http://gulaghistory.org/.** [Website] Free. Date reviewed: 2016.

Gulag: Many Days, Many Lives is an extensive study of the brutal system of forced labor camps in the Soviet Union endured by millions. Produced by the Roy Rosenzweig Center for History and New Media at George Mason University in association with the Gulag Museum at Perm-36 and the International Memorial Society in Moscow, the site features exhibits, archives, and resources. Funding came from several sources: The National Endowment for the Humanities, the Kennan Institute, and the Davis Center for Russian and Eurasian Studies at Harvard.

The home page of the site has links to the archives, exhibits, and resources in the upper-right-hand corner. Under the Archives link, users will find documents, photographs, art, and more. These can be browsed sequentially or by tag. A click on the Exhibits link directs users to the traveling exhibit produced by a partnership between the National Parks Service and the Gulag Museum of Perm. Called *Gulag: Soviet Labor Camps and the Struggle for Freedom,* this exhibit portrays life in Perm-36, a forced labor camp in the Ural Mountains. The exhibit recounts in vivid and painful detail conditions in the Gulag and the political system that put people there. The Resources link allows users to access an amazing bounty of material, including curriculum aimed at middle-and high-school students, a bibliography, and scholarly commentary on the Gulag system via sublinks. Under Teacher Resources users will find a downloadable curriculum entitled "GULAG: Soviet Prison Camps and Their Legacy," a Harvard-developed, three-day curriculum designed to accompany the traveling exhibition. Focusing on daily life in the camps, the Gulag system, and the legacy of the Gulag, the curriculum includes first-person accounts and artwork along with class assignments and homework. "Episodes in Gulag History'" presents conversations with scholars about the Gulag system and its legacy.

Highly recommended.—**ARBA Staff Reviewer**

C, P

148. Smele, Jonathan D. **Historical Dictionary of the Russian Civil Wars, 1916-1926.** Lanham, Md., Rowman & Littlefield, 2015. 2v. (Historical Dictionaries of War, Revolution, and Civil Unrest). $250.00/set; $249.99 (e-book). ISBN 13: 978-1-4422-5280-6; 978-1-4422-5281-3 (e-book).

    This two-volume work was compiled by Jonathan D. Smele, a scholar of Russian history who has focused his career on the civil wars. As part of the Rowman & Littlefield Historical Dictionary series, it is ostensibly written for high school and college students. While that audience does benefit, it also is a valuable addition to Russian scholars and specialists. Of particular note is the comprehensive, historiographic, 60-page essay which introduces this work. This essay details why this work incorporates a longer time frame in which to consider the civil wars and how the wars are more than just the Reds versus the Whites. Indeed, one of the key inclusions is the look at nationalist movements from the periphery of the Russian empire, such as in Latvia and Turkestan. The bulk of *Russian Civil Wars* is made up of 2,000 dictionary entries. These entries include bolded words to other entries. The extensive bibliography is broken out by region and broad subject areas and includes resources in English, Russian, or German. There is a chronology of events, and a few appendixes detailing the various governing institutions from this time. There are no images, including, unfortunately, no maps. The price may also be an impediment for some institutions. Recommended, highly so, for any libraries actively collecting in Russian history.—**Allen Reichert**

Latin America and the Caribbean

Dictionaries and Encyclopedias

C, P, S

149. **Iconic Mexico: An Encyclopedia from Acapulco to Zócalo.** Eric Zolov, ed. Santa Barbara, Calif., ABC-CLIO, 2015. 2v. illus. index. $189.00/set. ISBN 13: 978-1-61069-043-0; 978-1-61069-044-7 (e-book).

    If ever there were a need for an encyclopedia of Mexico aimed at a general audience, from high schools to public libraries, it is now. Obviously, electoral campaigns produce little serious analysis, but most honest observers agree that our relations with Mexico are in serious jeopardy. The reasons bear no repeating: everyone has heard too much nonsense about the country and its people.

    Going to the Internet for help is hit and miss, because, honestly, the wisdom of crowds is not always apparent. Better an experienced guide and a number of tutored, if not quite impartial, sources to lead people to somewhere worth going. That is what makes these two volumes very worthwhile. My copy of the *Shorter Oxford English Dictionary* defines an icon as "a person or thing regarded as a representative symbol of a culture, movement, etc.," and that is a good description of what this encyclopedia provides. It is a compilation of 100 "iconic" Mexican persons, places, things, or events that open a window to the country's wider culture and history. It includes famous historical personages, well-known authors, material artifacts, rock groups, and events of really transcendent importance in the shaping of contemporary Mexico. The editor, Eric Zolov, is a respected historian, and while the limits of space make leaving a good deal aside, one can make the case that this encyclopedia is a reasonable starting point. For one thing, the entries are, for the most part, clearly and engagingly written and avoid that bane of good literature, academese. They are also accessible without being oversimplified, and cover a broad spectrum of obvious and not-so-obvious starting points for the interested reader. Each entry has a sidebar or, in some cases, the translation of a historical text as a supplement. Where photos are helpful, there are photos. There is a timeline, a bibliography of English-language works, and an index that runs to 50 pages. In addition, each entry has its own bibliography, and these are good guides to further enlightenment.

Some of the entries dealing with popular culture are especially entertaining. "Acapulco" leads off ("Zócalo" for the record, concludes), and I was happy to find a reference to Frank Sinatra's "Come Fly With Me" prominently featured as a quintessential 1950s plug for that still lovely, if not untroubled, city. There is a very nice discussion of the celebrated author Elena Poniatowska that prompted me to go out and buy one of her books that I had neglected to read. Essays on Father Las Casas and Antonio López de Santa Anna may not break any new historical ground, but they are accurate, although trying to say something nice about Santa Anna is akin to washing dirt: it can't be done. There is a good piece, well considered, on the significance of the earthquake of 1985 in Mexico City that was every bit as important as the author maintains. While I tend to think of the Mexican art form "papel picado" as bigger in San Antonio, Texas, than in Mexico City, I guess I will have to look more closely in the future. Omitting the Mexican political singer Oscar Chávez in favor of El Tri is generationally defensible—or a matter of taste. The entry on the Niños Héroes monument in Mexico City is actually pretty courageous, because calling the story of the military cadets in the War of 1847 a myth can still get you in trouble there. I went and looked up Truman's visit to it (mentioned in the entry) on You Tube as a result. That's a pretty good recommendation for an encyclopedia entry.

These volumes are well done and well worth the price. I recommend them to anyone interested in Mexico, because, literally, there is something for everyone, even long-time students of the country and its history.—**Richard Salvucci**

World History

Dictionaries and Encyclopedias

C, P, S

150.   **Ancient History Encyclopedia. http://www.ancient.eu/.** [Website] Free. Date reviewed: 2016.

Ancient History Encyclopedia is a volunteer-run Website providing excellent and accessible resources on ancient history for high school and undergraduate students, teachers, and the general public. A team of specialists manages the site, which combines text content with a variety of digital resources. Overall it is well-organized and comprehensive. While the collection is more heavily weighted toward Western civilizations, a good effort has been made to be inclusive of global cultures. The search function works well: a search for "Roman Empire" called up 156 results, including articles, images, videos, and other resources, and results could be further limited by subject (such as daily life or warfare and battles). Users can also make a timeline search or use the "Explore" function to choose an area on a world map to research.

The heart of the site is made up of encyclopedia-style articles written by scholars in relevant fields. The articles are written in a clear and engaging style and are attractively presented, with images, maps, and videos accompanying the text. Other text resources include interviews with authors and scholars active in ancient history-related projects, features on current museum exhibitions, book reviews, and travel guides on locations of interest to ancient history enthusiasts.

This site provides maps of empires, cities, sites, and battle locations around the world. Finding the maps can be a bit tricky; however, clicking on "Maps" on the homepage takes the user to a page with just four large interactive maps, which is not the entire collection (to find other maps, the user can enter "maps" in the search bar and then select "images"). Nevertheless, the interactive maps are detailed and full of information; the map of the entire ancient world is especially impressive. The site's very extensive video collection draws from a variety of sources, including museums and other educational Websites. The site's large collection of high quality images can be found using a simple search on the "Images" page. A tool to convert ancient measurements to their modern equivalents will be useful to students working with primary sources.

The quality of this site's content and presentation is outstanding, and it is highly recommended for students and general users.—**ARBA Staff Reviewer**

C, P

151.   **The Encyclopedia of the Industrial Revolution in World History.** Kenneth E. Hendrickson III, ed. Lanham, Md., Rowman & Littlefield, 2015. 3v. illus. index. $240.00/ set; $239.99 (e-book). ISBN 13: 978-0-8108-8887-6; 978-0-8108-8888-3 (e-book).

This three-volume set provides over 1,000 entries, written by 64 contributors (both academics and independent scholars), on a wide range of subjects related to the industrialization of the world. Individuals such as inventors, industry leaders, and politicians are profiled and their contributions discussed. Technological advances, such as the steam engine, the sewing machine, and refrigeration are explained within their historical context. Social topics like immigration, imperialism, and even romanticism are addressed. (The work at times seems more diverse or eclectic, as well as more selective, than a reader might expect. For instance, there are articles on "cell phones," "Gulf War (2003)," "Three Mile Island," and "superconductors," but none on India or any of the Middle East countries, despite reference to these areas in the introduction.)

A couple of remarks concerning the production of this work are necessary. Very few entries have references more recent than 2007 in the "Further Reading" section, possibly indicating a long gestation period for this complex work. Images seem to lack adequate contrast, giving them an overall grayish look. The writing, however, is clear; articles often contain cross-references to other entries which provide context for the original text being read. There is a comprehensive, 48-page index which is quite helpful, too. For students of the period and the evolution of industrialization around the world, this resource will be welcome. Public and academic libraries should consider.—**Mark Schumacher**

C

152.   **Oxford Classical Dictionary. http://classics.oxfordre.com/.** [Website] New York, Oxford University Press. Price negotiated by site. Date reviewed: 2016.

The *Oxford Classical Dictionary* (the "OCD" as it is always known) has been for more than a half century one of the great reference works of all time. Its clear writing, its authorship by hand-picked academics of the highest pedigree, and its coverage in one volume of the entire Greco-Roman world all made the OCD the "go to" resource for undergrads, buffs, graduate students, and scholars around the world. After its first edition (in 1949), new editions followed up to 2012 (the fourth edition, with 6,000+ entries, see ARBA 2013, entry 24). Now comes the digital OCD, launched formally in March 2016 as a member (probably the premier member) of the Oxford Research Encyclopedias suite. After spending a few hours with this new OCD, your reviewer (a constant user of the second edition many years ago in graduate school) considers the digital OCD an excellent and worthy successor to its dog-eared print ancestors. The two most important reasons this is so are, one, that a digitized OCD means that the simplest search can instantaneously retrieve all text mentions of the search term, freeing the user from relying only on the main entry and its official cross-references, and, two, OCD's promise of constant additions to and revision of the core material means the world will not have to wait a decade or more for important articles to reach their audience.

There are other reasons to love the new OCD. As expected, the new OCD contains both new and revised articles, everything from Gladiatorial Combat to Matriarchy. There is a commitment to add video in the near future. One can hardly wait! How does the digital OCD perform in testing? Entries are easily available via simple and advanced searches. For those keen on bibliography, most items are linked directly to their Google Books and World Cat pages. This is a huge boon for researchers wishing to dig deeper into the subject. To take advantage of the digital format, systematic browsing is enabled by drilling into the 25-odd subfields that the editors have determined best represent the OCD's summation of the classical world. Most of these categories cover expected topics such as Greek History and Historiography, Material Culture, Ancient Economy, and so on. But one category, Gender Studies, represents a field of scholarship that would never have appeared in the first editions of the OCD. Who says the field of Classics is a static one?

How does the subfield browsing work in practice? A sample drill-down into Roman History and Historiography retrieved 1,107 hits (fully a sixth of the entire database), beginning with Acclimation and ending with Zenobia (that's Zenobia of Palmyra, by the way, recently and sadly sacked by the Islamic State). What one does not find, unfortunately, is a major entry actually on "Roman History and Historiography" that might provide full context. (There is a "Roman Historiography" entry, but it took the reviewer some time to find it from within the subfield's list of entries.) This is a very minor quibble. The subfield organization is a legitimate way for OCD editors to tie together related entries as well as to enable the serendipitous browsing that has always been so irresistible a feature of print OCD.

Final verdict—the reviewer loves and highly recommends OCD's digital version to all libraries serving patrons and students who study and appreciate the classics. That said, the reviewer will also continue to own and treasure his print version of the OCD.—
Vincent Burns

Handbooks and Yearbooks

C, P, S

153.   **Alpha History: http://alphahistory.com.** [Website] Free. Date reviewed: 2015.

Alpha History is a nonprofit online textbook and resource center that provides free information on 11 popular history subjects. It contains a simple and attractive layout with over 3,000 pages of historical sources, including topic summaries, documents, graphics, maps, timelines, glossaries, and even quizzes, essay questions, crosswords, and word searches for interactive fun.

The Website is based in Australia and is organized by several esteemed authors from around the globe. The targeted age group is 15 and older, so this Website would be a fantastic resource for high school students looking for concise and interesting content about a variety of historical events. The events included in *Alpha History* are: the American Revolution, French Revolution, World War I, Russian Revolution, Weimar Republic, Nazi Germany, The Holocaust, The Cold War, Conflict in Vietnam, Chinese Revolution, and Northern Ireland. Each subject can be found on the left side of the homepage; users will be able to navigate through the Website with ease to gather information on their desired topic. Each event has an extensive glossary that will benefit students who are unfamiliar with the content.

To further appeal to the student population, the homepage also includes *Alpha History's* Twitter feed, which provides blurbs of interesting historical information with links to external pages. Additional features include low-cost mobile apps for the iPad, iPhone, and iPod Touch, as well as e-book apps for different history subjects and advertisement-free quiz apps for iOS devices. This impressive collection of literature is continually updated, making the site an ideal and highly recommended resource for students, teachers, and history buffs alike.—**ARBA Staff Reviewer**

C, S

154.   Ciment, James. **How They Lived: An Annotated Tour of Daily Life through History in Primary Sources.** Santa Barbara, Calif., Greenwood Press/ABC-CLIO, 2015. 2v. illus. index. $205.00/set. ISBN 13: 978-1-61069-895-5; 978-1-61069-896-2 (e-book).

Scholar James Ciment's two-volume set focuses on a wide variety of primary sources related to daily life of ordinary people—the regular, repeated experiences that provide a historical context or provide knowledge about the economy, culture, or art of a time and society. An illustration or description of the source accompanies information that provides context for the source, and this context helps the reader understand the source and its relation to the society. Whether the entry is medicine practiced by a medieval Arab doctor, instructions on how an orator should dress from first century Rome, a description of Chinese foot-binding in the late nineteenth century, or Victorian mourning wear, these varied sources comprise this title of historical information. Each volume covers a different historical period; volume one deals with the ancient and medieval world, and volume two encompasses 1500 to the present day, and includes an index and a short bibliography of other daily life readings. Students and scholars of history, as well as teachers seeking sources to support the Common Core, will find this title of interest.—**Denise A. Garofalo**

P, S

155. D'Efilippo, Valentina, and James Ball. **The Infographic History of the World.** New York, Firefly Books, 2014. 223p. illus. maps. $35.00. ISBN 13: 978-1-77085-316-4.

The Infographic History of the World is a terrific volume that examines our planet's history from the very beginning to modern times by analyzing data in graphical form. The book is divided into four parts: In the Beginning, Getting Civilized, Nation Building, and the Modern World. The largest section is the Modern World by virtue of the fact that more data exists in present times than in the past. The book starts out in a primitive form and finishes with a modern flair from the quality of the paper to the color and style of the graphics to give the reader a sense of history's progress. The scope of the work is well stated on the "How to Read the Book" page. The authors are smart to state that they certainly could not include all aspects of world history. The authors are creative in matching the style of each graph to the data that is represented in a complementary fashion. *Infographic History* would do well in any library. The work is best suited for anyone middle school age and up who likes works of a visual nature. The graphical nature of the book gives perspective to data better than just stating statistics in a paragraph. A couple of good examples are the timeline of human existence (All in the Family, p. 46) that portrays the time and duration of many near-human species over the last 2.3 million years to the present or the comparison charts of current and historical carbon emissions (The world in Carbon, p. 160-161) per person and geographical area. The appendix explains where the authors got their sources and how they analyzed them. Timelines and graphs are certainly nothing new, but D'Efilippo and Ball create theirs in a fun, creative, and well-chosen way.—**Sue Ellen Knowlton**

C, P

156. **Defining Documents in World History: Ancient World (2700 B.C.E.-c.500 C.E.).** Michael Shally-Jensen, ed. Hackensack, N.J., Salem Press, 2015. 289p. index. $175.00. ISBN 13: 978-1-61925-771-9.

This primary source collection, another entry in the Defining Documents series published under the Grey House/Salem Press banner, represents the first title in a new subseries: *Defining Document in World History: Ancient World.* Like the original series' prior U.S.-focused titles, the present title is edited by Michael Shally-Jensen.

The core of this slim collection is the documents and their analyses. Documents excerpted originated in Mesopotamia, Egypt, Asia (China and India), Greece, Rome, and "Distant Lands" (which turn out to be Europe and modern-day Guatemala). The title contains 40 primary sources (running one to two pages to ten or more pages), prefaced with a scene-setting overview, "defining moment" description, and some basic data (date, region, author). After the primary source itself and a brief glossary (printed in a shaded box) come the analysis essay and "essential themes." Closing each section is a brief list of further readings.

Compilation of ancient documents in translation today presents particular challenges to teachers, students, and publishers: are the primary sources standard canonical texts or do they represent potentially new and unfamiliar texts to most students; are the translations fresh and recent or do they rely on early-twentieth-century translations (which sometimes require a translation of their own!); and do the primary sources well represent the entire "ancient" history of the world or do they largely come from well-studied Greece, Rome, Egypt, and Mesopotamia?

Judged by these criteria, this document collection fares relatively well in geographic diversity: eight of the forty documents originated in Asia. The document selection itself is relatively traditional: Code of Hammurabi, Epic of Gilgamesh, Sun Tzu, Bhagavad Gita, Thucydides, the funeral oration of Pericles, Cicero, and so on. The translations, alas, often can be traced back to out-of-copyright early-twentieth-century compilations which run the risk of being less than relevant or compelling to modern students. Fortunately, the analytical materials go some distance toward making the primary sources relevant to students.—**ARBA Staff Reviewer**

C

157. **Histories of Everyday Life in Totalitarian Regimes.** Thomas Riggs, ed. Farmington Hills, Mich., St. James Press/Gale Group, 2015. 3v. illus. maps. index. (The Literature of Society Series). $550.00/set. ISBN 13: 978-1-55862-927-1; 978-1-55862-931-8 (e-book).

This three-volume set presents 300 articles, written by 43 contributors, on a diverse range of topics relating to the world of twentieth- and twenty-first-century totalitarianism. Focused on Nazi Germany and the Soviet Union, it also provides information on other countries, including China, Fascist Italy, North Korea, and Cuba. The volume titles reflect this broad coverage, too: *Personal Experiences, Effects of Totalitarianism,* and *Literary Approaches.*

Each of the entries is three to four pages long, and each follows the same format: "overview, historical and literary context, themes and styles, critical discussion, sources and further reading" (p. xviii). Therefore, although only small excerpts of the original texts are presented (in most cases), readers will have a clear understanding of the work's place and importance within a reflection on totalitarianism. Roughly two-thirds of the entries are biographical or autobiographical in nature; many are texts published since 2000. Classic texts, such as *Animal Farm, Fahrenheit 451,* and *The Trial* are also included, as are plays, poems, and songs.

A somber work by its topic, this set provides the reader a fine introduction to the literature exploring life under the harshest regimes of our recent past. The text is clear, organized, and easy to comprehend, so readers of all levels will benefit from it. Given the cost, however, purchase is most appropriate for large public and academic libraries.—**Mark Schumacher**

C, P, S

158. **Internet History Sourcebooks Project. http://legacy.fordham.edu/halsall/.** [Website] Free. Date reviewed: 2016.

The *Internet History Sourcebooks Project* (ISHP) collects primary source material in ancient, medieval, and modern historical topics. In addition, it provides subsidiary source materials on regional (African, Indian, Islamic, etc.) and thematic (science, women, LGBT, law, film) history. While designed for use by teachers, its resources can also assist students and researchers.

Each sourcebook begins with an introduction describing how and why to read and use primary sources, and then moves into thematically organized collections of primary documents. Some are hosted on the IHSP site; others are linked. Wherever possible, original citations are listed at the foot of the document. In addition, secondary sources introduce history, theory, and critiques. Where possible, the site links to additional archives including maps, music, and images.

This site offers access to primary sources on many topics that teachers can integrate into the classroom. ISHP is a highly recommended reference.—**ARBA Staff Reviewer**

C, P, S

159.   **Modern Genocide: The Definitive Resource and Document Collection.** Paul R. Bartrop and Steven Leonard Jacobs, eds. Santa Barbara, Calif., ABC-CLIO, 2015. 4v. illus. maps. index. $415.00/set. ISBN 13: 978-1-61069-363-9; 978-1-61069-364-6 (e-book).

This 2,200-page set examines 10 major genocides of the twentieth and early twenty-first centuries: Armenia, Bosnia, Cambodia, Darfur, East Timor, Guatemala, Herero (Namibia), the Holocaust, Kurdistan, and Rwanda. Each section, ranging from 120 to 420 pages, includes a set of essays [Overview, Causes, Consequences, Perpetrators, Victims, Bystanders, International Reaction].Those are followed by an A-Z list of entries discussing people, places, documents, and events of importance (each with "Further Reading" references), and a group of primary resources concerning the genocide, including legal documents, statements by political leaders, trial transcripts, and government declarations. Each section ends with an English-language bibliography and a list of contributors to that section.

The essays provide useful information to those beginning research into these tragedies. The entries and documents are more specialized and detailed for readers with some background on the subject. Any library with patrons investigating these events will benefit from having this set.—**Mark Schumacher**

C, P, S

160.   **1914-1918 Online: International Encyclopedia of the First World War. http://www.1914-1918-online.net/.** [Website] Free. Date reviewed: 2016.

1914-1918-Online: International Encyclopedia of the First World War is a collaborative English-language, Web-based reference encyclopedia resource covering World War I. The encyclopedia is project-managed in Germany, primarily at Freie Universität Berlin. Released in 2014, the project's approach looks at the First World War as a truly global conflict as opposed to the traditional emphasis on England, France, and Germany. The plan is to include more than 1,000 entries; as of this writing, the database includes 853 published articles. An additional 782 (listed as "unpublished articles" in the Articles A-Z section) remain unavailable, including such essential entries as Erich Ludendorff, Philippe Pétain, Joseph Joffre, the Battle of Amiens, and the Battles of the Marne, among others. While the current coverage of the war is good, clearly there remains much work to be done.

Submitted entries to the encyclopedia undergo academic review before they are accepted for publication. The project includes concise encyclopedic entries as well as broader thematic or regional essays tied to key topics or regions. Individual entries are generally very good, but in many cases tend more toward an academic audience than to general readers or students. Some of the project's published entries are shorter than one might expect considering the intended scope and depth of the project, leaving the reader to look elsewhere for more information.

The encyclopedia has a number of innovative approaches for accessing the content, including by themes, by regions, by subjects, and by timeline. The bibliography is excellent, with over 6,000 entries, which fortunately can be filtered by regions, themes, and languages. Similarly, an index with over 6,000 entries, filterable by name, place, and subject leads users to entries across the entire collection of content. The entries are connected with an impressive array of lists and graphs that provide many different ways to view the relations between entries. Entries can be exported in PDF, EPUB, and Kindle format, and can be linked to social media via buttons for Facebook, Google+, and Twitter. Images from the war are side-related to individual entries, but they are not integrated into the accompanying text for a closer association with the narrative.

In short, this is a useful but still in-progress scholarly resource on the First World War, with forward-looking technical, search, and social media features; those looking for an introduction to the war for students would be better served with other resources.—**ARBA Staff Reviewer**

P, S

161.   Price, Bill. **Fifty Foods that Changed the Course of History.** New York, Firefly Books, 2015. 223p. illus. index. $29.95. ISBN 13: 978-1-77085-427-7.

Presents 50 foods that have changed the world, discussing them in chronological order from the days of hunters and gatherers to the present. Entries vary in length from approximately two pages to eight pages. Each entry provides a place of origin, dates of origin, and type of food as well as sidebars and color photographs and illustrations. Readers will find historical context and brief introductions for each entry. Even though entries do not have notes or references, suggested further readings appear at the end of the book along with Website recommendations and an index. The 50 entries include several beverages—beer, tea, gin, American whiskey, Coca-Cola, and Starbucks coffee. Readers will find expected foods like bread, beef, corn, and the potato alongside foods that might not immediately come to mind, such as Spartan black broth, Roquefort cheese, madeleines, Anzac biscuits, and Swanson TV dinners. This eclectic mix, however, is partly what makes this a fun book to read.

This book does double-duty as both a good read and as food for thought for further research. Recommended for public and school libraries.—ARBA Staff Reviewer

C, P, S

162.   **Untold Lives Blog. http://britishlibrary.typepad.co.uk/untoldlives/.** [Website] Free. Date reviewed: 2016.

The Untold Lives blog, housed on the British Library Website, functions in an unusual way, in that its curation is very specific and unpredictable. It is not a comprehensive research tool, but rather a starting point that highlights otherwise obscure moments and facts. For example, a recent timely post featured an exploration of the leap year tradition of women proposing to men, and some of the varied perspectives on that tradition. Other recent features include pieces concerning Samuel Pepys, architect Sir Christopher Wren, Muslim burial ground design, and a slave governor. There are numerous others, with each piece providing a jumping off point to further discovery. *Untold Lives* also utilizes Twitter, which cleverly exploits the tidbit nature of the content.

From the blog: "The British Library's collections contain stories of people's lives worldwide, from the dawn of history to the present day. They are told through the written word, images, audio-visual and digital materials. The *Untold Lives* blog shares those stories, providing fascinating and unusual insights into the past and bringing out from the shadows lives that have been overlooked or forgotten...The blog contains many links to act as signposts to research information and online resources that you can explore for work or pleasure." There is a link to the History and Classics Web page, which does offer a traditional interface for research sources and topics. The blog functions as an appetizer for the history department of the British Library, offering a pop take on conventionally academic pursuits.

Untold Lives also has a tags section: you can click on a descriptor, such as "Philatelic," to land on a piece about stamps issued in the 1920s and 1930s in the Middle East. It is a distinctive approach to information dissemination. Though not recommended for pointed research efforts, the factoid roulette wheel design of the blog makes for an enjoyable visit for anyone interested in the daily life genre of history studies.—**ARBA Staff Reviewer**

S

163.   **U*X*L World Eras.** Carnagie, Julie, ed. Farmington Hills, Mich., U*X*L/Gale, 2016. 10v. illus. index. $780.00/set. ISBN 13: 978-1-57302-967-4.

This ambitious set attempts to provide a detailed overview of major periods of human history, organizing each volume into nine sections covering topics such as geography, art, family life, and science in periods such as ancient Mesopotamia, ancient Egypt, and the Industrial Revolution in Europe. Four additional volumes specifically focus on non-European periods: Ancient Mesopotamia, West African Kingdoms, Rise and Spread of Islam, and Imperial China. A glaring omission in the set is the lack of any volume focused on great civilizations in the Americas such as the Aztecs, Incas, or Mayas.

Each volume in the set is self-contained with an introductory overview, volume-specific index, and the many maps, illustrations, and glossaries that render the UXL sets so readable and visually interesting for students. Sidebars contain copious quotations from original sources such as poems from the cultures being analyzed. The final volume ends with the onset of World War I.—**Delilah R. Caldwell**

P, S

164.   Westfahl, Gary. **A Day in a Working Life: 300 Trades and Professions through History.** Santa Barbara, Calif., ABC-CLIO, 2015. 3v. index. $310.00/set. ISBN 13: 978-1-61069-402-5; 978-1-61069-403-2 (e-book).

This three-volume set traces the various types of work that mankind has undertaken over the last 30,000 years, from cave painters and animal herders to video game and Website designers. Each entry is about four pages long, and provides a brief "Further Reading" list and a document, often a primary source, related to the job or profession. An extremely wide range of occupations is presented, from emperors, gladiators, and Islamic alchemists, to Victorian fire fighters, magicians, and twentieth-century dictators and astronauts. Readers can also examine the evolution of occupations, such as "soldiers" from the Hittite civilization to the Second World War.

Text editing is unfortunately sloppy at times: words are omitted or misused and occasional incorrect names and dates are included. This work is nevertheless recommended, primarily to high school and public libraries, whose readers will learn much about the work done across many centuries.—**Mark Schumacher**

C, P, S

165.   **World History Sources. http://chnm.gmu.edu/worldhistorysources/index.html.**
[Website] Free. Date reviewed: 2016.

World History Sources is a Web-based resource intended to help teachers and students find and analyze primary sources for world history. The project was created by The Center for History and New Media (CHNM) at George Mason University. It is organized around four sections: Finding World History, Unpacking Evidence, Analyzing Documents, and Teaching Sources. The Finding World History section is a collection of reviews by a team of world history scholars of world history primary source archives, organized both by region and by time period. A helpful introductory framing essay in this section explores the myriad problems and issues involved with the use of online world history primary source materials: questions of authority, difficulties of translation, and more. Unpacking Evidence is a set of guides to the proper analysis of eight different types of primary sources: images, objects, maps, music, newspapers, official documents, personal accounts, and travel narratives. Each guide features an introduction to that type of source, provides sample questions to ask about that type, and a collection of resources designed to show how historians learn about the past using this type of source. The Analyzing Documents section features additional resources about each of those eight types of sources, including illustrated audio mini-lectures by the project's scholars. Teaching Sources is a collection of 16 case studies on how to use primary sources, ranging from Hammurabi's Code to Sgt. Pepper's Lonely Hearts Club Band. These case studies, written by world history high school and college instructors using their own experience, will be of greatest use to teachers looking for compelling ways to use primary sources in their own classrooms. The scholars who worked on the project throughout are excellent, and the content is thoughtful and of high quality. One caveat is that many of the reviews of the online source archives date as far back as 2003 and do not appear to have been recently updated; a matter of some concern considering the transitory nature of Websites.—**ARBA Staff Reviewer**

10 Law

General Works

Handbooks and Yearbooks

C, P

166.   Epstein, Lee, Jeffrey A. Segal, Harold J. Spaeth, and Thomas G. Walker. **Supreme Court Compendium: Data, Decisions, and Developments.** 6th ed. Thousand Oaks, Calif., CQ Press / Sage, 2015. 840p. index. $195.00. ISBN 13: 978-1-4833-7660-8; 978-1-4833-7659-2 (e-book).

With the recent death of Justice Antonin Scalia and the controversy over the nomination of his successor, there has been heightened public interest in the Supreme Court. The larger part of this resource consists of 179 tables within nine chapters. Except for a general introduction and brief prefaces to each chapter, there is no text, making this a kind of statistical abstract. The topics include the Supreme Court as an institution; its review process, caseload, and cases; its opinions, decisions, and outcome trends; and its political and legal environments; the justices' backgrounds, nominations, confirmations, postconfirmation activities, departures from the Court, oral arguments, votes, and opinions; public opinion related to high-profile issues adjudicated by the Court; and the impact of the Court in American society. These last two topics do not present data on the Court per se, but draw on public opinion polls and statistical data on events related to areas in which the Court has been involved (e.g., "Legal Abortions, 1966-2008"). The editors provide source information for each of the tables. The greatest value of this compendium is in allowing researchers to see comparative data in specific areas; it is not the place to find a general overview of the court or its justices. The biographical information on the justices, while ample, is fragmented into numerous tables (e.g., family background; education and legal training; marriages and children). Some of the data is gleaned from social science research of an advanced nature (e.g., "Means and Medians in Economic Liberties Cases, 1946-2013 Terms"). This is a valuable resource, but will be best used by those seeking comparative information on specific topics. Recommended for large public, academic, and law libraries.—**Jack Ray**

C, P

167.   Hudson Jr., David L. Based on the prior edition by Kathleen A. Hempelman **Teen Legal Rights.** 3d ed. Santa Barbara, Calif., Greenwood Press/ABC-CLIO, 2015. 354p. index. (Contemporary World Issues). $89.00. ISBN 13: 978-1-61069-699-9; 978-1-61069-700-2 (e-book).

Teen Legal Rights, third edition, (see ARBA 2001, entry 541) is a straightforward volume that explains the rights of teens in a comprehensive manner, yet in language that teens (and their parents) can easily understand. It would be helpful to everyone, not just teens. For instance, it explains in understandable terms the theory of "no fault insurance," the legality of dress codes at work, what a "stop and frisk" search is, and a myriad of other everyday legal concepts.

Teen Legal Rights includes 19 chapters covering issues from young adult's rights at school, work, and home, to marriage, contracts, and conduct in the virtual world. Fifty state comparison charts are included as tables where applicable—for example, the table Marriage Laws by State specifies the age each state deems a teen able to consent to marry, both with and without parental consent. A list of the all the tables in the volume is provided after the table of contents.

Sprinkled throughout the volume are "Do You Have the Right?" segments which provide hypothetical legal situations, setting out a typical fact pattern and then providing questions designed to illuminate the intricacies of the problem. These would provide material for excellent discussions in a classroom setting.

At the end of each chapter a list of additional readings on the topics covered is provided, as well as other information sources, online sources, and hotline information where applicable. A comprehensive glossary and index are included at the end as helpful aids.

Teen Legal Rights is an accessible work that would be a valuable addition to any public library or academic library through the college level. Parents and teens alike would find it of interest and a highly usable resource when researching the legal rights of young people.—**Alicia Brillon**

C, P

168.   **National Survey of State Laws.** 7th ed. Richard A. Leiter, ed. Getzville, N.Y., William S. Hein, 2015. 829p. $225.00. ISBN 13: 978-0-8377-4026-3.

This smartly arranged book records the changes made to a wide variety of state laws since 2008. Covering eight general categories of law (Business and Consumer, Criminal, Education, Employment, Family, General Civil, Real Estate, and Tax), the book presents these changes in an easily referenced table format, wherein readers can compare each specific law from state to state.

Each category is further broken down into more specific topics. For example, the Education Law section details legislation concerning compulsory education, corporal punishment in public schools, prayer in public schools, and privacy of school records. Specific topics are arranged alphabetically. Each topic includes an overview which examines the history of the particular laws, national and state outlooks, and any current issues or debate concerning the law.

Specific topics are then examined in a table demarcated by state and applicable headings (so that headings will differ from topic to topic). For example, the topic of gun control within the Criminal Law section uses the headings of Code Section, Illegal Arms,

Waiting Period, Who May Not Own, and Law Prohibiting Firearms On or Near School Grounds. The Code Section heading is particularly useful to readers who would like to peruse the actual text of the law. The table structure makes it extremely easy to compare laws across states. Using the same example of gun control, we can see how California law mandates a 10-day waiting period after the purchase of a gun, while Colorado mandates none.

The appendix of this recommended work references statutory compilations for each state and conveys abbreviations if applicable. This book would be put to great use by students of law, those just beginning their law careers, and more.—**ARBA Staff Reviewer**

C

169.   **US Constitutional Law. https://global.oup.com/academic/product/us-constitutional-law-9780199363605?cc=us&lang=en&.** [Website] New York, Oxford University Press. Price negotiated by site. Date reviewed: 2015.

US Constitutional Law is available as part of Oxford's Constitutional Law Product Family, which also contains *Oxford Constitutions of the World. US Constitutional Law* provides researchers with a comprehensive reference source that combines primary materials with expert commentary to offer a picture of the historical development of constitutionalism at the state and federal levels. Searches are available across both databases in the product family, even if a library only subscribes to one product. *US Constitutional Law* users can access the full text of current and historical state constitutions, as well as article-by-article commentaries on historical development from the Oxford Commentaries on the State Constitutions of the US series. New materials are added regularly and commentaries are amended as necessary. Additions planned for 2015 include the first volumes on the colonial era and founding period from Howard Gilman and Mark Graber's American Constitutionalism series, a documentary archive on the whole history of U.S. constitutionalism, the updated new edition of Neil Cogan's *The Complete Bill of Rights*, and Bernard Schwartz's Unpublished Opinions series.

Searchers can use the quick search box from the home page or search using three main links: Browse All, Content Type, and State. Under these main links are advanced search options that allow users to narrow results. Once content is selected, tools to the right provide the ability to share results or to create personal profiles, among other things. Further tools on the left side of the screen include the Oxford Law Citator, which links to material form Oxford's online law resources and carefully selected third-party Websites. The citatory record contains citation details, links to content, and more, a service free of charge to subscribers of any of Oxford's online law products. Another interesting search feature is the interactive map of U.S. State Constitutions, which takes users from a simple click on Delaware, for instance, to the relevant secondary and primary sources.

Several features support librarians—direct object identifiers, downloadable MARC records, and ample help options. Subscriptions are available to libraries, organizations, and institutions; pricing depends on the size and type of institution and the number of users. This well-curated collection of primary and secondary sources is highly recommended to academic libraries and research institutions that need access to comprehensive, easily comparable, historical data pertaining to constitutional development.—**ARBA Staff Reviewer**

C

170.   **Whistleblowing Law.** Robert G. Vaughn, ed. Northampton, Mass., Edward Elgar, 2015. 2v. $695.00/set. ISBN 13: 978-1-78341-256-7.

The most commonly accepted definition of whistleblowing, quoted more than once in this resource, is "the disclosure by organization members (former or current) of illegal, immoral or illegitimate practices under the control of their employers, to persons or organizations that may be able to effect action." This source is not a textbook or treatise on whistleblowing, but rather a collection of 31 reprinted articles (primarily from law journals and the *Journal of Business Ethics*) and three book chapters. Vaughn's introduction is largely an overview of these various contents, which are thematically organized. Taken as a whole, these articles and chapters highlight many aspects of the history of and controversies surrounding the development of whistleblowing law, globally as well as in the United States. While whistleblowing has been more generally accepted in democratic societies that value individual rights than in societies in which loyalty to the group is the prevailing norm, the articles document how, even in the United States, protection of whistleblowers against retaliation that has been mandated by legislation often is not realized by courts and administrative agencies. While lip service is paid by organizations, their reactions are typically hostile. A number of issues and questions are explored in this collection: Should the whistleblower be required to report first to responsible superiors in the organization before going to external regulatory bodies or even the media? Should there be financial inducements to encourage whistleblowing or, conversely, penalties imposed for failing to report misdeeds? Is the public revelation of matters that may compromise national security, a la Edward Snowden, ever justifiable? Although governmental transparency is increasingly touted in the United States, one author's research surprisingly revealed that the more the public knows about government, the less they trust it. This collection is a thought-provoking and useful resource for academic and law libraries.—**Jack Ray**

Criminology and Criminal Justice

Dictionaries and Encyclopedias

C, P

171.   **Encyclopedia of Criminal Justice Ethics.** Bruce A. Arrigo, ed. Thousand Oaks, Calif., Sage, 2014. 2v. index. $370.00/set. ISBN 13: 978-1-4522-7411-9.

This two-volume set presents a diverse look at topics dealing with ethics in the criminal justice system. Entries include topics such as Postcolonialism, Jacques Lacan, Vice, Attorneys, Socrates, Insanity Defense, Public Shootings, and Pariah Underground Economy. The editor's introduction groups the 381 articles into eight categories: history, philosophical concepts, policing ethics, legal ethics, issues in offender treatment and rehabilitation, cases and controversies, science and culture, and politics and social justice. (This same categorization, with the articles in each section, is provided in the "Reader's Guide" at the beginning of the set.)

Entries range from one-and-a-half pages to seven pages, and each one has cross-references and a brief reading list. Three appendixes provide information on capital punishment, the FBI's code of ethics, and a document from the International Criminal Court. Organized along the same clean lines as a number of other Sage encyclopedias published recently, this set (also available online) provides much useful information on an important topic often in the news. It is highly recommended for academic and major public libraries; other libraries, if the cost is manageable, should consider it as well.—**Mark Schumacher**

Handbooks and Yearbooks

C, P, S

172.   Altschiller, Donald. **Hate Crimes: A Reference Handbook.** 3d ed. Santa Barbara, Calif., ABC-CLIO, 2015. 372p. illus. index. (Contemporary World Issues). $58.00. ISBN 13: 978-1-61069-946-4; 978-1-61069-947-1 (e-book).

Donald Altschiller is the distinguished author of eight reference books. In addition, he has published articles in the *Wall Street Journal, Chronicle of Higher Education, Boston Globe,* and the *Los Angeles Times.* Altschiller's impressive resume documents noteworthy contributions that include numerous essay entries in encyclopedias.

Hate Crimes: A Reference Handbook, third edition, represents an essential and comprehensive reference on bias-motivated violence committed in the United States. Debate, discussion, and legislation swirl around hate crime victims who suffer consequences because of their race, religion, ethnicity, skin color, or sexual orientation. *Hate Crimes* assists readers to explore and comprehend complex and divisive realities. This is an introductory, one-volume, academic and professional resource that provides an overview for scholars, researchers, lawyers, and students. Individuals interested in enhancing their expertise will find this text beneficial. Chapter themes integrate diverse approaches (historical, sociological, criminological, and victimology) that enhance understanding and in-depth examination of associated discussions and topics. Related legal issues expand inquiring minds and serve as another primary theme. For example, chapters document U.S. Supreme Court decisions and federal and state legislation regarding hate crimes.

Well-documented chapters focus on the recurrent and disturbing social dynamics of hate crimes. In addition, pertinent discussions address government and activist approaches to combat the hate crime phenomenon that ignites an atmosphere of prejudice and social restlessness. Furthermore, contemporary hate crimes committed on America's college campuses emphasize the need to acknowledge and combat this disturbing occurrence. According to the author's research, in multicultural America, the perpetrators occasionally resemble the diverse racial, ethnic, and religious spectrum of our society. Interestingly, the chronology chapter documents incidents that contradict the prevailing perception that hate crimes are almost solely committed by white racists. African Americans have harassed and abused Asian Americans; American Muslims have torched synagogues and physically attacked American Jews; Hispanics have beaten African Americans; and diverse minority groups harass and assault gays, lesbians, and transgendered individuals.

The developers and designers of *Hate Crimes: A Reference Handbook* considered many options in their effort to produce a superior product. For example, the photograph on the book's cover arouses strong emotions when one first observes the image of an impromptu memorial. The photograph represents a makeshift memorial and protest over the shooting of a gay man, Mark Carson, murdered by a stranger yelling anti-gay slurs in West Village, New York City on May 20, 2013. *Hate Crimes* presents a unique listing of audio-visual sources, including the most comprehensive annotated entries of magazine articles and other books on the topic; provides the most comprehensive source for U.S. congressional hearings and legislation on hate crimes and supplies a wide range of viewpoints on the philosophical and legal arguments both in support of and in opposition to hate crime legislation. The work also clarifies nomenclature in a helpful glossary; uses reader-friendly fonts; offers bold headings that prepare readers for new topics, enhance presentation, and facilitate content organization; documents the source and story behind authentic pictorial images that appear at the beginning of individual chapters; offers case studies that appear for emphasis and illustrate the significance of the problem; and offers extensive reference sections at the conclusion of each chapter.

Hate Crimes: A Reference Handbook includes seven well-appointed and organized chapters. The preface provides an overview of the book and highlights infamous hate crimes. The third edition offers new material and discusses controversies about related legal implications. Chapter one emphasizes the history of hate legislation and the Civil Rights Act of 1968. Significant legislative acts and Supreme Court decisions offer insight into the evolution of the legal requirements for prosecution. Chapter two, "Problems, Controversies, and Solutions," examines laws directed to punish and prevent hate crime and the opposition to these laws. Like many current issues, the topic of hate crimes draws diverse opinions ranging from the philosophical, legal, and ideological perspectives. Chapter three, "Perspectives," includes essays offering divergent viewpoints. Chapter four, "Profiles," introduces brief biographies of some notable experts on hate crimes, racial and religious bigotry, and political extremists. Chapter five, "Data and Documents," contains research materials on hate crimes. Chapter six, "Resources and Further Research," while unavoidably selective, provides students and researchers with annotated citations to significant and diverse publications on hate crimes. The number and documentation of individual hate crimes committed in the United States over the past few decades is too great to list. In chapter seven, "Chronology," carefully selected entries document the severity of the concern. The list also mentions international hate crimes that demonstrate the adverse impact on a global community. The appendixes (Glossary of Terms, Index System, and About the Author) offer additional content that enhances opportunities for integration and application of concepts.

Hate Crimes: A Reference Handbook highlights the significance of gaining an understanding of the social dynamics of hate crimes. The author's perspective endorses encouraging changes concerning the three branches of government that continue to evolve in combating these crimes. The FBI, state, and local law enforcement agencies have become more vigilant in enforcing hate crimes statutes. The following agencies will find this text of value: government agencies; law enforcement agencies; public and private libraries; and high school, community college, and university libraries. Donald Altschiller accomplished his overall objective to provide readers with an effective analysis and discussion of hate crime. The author offers insight into a topic that he acknowledges as being depressing. However, he proposes that one should never lose perspective about the basic goodness and humanity of our fellow citizens. Altschiller accomplishes his objective, remains focused, and offers a major contribution to understanding the role of hatred and violence in our society.—**Thomas E. Baker**

C, P

173.   **Crime in the United States 2015.** 9th ed. Shana Hertz Hattis, ed. Lanham, Md., Bernan Press, 2015. 664p. maps. index. $105.00; $105.99 (e-book). ISBN 13: 978-1-59888-765-5; 978-1-59888-766-2 (e-book).

Using information provided by the FBI, the large volume of statistics provides detailed information on both crime and law enforcement in the United States. Following a brief overview of the nine categories of crime presented here and an explanation of the Uniform Crime Reporting Program, the book presents 94 tables of data, dealing with crimes committed, persons arrested, law enforcement personnel, and hate crimes. Several of the tables provide information at the local level, such as the 10-page "Offenses Known to Law Enforcement, by Selected State and University and College," outlining campus crime. For anyone seeking detailed, authoritative data on crime in America, this resource will be the place to look.—**Mark Schumacher**

C, P

174.   Martinez, J. Michael. **The Greatest Criminal Cases: Changing the Course of American Law.** Santa Barbara, Calif., Praeger/ABC-CLIO, 2014. 266p. illus. index. $48.00. ISBN 13: 978-1-4408-2868-3; 978-1-4408-2869-0 (e-book).

In studying many of the landmark rulings that have changed the face of a law, scholars can often become mired in complex legal jargon and the technicalities a case may endure as it moves through a complicated court system. No major legal ruling has ever been considered straightforward and simply resolved, and yet it is imperative that such cases be clearly understood. This book strips away many of the complexities of some of the most groundbreaking and emblematic legal decisions and engagingly presents the human stories from which they emanate.

The author has chosen 14 cases spanning over a century and meeting compelling criteria. Readers can observe the origins and evolutions of legal principles we take for granted today, such as the Exclusionary Rule, whereby certain evidence becomes inadmissible in court, or the notion that criminal defendants have a "right to remain silent," aka the Miranda Right. The book also engages readers in the rich narrative behind the cases. An example is the story of "The Scottsboro Boys," where we see how the poverty and hopelessness of The Great Depression, along with vitriolic racial and regional divisiveness set the stage for the dubious court proceedings in *Powell vs. Alabama.* And there is the case of *Gideon vs. Wainwright,* which decided whether all defendants (as opposed to capital defendants only) had a right to counsel. This case included a cast of characters ranging from an irascible drifter to a future Supreme Court Justice.

Each chapter excellently captures the flavor of the times in which these cases were tried, demonstrates the delicate line between government authority and individual liberty, and provides a clear link between the initial ruling in the case, its precedents, and its impact today.

From an adultery-born street murder to our current "war on terror," this book delves into the vast historical milieu that has shaped our greatest legal rulings, and can genuinely be appreciated by history lovers and legal scholars alike.—**Laura Herrell**

C, P, S

175.   Sheridan, Matthew J., and Raymond R. Rainville. **Exploring and Understanding Careers in Criminal Justice: A Comprehensive Guide.** Lanham, Md., Rowman & Littlefield, 2016. 296p. index. $38.00; $37.99 (e-book). ISBN 13: 978-1-4422-5430-5; 978-1-4422-5430-5 (e-book).

Written by two people with extensive experience as practitioners in the criminal justice system and academics in college-level programs, this book is intended for use as a text in courses about jobs in the criminal justice profession but also as a reference for criminal justice program administrators as they guide undergraduates through their programs.

The book systematically covers an enormous amount of information in the following chapters: "Introduction: Why Another Book on Criminal Justice Careers?," "Exploring Careers in Criminal Justice," "Careers in Law Enforcement," "Careers in Corrections," "The Courts, Its Actors, and Its Functions," "The Federal Government," "Getting the Job, Entering the Field, and Career Advancement," "Criminal Justice Ethics," and "Life after the Career." The book also includes 16 valuable appendixes, the longest of which includes 16 profiles of people who have worked in the criminal justice system. In the appendixes, readers will find sample cover letters, a guide to interview questions, a sample resume, a list of federal law enforcement agencies in the United States, and much more. These appendixes are followed by notes and a bibliography of references and suggested readings. The index is particularly helpful for someone who wants to look up a specific topic like the CIA or Immigration and Customs Enforcement, as well as subjects like stress and tuition. There is a separate name index.

This practical guide to criminal justice careers is recommended for high school or college career counseling centers; high school, college, and public libraries; and for criminal justice practitioners or professors.—**ARBA Staff Reviewer**

Employment Law

Handbooks and Yearbooks

C

176.   **Comparative Labor Law.** Matthew W. Finkin and Guy Mundlak, eds. Northampton, Mass., Edward Elgar, 2015. 491p. index. $285.99; $256.00 (e-book). ISBN 13: 978-1-7810-0012-0; 978-1-7810-0013-7 (e-book).

The 37 authors of the various chapters are all academic professors and lecturers of law from 16 countries. Each chapter, though focused on a particular area, presents information based on labor law in the country under study. The objective was to identify theoretical or policy-oriented commonalities, or trends. It is not organized in a traditional county-by-country format, but the countries are included in the index. Authors used comparative methodology to explain legal diversity or to reveal differences. Some authors used "ideal types" and looked for these characteristics in the labor law of countries they compared. In chapter six, for example, the authors examine and compare autonomy, privacy, and dignity under technological oversight in the United States, Germany, and Japan, commenting on specific technology oversight, employers' access to employee social media, geolocation, and biometric identification.

Each chapter includes an introduction, conclusion, and bibliographical references. The editors do an excellent job of explaining the many different ways authors compare the information. What is lacking is analysis of the conclusions reached or trends to watch unfold in the future. The authors of each chapter present their findings, but these need to be summarized.

Highly recommended for academic law libraries and for government law libraries.—**Ladyjane Hickey**

C, P

177.   Feldacker, Bruce S,, and Michael J. Hayes. **Labor Guide to Labor Law.** 5th ed. Ithaca, N.Y., Cornell University Press, 2014. 625p. index. $89.95. ISBN 13: 978-0-8014-5225-3.

The *Labor Guide to Labor Law* is a comprehensive guide, written from the labor perspective. Originally intended primarily for union officials, it focuses on issues of particular concern to the labor movement. Topics covered include: the history and structure of federal labor legislation, collective bargaining, union organizing rights, employees' rights, union regulation of work, fair representation, equal employment opportunity, and the federal-state relationship in labor relations. Review questions, which can be used to facilitate in-class discussions, are provided at the end of each chapter. Additionally, each chapter includes a list of basic legal principles, which explains the law and provides citations to relevant case law and National Labor Relations Board (NLRB) decisions. Recommended readings give further opportunities to add depth to student understanding and class discussions.

Since its first edition, published in 1980, *Labor Guide to Labor Law* has provided a straightforward explanation of current labor law principles. The structure of the fifth edition remains essentially the same; however, the content has been substantially revised.—**Lisa Schultz**

Environmental Law

Handbooks and Yearbooks

C, P

178.   Burch, John R., Jr. **Water Rights and the Environment in the United States: A Documentary and Reference Guide.** Santa Barbara, Calif., Greenwood Press/ABC-CLIO, 2015. 442p. index. (Documentary and Reference Guides). $100.00. ISBN 13: 978-1-4408-3802-6; 978-1-4408-3803-3 (e-book).

The problem of water: it seems that there is either too much of it (flooding) or too little (drought). This work examines how we Americans have historically grappled with both ends of the aqueous spectrum, along with more recent issues, such as pollution and climate change. It does so by providing the verbatim text, usually excerpted, of court cases, legislation, treaties, studies, and other such primary source material detailing who gets what and why. Sixty-six written records are thus examined.

Each document is presented in a standard four-part format. A "Snapshot" section gives the reader a bulleted list of basic facts, such as date of creation, geographic location, and the reason for its inclusion in this collection. This is followed by the actual record concerned, the title of which doubles as a chapter heading. An "Analysis" segment helps to digest and interpret the foregoing material, which is oftentimes written in "legalese" or other technical language. Furthermore, it places the material in its cultural and historical context, which goes a long way towards sense making. Lastly, a short bibliography entitled "Further Reading" provides additional pertinent literature regarding the matter at hand. Special features include an introductory essay that gives a well-written overview of the contents of the book, along with a series of sidebar articles entitled, "Did You Know?" that gives interesting ancillary information.

The author is well versed on this topic; included among his published works is *Encyclopedia of Water Politics and Policy in the United States* (Congressional Quarterly Press, 2011, which was coedited along with Steven L. Danver; see ARBA 2012, entry 773). Burch holds a PhD in history from the University of Kentucky and currently serves as Dean of Library Services at Campbellsville University.

Considering the vital importance of water distribution and usage in this country, this engaging and informative work would be an appropriate purchase for all public and academic libraries.—**Michael Francis Bemis**

Human Rights

Handbooks and Yearbooks

C, P

179.   Bouchet-Saulnier, Françoise. **The Practical Guide to Humanitarian Law.** 3d ed. Lanham, Md., Rowman & Littlefield, 2014. 797p. index. $88.00pa.; $87.99 (e-book). ISBN 13: 978-1-4422-2141-3; 978-1-4422-2113-0 (e-book).

Humanitarian law is certainly an important topic, what with natural disasters, deadly armed conflicts, millions of refugees moving across national borders, and correspondingly bitter debates over how they are to be helped and officially categorized. This scholarly encyclopedia has over 200 long entries that examine particular aspects of various important legal topics, and how the interpretation of and implementation of humanitarian law has evolved over time. The author notes in the introduction that this work emphasizes "the perspective of victim's rights and aid organizations [,]" and that the weakest need to be protected "from interpretation of the law by dominant actors such as States and armed forces."(p. xvi) The entries include many references to international agreements, official documents, court decisions, and procedures of organizations, so that one can track down the original source material. Boxed sections of text highlight other important points of information that should be considered for an issue. *See also* indicators are located throughout the text. At the end of the entry there are cross-references to other parts of this guide, and a bibliography of resources for additional information, such as the United Nations Office for the Coordination of Humanitarian Affairs (http://www.unocha.org/). The work was originally published in 2002, and had a second edition in 2007. It provides more discussion than Connie de la Vega's *Dictionary of International Human Rights Law* (Elgar, 2013). The author is the legal director of Medecins Sans Frontieres (http://www. doctorswithoutborders.org), which sponsored this work. The book is also available in electronic format through various platforms. This easy-to-use reference book is useful for both practitioners and policy-makers, those working in governments, Non-Governmental Organizations or Inter-Governmental Organizations, law libraries, and collections serving graduate students and upper level undergraduates.—**Daniel K. Blewett**

C, P

180.   **Sexual Harassment in Education and Work Settings.** Michele A. Paludi, Jennifer L. Martin, James E. Gruber, and Susan Fineran, eds. Santa Barbara, Calif., Praeger/ABC-CLIO, 2015. 347p. index. (Women's Psychology). $79.00. ISBN 13: 978-1-4408-3293-2; 978-1-4408-3294-9 (e-book).

Sexual Harassment in Education and Work Settings: Current Research and Best Practices for Prevention is a volume in the series on Women's Psychology that examines sexual harassment in K-12 classrooms, in higher education institutions, and various workplace settings. The contributors of this book intend it to be a resource for those who want to make education institutions healthier places for women. The volume is arranged into sections that allow the reader to understand the nature of sexual harassment, the workplace organizational culture, pervasiveness of sexual harassment, Title IX, prevention programming, and coping strategies.

This text expands the definition of sexual harassment to more than that of males in the workplace telling inappropriate jokes and giving unwanted advances to female coworkers. Rarely do we think of sexual misconduct in education spaces occupied by children and young adults. According to Paludi, "the incidence of sexual harassment among undergraduate students by their peers ranges between 20% and 80% each year." According to the contributors it is the responsibility of the educational institutions to develop policies and procedures that deal with sexual harassment and that it is imperative that student's complaints are taken seriously with little stereotyping.

This volume is a valuable resource for college students, parents, and members of the workforce that need ongoing training and education in order to minimize and eradicate sexual harassment. This book can also be utilized by educators and education administrators who wish to develop policies and procedures for dealing with sexual harassment. Readers can have access to recent studies completed on the subject and the valuable data retrieved. The contributors expose the reality of sexual harassment in both K-12 and higher education institutions.—**Shireen Lalla**

International Law

Handbooks and Yearbooks

C

181.   **International Labour Law.** Barbara J. Fick, ed. Northampton, Mass., Edward Elgar, 2016. 882p. (International Law). $430.00. ISBN 13: 978-1-4422-4500-6.

This compendium of articles, the ninth volume in the Edward Elgar International Law series, focuses on the role of the International Labour Organization (ILO) in protecting core labor rights and on efforts to enforce those protections amidst a changing world economic and political environment. Editor Barbara J. Fick, Associate Professor of Law at the University of Notre Dame Law School and an acknowledged authority in the field, has selected 27 articles from the *International Labour Review,* the *Comparative Labor Law and Policy Journal,* the *European Journal of International Law,* and other journals, plus some book chapters and working papers. She points out in her introduction that globalization "has inserted a new player into the international labor regime" and that multinational corporations have had a growing influence on domestic labor policies. The task of the ILO has thus become more difficult as nations compete for foreign investment. The book aims to provide the reader with an understanding of the ILO's policies and practices, the core labor standards, and the ways that labor rights can be protected in the context of the many current challenges. Part one focuses on the ILO's role in international labor law, part two on the substantive content of the core labor rights, part three on enforcement mechanisms outside the ILO, and part four on the future of international labor law. Insofar as possible, the articles have been reproduced as they were originally published, using facsimile reproduction. All the articles are footnoted; there is no index. The earliest article dates from 1977 but the great majority are from 2010 or later. This volume, pulling together as it does relevant and significant scholarship on labor rights and the ILO, will be a valuable reference for students, researchers, and policy-makers concerned with labor rights and international law.—**ARBA Staff Reviewer**

C

182. **Research Handbook on International Financial Crime.** Rider, Barry, ed. Northampton, Mass., Edward Elgar, 2016. 797p. index. (Research Handbooks in Financial Law). $345.00. ISBN 13: 978-1-78347-578-0; 978-1-78347-579-7 (e-book).

This is the sixth volume in the series entitled Research Handbooks in Financial Law and has been compiled to be of interest to both scholars and practicing lawyers in this increasingly important field of financial crime. The majority of the contributors were educated in the United Kingdom.

The articles deal with matters related to the commission and the resulting consequences of economically motivated crime especially financial crime as impacted by different legal systems and traditions.

The articles have been grouped into seven topical areas which include: the enterprise of crime, business crime, the financial sector at risk, fraud, corruption, the proceeds of financial and economic crime and the enforcement and control of financial crime. The length of these 60 articles varies from 11 to 15 pages. A list of the cases cited in all the articles will be found at the front of the book.

Considering the number of financial crimes that have been in the headlines recently, this book will serve as a useful framework in providing the reader with practical information on what constitutes a financial crime and how it impacts society.—**Judith J. Field**

C

183.   **Research Handbook on International Marine Environmental Law.** Rosemary
Rayfuse, ed. Northampton, Mass., Edward Elgar, 2015. 492p. index. (Research Handbooks
in Environmental Law). $265.00. ISBN 13: 978-1-78100-476-0; 978-1-78100-477-7
(e-book).

   This research handbook from Edward Elgar deals with a timely and important
topic—the conservation and sustainable use of marine biological diversity beyond areas
of national jurisdiction. As the foreword by David Freestone, executive director of the
Sargasso Sea Commission, points out, oceans beyond areas of national jurisdiction "are
the last great global commons areas on Earth" and cover nearly half the surface of the
planet. The book, intended to provide a critical survey of current legal research relating
to protection of the marine environment, has six parts: the legal framework for protection
of the marine environment, pollution, seabed activities, protection of marine diversity,
regional approaches to legal protection, and climate change. Editor Rosemary Rayfuse,
professor at UNSW Australia (formerly called The University of New South Wales) and
conjoint professor at Lund University, Sweden, has pulled together contributions from
24 distinguished legal scholars from five continents to tackle these subjects. Chapters
include "Principles of international marine environmental law," "Protection of the marine
environment from offshore oil and gas activities," "Protecting marine species," and much
more. Each chapter has explanatory notes, and a comprehensive index enables the reader
to locate the pertinent information sought. This book is recommended for libraries serving
scholars and practitioners dealing with international law as well as government agencies
and readers concerned with the environment and preservation of marine biological
diversity.—**ARBA Staff Reviewer**

11 Library and Information Science and Publishing and Bookselling

Library and Information Science

General Works

C, P, S

184.   Gorman, Michael. **Our Enduring Values Revisited: Librarianship in an Ever-Changing World.** Chicago, American Library Association, 2015. 256p. $45.00pa.; $40.50pa. (ALA members). ISBN 13: 978-0-8389-1300-0.

Michael Gorman has an extensive list of publications on librarianship, and this title updates his 2000 publication of *Our Enduring Values: Librarianship in the 21st Century,* which was published before such significant world events as 9/11, the Afghanistan and Iraq wars, the Great Recession, and other events and trends that have affected public perception of libraries and the challenges we face. Gorman sees patterns in wide-ranging phenomena and discusses their significance in light of topics such as "The Value of Libraries," "The Library as Place," "Stewardship," "Service," "Intellectual Freedom," "Literacy and Learning," "Equity of Access," and "Privacy," among others. The 14 relatively short chapters (most under 20 pages) present much to contemplate on the values librarians attempt to uphold. His views are not black and white; rather he delights in exploring the areas of nuanced decision-making in libraries. At times he seems objective, and at other times, merely argumentative. Highly recommended for circulating and professional collections in all libraries, but not a reference book.—**Rosanne M. Cordell**

S

185.   **Information Services Today: An Introduction.** Hirsh, Sandra, ed. Lanham, Md., Rowman & Littlefield, 2015. 514p. $55.00; $54.99 (e-book). ISBN 13: 978-1-4422-3958-6.

This textbook provides an extensive overview of the many fields and specializations of information services, the wide variety of careers available, and the expanding roles of information services. A variety of management and technical skills needed and information issues such as ethics are discussed. School media specialists will be interested in the chapters on school libraries, teaching users, the creation culture and Makerspaces, and concepts such as the learning commons. A lengthy guide to abbreviations and a thorough glossary help the reader appreciate the increased depth of the field. Tables, pull quotes, and discussion topics within chapters add to its value.—**Mary Alice Anderson**

Libraries

College and Research Libraries

C

186.   **ACRL Insider. http://www.acrl.ala.org/acrlinsider/.** [Website] Free. Date reviewed: 2016.

The mission of ACRL Insider is to keep the world current and informed on the activities, services, and programs of the Association of College & Research Libraries (a division of the American Library Association), including publications, events, conferences, and eLearning opportunities.

With this mission, it's important that the Website be up to date, and this one is. Its main feature is a set of posts that range in topic from the ACRL member of the week to announcements about the latest issue of *Keeping Up With...,* ACRL's online current awareness publication, featuring concise briefs on trends in academic librarianship and higher education. Other recent posts include an ad looking for new mentors for the ACRL Dr. E.J. Josey Spectrum Scholar Mentor Program, which links library school students and new librarians with established academic librarians for mentoring and professional guidance. The blog highlights professional workshops and profiles board-of-director candidates.

The format of the site is clear and attractive, with a set of main links across the top and a large scrolling photo banner underneath. The main page features a link to the newest blog content; a "Libraries in Transition" video, created for the 75th anniversary of the ACRL; a link to ACRL publications; Instagram photos; archives; a link to the ACRL's Twitter feed; and a delightful link to *Goodreads,* where ACRL members of the week share what books they're reading.

While a link to a Google calendar is available, no events show up. The blog appears to be a better place to find information. Clicking the "About" link takes users to the same Web page as the "Posts" link. What you see on the home page is basically what you get; the site doesn't have much depth, but most users will be interested in the information found on the blog, and a "subscribe" link makes it easy to get publications and information by e-mail or RSS feed.

In short, *ACRL Insider* is the go-to resource for librarians and others who want to stay abreast of the ACRL's varied activities and resources.—**ARBA Staff Reviewer**

C

187.   **Creating Leaders: An Examination of Academic and Research Library Leadership Institutes.** Irene M.H. Herold, ed. Chicago, American Library Association, Association of College and Research Libraries, 2015. 380p. index. (Publications in Librarianship series). $78.00pa. ISBN 13: 978-0-8389-8763-6.

This is the first book to systematically examine leadership training institutes for academic librarians, some of which have been running for decades. The 18 chapters each focus on a single program, including five that are defunct, and are written by librarians who participated in them. The authors, who are nearly all university library directors, associate directors, or department heads, are ideally positioned to provide insights into the benefits of preparation for leadership roles. In addition to reflecting on their personal experiences, the authors recount the institute's history, outline its curriculum, suggest ways to improve the program, and discuss specific leadership theories, if any, that underpin it. Most chapters also review publications about the institute, although the literature is generally scant, which reinforces the value of this collection. The book is divided into six parts. In part one, an institute open to all academic librarians is described. In part two, four institutes aimed at specific populations within academic librarianship are profiled—theological librarians; college library directors; librarians at historically black colleges and universities; and medical librarians. Part three focuses on four programs that develop leaders for Association of Research Libraries and large research libraries. Part four examines six institutes that span multiple types of libraries, including academic. Part five covers three programs that are open to a broad spectrum of academic personnel including librarians; two of the three are specifically for women in administrative roles. Across the categories, the majority of the institutes are intended for mid-career librarians, but a few target entry-level librarians or those already in senior positions. The formats vary widely, from intensive workshops to Webinar series to residential programs lasting one to three weeks. Many build in a strong mentoring component; several revolve around campus visits. Most of the chapters report the results of formal or informal surveys of program graduates. In part six, editor Irene Herold presents tabular comparisons of the 18 programs on several dimensions, including how they were formed, size, longevity, enrollment process, and curriculum. Although she uncovers little evidence that such programs actually develop leadership skills, it is clear from participants' testimonies that they increase librarians' self-knowledge, instill confidence, and create supportive collegial networks. Librarians who are considering applying for one of the still-active programs can benefit from the information and first-hand accounts gathered together in this book, as can directors who may be pondering the value of supporting a librarian's participation. Therefore, *Creating Leaders* is recommended for all academic libraries.—**Susan E. Searing**

C

188.   **Difficult Decisions: Closing & Merging Academic Libraries.** Sara Holder and Amber Butler Lannon, eds. Chicago, American Library Association, Association of College and Research Libraries, 2015. 253p. $58.00pa. ISBN 13: 978-0-8389-8791-9; 978-0-8389-8793-3 (e-book).

During three branch library consolidations, McGill University librarians sought advice and best practices from colleagues and library literature during the process. They discovered that while many librarians have experienced change and transition, their experiences are not shared in the literature. The McGill University librarians decided to gather case studies and other research from American libraries about their institutional experiences on library restructuring. This edited volume compiles case studies from 11 institutions, including McGill University Library, University of Illinois Library at Urbana-Champaign, Welch Medical Library, Purdue University Libraries, Columbia University Libraries, University of California-San Diego, University of California-Berkeley, University of Idaho's University Libraries, University of British Columbia Library, Georgia Regents University Libraries, and University of North Georgia Libraries. These institutions are mostly large, research libraries with some consortia. The case studies document transitions and illustrate a variety of problems including staff morale, collection weeding, and logistics. Twelve of the 14 chapters are case studies of mergers, downsizing, weeding, branch closings, service consolidations, and staff and budget reductions. One chapter outlines a failed merger of a library and IT department. This unusual case study describes where the failure occurred and what could have been different to ensure a better outcome. Chapter 12 describes the planning and implementation of a consolidated library Website and a section of chapter 3 describes how a cohesive library Website was created from several, unique library Websites. All chapters include bibliographical references. The text also includes tables, charts, graphs, illustrations, and planning documents. These case studies are valuable for administrators, librarians, and change agents in university settings. Smaller-size institutions may find nuggets of information that would assist in preparation for change. The keys to success are planning and communication.—**Linda M. Turney**

C

189.   **Digital Humanities in the Library: Challenges and Opportunities for Subject Specialists.** Arianne Hartsell-Gundy, Laura Braunstein, and Liorah Golomb, eds. Chicago, American Library Association, Association of College and Research Libraries, 2015. 287p. $68.00pa. ISBN 13: 978-0-8389-8767-4.

Although there are other books on digital humanities scholarship, this edited work is intended to help subject librarians understand the possibilities in this area and navigate relationships among faculty, students, and fellow librarians. The book is divided into four parts. Part one explores the reasons why subject specialists should acquire digital humanities skills. Part two provides examples of how librarians can become involved in digital humanities. Part three discusses successful library initiatives involving collaborations or in establishing spaces to accommodate digital humanities projects in the library. Finally, part four provides case studies on individual projects from start to completion. In most chapters, examples are given of actual projects or collaborations. Each chapter has a bibliography of about two dozen resources, and collaborators do a good job of mentioning other resources that can be helpful to librarians new to digital humanities. An appendix includes a list of tools and resources referenced in the book, followed by brief biographies of the contributors. Overall, if you are looking for a handbook on digital humanities, this isn't it. Rather it provides a "here's what we did" approach to understanding how subject librarians can become more involved in digital humanities. At close to 300 pages the book is sufficiently descriptive, and most librarians new to the topic will learn something. Recommended for all academic libraries.—**Kevin McDonough**

C

190.   Nelson, Bryce. **The Academic Library Administrator's Field Guide.** Chicago, American Library Association, 2014. 224p. index. $72.00pa. ISBN 13: 978-0-8389-1223-2.

Being in an academic library administration requires a diverse set of skills in leadership, management, communication, and supervision. Administrators often find a lack of time and resources to develop and improve on their skill sets. The purpose of *The Academic Library Administrator's Field Guide* is to provide an overview of the topics and decision-making approaches that fit the role of an academic library administrator. Administrators at any level of experience will find this book useful in exploring areas that they may not have previously thought about or realized the importance of in the fulfillment of their responsibilities within the college or university environment. The book is divided into three parts: being politically active where the director has a role in positioning the library as a part of the college or university's mission; managing and leading staff to the fulfillment of the library's mission; and supervising operations where the library's services are managed at a high level. Each chapter provides an assertion, commentary, and application examples for the relevant topics that administrators face in their roles. Each chapter also provides recommended reading materials for a more in-depth study on a particular topic. This book succeeds in its purpose, in both layout and content, of providing overview information that can be examined on an individual topic level or as a whole study. An administrator would find it simple to pick up this book, find a particular item of interest, and obtain an overview of its importance and how to apply it to daily activities.—**Lee Sochay**

C

191.   **Practical Strategies for Academic Library Managers: Leading with Vision through All Levels.** Frances C. Wilkinson and Rebecca L. Lubas, eds. Santa Barbara, Calif., Libraries Unlimited/ABC-CLIO, 2015. 168p. index. $65.00pa. ISBN 13: 978-1-61069-889-4; 978-1-61069-890-0 (e-book).

In this highly practical guide, experienced managers share their wisdom on traditional as well as emerging functions in academic libraries. Steven Mandeville-Gamble (University of California, Riverside) advises on communicating and implementing an organization's vision, with an emphasis on internal audiences. The volume's editors, Rebecca L. Lubas (Claremont Colleges) and Frances C. Wilkinson (University of New Mexico) contribute an essay on reorganizations, in which they identify common impetuses for revamping library organization structures and outline basic strategies for successful "reorg" processes. Pat Hawthorne (University of Nevada, Las Vegas) provides a primer on the core functions of human resources management: recruitment; orientation of new employees; supervision; management of teams; retention and staff development; and self-improvement as a manager. Susan E. Parker (UCLA) demystifies the complex topic of budgeting, which perplexes and frightens many first-time managers. Loreen S. Henry (University of Texas, Dallas) takes a broad view of marketing, publicity, and outreach; she focuses on clarifying the purpose of a marketing campaign, defining the target audience, and understanding what users want before framing the message. Mary Ellen Spencer (University of Oklahoma) and Sarah Barbara Watstein (University of North Carolina, Wilmington) offer a wide-ranging yet detailed overview of issues involved in conceptualizing, planning, and managing library facilities. Nina Davis-Millis (MIT) shares succinct wisdom on managing library information technology and IT staff. The relatively new concept of blended librarianship is explained by Anne E. Pemberton (University of North Carolina, Wilmington), who not only elaborates the benefits of combining traditional library expertise with instructional technology skills, but also illustrates how blended librarianship requires systems thinking that can be applied to many aspects of management. Finally, consultant Nancy Bolt analyzes the Colorado Digitization Project as a case study of collaboration between an academic library and other cultural heritage institutions, paying particular attention to managerial and leadership roles. Although the nine chapters vary in length, approach, and quality, taken as a whole this volume will be a lifesaver for new managers in academic libraries. As Maureen Sullivan notes in her foreword, most academic library managers are hired or promoted because of their record in a functional area of library practice, and the transition to a managerial role often feels daunting. This volume both informs and reassures new managers, and thus is an excellent choice for any academic library professional collection. In addition, many of the chapters would be useful in courses on library administration.— **Susan E. Searing**

C

192.   Puckett, Jason. **Modern Pathfinders: Creating Better Research Guides.** Chicago, American Library Association, Association of College and Research Libraries, 2015. 156p. $42.00pa. ISBN 13: 978-0-8389-8817-6.

Research guides are a mainstay in today's academic libraries. Whether they are developed online using proprietary software or created via word processors, librarians have adopted these guides as a communication tool for their patrons. *Modern Pathfinders: Creating Better Research Guides* by Jason Puckett provides background knowledge, theory, and application to help librarians design and implement more effective guides for their patrons. The book is not software specific and uses proven ideas supported by user experience design that anyone can apply.

This compact book includes a descriptive table of contents and introduction followed by six chapters that cover a variety of relevant topics with an important focus on learning objectives. Lengthy notes and references provide additional resources for those wanting to dig deeper. Puckett uses best practices, examples, and screenshots from various research guides to support the content. All stages of designing a guide are covered from pre-planning to design, development, and assessment.

In addition to providing specific examples for application, Puckett incorporates and applies learning styles and instructional theory while focusing on student outcomes. The book includes a terminology list which is helpful for librarians new to the concept of research guides. Puckett acknowledges common issues or mistakes and includes how to use Web analytics to increase efficiency and user experience. This book is highly recommended for academic libraries, and librarians of all experience levels will find the material relevant, useful, and accessible.—**Jessica Crossfield McIntosh**

Public Libraries

P

193.   Nichols, Joel A. **Teaching Internet Basics: The Can-Do Guide.** Santa Barbara, Calif., Libraries Unlimited/ABC-CLIO, 2014. 143p. $22.50pa. ISBN 13: 978-1-61069-741-5; 978-1-61069-742-2 (e-book).

This is a guide designed primarily for public librarians who teach Internet literacy. The guide is well-organized and designed to move learners from the basics of browsers through more advanced tasks such as online communities. Each chapter is a complete workshop plan that includes lesson outcomes, hands-on activities, and potential problems along with suggested solutions. Appendixes include free online courseware, additional resources, and sample handouts, as well as a reproducible glossary of key concepts. A few of the lessons may not be appropriate in a school setting; many can be found in other formats online.—**Alda Moore**

P

194.   **Public Library Video Online: Premium. http://www.alexanderstreet.com/products/public-library-video-online-premium.** [Website] Alexandria, Va., Alexander Street Press. Price negotiated by site. Date reviewed: 2016.

The Alexander Street *Public Library Video Collection* provides video streaming access to over 42,000 videos with the aim to "serve the needs of today's public library patrons." This is certainly a vast and varied audience; hence, the collection includes a wide, diverse, and multidisciplinary selection of content including documentaries, newsreels, commercials, how-to videos, and performances. Subjects represented include American and world history, current events, art, science, cooking, etc. Content is provided from a wide range of sources including major, well-known providers (such as A&E, ABC, PBS, and NBC), to lesser-known independent and private filmmakers.

The video collection can be searched by keyword and browsed by title, discipline, people, and series. Searches can be refined by several criteria including persons and places discussed, content type (i.e., documentary, interview, performance, instructional material, etc.), subject, and date.

Users are allowed to add their own bookmarks to the videos, and they can cite and share the videos, save favorites to a playlist, and generate a permalink embed code—an option very useful for teaching or research. Users are also able to make and save their own video clips allowing many different and useful applications for both teachers and students such as building an engaging lesson, presentation, or report. Each video has a visual table of contents to help users easily navigate the videos by memorable scene.

All of the videos are fully transcribed. The transcript is synced with the video time code allowing users to click on any word or phrase in the transcript and jump to the corresponding place in the video. While still very useful, the transcripts were noted to contain several flaws, misspellings, and incorrect words choices. This can likely be attributed to machine/algorithm-based transcription.

This resource is recommended for public libraries interested in expanding their video offerings. It is a high-quality, user-friendly resource that can serve a large and diverse audience. There is a lot of content that will appeal to patron's recreation and entertainment needs, but the majority of the content is geared for more educational and research pursuits. Libraries looking for a more recreation/entertainment-oriented service might need to supplement with other materials.—**Kristin Kay Leeman**

School Libraries

S

195.   Cavanaugh, Terence W. **eBooks for Elementary School.** Santa Barbara, Calif., Libraries Unlimited/ABC-CLIO, 2014. 206p. index. $45.00pa. ISBN 13: 978-1-61069-849-8; 978-1-61069-850-4 (e-book).

The time for using e-books is here and educators need to embrace the technology that allows using different kinds of reading to engage and teach. Cavanaugh lays out a list of possibilities for different kinds of teachers, and different readers. There are many sources and good ideas for all teachers in this book. The suggestions for getting started provided lots of help and encouragement. Many of the Web addresses listed might be familiar, but the author also includes step-by-step ways to use them. It would be helpful if a district orders several copies to circulate. This is a book librarians can pore over again and again, taking away something each time. An index rounds out the publication.—**Leslie Greaves Radloff**

S

196.   Harvey, Carl A., III, and Linda L. Mills. **Leading the Common Core Initiative: A Guide for K-5 School Librarians.** Santa Barbara, Calif., Libraries Unlimited/ABC-CLIO, 2014. 230p. index. $22.50pa. ISBN 13: 978-1-61069-491-9; 978-1-61069-492-6 (e-book).

This text begins with a brief history of the Common Core State Standards and connections to the AASL standards. The next three chapters address the impact of Common Core on the administration, instruction, and growth of the library. The chapters on administrative, professional development, and advocacy impacts will be helpful to librarians and school administrators still struggling to figure out the role of the library. Budgeting, collection development, technology, facilities, policies, procedures, and professional development are each covered with sound advice and insight. Sample lessons for each grade level provide models for integrating Common Core Standards in collaborative and independent instruction. Appendix materials include student and staff surveys, bibliographies of print and electronic resources, and graphic organizers.—**Holly Whitt**

S

197.   Hopwood, Jennifer L. **Best STEM Resources for NextGen Scientists: The Essential Selection and User's Guide.** Santa Barbara, Calif., Libraries Unlimited/ABC-CLIO, 2015. 279p. index. (Children's and Young Adult Literature Reference Series). $65.00. ISBN 13: 978-1-61069-721-7; 978-1-61069-722-4 (e-book).

STEM (science, technology, engineering, and math) is a clearly defined emphasis in schools today. How do school librarians integrate STEM into their programming? *Best STEM Resources for NextGen Scientists: The Essential Selection and User's Guide* gives an overview of materials to support STEM curriculum.

Author Jennifer L. Hopwood currently works as a training coordinator for the Southern Maryland Regional Library Association and an online adjunct professor for Rasmussen College. A former youth services librarian, Hopwood has depth in her STEM experiences as she has carried out programs on a regular basis and contributes information to STEM publications.

This resource is available in print or e-book format. The cover is inviting and suggestive of exploration and innovation. A clear table of contents enables the user to find specific resources with ease. Chapter headings are clear making the information accessible. The indexes are particularly valuable; an Author Index, Title Index, and STEM index provide three access points to resources and information. The STEM index is divided into the four subjects, allowing librarians to focus on just some or all of the topics.

The first two chapters define and explore the library's role in STEM curriculum. As the title states, the primary purpose of this text is as a collection of STEM resources. Most chapters are listings of books, both fiction and non-fiction, from preschool through young adult, and Chapter 10 relates to professional development titles. There are no graphics within the book, save useful tables for each resource to show which of the four study areas the book pertains to (science, technology, engineering, or math). The tables are practical as they allow the user to quickly surmise the usefulness of a resource. Largely, the book lists are well annotated and contain strong titles both current (*Parrots Over Puerto Rico,* 2014) and from the distant past (*The Voyages of Doctor Doolittle,* 1923). Chapter nine, "New Media for STEM Education" is a collection of apps and Websites, but it is questionable whether CDs could be considered "new media."

Hopwood has done due diligence with *Best STEM Resources for NextGen Scientists: The Essential Selection and User's Guide.* Age groupings of resources that are suitable for STEM programming are valid and applicable to this curriculum. This book has programming ideas but that is not the focal point; school librarians trying to find resources to accentuate their STEM curriculum will find this collection supportive of learning plans and library programs. Recommended.—**Janis Minshull**

S

198.   Kelsey, Mark. **Cataloging for School Librarians.** Lanham, Md., Rowman & Littlefield, 2014. 316p. $44.00pa.; $43.99 (e-book). ISBN 13: 978-1-4422-3246-4; 978-1-4422-3247-1 (e-book).

Many school media specialists have never had a cataloging class; they rely on MARC records from vendors. Not only is this book a valuable refresher for professionals who aren't sure how to catalog a Web page, etc., it is a clearly written, step-by-step, easy-to-understand handbook for the many clerks and paraprofessionals in school libraries who have never had a cataloging class. This handbook explains where to get complete records, how to correct your current records, and includes a "what if" critical thinking section at the close of each chapter to help expand the reader's understanding. This book should be in every school library, read by every person who manages the local catalog, and kept nearby as a handy reference. Two appendixes, a glossary, and a bibliography complete the work.—**Claire Berg**

S

199.   **School Library Management.** 7th ed. Gail K. Dickinson and Judi Repman, eds. Santa Barbara, Calif., Libraries Unlimited/ABC-CLIO, 2015. 335p. index. $60.00pa. ISBN 13: 978-1-61069-140-6; 978-1-4408-3456-1 (e-book).

This is a compilation of articles from *Library Media Connection,* and is aimed at anyone in the library profession, from preservice library students to beginning librarians, as well as experienced practicing librarians. Five chapters cover establishing the library's place in the school; how librarians are putting into practice the concepts of intellectual freedom, access, and equity; current practices including ISTE technology standards and Common Core; keeping libraries current and relevant in difficult economic times; the future of school libraries; and the profession in general. This edition includes more writing about technology, and offers "TIPS and Other Bright Ideas" from the print publication. Each chapter starts with an Editor's Note. This is a reflective look at current practices that make school libraries relevant and necessary. This is a great reference book for all school librarians.—**Tracy A. Fitzwater**

C, S

200.   Spisak, Jen. **Multimedia Learning Stations: Facilitating Instruction, Strengthening the Research Process, Building Collaborative Partnerships.** Santa Barbara, Calif., Libraries Unlimited/ABC-CLIO, 2015. 223p. illus. index. (Tech Tools for Learning). $45.00pa. ISBN 13: 978-1-4408-3517-9; 978-1-4408-3518-6 (e-book).

The Tech Tools for Learning series introduces K-12 teachers and librarians to innovative technologies for the classroom and school media center. In this new volume, award-winning middle school librarian Jen Spisak provides detailed instructions for setting up learning stations to support standards-based curricula and to encourage students to take responsibility for their own learning. Students develop information literacy skills, acquire content knowledge, and hone their critical thinking ability as they rotate among stations to explore diverse resources on a topic, including databases, Websites, books, videos, podcasts, educational apps, manipulatable objects, and more. In the first third of the book, Spisak carefully lays out everything a librarian needs to know to implement multimedia learning stations and reap positive effects on student learning and librarian-teacher collaboration. Boxed testimonials from students and teachers further attest to the value of the station approach. Spisak emphasizes that learning stations appeal to students with diverse learning styles, facilitate both individual and group work, align well with any stage of research, and can be applied to a wide range of topics. One chapter is devoted to framing questions to propel and demonstrate learning, based on Bloom's taxonomy. Other chapters address the logistics of rotating students among the stations and designing assessments. Spisak provides a step-by-step guide to designing stations and recommends techniques for organizing and implementing them. The final two-thirds of the book contain 15 examples of stations for curricula in English (e.g., contextualizing the novel, *The Giver*), history (e.g., the Harlem Renaissance), math (e.g., fractions), and science (e.g., cells). Each example identifies the appropriate grade range, from middle school through high school, and relevant state standards (Virginia is given as an example) as well as the American Association of School Librarians (AASL) standards. Modifications for special education students are suggested. The number of stations per topic varies from three to eight. Each individual station is described in detail, including what students do, the questions they must answer, and what level of Bloom's taxonomy is addressed. Lists of the specific online and physical materials needed at each station follow, and assessment strategies for the unit are spelled out. Although learning stations are not a new concept, in this book Spisak blends traditional approaches with multimedia content and online interactivity to provides a start-to-finish recipe for success. A librarian who has not previously experimented with learning stations can take the plunge by adapting one of Spisak's detailed models. Those already using the station method will find inspiration to update their practice. This work is recommended for all secondary school librarians' professional reading shelves, as well as academic libraries that support the education of K-12 librarians and classroom teachers.—**Susan E. Searing**

S

201.   Weisburg, Hilda K., and Ruth Toor. **New on the Job: A School Librarian's Guide to Success.** 2d ed. Chicago, American Library Association, 2015. 223p. index. $40.00pa. ISBN 13: 978-0-8389-1264-5.

This book is an update to the earlier edition published seven years ago. Written by two retired school librarians with a great deal of experience between them, this book is excellent for new school librarians or veterans who are switching schools or just want to refresh their "game." The book is well-organized; an appendix includes Essential Resources and a list of Jobbers and Vendors. This title will help a new school librarian prepare for everything that first year—from advice for getting ready for the job interview, to organizing and cleaning out that first space, to getting along with a new school community. This book seems to have everything you need to know that you did not learn in library school. The book includes a useful glossary, table of contents, and index.—**Valerie Byrd Fort**

Special Topics

Archives

P

202.   Schull, Diantha Dow. **Archives Alive: Expanding Engagement with Public Library Archives and Special Collections.** Chicago, American Library Association, 2015. 324p. index. $79.00pa. ISBN 13: 978-0-8389-1335-2.

Despite the omnipresence of emphasis on digital projects and digitization in Library and Information Science (LIS) literature, building, maintaining, and expanding traditional print archival collections, sometimes with digital augmentation, remains a key role for academic and public library archives and special collections. This compendium of case studies demonstrates that the desire to highlight and expand public access to and engagement with unique local collections remains a critical part of public library operations nationwide.

It opens with an introduction describing using digital technologies and programming to make unique archival and special collections more accessible to local, national, and even international users. This work is broken up into 10 thematic sections covering art and archives, community archives, educational initiatives, emerging institutional models, exhibitions and related programs, interactive archives, lectures, conferences, and broadcast programs, national and international programs, oral history and community documentation projects, and tours, commemorations, and special events.

Examples of specific initiatives covered within these thematic sections include discoveries from the Free Library of Philadelphia's Fleisher Collection of orchestral music; the Community Archivist Program at the Austin, Texas, Public Library's Austin History Center; the Pittsburgh Iron and Steel Heritage Collection at Pittsburgh's Carnegie Library; the Jerome Robbins Dance Division at the New York Public Library's Performing Arts Division; a history of Kansas City, Missouri, stockyards in the metropolis' public library; the Allen County Community Album of genealogical information made by this Fort Wayne, Indiana, library's renowned collections in the field; the Central Arkansas Library System's Korean War Project; the Madison, Wisconsin, Public Library inviting individuals to bring 8 and 16 mm home movie for free onsite film inspections by experts and for public screenings; a Nashville, Tennessee, Public Library project documenting the impact of major 2010 flooding on Tennessee's capital city by creating a digital portal repository; and the La Crosse, Wisconsin, Public Library creating interpretive tours of community buildings and neighborhoods characterized by scripted walking tours, a stage production, self-guided online tours, and trolley tours.

These examples show that local libraries are seeking to expand public access to their unique archival and special collections by creative marketing and taking advantage of emerging digital technologies. Recommended for libraries interested in expanding and promoting regional history collections.—**Bert Chapman**

Cataloging and Classification

C, P, S

203.   Broughton, Vanda. **Essential Classification, Second Edition.** Chicago, American Library Association, 2015. 421p. index. $95.00pa.; $85.50pa. (ALA members). ISBN 13: 978-0-8389-1369-7.

Broughton (Information Studies, University College, London) updates the first edition (2004) while maintaining its basic structure. The first part reiterates the theoretical basis of classification: types of classification schemes, content analysis, and controlled indexing languages. The book then discusses the three major classification schemes used in the world today: Library of Congress (LC), Dewey Decimal Classification (DDC), and, in a bow to her European colleagues, Universal Decimal Classification (UDC). The author also devotes two chapters to the structure and application of Library of Congress Subject Headings. The text ends with chapters devoted to faceted classification, managing classification, and classification in the digital era respectively. This last chapter, the one major update to this edition, delves into contemporary classification digital topics like information architecture, folksonomies, visualization tools, and the semantic Web. A practical glossary and a comprehensive bibliography round out the text.

The two other classics competing for attention in this arena also discuss subject access and analyze the major classification systems. However, Daniel Joudrey, Arlene Taylor and David Miller, *Introduction to Cataloging and Classification* (Libraries Unlimited, 2015, 11th ed.) add a discussion of Sears' List of Subject Headings and include other classification systems like Bliss and National Library of Medicine, which one would expect in an introductory text. Lois Chan and Theodora Hodges, *Cataloging and Classification* (Scarecrow Press, 2007, 3rd ed., see ARBA 2008, entry 528; fourth edition due 2016) treat subject headings more fully by including Sears, Faceted Application of Subject Terminology (FAST), and NLM's Medical Subject Headings (MeSH) and deal with even more alternative classification systems. Both give UDC short shrift.

Broughton is a noted contributor to the field, having authored most recently *Essential Library of Congress Subject Headings* (Neal-Schuman, 2012) and *Essential Thesaurus Construction* (Facet, 2013). She serves a leadership role on the editorial teams of the Bliss Bibliographic Classification and Universal Decimal Classification.

The book's greatest strengths are its focus exclusively on classification (i.e., without the descriptive cataloging element), a strong theoretical component, and greater focus on UDC. The additional inclusion of profuse examples, exercises (with answers), and bulleted summaries makes the book useful as an introductory library science text, a self-learning manual, or a refresher.—**Lawrence Olszewski**

C, P, S

204.   Coyle, Karen. **FRBR, Before and After: A Look at Our Bibliographic Models.** Chicago, American Library Association, 2016. 179p. index. $50.00pa.; $45.00pa. (ALA members). ISBN 13: 978-0-8389-1345-1.

In *FRBR, Before and After* Karen Coyle provides a critical look at the Functional Requirements for Bibliographic Records, more commonly known as FRBR. The book is divided into two parts; the first is an overview of the evolution of cataloging theory, data models, and technology. In the second part Coyle takes a close look at FRBR and the entities the model describes and provides a compelling argument for how bibliographic models must move to an integrative approach as data and technology continue to evolve. Coyle, drawing on over 30 years expertise, exposes some of the weaknesses of FRBR and the concept of the "work" in libraries within an ever-changing landscape of what library resources look like and how users try to find them. Written at a technical level this book is best for those with experience in cataloging or who would like to brush up on their knowledge of bibliographic data theories.—**Andrea C Kepsel**

C, P, S

205.   Hart, Amy. **RDA Made Simple: A Practical Guide to the New Cataloging Rules.** Santa Barbara, Calif., Libraries Unlimited/ABC-CLIO, 2014. 176p. index. $22.50pa. ISBN 13: 978-1-61069-485-8; 978-1-61069-486-5 (e-book).

In clear, concise language and well-organized chapters, this manual provides information for cataloging librarians moving to RDA. Hart has written an introduction to RDA specifically for general catalogers and not specialists. The book provides the basics, with bulleted points, charts, and lists that make it easy to find information. The book provides succinct descriptions, and deals with special topics such as MARC bibliographic fields impacted by RDA and collaborations/compilations. A final chapter provides a variety of real cataloging examples; they quickly show what has changed. While it contains much information, each chapter includes an introductory paragraph and a conclusion. This handbook would be helpful as an introduction to RDA for working catalogers or library students taking cataloging classes. Library directors may also find it useful, especially the chapters on planning and implementation. A bibliography and an index round out the work.—**Mary Northrup**

C, P

206.   Moulaison, Heather Lea, and Raegan Wiechert. **Crash Course in Basic Cataloging with RDA.** Santa Barbara, Calif., Libraries Unlimited/ABC-CLIO, 2015. 164p. index. (Crash Course Series). $45.00. ISBN 13: 978-1-4408-3776-0; 978-1-4408-3777-7 (e-book).

Crash Course in Basic Cataloging with RDA provides both students and professionals with the adopted RDA procedures. This volume is designed for readers who are interested in cataloging but not experts in cataloging. This book describes the basic needs and reasoning behind the RDA rules and everything that accompanies RDA cataloging. Authors Heather Lea Moulaison and Raegan Wiechert both have extensive experience in teaching information organization and cataloging. The authors wrote this book to provide "a practical standpoint for non-catalogers," and the book succeeds admirably in this. Supplementary items include figures, sidebars, tables, images, three appendixes, and an index.

Since the book assumes the reader has had no prior history or knowledge with cataloging, information starts from the ground up. The 10 chapters in this book cover computer systems, different formats, MARC, encoding library data, RDA, access points, subject headings, Dewey Decimal Classification, and Library of Congress Classification. The inclusion of visual items such as images and figures is a great addition, given the target audience. These visual items range from screenshots of the Web interface of a catalog to a comparison of Bibframe version record versus MARC version record to MARC fields along with their explanations of use. These visual aids are beyond beneficial to those just starting their cataloging career as the material can be overwhelming. For example, the included flowchart on the decision and reasoning of adding access points enhances the understanding of readers with no cataloging experience and is much more effective than a text-only explanation. Finally, the book's appendixes provide examples of MARC record, RDA record, free and subscription-base Web resources, and other professional resources to further the readers' cataloging knowledge. The authors acknowledge that cataloging rules, protocols, and products can (and most likely will) change in the future, but presently this would be a great resource for students and nonprofessionals who need to learn the basics of cataloging.

This resource is highly recommended for academic and public libraries.—**Sara Mofford**

Children's and Young Adult Services

P, S

207.   Alessio, Amy J., and Heather Booth. **Club Programs for Teens: 100 Activities for the Entire Year.** Chicago, American Library Association, 2015. 165p. index. $49.00pa.; $44.10pa. (ALA members). ISBN 13: 978-0-8389-1334-5.

Club Programs for Teens: 100 Activities for The Entire Year is a hands-on guide for development of young adult clubs at school or public libraries. Authors Amy J. Alessio and Heather Booth share years of experience as teen librarians in the public sector and have published other books on teen services.

This paperback's cover is bold and engaging though photos are gender limiting; girls are shown baking and sewing, boys are using technology. Turning inside, this American Library Association (ALA) publication is comprised of a table of contents with 14 chapters representing teen club themes. The introduction is worthy of reading as it imparts overview tips such as "groups generally require four to six months to catch on," and the introduction also includes thoughts on how to handle a teen club scenario that isn't working. The book concludes with an effective index.

With club themes including "Crafting for Charity" and "Green Teens," each section offers multiple program suggestions. Some ideas overlap with other themes, and are duly noted in the CROSSOVER listing for each activity. Each activity may incorporate the following: a summary, the crossover, a shopping list, "make it happen" (the process), variation, online, and resources. The resource sections are slight, and only very rarely include books. The index is in-depth so it makes it an easily used book. Clear organization makes this a "go-to" guide for anyone doing club programming with teens. An evaluation process for programming, rated leveling for difficulty, or estimated preparation time are not part of this guide; such added information would save busy librarians time in deciding which activities best suit their planning time and their teen community.

Activity write-ups are generally all-inclusive but some are lacking, particularly for novice librarians. For instance, "A Picture's Worth..."(p 104) is an activity in using photography as a newsworthy story. Nowhere does it mention the need for permission in certain photographic settings. Author events are quite common and, yet, only get a brief mention. The "Traveling App Showdown"(p 145) neglects to include a shopping list whether it be a hand-held device or a computer and projector. The final chapter on more ideas for clubs is only four pages and is more of a listing of club themes and lacks activity details. It does reference *A Year of Programs for Teens* (see ARBA 2008, entry 534) and *A Year of Programs for Teens 2* (see ARBA 2012, entry 601), both coauthored by Alessio, which offer additional support for staff who organize teen programming.

Overall, *Club Programs for Teens:100 Activities for the Entire Year* gives the nuts and bolts of young adult programs from planning, to budget, through "how to make it happen." Suggestions are timely, engaging, and have potential to build a strong teen presence in school and public libraries. Activities can be modified for other age groups and program resources adjusted according to budgetary restrictions which makes this guide a flexible programming tool. Useful to librarians and educators seeking new ideas for teen engagement, this book will be the catalyst for your own club whether using one theme or intertwining many. Recommended.—**Janis Minshull**

P

208.   Alessio, Amy J., Katie Lamantia, and Emily Vinci. **A Year of Programs for Millennials and More.** Chicago, American Library Association, 2015. 194p. index. $49.00pa.; $44.10pa. (ALA members). ISBN 13: 978-0-8389-1332-1.

Defining millennials as "young adults in their late teens, 20s, 30s, and 40s," the authors strive to fill a gap in the literature on public library programming, which tends to focus on children, younger teens, and seniors. Alessio, LaMantia, and Vinci provide detailed outlines for program planning, promotion, set-up and delivery keyed to the 12 months of the year. Alessio and LaMantia are teen librarians and Vinci is a readers' advisory specialist; all work at the Schaumburg Township District Library in Illinois. Alessio is coauthor, with Kimberly A. Patton, of *A Year of Programming for Teens* (see ARBA 2007, entry 510) and *A Year of Programming for Teens II* (see ARBA 2012, entry 601); this new work focused on an older demographic mimics the format of her earlier titles. The authors describe four or five programs for each month. Some of the suggestions are calendar-dependent (e.g., Un-Valentine's Day, Oscar Night, and Mardi Gras programs in February), but others seem designed to fill in months without major holidays or happenings (e.g., '80s Night in April and Microwave Magic in July). For each event, they specify the preparation time, length of program, optimal number of participants, and suggested age range. They also provide shopping lists, planning timelines, variations to appeal to different ages or to incorporate an online component, suggestions for marketing, and tips to guarantee the events run smoothly. The introduction to the book differentiates among the needs and interests of the age groups within the millennial generation. A final chapter describes 10 "clubs that keep them coming back" for ongoing programs about fitness, trivia, crafts, movies, and more. The index aids in identifying programs that, for instance, involve food or target parents. Overall, this is a well-organized and easy-to-consult sourcebook. Librarians can use it in conjunction with Brett W. Lear's *Adult Programs in the Library,* 2d ed. (ALA, 2013), which likewise presents program exemplars along with deeper discussions of mission, fundraising, publicity, and evaluation. Both works are excellent additions to public library professional collections; *A Year of Programs for Millennials and More* might also inspire academic librarians who wish to engage traditional-aged and older students.—**Susan E. Searing**

P

209.   Ernst, Linda L. **The Essential Lapsit Guide: A Multimedia How-To-Do-It Manual and Programming Guide for Stimulating Literacy Development from 12 to 24 Months.** Chicago, American Library Association, 2015. 276p. index. $72.00pa.; $64.80pa. (ALA members). ISBN 13: 978-1-55570-761-3.

In this exhaustive guide, the author, an expert children's librarian, compiles and updates practical information from her two earlier works, *Lapsit Services for the Very Young* (Neal-Schuman, 1995) and *Lapsit Services for the Very Young II* (Neal-Schuman, 2001). Like the earlier books, this guide presents a wealth of suggestions for storytime programs enhanced with movement and creative activities, all designed to foster language development in infants and pre-toddlers (12 to 24 months) through interactions with their parents or caregivers. Part one provides important context by presenting concise background on early childhood development, identifying adult program participants (e.g., bilingual families, teen mothers, grandparents), and recommending ways to make all components of library services, from facilities to collections to outreach, responsive to the needs of the very young. The heart of the book is part two, which focuses on programming. Detailed tips deal with everything from planning and publicity to room set-up and program pacing. An annotated bibliography of some 180 titles for reading aloud is arranged by author, but the topical index that follows immediately allows one to discover stories about, for instance, animals or seasons or stories that rhyme. Over 30 pages are devoted to nursery rhymes, finger plays, and short songs that audiences can perform along with the librarian. Ernst recommends combinations of stories and activities for more than 20 themes (e.g., animals, bedtime, food) but stresses that non-themed programs also succeed. As models for program planning, she offers sample outlines for 20-30 minute sessions that alternate listening to stories with active play. A chapter on "enhancements" adds ideas for incorporating music, flannel boards, puppets, crafts, and more, as well as displays and handouts for the adult participants. Librarians with small budgets will appreciate Ernst's instructions for making materials such as rhythm instruments from scratch. An appendix offers 21 reproducible handouts and templates, most intended to encourage adult participants to initiate similar activities at home with their little ones. The complete set of materials is also available for downloading/printing at http://alaeditions.org/Webextras, along with a compilation of the bibliographies and resource lists that appear throughout the book, a copy of the rhyme lyrics from part two, and nearly 50 video clips of the author performing rhymes and finger plays. Since Ernst began sharing her wisdom over 20 years ago, library programming for babies and toddlers has grown in popularity, making this new work an essential purchase for public libraries that serve this age group.—**Susan E. Searing**

C, P, S

210.   Lyons, Reneé Critcher. **Teaching Civics in the Library.** Jefferson, N.C., McFarland, 2015. 224p. illus. index. $39.95pa. ISBN 13: 978-0-7864-9672-3; 978-1-4766-2092-3 (e-book).

This timely work by Reneé Critcher Lyons, Assistant Professor in the School Library Media Program at East Tennessee State University, arrives on the heels of various new K-12 standards initiatives that place a renewed emphasis on civic readiness. The book pairs a basic background on the connection between libraries and civic education with practical activity ideas for a public or school library setting. While passing mention is made of "Socrates Cafés" and other programming ideas for adult patrons, public libraries considering this title for purchase should be aware that this book will be of interest primarily for a youth services audience. Chapters one through five provide an excellent, accessible introduction to the subject of democracy education and the critical leadership role the library has historically played in this field—a role the library should, the author contends, continue to play. Of particular interest to school librarians will be chapter five, "21st Century Role of School and Public Libraries," which connects the dots between the American Association of School Librarians' Standards for the 21st-Century Learner and civic learning goals from social studies standards, such as those outlined in the College, Career, and Civic Life (C3) Framework. Chapter six offers readers an annotated list of clustered titles for students grades K–12 "for collection development modeling purposes."

While readers may appreciate the list of titles vetted by an expert here, of even greater use will be the superb list of title evaluation criteria on page 69, which librarians will want to consult when considering any effort to develop a civics collection for youth. Subsequent chapters provide dozens of creative, ready-to-use activity ideas and resources organized by grade level. Lyons' passion for the Founding era resonates throughout this book and is contagious. However, Lyons' focus on this period comes at the expense of other essential moments in American history—with a few exceptions, those looking for civics-related resources and activity ideas set against the backdrop of later periods will need to look elsewhere. Readers wading for the first time into the treacherous waters of discussing political issues in the classroom may also have benefitted from additional guidance on building stakeholder support for their efforts to make the library a hub of civic learning and on anticipating and preparing for potential challenges to materials and programs. The work overall remains a vital contribution to an important and underexplored topic which has seen few book-length studies and none with as practical an approach as Lyons' book. Given the renewed emphasis on civic skills in K-12 standards, the book is recommended for purchase for libraries that support LIS education, school libraries, and those public libraries interested in initiating or growing civics-related programs for young patrons.—**ARBA Staff Reviewer**

P, S

211.   Torres-Roman, Steven A., and Carson E. Snow. **Dragons in the Stacks: A Teen Librarian's Guide to Tabletop Role-Playing.** Santa Barbara, Calif., Libraries Unlimited/ABC-CLIO, 2014. 212p. index. $45.00pa. ISBN 13: 978-1-61069-261-8; 978-1-61069-262-5 (e-book).

Public and school librarians who are thinking of adding tabletop role-playing games (RPGs) to their collection or programming will find this book to be an invaluable reference. Role-playing games create a structured and imaginative environment for players to complete quests, engage in storytelling, solve problems, and play make-believe. This book introduces readers to the genre and general vocabulary of RPGs; it suggests a core collection of RPGs for libraries and offers a more comprehensive list of game reviews and additional resources. It also includes ideas and considerations for cataloging, shelving, advertising, and programming. This book offers a tremendous single volume introduction to the world of tabletop RPGs and their potential place in the library. An index rounds out the work.—**Ellen Range**

P

212.   Velásquez, Jennifer. **Real-World Teen Services.** Chicago, American Library Association, 2015. 116p. index. $50.00pa.; $45.00pa. (ALA members). ISBN 13: 978-0-8389-1342-0.

This engaging title is directed at teen services librarians and library science students, but administrators and generalists can also benefit from its guidance and advice for real-world situations. In six fun-to-read chapters, Velásquez covers a wide range of topics inspired by her own experiences and by the questions she has received from practicing teen services librarians and from students in her introductory course on teen services. She focuses on the why of teen library services and demonstrates the importance of trusting teen ideas and desires regarding library experiences.

In the first chapter, "Teen Library Space," Velásquez discusses the importance of creating a designated place for teen library users, highlighting pitfalls and remedies, incorporating youth ideas in space development, and providing real world examples of how to claim space. For example, one space-claiming tactic allows teens to customize bookshelves and book carts. "Programming for Teens," chapter two, addresses myriad issues such as why teens don't attend programs, the difficulties of obtaining funding, and the resistance of colleagues, suggesting that successful teen programming not only responds to what teens want but also involves teens in program planning. The next chapter, "Crafting Service Dynamics and Modeling Service Strategies," examines the need for teen services librarians to educate all library staff about serving teens and addresses the creation of a reader's advisory strategy. Chapters four and five, "Rules, Conduct Codes, and Behavior," and "Access, Control, and Privacy" provide valuable guidance for the development of library use rules and the policies regarding how the library treats its users. In these chapters, readers will find ideas about maintaining professionalism, knowing when to call in the authorities, establishing library policies about teen privacy and truancy issues, and much more. The final chapter uses a question and answer format to address common situations like teaching colleagues how to answer teen services questions at the reference desk or the impulse to give teen patrons money, rides, a place to stay, etc.

All chapters begin with bullet point lists of key considerations and end with "soapbox moments" and references. An index rounds out the work. Highly recommended for anyone interested in the real world of teen librarian services.—**ARBA Staff Reviewer**

Collection Development

C, P, S

213.   Arndt, Theresa S. **Getting Started with Demand-Driven Acquistions for E-Books: A LITA Guide.** Chicago, American Library Association, 2015. 99p. index. $65.00pa. ISBN 13: 978-0-8389-1314-7; 978-0-8389-1322-2 (e-book).

Demand-driven acquisitions has been a hot topic within the library industry in recent years. Published for ALA's LITA division, Ardnt has crafted a brief yet thoughtful introduction to demand-driven acquisitions (DDA). While many library professionals have heard the acronyms and perhaps have even had exposure to this acquisitions method, Arndt's guide provides explanations and helpful checklists of considerations, as well as her library's recent experience with implementing demand-driven acquisitions.

This guide is geared towards libraries or librarians who are investigating demand-driven acquisitions for the first time (although experience with purchased or subscribed e-books is assumed and is stated as such in the introduction). However, this book may also be useful for library school students and recent graduates.

The author begins with an overall explanation of demand-driven acquisitions as well as alternate names and acronyms for terms frequently referenced in the context of DDA. The next five chapters are divided by topics such as budgeting, cataloging aspects of DDA, DDA within a consortium, etc. Some considerations—inclusion of DDA records in the library catalog, in the discovery layer, or both—are repeated in multiple chapters, assumedly due to increased importance of these particular issues. Within the appendixes of this guide, a sample DDA implementation schedule is provided as is a glossary and index.

Inasmuch as the author states her own experience of desiring a comprehensive checklist of considerations when implementing demand-driven acquisitions (and does provide this divided throughout the book) nowhere are these checklists provided in entirety. The complexity and difficulties of de-duplication are somewhat over-simplified. Furthermore, the author's perspective seems to be limited to DDA via a library service provider, thus some topics would benefit from additional details and/or perspectives.

This concise (99 pages) guide's affordable price ($65) and availability in both print and eBook formats make it a worthwhile addition for many technical/access services departments' professional literature collections. It is appropriate for all libraries who have not yet implemented demand-driven e-book acquisitions at their libraries and are interested in a holistic view of the considerations this process entails.—**Kat Landry Mueller**

C, P, S

214.   Wilkinson, Frances C., Linda K. Lewis, and Rebecca L. Lubas. **The Complete Guide to Acquistions Management.** 2d ed. Santa Barbara, Calif., Libraries Unlimited/ ABC-CLIO, 2015. 208p. index. (Library and Information Science Text Series). $60.00pa. ISBN 13: 978-1-61069-713-2; 978-1-61069-714-9 (e-book).

A great deal has changed in the more than a dozen years since the first edition of this book (see ARBA 2005, entry 626). The text has been completely revised and updated to reflect shifts in publishing and library processes. A new chapter on choosing vendors is one of the longest chapters; it includes recommendations for writing a request for proposal (RFP) and evaluating vendor performance. Previously separate treatments of serials and electronic resources are combined into a single chapter on acquiring continuing and electronic resources through subscriptions and licenses. Other chapters cover: the organization of acquisitions departments; the publishing industry; outsourcing; acquisitions systems; monographic content; used and antiquarian materials; gift and exchange programs; "decisions of permanence" (i.e., preservation and binding); and professional ethics. The authors conclude by asserting the value of acquisition librarians' perspectives as libraries choose and implement discovery and delivery services. The appendixes contain a wealth of useful reference material, including: a list of companies that offer automated acquisitions systems; acquisitions-related conferences and seminars; electronic discussion lists; Internet sites; journals; organizations; Web-based reference tools; and a glossary. Although the volume fits in the textbook genre, few LIS schools these days offer courses devoted to acquisitions librarianship. Librarians forced to learn the business of acquisitions on the job, however, will find this new edition invaluable. Although the authors are all academic librarians, any large library faces the challenges outlined here and will benefit from their sage, clearly presented advice. The detailed table of contents and subject index makes this a handy desk reference for anyone working in this area or desiring to learn more about it.—**Susan E. Searing**

Customer Service

C, P

215.   Hands, Africa S. **Successfully Serving the College Bound.** Chicago, American Library Association, 2015. 168p. index. $50.00pa.; $45.00pa. (ALA members). ISBN 13: 978-0-8389-1272-0.

American public libraries play an important role in filling the information needs of their users. New immigrants from different countries with different cultures, religions, languages, and little knowledge of computers come to the United States every year and use public libraries. Therefore, the role of librarians serving them has changed in the twenty-first century; this role includes helping immigrants prepare for college. This new book written by Africa S. Hands will fill the needs of college-bound students of all ages. The book has eight well-written chapters full of information for public librarians who have to play a new role in the present information age. The new law passed by the President Obama administration to give free education to all students in community colleges will further encourage college-bound students to seek more information through public libraries and librarians. The book includes four appendixes which will further help all interested parties find more information on going to college with the help of public libraries and academic libraries. The book also provides good suggestions for librarians to develop collections on the subject in all formats in order for their libraries to help library users of all ages. This book is certainly well written and fills a major gap in the library literature. It is recommended for all public and academic libraries.—**Ravindra Nath Sharma**

C, P, S

216.   Hernon, Peter, Ellen Altman, and Robert E. Dugan. **Assessing Service Quality: Satisfying the Expectations of Library Customers.** 3d ed. Chicago, American Library Association, 2015. 218p. index. $75.00pa.; $67.50pa. (ALA members). ISBN 13: 978-0-8989-1308-6.

First published in 1998 and revised in 2010 (see ARBA 2011, entry 590), the third edition of this indispensable guide reflects the latest developments in library service assessment theory and technique. Peter Hernon is a professor emeritus at Simmons College and a pioneer in the field of library assessment. Ellen Altman, who collaborated with Hernon on the earlier editions, is also a retired LIS professor. The new member of the authorial team, Robert E. Dugan, is the dean of libraries at the University of West Florida and has also published previously about library metrics. The organization of the book closely follows the first two editions, although some content is repositioned within the volume; for example, descriptions of techniques for eliciting user feedback are gathered into a new chapter titled "Different Ways of Listening to Customers." The authors begin with an essay on the concepts of customer service and service quality and then probe several key factors that affect service, e.g., customers' desire for self-sufficiency. They expound on mission, vision, goals, and values in the context of the library-as-system. The meaty chapter on "Measuring and Evaluating the Components of High-Quality Service" suggests 11 core questions to guide service evaluation, such as "how much?," "how prompt?," and "how reliable?" Under "how valuable?" the discussion of ROI (return on investment) is considerably expanded from the previous edition, as befits the current popularity of this metric. The authors make a key distinction between "countable" and "evaluateable" measures, and they present a conceptual framework that regards library service from the perspectives of the library, customer, decision-makers, and society. A brief chapter cautions about the pitfalls of working with quantitative data. Special emphasis is given to customer comment and complaint channels, surveys, and focus group interviews, with a chapter devoted to each mode of data collection. Another chapter recommends specific customer-related metrics for both academic and public libraries. The remainder of the book addresses techniques to measure customer satisfaction (which, the authors stress, is not the same as service quality), methods for interpreting and presenting data, and ways to incorporate service quality assessment into strategies for continuous improvement through engagement with customers. The book has a very detailed index but, unlike the earlier editions, lacks a bibliography. However, each chapter includes endnotes which cite both classic and recent publications. Over 60 charts, figures, and sample forms have been redesigned for greater visual impact. While most of the information is recycled from the last edition, every page shows evidence of careful revision to the text. Some older examples and quotations have been dropped, while new material has been added and content updated as needed. With the recent creation of assessment librarian positions in many academic libraries, as well as increased attention to the user experience across both physical and virtual library services, this new edition should find a wide readership among all types of librarians as well as LIS students.—**Susan E. Searing**

Digitization and Digital Libraries

C, P

217.   **Queers Online: LGBT Digital Practices in Libraries.** Rachel Wexelbaum, ed. Sacramento, Calif., Library Juice Press, 2014. 239p. index. (Gender and Sexuality in Information Studies). $35.00pa. ISBN 13: 978-1-936117-79-6.

A dozen contributions explore varied approaches to representing and preserving online the history and culture of LGBTIQ communities (lesbians, gay men, bisexuals, transgender, intersex, and queer). In section one, "Queering the Online Realm," four chapters situate digital information projects within the larger contexts of LGBTIQ theory and archival practice. Setting the tone for the rest of the book, the first chapter draws on the author's own experiences of using the Internet to explore his gay identity. He asserts that online spaces have supplanted physical spaces as the nexus for gay community-building and should therefore be preserved as historical artifacts. The following chapter makes a persuasive, theory-steeped argument that a particular pornographic Website has value as a public history repository. A survey of Web directories by and about transgendered people from 1994 to the present exposes multiple barriers to seeking transgender information on the Web; the author offers practical recommendations for meeting the online information needs of transgendered people. Acknowledging the dominance of Wikipedia as an information source, the final chapter in this section describes (with photos) Wikipedia edit-a-thons sponsored by the Tom of Finland Foundation and advocates for holding such events to improve access to accurate queer information. Section two focuses on the digitization of print and realia collections. A long-time volunteer at the Lesbian Herstory Archives in New York City explains how decisions about digitization are guided by the archives' principles. Included in the chapter are interviews with other volunteer staff who lead efforts to digitize photographic and audio materials and to create a Web-based catalog. The other chapters in this section address the legal and ethical nuances of copyright and privacy rights that affected digitization projects in Canada and Australia. Section three, titled "The Nuts and Bolts of Queer Digitization Projects," recounts the goals, challenges, and outcomes of three innovative projects: Open Up!, a Dutch effort to collect and digitize materials from Central, Eastern, and Southeastern Europe; the Matthew Shepard Web Archive at the University of Wyoming that captured and preserved Websites about the gay student's murder and its impact on the local community and worldwide movement for LGBTIQ rights, 10 years after the event; and the LGBT Religious Archives Network, which serves as a portal to existing archival collections and provides direct access to biographical profiles and oral histories of LGBTIQ religious leaders of many faiths. Section four offers two short chapters by editor Wexelbaum that bring to light continuing obstacles to information access: censorship in libraries, and the paucity of LGBTIQ e-books. The discussion of e-books is informed by her recent survey of LGBTIQ reading habits as well as background on how libraries acquire electronic content. Taken together, these dozen chapters make a compelling case for the centrality of the Web as a platform for LGBTIQ information. They advocate strongly for LGBTIQ communities to shape online spaces that meet their information needs, document their histories, and counter misinformation and prejudice. This work is recommended for all academic and public libraries.—**Susan E. Searing**

Fundraising

C, P, S

218.   Maxwell, Nancy Kalikow. **ALA Book of Library Grant Money.** 9th ed. Chicago, American Library Association, 2015. 348p. index. $180.00pa. ISBN 13: 978-0-8389-1211-9.

This book aims to provide librarians, fundraisers, and researchers with quick, convenient access to information on the major U.S. funding sources for library grants. They include private and corporate foundations, corporate direct givers, library and nonprofit organizations, and government agencies. Each entry is arranged alphabetically and includes the pertinent information a grant seeker would need to begin researching a potential funder. A section on grant-related organizations and resources offers grant seekers help to do their research, write proposals, administer, and evaluate a project. Indexes include grantors by total grant value, grantors by state, named grants/programs, and professional library organization grantors. The introduction takes the novice grant seeker through the essential steps of becoming "grant ready." The book will pay for itself with the first grant and should be part of any library grant seeker's collection. Four indexes round out the book.—**Norman Desmarais**

Information Literacy

C

219.   Bowles-Terry, Melissa, and Cassandra Kvenild. **Classroom Assessment Techniques for Librarians.** Chicago, American Library Association, Association of College and Research Libraries, 2015. 118p. $36.00pa. ISBN 13: 978-0-8389-8775-9.

Although there is no dearth of material on assessing information literacy instruction (see, for example, *A Practical Guide to Information Literacy Assessment for Academic Librarians* by Carolyn J. Radcliff et al., ARBA 2009, entry 568), this new book is unique in its depth of treatment of a single method, classroom assessment techniques, or CATs. Bowles-Terry, Head of Educational Initiatives for the University of Nevada, Las Vegas, library, and Kvenild, Head of the Learning Resource Center at the University of Wyoming library, define classroom assessment as "a learner-centered, formative assessment practice that allows instructors to find out what students are learning in the classroom and how well they understand it" (p. xi). The authors illustrate how academic librarians can employ CATs to promote student learning and improve their own teaching. Their examples span the spectrum from one-shot class sessions to librarian-taught credit courses. The authors include techniques well suited to situations when librarians are temporarily embedded in courses for the duration of an assignment, and they illustrate the use of CATs in online as well as face-to-face teaching. Two dozen different techniques are grouped in six categories depending on the characteristic to be assessed: prior knowledge and understanding; skill in analysis and critical thinking; skill in synthesis and creative thinking; skill in application; attitudes and self-awareness; and learner reactions. The authors describe the particular strengths of each CAT and when to employ it. For example, the Defining Features Matrix CAT is recommended when students must compare different information sources, whereas Concept Maps are useful when students are selecting a topic to research. Concept Maps is just one example of a familiar tool that is often used for pedagogical purposes, but Bowles-Terry and Kvenild zero in on its strengths for assessing learning. Some of the CATs included in this book, such as the Minute Paper and Think-Pair-Share, are widely practiced in library instruction, but others, such as Chain Notes, will be new to most readers. Bowles-Terry and Kvenild provide several examples of employing each CAT with different types of students, learning outcomes, and instructional frameworks. For many of the CATs, they also suggest variations on the basic technique. A cornerstone of their approach to classroom assessment is scoring the responses and providing feedback to the students, either by immediately sharing the results and modifying the session's agenda as needed to focus on areas where confusion lingers, or by analyzing responses after the class and following up with research guides, email messages, additional sessions, and the like. The sheer variety of CATs described in this practical, well-written guide guarantee that any instruction librarian, no matter what her teaching style, will be inspired to incorporate CATs into her classroom lessons. For this reason, every academic library should own at least one copy, and many instruction librarians will want personal copies.—**Susan E. Searing**

C

220.   **Metaliteracy in Practice.** Trudi E. Jacobson and Thomas P. Mackey, eds. Chicago, American Library Association, 2016. 224p. index. $70.00pa.; $63.00pa. (ALA members). ISBN 13: 978-0-8389-1379-6.

This collection of case studies is a companion to the coeditors' recent influential book, *Metaliteracy* (see ARBA 2015, entry 416), which articulated four goals for developing metaliterate learners: evaluate content critically, including dynamic, online content that changes and evolves, such as article preprints, blogs, and wikis; understand personal privacy, information ethics, and intellectual property issues in changing technology environments; share information and collaborate in a variety of participatory environments; and demonstrate ability to connect learning and research strategies with lifelong learning processes and personal, academic, and professional goals. (For objectives associated with each goal, see https://metaliteracy.org.) Students no longer merely discover and consume information but actively create, repurpose, and share it. Jacobson, Head of the Information Literacy Department of the University of Albany Libraries, and Mackey, Vice Provost for Academic Programs at SUNY Empire State College, therefore argue that librarians must progress beyond teaching traditional information literacy skills. They specify four domains within the concept of metaliteracy: behavioral, cognitive, affective, and metacognitive. Eight of the chapters in this collection present case studies by academic librarians (typically partnered with faculty from other disciplines) who have designed, revised, assessed, and/or analyzed strategies to incorporate metaliteracy as both a learning outcome and a pedagogical method. The contributors explore elements of curricular design, information politics, social media as teaching tools, students as information creators, and other topics, while thoughtfully and honestly reflecting on their own experiences as teachers. Techniques to foster student empowerment are foregrounded in several of the chapters. Of the four domains, metacognition is discussed most often; these teachers grappled with promoting and then assessing students' awareness of their own mental processes as they interact with information. The case studies provide sufficient detail about assignments, assessments, and the process of curriculum development for readers who may wish to adopt these innovative approaches. Lending context to their experiences, the authors review relevant literature on pedagogy from librarianship, higher education, and their academic disciplines, and several observe how the concept of metaliteracy parallels and enriches disciplinary or campus-mandated learning objectives and competencies. The final chapter departs from the case study format. Instead, it offers a reflection on the meaning of "metaliteracy-as-agency," drawing on the ideas of social theorist Pierre Bourdieu. This eight-page essay is peppered with rarified academic jargon, overloaded with quotations, and adorned with 102 endnotes. Yet placed at the end of the book, it adds thought-provoking depth to the scholarly, praxis-centered studies that precede it. *Metaliteracy in Practice* is a timely publication—first, because the notion of metaliteracy has captured the attention of many academics, and second, because metaliteracy learning goals dovetail with the new ACRL Framework for Information Literacy in Higher Education. This book can be a source for inspiration and practical ideas to refresh the information literacy program of any academic library.—**Susan E. Searing**

C

221. **Teaching Information Literacy: Threshold Concepts Lesson Plans for Librarians.** Patricia Bravender, Hazel McClure, and Gayle Schaub, eds. Chicago, American Library Association, Association of College and Research Libraries, 2015. 251p. $48.00pa. ISBN 13: 978-0-8389-8771-1.

The editors (all from Grand Valley State and all librarians with liaison responsibilities) have compiled 34 lesson plans on the six information literacy frames (Scholarship as Conversation, Research as Inquiry, Authority is Constructed and Contextual, Information Creation as a Process, Searching as Strategic Exploration, and Information has Value) identified by the Association of College and Research Libraries (ACRL) in its 2015 Framework document. The 43 contributors' lesson plans are formatted consistently to include Learning Goals, Anticipatory Set, Lesson Objectives, Input/Modeling, Check for Understanding, Guided Practice, and Independent Practice. The lessons are short enough to cover in a one-hour session such as is common for information literacy courses, and could be adapted to be part of a one-shot instruction session. Materials needed for each lesson are listed, and handouts are included as an appendix and online at www.ala.org/acrl/files/handouts.pdf. Other appendixes are a list of lessons with overlapping threshold concepts, the ACRL Framework document, "Implementing the Framework" which includes sections for faculty and administrators, "Background of the Framework Development" covering a history of its development, "Sources for Further Reading" about information literacy and threshold concepts, and "Recommended Reading" about the framework. This is not a traditional "reference" book but will be most useful in a professional collection, possibly with a second circulating copy. It will be invaluable to academic librarians incorporating the information literacy frames in instruction sessions and information literacy courses. Highly recommended.—**Rosanne M. Cordell**

Information Technology

S

222.   Connolly, Matthew, and Tony Cosgrave. **Using iPhones, iPads, and iPods: A Practical Guide for Librarians.** Lanham, Md., Rowman & Littlefield, 2014. 210p. index. (Practical Guides for Librarians). $65.00pa.; $64.99 (e-book). ISBN 13: 978-1-4422-2687-6; 978-1-4422-2688-3 (e-book).

The primary audience for this book includes librarians and library IT staff with clear, easy-to-follow instructions for using iDevices for a variety of purposes across all types of libraries. The authors open with a general introduction that examines the Apple advantage and its implications for libraries. The remaining chapters are divided into three parts: iDevices in the Hands of Library Patrons; Lending iDevices to Library Patrons; and iDevices in the Hands of Librarians and Staff. Within each, chapters provide step-by-step guidance to every conceivable situation. The appendix lists and describes a selection of useful apps. Figures and tables are interspersed throughout the text. Each chapter ends with key points as well as a list of references. This title is a good purchase if your school is considering iDevices. There is an appendix of recommended iDevice apps and an index.—**Susan Yutzey**

C, P, S

223.   **More Library Mashups: Exploring New Ways to Deliver Library Data.** Nicole C. Engard, ed. Medford, N.J., Information Today, 2015. 362p. illus. index. $45.00pa. ISBN 13: 978-1-57387-498-4.

A follow-up to Engard's 2009 *Library Mashups,* this collection introduces 21 new mashup projects created by Engard and 24 library professionals from all types of libraries. Engard, the vice president of education at ByWaters Solutions where she educates librarians about open source software, brings together projects for the novice and the experienced programmer, for those who engage in systems and Web programming on a regular basis, and for those who are just starting to consider the idea of using mashups in their libraries of any size. Focusing solely on free, open-source products, the book is organized into five sections: the basics, library Websites, library catalog data, visualizing data, and value-added services. The book begins with four basics of mashups for libraries that can be done by any person such as data play, map mashups, visualizing library data, and delivery access; the volume next offers three chapters on library Websites, specifically using Drupal and APIs. The third part offers four chapters on enhancing the library catalog data such as searching databases through Twitter, putting library catalog data on the map, next generation cataloging, and delivering catalog records using Wikipedia current awareness. The fourth part focuses on visualizing data over four chapters, while the final section offers six chapters in ways to integrate value-added services such as a book suggestion app, single sign-on integration, and developing custom workflows. Each chapter is written by practicing librarians who have implemented the mashup and offers guidance, tips, tricks, successes, and failures that have occurred during the creation and implementation at the specific library. While the extensive knowledge can be overwhelming to the uninitiated, the opening part will be approachable and achievable by anyone, offering a sense of accomplishment and hopefully a desire to go forward with more advanced mashups in time. Public, school, academic, and special libraries will benefit from the ideas and tips offered in this book.—**Sara Marcus**

C, P, S

224.   **Technology Disaster Response and Recovery Planning: A LITA Guide.** Mary Mallery, ed. Chicago, American Library Association, 2015. 114p. index. $59.00pa.; $53.10pa. (ALA members). ISBN 13: 978-0-8389-1315-4.

Like other volumes in the highly regarded LITA Guide series, this small book presents a succinct and practical introduction to an important topic for library IT managers and other library staff responsible for digital collections and services. The contributors are expert consultants and librarians with first-hand knowledge of disaster preparation and recovery. Part one focuses on planning for disaster response. As the editor's brief initial chapter points out, librarians who are developing or revising plans to protect physical collections and library facilities can draw on a relatively rich professional literature with detailed recommendations, policy templates, and checklists; see, for example, the third edition of *Disaster Response and Planning for Libraries* by Miriam B. Kahn (see ARBA 2013, entry 548). Planning to mitigate the effects of IT outages and prevent the loss of digital collections is more recent and less well documented. This book begins to remedy the disparity. Liz Bischoff and Thomas F.R. Clareson advocate for thoroughly inventorying digital collections and assessing the risks to both collections and technical infrastructure; they recommend tools to facilitate these tasks. Donia Conn explains how dPlan, an online tool from the Northeast Document Conservation Center, can be used to develop a disaster recovery plan that applies to IT resources. Stating that successful responses to library disasters depend on a well-wrought communications plan, Denise O'Shea delivers a basic lesson in crisis communication, but she notes that IT outages may interfere with using the library's Website, email, or social media to get the word out to employees and patrons. A template for communications planning is supplied as an appendix. In what may be the most valuable chapter in the guide, Marshall Breeding examines the role of cloud computing in disaster mitigation. He clearly explains various options for locating library services in the cloud and using the cloud for back-up data storage. Although Breeding's chapter is titled "Future Trends," most of the cloud-based options he describes are available today, and forward-looking libraries are already beginning to utilize them. Part two presents two case studies of how libraries recovered from disasters that interrupted their IT operations. Oddly, since the editor and other authors identify a wide spectrum of possible disasters that can befall libraries—including weather-related natural disasters, fires, local technology failures, Internet outages, and security breaches—both case studies revolve around floods. The lessons they present, however, are applicable to most emergency situations and plans. Paul A. Soderdahl recounts the severe flooding at the University of Iowa in 2008 that tested a brand-new plan. The plan was reactivated in 2013 when the river again threatened to breach its banks. Soderdahl shares insights from both occasions. Clareson briefly examines disaster responses by three libraries in the wake of Hurricane Sandy in 2012. The volume concludes with an index. Although aimed primarily at academic librarians and IT staff, this handy guide will be useful in almost all libraries with digital content and services to protect. It can also serve to introduce LIS students to an important and evolving area of practice.—**Susan E. Searing**

C, P

225.   van Hooland, Seth, and Ruben Verborgh. **Linked Data for Libraries, Archives and Museums: How to Clean, Link and Publish your Metadata.** Chicago, American Library Association, 2014. 272p. index. $88.00pa. ISBN 13: 978-0-8389-1251-5.

In the age of information and technology many books have been written on the subject of libraries and technology but the book under review is very different. It has been written by two Europeans, a library educator and an engineer/researcher. The book has seven well-written chapters on the subject of linked data and its importance. Each chapter starts with learning outcomes and is focused on the practical steps which will help librarians and others to learn more about the global pool of linked data and its importance in creating a global database. Five chapters include case studies of libraries and museums which will further help librarians and others to understand the subject. The authors are of the view that in the age of technology even the car navigation systems, phones, and fridge will start consuming linked date in the near future. Therefore, it is possible that the linked data will create a global database for the benefit of all institutions. The book introduces readers to practical steps to understand how libraries can help their institutions to join and create a global database. It is the business of libraries, archives, and museums to collect and preserve information for their users. Therefore, it is important to maintain powerful URLs. The technology has certainly influenced the world and the humans can also leave a mark on the technology by creating the linked database. The book is an excellent addition to the library literature and is recommended highly for all libraries, archives, and museums.— **Ravindra Nath Sharma**

Library Cooperation

C, P, S

226.   **Going Beyond Loaning Books to Loaning Technology: A Practical Guide for Librarians.** Sander, Janelle, Lori S. Mestre, and Eric Kurt. Lanham, Md., Rowman & Littlefield, 2015. 158p. illus. index. (Practical Guides for Librarians). $65.00pa; $64.00 (e-book). ISBN 13: 978-1-4422-4499-3; 978-1-4422-4500-6 (e-book).

Thirteenth in the series Practical Guides for Librarians, *Going beyond Loaning Books to Loaning Technologies* is a useful resource for librarians. Available in paperback and e-book formats, this text details the emergence of a loanable technology program at libraries.

Adaptable to school, public, and academic libraries, most of the information is based on the model for creating an expanding loanable technology program at the University of Illinois at Urbana Champaign (UIUC). The guide is a step-by-step process in eleven chapters, including two appendixes, tables, and figures. Additionally, shaded text boxes in each chapter highlight information and tips. Chapters close with key points and references, and the book concludes with an index.

Overall, the organization of this book is quite good, though a few organizational flaws exist. Black-and-white photos are helpful but lack engagement. In a few instances, "Figures" show forms (Equipment Loan Form, p.75 and 105) which would be best if placed in closer proximity. Or, more logically, another appendix with all forms would be more useful to librarians. Final evaluation of technology programming, as discussed in Chapter 11, lacks any assessment form examples.

Authors Sander, Mestre, and Kurt clearly outline the steps necessary for a technology loaning program expansion. Sequential information will be useful for librarians seeking expansion of loaning services in the realm of technological equipment. Topics from initial identification of community needs through final assessment of successes and failures give this topic the A-Z of program development.

Libraries are repositories for a vast array of items, many of which are for borrowing. Looking beyond traditional lending, this book embraces the future by encouraging and guiding staff in the new age of loaning. Librarians will find this guide useful in exploring a library's niche for loaning these technologies. From e-books to cameras, gaming devices to projectors, *Going Beyond Loaning Books to Loaning Technologies* provides a guide to everything from the initial concept to the training of staff. Written with purpose, librarians will want this title on the professional development shelf. Highly Recommended.—**Janis Minshull**

C, P, S

227.   Nyquist, Corinne. **Resource Sharing Today: A Practical Guide to Interlibrary Loan, Consortial Circulation, and Global Cooperation.** Lanham, Md., Rowman & Littlefield, 2014. 213p. index. $65.00pa.; $64.99 (e-book). ISBN 13: 978-0-8108-8803-6; 978-0-8108-8804-3 (e-book).

Living in an interspace between circulation, reference services, and acquisition departments, Interlibrary Loan–ILL (or Interlibrary Services–ILS as it is called in some institutions) is a highly utilized yet underpromoted division within the library world. Corinne Nyquist (librarian, Sojourner Truth Library at State University of New York, New Paltz) seeks to address this under promotion by means of a "how-to" text geared to both new and more experienced librarians. Because ILL is rarely covered within traditional library/ information science programs, Nyquist covers everything from the early history and philosophy of consortial services through the departmental politics of ILL- where do ILL librarians report? To circulation? To reference? To acquisitions? Are they their own unit? Nyquist closes with appendixes for local, state, national, and international ILL codes, open access agreement, and purchase on demand plan templates.

A well-written, comprehensive work on consortial library services, Nyquist certainly succeeds at educating all librarians on the necessity of ILL to patrons in all manner of libraries. As stated in the introduction (written by Collette Mak, Head of Access Services, Notre Dame University), Nyquist's book joins a small but growing number of texts geared towards excellent user service in an increasingly networked world. Of particular interest is Nyquist's chapter nine, "Conundrums" where she elucidates on the myriad of issues ILL runs into: journal cancelations forcing up patron requests while database licensing makes articles more difficult to acquire, problems with citations stopping ILL requests, and encouraging better metadata so that technology can better verify even partial citation, etc. Although chapter nine was a particular standout, each chapter holds its own in this text, making Nyquist's book useful for any librarian working within ILL.—**Rachel Meredith Minkin**

Library Facilities

C, P, S

228.   Albrecht, Steve. **Library Security: Better Communication, Safer Facilities.** Chicago, American Library Association, 2015. 184p. index. $55.00pa.; $49.50pa. (ALA members). ISBN 13: 978-0-8389-1330-7.

Library Security: Better Communication, Safer Facilities author, Dr. Steve Albrecht, is an internationally known expert on workplace violence, safety, and security and an author, speaker, trainer, and consultant. Dr. Albrecht is retired from the San Diego Police Department and is also board certified in human resources, security, and employee coaching. In addition, Albrecht manages a consulting firm that specializes in high-risk customer service skills. His expertise in law enforcement and conflict resolution in libraries offers positive leadership responses. This experience combines with his sense of humor to produce a literary contribution that is helpful, unique, and timely. Readers will enthusiastically determine that the pages address essential learning lessons for library administrative personnel and staff. Law enforcement agencies will also gain an awareness of related library security concerns after reading this informative handbook.

This one-volume professional resource contains nine chapters that offer opportunities to evaluate and implement essential safety and security requirements. Furthermore, the author's candid comments empower readers and motivate colleagues to maintain a safe library community and environment. Chapters cover the library work environment; the enforcement of a library code of conduct; difficult patrons and the challenges posed by certain such patrons as teenagers, the mentally ill, and the homeless; how to assess and manage threats; workplace violence; conducting a site security survey; the cultivation of community partnerships; and staff development for a safer library.

Library Security offers essential reading for public libraries. High school, community college, and university library colleagues also benefit along with local enforcement and security agencies. Steve Albrecht makes a literary contribution that warrants praise for readability and vision that encourages safety and due diligence in libraries that once served communities as quiet refuges from the noise of the world.—**Thomas E. Baker**

P

229.   Charbonnet, Lisa. **Public Library Buildings: The Librarian's Go-To Guide for Construction, Expansion, and Renovation Projects.** Santa Barbara, Calif., Libraries Unlimited/ABC-CLIO, 2015. 220p. illus. index. $65.00pa. ISBN 13: 978-1-4408-3858-3; 978-1-4408-3859-0 (e-book).

Lisa Charbonnet, a public library director-turned-consultant with experience in both renovating a public library and constructing a new branch, covers an astonishing amount of detail in this dense but readable guide. In a reassuring, conversational tone, she leads readers along the path from the initial vision for a new or remodeled space to postconstruction maintenance. Each chapter is devoted to a major stage in the process: getting started (understanding the community and setting goals); site selection and acquisition; securing funding; forming a project leadership team; programming and space planning; preconstruction planning; construction; wrapping up and moving in; and postconstruction sign-off and ongoing maintenance. The eight-page table of contents lists every heading and subheading in the text, making it easy to zero in on essentials like the requirements for different spaces (meeting rooms, shelving, staff workspaces, etc.). Charbonnet stresses essential behind-the-scenes space for storage and technical processing that may be overlooked by architects. Rather than dictate solutions, she frequently highlights the pros and cons of decisions. For example, she explains how using volunteers to help with the physical move requires more managerial effort than contracting with a mover, but it can save money and increase community enthusiasm for the new facility. Bulleted lists of considerations and questions about the anticipated uses of new spaces are extremely helpful. Boxed quotations from a handful of public library directors are sprinkled throughout the book; they provide honest glimpses of what has worked and what can go wrong. There are a number of works in the library literature about planning and managing library building and renovation projects, yet this book surprisingly lacks a bibliography—perhaps its only significant flaw. However, the author does employ endnotes to point to published standards and formulas, as well as documents from the two projects she led. Additional model documents and policies are reproduced as appendixes, accompanied by a glossary of terms. *Public Library Buildings* sets a new standard for such guides, and therefore it belongs in most public library professional collections and in all libraries supporting LIS education. The second edition of *Countdown to a New Library: Managing the Building Project,* by Jeannette A. Woodward (ARBA 2011), which is similar in content and approach, is another excellent resource for library directors and building planners.—**Susan E. Searing**

C, P, S

230.   Mathews, Brian, and Leigh Ann Soistmann. **Encoding Space: Shaping Learning Environments that Unlock Human Potential.** Chicago, American Library Association, Association of College and Research Libraries, 2016. 176p. illus. $62.00pa. ISBN 13: 978-0-8389-8825-1.

People go to libraries because the space gives them something. That physical space can provide great significance. In the future, libraries will speak to the human experience, promoting a feeling of well-being and openness to learning. The subtitle of *Encoding Space* describes this vision well; "shaping learning environments that unlock human potential".

A paperback book of 175 pages, the deceiving cover uses subtle tones of black, grey, and white; light bulbs decorate the cover, alluding to inspiration. Inside, the book comes alive with insight on what library facilities can be and how the philosophy of space really does matter.

Authored by Mathews of the Virginia Tech Libraries and in collaboration with interior designer Soistmann, the structure of the book encourages thinking outside the box on library design. Beginning with an unusual visual Journey Map (table of contents), Mathews and Soistmann epitomize exploration of space as unique and without boundaries. The book engages librarians and administrators with invigorating text and intersperses Soistmann's black-and-white drawings and color renderings throughout. The book concludes with notes, references, and attributions, as well as acknowledgements.

Mathews suggests there is more to a physical library space than bricks and mortar, asking readers what library environments best inspire people and what spaces a library community needs. The author also challenges preconceived notions of what a library space must adhere to; boundaries are pushed and new physical spaces that inspire confidence and exude accomplishment are suggested. Section topics include the Importance of Place, Conceptual Transitions, and Well-Being.

The text broadens concepts of architecture with intellectual and stirring conviction using graphics that support the contention. The argument that providing space, collections, and service is no longer enough is supported by the case that library environments must be alive and changeable to accommodate the needs of the community. Mathews states "at its heart, the future of library buildings is rooted in stimulating the mind, and inviting people to pause, ponder, and produce" (154).

The book lacks concrete architectural designs but is successful as a springboard to facility development or expansion. *Encoding Space* is the spark to ignite conversation on how to best design engaging space. Mathews and Soistmann's publication tosses open the door to possibilities and provokes library staff and administration to imagine what an amazing space can bring to library users. This book ameliorates traditional ideas of how library design evolves and cleverly demonstrates the philosophy of library space as a catapult for great thinking. Highly recommended.—**Janis Minshull**

Library Instruction

S

231.   Buchanan, Heidi E., and Beth A. McDonough. **The One-Shot Library Instruction Survival Guide.** Chicago, American Library Association, 2014. 136p. index. $48.00pa. ISBN 13: 978-0-8389-1215-7.

What a wonderful little book this is. It has information to help new and seasoned librarians work better with teachers, manage time, and evaluate the success of lessons and programs. There is an extensive bibliography included to further reading as well. The chapters are easy to understand and have case scenarios to help the reader understand what the lesson would look like in practice. This book just might be the ticket to jump-start a ho-hum library program. An index rounds out the work.—**Catherine Vinson**

S

232.   Markgraf, Jill, Kate Hinnant, Eric Jennings, and Hans Kishel. **Maximizing the One-Shot: Connecting Library Instruction with the Curriculum.** Lanham, Md., Rowman & Littlefield, 2015. 188p. $55.00pa.; $54.99 (e-book). ISBN 13: 978-1-4422-3866-4; 978-1-4422-3867-1 (e-book).

This book is a case study of how university librarians collaborated with faculty to integrate information literacy instruction in a selected curriculum. The authors address the challenges of institutional reality, instructing students, and collaborating with faculty. They initially developed lessons for students in composition classes; their approach was expanded for science and nursing classes. The narrative explains lesson goals, planning processes, lesson activities, helping faculty understand the importance, scaffolding, and assessment. Selected worksheets, research guides, and less on study outlines are featured. The information will be helpful to high school and postsecondary librarians implementing a similar program.—**Mary Alice Anderson**

Library Management

P

233.   Bizzle, Ben, and Maria Flora. **Start a Revolution: Stop Acting Like a Library.** Chicago, American Library Association, 2015. 208p. illus. index. $52.00pa.; $46.80pa. (ALA members). ISBN 13: 978-0-8389-1267-6.

An excellent book written by Ben Bizzle and Maria Flora, two nonlibrarians for the benefit of all public libraries and librarians, it not only shows librarians how to introduce changes successfully in public libraries with the help of technology and effective teamwork, but also how to present the proposed changes to administrators, decision-makers, and the library board for approval. It is based on a practical and successful experience of a technology expert who changed the face of a library in five years—the library won a national award from the American Library Association. The book has eight well-written chapters including the "Digital Library"; "Going Mobile: Face Book Advertising"; "Marketing in the Real World"; "Making Pretty Pictures"; "Convincing the Decision Makers"; and "Start Your Own Revolution." It also includes three very practical Appendixes on "Twitter,""Pinterest," and "More Convincing the Decision Makers." Every chapter is full of information based on the practical experience of one author who successfully suggested changes to introduce technology in a public library in Arkansas, including a Website for the library and an online catalog and access to the library information and holdings through smart mobile phones, to attract successfully more readers and members to the library. It also discusses a successful marketing campaign using technology and traditional means of advertising to make the library more popular and attractive. Finally, the book discusses how the good teamwork of librarians, staff, and administrators can convince the Library Board, the decision makers, to approve the proposed changes in public libraries for the benefit of all users. This book is highly recommended for all public libraries in the United States.—**Ravindra Nath Sharma**

C, P, S

234.   Giesecke, Joan, Jon Cawthorne, and Deb Pearson. **Navigating the Future with Scenario Planning: A Guidebook for Librarians.** Chicago, American Library Association, Association of College and Research Libraries, 2015. 118p. $36.00pa. ISBN 13: 978-0-8389-8751-3.

To update her useful guide, *Scenario Planning for Libraries* (ALA, 1998), Joan Giesecke, former dean of libraries at the University of Nebraska-Lincoln, was joined by three experienced library administrators: Jon Cawthorne, West Virginia University; Deb Pearson, University of Nebraska-Lincoln; and Tyler Walters, Virginia Tech. Together they give readers the conceptual tools to develop multiple plausible futures as a basis for strategic planning. Scenarios for library planning sometimes come ready-made, such as the *ARL 2030 Scenarios: A User's Guide for Research Libraries* (Association of Research Libraries, 2010), *Futures Thinking for Academic Librarians: Higher Education in 2025* by David J. Staley and Kara J. Malenfant (ACRL, 2010), or scenarios developed by the library's parent institution. However, the authors of this book argue that adopting externally developed scenarios misses the benefits of organizational learning and leadership development that result from a full-fledged scenario planning process. In part one, four short chapters explain the theory and history of scenario planning and the steps in the process, including writing scenario stories (several more or less standard "plots" are described) and developing strategies based on the scenarios. While this isn't rocket science, if a library is going to engage in scenario planning, it is worth doing well. This overview is sufficient to inspire such an undertaking and to set planners on a firm path forward. Part two consists of five chapters, each exploring a different complementary topic. One chapter recommends the incorporation of other research methods into scenario planning and briefly explains the Delphi method, semistructured interviews, case studies, and stratified and purposive sampling. Another chapter reviews published scenarios on the future of higher education, research, and university libraries; this material is secondary to the book's central purpose but is nevertheless thought-provoking. A third chapter discusses the benefits of scenario planning for library leaders who strive to think deeply about organizational culture and to approach change creatively. The book concludes with two case studies. The first analyzes the responses of academic library human resources directors to scenarios that require changes in the workforce. The second revisits a case from the 1998 edition, where scenarios informed decision-making about the allocation of a student fee for information technology. The volume has a bibliography but no index. Although this book is slanted toward academic librarians' needs, scenarios can be a useful tool for public, school, and special librarians too. This book belongs in most professional collections, as well as libraries that support LIS education.—**Susan E. Searing**

C, P

235.   Hernon, Peter, Robert E. Dugan, and Joseph R. Matthews. **Managing with Data: Using ACRLMetrics and PLAmetrics.** Chicago, American Library Association, 2015. 216p. index. $85.00pa.; $76.50pa. (ALA members). ISBN 13: 978-0-8389-1243-0.

In these days of budgetary constraints, it is imperative that libraries present relevance, usefulness, and value to their stakeholders. In order to accomplish this, data and the methods in which to appropriately use the data need to be incorporated into the management process that guides the making of decisions and the application of policies. The purpose of *Managing with Data: Using ACRLMetrics and PLAmetrics* is to build a foundation for using these data services to foster the decision-making process to manage the facilities, collections, and services of the library.

The theme of the purposeful use of metrics in evidence-based management is developed in each of the 11 chapters to address the areas of concern of providing the resources and services to fit the needs of the institution (academic library) or community (public library). This book is a practical guide in gathering data from the appropriate data sets, compiling the data for the relevant study, and encouraging the reader to draw conclusions that can improve services, facilities, and collection development. Each chapter provides the opportunity to gain real experience through examples and exercises that utilize complimentary access to a subset of data from the two data services. This approach solidifies the ideas presented and encourages the reader to expand upon these themes to incorporate other sources of data to fashion a management process that addresses the mission and visions of the institution or the community. Libraries are localized to a community or institution, so this book does not aim to provide a set of standard analyses, but, by developing benchmarking and analysis of peer library best practices, strategies can be applied to improve efficiencies, services, and outcomes demonstrating relevance and value.

The book's coauthors bring many years of experience within the LIS management field and they have all been a part in award-winning publications concerning planning, assessment, evaluation, and management of libraries. This book would serve students in LIS masters programs studying library management as well as current and future department heads and directors in public and academic libraries looking to improve skills in assessment, decision-making, and communicating value to stakeholders.—**Lee Sochay**

C, P, S

236.   **Running a Small Library: A How-To-Do-It Manual for Librarians.** John A. Moorman, ed. Chicago, American Library Association, 2015. 276p. index. $80.00pa; $72.00pa. (ALA members). ISBN 13: 978-0-8389-1273-7.

This book was written to help administrators of small libraries run them. Small libraries are often run by individuals who did not train for the job of chief administrator. Small libraries are run with small budgets and small staffs. This book is written to help administrators of small libraries by providing explanations and best practices for the various operations of the library. The book consists of five parts (Introduction, Administration, Public Services, Collection Development, Computers and Automation) and a resource section. Each section is made up of chapters written by 14 library practitioners with expertise in the subject under discussion. Most chapters are 5-10 pages long and include a table of contents on the first page of the chapter. At the end of each chapter the author includes references and suggested further reading. Topics covered range from budget basics to book selection and weeding. The Sourcebook, completely updated from the first edition, contains lists of State Library Agencies, Book and Periodical Vendors, Library Furniture and Supply Vendors, Automation Vendors, Professional Organizations, and Professional Statements. Very brief biographies of the authors are included, followed by an index.

The information in the book is very basic. It would be most helpful to new administrators who come to the job with very little training or experience. It will also be useful to librarians taking on new duties in unfamiliar segments of library work. Recommended.—**Joanna M. Burkhardt**

Museum Studies

C

237.   Latham, Kiersten F., and John E. Simmons. **Foundations of Museum Studies: Evolving Systems of Knowledge.** Santa Barbara, Calif., Libraries Unlimited/ABC-CLIO, 2014. 155p. illus. index. $55.00pa. ISBN 13: 978-1-61069-282-3; 978-1-61069-952-5 (e-book).

As of early 2016 there are over 60 graduate degree programs in museum studies and museology in the United States, according to the American Alliance of Museums. This book is intended to serve as a core text for them. It is not a how-to manual for museum practitioners, but a classic introductory text that covers the history, structure, functions, and values of the field. The authors are well qualified to provide an overview of the field and its theoretical frameworks. Latham established the museum studies specialization within the School of Library and Information Science at Kent State University; like her coauthor Simmons, she has had a varied career in museum education and museum practice. Their combined experience spans history, science, and art museums; and both are published scholars. "Reality checks" highlighted in text boxes throughout the book draw on their experiences to illustrate the intersection of theory and practice. Following an introduction that defines "museum," discusses legal and ethical responsibilities of museums, explains what museum studies is, and outlines the historical development of museums, the core content is organized around the basic categories of how, what, who, where, and why. The "How" chapters examine museums through the lens of systems theory and explain their functions: preservation, which includes restoration, conservation, and collection management; research; and communication. The "What" chapters differentiate among types of museums and discuss their collections, focusing on what makes a museum object meaningful. As befits an LIS approach to museum studies, the authors ground this section in the concept of the "document" as articulated by Michael Buckland and

Suzanne Briet. The "Who" chapter on museum workers identifies over 30 different tasks fulfilled by employees or volunteers, while the chapter on museum users looks not just at demographics but also at users' varied reasons for visiting museums and the challenge of universal design. The "Where" chapter discusses the effects of globalization on museums, and the final "Why" chapter explores perceptions of museums' value to humanity now and in the future. This concise textbook is intended to be supplemented by additional readings. This is an essential purchase for libraries that support museum studies courses. Most general LIS collections should acquire a copy as well, because students are increasingly interested in how LIS concepts and skills can be applied beyond traditional employment in libraries. Readers looking for a more practical introduction to museum work might prefer the concise *Museums 101* by Mark Walhimer (Rowman & Littlefield, 2015) or the more substantial *Museum Basics,* 3rd ed., by Timothy Ambrose and Crispin Paine (Routledge, 2012).—**Susan E. Searing**

Readers' Advisory

P, S

238.   Alessio, Amy J. **Mind-Bending Mysteries and Thrillers for Teens: A Programming and Reader's Advisory Guide.** Chicago, American Library Association, 2014. 152p. index. $54.00pa. ISBN 13: 978-0-8389-1204-1.

This book offers an explanation of the mystery genre and all its subgenres of interest to teens. The author offers a cross-referenced annotated list of representative books in each subgenre, along with authors. While the lists are not exhaustive, the examples will get a YA or teen librarian up to speed quickly if he or she is not that familiar with mysteries. The author also includes booktalking examples and programming and marketing ideas. Also included is a book discussion guide over a variety of books. Titles are listed by subgenre and by author in the appendixes, making it easy to find something specific, and genres, titles, and authors are also listed in the index for quick reference.—**Richard Fanning**

P, S

239.   Cart, Michael, and Christine A. Jenkins. **Top 250 LGBTQ Books for Teens: Coming Out, Being Out, and the Search for Community.** Chicago, Huron Street Press/ American Library Association, 2015. 164p. illus. index. $21.95pa. ISBN 13: 978-1-937589-56-1.

The Top LGBTQ Books for Teens provides an annotated bibliography of the best fiction, graphic novels, and nonfiction for gay, lesbian, bisexual, transgender, and questioning teens in middle and high school, published for the most part since 1994. The authors formerly collaborated on *The Heart Has Its Reasons: Young Adult Literature with Gay/Lesbian/Queer Content, 1969-2004* (Scarecrow, 2006).

The current title opens by addressing the evolution of LGBTQ literature and the inclusion criteria, before presenting 195 titles from a variety of genres. The preface to this section includes an explanation of the codes given to each book in the bibliography, designed to help place the titles within the larger community of YA literature with LGBTQ content. HV stands for homosexual visibility, GA for gay assimilation, and QC for queer consciousness. The sections on graphic novels and nonfiction are followed by one on professional resources available to librarians, teachers, parents, counselors, and any adult who works with LGBTQ teens. An index rounds out this fine work that can be used to great effect by librarians at public, college, and middle/high school libraries.—**ARBA Staff Reviewer**

P, S

240.   Isaacs, Kathleen T. **Excellent Books for Early and Eager Readers.** Chicago, American Library Association, 2016. 264p. index. $52.00pa.; $46.80pa. (ALA members). ISBN 13: 978-0-8389-1344-4.

Isaacs's guide to intriguing works for young bibliophiles introduces transitional readers and classics by cover art, title, author, illustrator, publisher, and type as well as interest and reading level, for example, *The Librarian Who Measured the Earth* and *Where the Sidewalk Ends.* The selections reach back to old favorites as beloved as *D'Aulaires' Book of Greek Myths,* O'Brien's *Mrs. Frisby and the Rats of Nimh,* and Randall Jarrell and Maurice Sendak's *The Bat-Poet.* Beyond fiction, the compilation spotlights biographies of Louisa May Alcott and U.S. marshal Bass Reeves and nonfiction introductions to the Boston Tea Party, octopi, marsupials, dinosaurs, and Steve Jenkins's cross-category bestseller *The Animal Book.* Keys to the success of this work lie in its appealing book summaries and two-part indexing by title, author, and subjects as variant as the Galapagos Islands, Honus Wagner, and boarding schools. A must-have work for belabored public and school librarians and teachers, as well as home-schooling parents. Highly recommended— **Mary Ellen Snodgrass**

Reference Services

C, P

241.   **Reimagining Reference in the 21st Century.** David A. Tyckoson and John G. Dove, eds. Ashland, Ohio, Purdue University Press, 2014. 418p. (Charleston Insights in Library, Archival, and Information Sciences). $29.95pa. ISBN 13: 978-1-6124-9366-4; 978-1-5575-3698-3 (e-book).

"Is reference still a useful component of library services?" So begins this provocative and uber-current essay collection on one of the great questions of librarianship. Veteran librarian and reference scholar David Tyckoson teams with publishing consultant John Dove to assess the status of the reference service provided by librarians today and how it will be done in the future. Nine essays and 23 case studies are followed by Tyckoson and Dove's concluding "Where Do We Go From Here?" chapter. The core of this last is a list of key trends the editors see as critical to future reference and user services: 1) twenty-first-century literacies, 2) lifelong learning, 3) filter failure and filter success (an understanding of the "filters" necessary for modern information processing), 4) the hidden Web, 5) inclusivity, and 6) changing technology. The book is particularly noteworthy for chapters by Wikimedia Foundation board member (Phoebe Ayers), the general editor of ALA's Guide to Reference (Denise Bennett), and Jessica Moyer of the University of Milwaukee who proposes the combination of two traditional library services ("Readers' Advisory Services As Reference Services"). The case studies run the reference gamut: using LibraryThing for Libraries (https://www.librarything.com/forlibraries) as a discovery tool for patrons at a public library in Massachusetts, crowdsourcing reference, "peer reference" tutoring, 24/7 global virtual reference, embedded librarianship, and much more.

This title is published as part of Purdue's Charleston Insights in Library, Archival, and information Sciences series of Purdue University, overseen by Katina Strauch and Tom Gilson of the College of Charleston. The purpose of the series—like that of the Charleston Conference itself—is to provide a forum for discussion of issues of interest to librarians, publishers, and vendors. Likewise, the editors of this volume sought out contributions from all segments of the librarian and publishing community.—**Vincent Burns**

C, P

242.   **Reinventing Reference: How Libraries Deliver Value in the Age of Google.** Katie Elson Anderson and Vibiana Bowman Cvetkovic, eds. Chicago, American Library Association, 2015. 176p. index. $65.00pa.; $58.50pa. (ALA members). ISBN 13: 978-0-8389-1278-2; 978-0-8389-1286-7 (e-book).

The goal of Anderson's and Cvetkovic's book is to envision the future of the librarian profession and library reference services as libraries continue to face challenging times, and presumably become less relevant. In a conventional three-part format including nine chapters, the book's contributors present a deeper understanding of current trends in reference services and suggest how the future of these services will look based on historical events in the profession. In part one, contributors thoughtfully describe the history of reference, its professional standards and ethics, and the changes in reference services caused by advances in technology. Following in part two, writers provide descriptions of the current state of reference in academic, school, public, and special libraries; however, these chapters suffer from a lack of a consistent theme. Last of all, the writers in part three offer a vision for the future of libraries and, in particular, reference services. The first two chapters of part three offer useful discussions on topics ranging from the effects of digital rights management, artificial intelligence, crowd sourcing of information, and emerging technologies to descriptions of the seven categories of reference service "strategies." Part three's last chapter is quite optimistic by playfully outlining what reference services will look like in the year 2052. Finally, even though the editors recognized that the book would be out of date by the time it was published, the real value of the book will be found by library staff that isn't well versed in the historical and current trends of reference services. They should find this book as a good starting resource for the subject.—**Jennifer Brooks Huffman**

Research

C

243.   Roemer, Robin Chin, and Rachel Borchardt. **Meaningful Metrics: A 21st-Century Librarian's Guide to Bibliometrics, Altmetrics, and Research Impact.** Chicago, American Library Association, Association of College and Research Libraries, 2015. 241p. index. $60.00pa. ISBN 13: 978-0-8389-8755-1.

In the academic world of researchers citing each other to increase impact factors, predatory publishers, and administrators searching for faculty that will bring the most prestige to their departments, what metrics are meaningful and can they really be measured with certainty? Assessment is the bane of all educators in this day and age, and librarians are being asked to aid faculty and administrators to assess their impact on the scholarly world and their campus communities. At the same time, librarians and library administrators must be able to do this for their own work. Authors Robin Chin Roemer and Rachel Borchardt provide a variety of excellent sources and activities to help the student librarian as well as the experienced practicing academic librarian answer the question above. Covering information about bibliometrics (the traditional tracking of influence through numbers and sources of bibliographic citations) and altmetrics (tracing influence by using alternative, often Internet-generated methods), and providing understandable descriptions of core tools, this book will be of use to students and academic writers as well as by the librarians for whom it was written. The glossary at the end is helpful for all three groups and would be worth the space for the acronym definitions alone. The various tools highlighted throughout the book will be very useful to the new and experienced information professional. An index would be a nice addition to a second edition. This practical how-to guide would also be a great help to anyone expected to measure the impact of written material, be it scholarly, social, political, environmental, or beyond.— **Diane J. Turner**

Storytelling

C, P, S
244.   Freeman, Judy, and Caroline Feller Bauer. **The Handbook for Storytellers.** Chicago, American Library Association, 2015. 416p. $65.00pa.; $58.50pa. (ALA members). ISBN 13: 978-0-8389-1100-6.

Caroline Feller Bauer's groundbreaking *Handbook for Storytellers* (1977) was the definitive guide to library storytime programming until it was superseded by her *New Handbook for Storytellers* (1993). In collaboration with Bauer, who died in 2013, Judy Freeman has thoroughly revised, expanded, and split this classic into two separate works. (The companion volume, published simultaneously, is titled *The Handbook for Storytime Programs.* Freeman is a former school librarian, teacher of graduate courses in storytelling, and author of several books on storytelling and children's literature; anecdotes from her and Bauer's experiences with young listeners provide useful and amusing background. A third of the book deals with the basics of planning, publicizing, and conducting a storytelling event. Detailed practical information ranges from sources for purchasing puppets and other objects to augment storytime activities, to advice on avoiding common performance pitfalls. The other two-thirds highlight sources for stories. In a chapter on folklore, Freeman covers beast tales, trickster tales, humorous stories, pourquoi (how and why) stories, scary stories, fairy tales, fables, myths, and religious stories, following the model set out in Bauer's last edition. The subsequent chapter presents additional folk and fairy tales arranged by continent. A chapter titled "More Stories to Tell" is a grab bag of modern retellings and parodies of folk and fairy tales, literary tales, and biographical stories, plus a short section on crafting and telling family stories. The final chapter recommends Freeman's and Bauer's favorite storybooks, tags them by age level, and organizes the citations by subject. Here, and throughout the book, Freeman has significantly updated the source lists, eliminated most out-of-print titles, and provided one-sentence annotations for all entries. In addition, many illustrative stories are presented in their entirety, making this a handy first stop for anyone needing to quickly plan a story program. Although the book is aimed at beginning storytellers, even the most experienced tellers will be inspired and discover new sources because the handbook is brimming with ideas for engaging listeners through riveting tales, interactive play, props, and other techniques. Freeman writes in a fluent, conversational style, and the content is well organized, although the work would succeed better as a reference tool if its table of contents included the chapter subheadings. There are many books available on the art of storytelling. For example, many libraries already own the fourth edition of *Storytelling: Art and Technique,* by Ellin Greene and Janice M. Del Negro (see ARBA 2011, entry 597), which covers similar ground but overlaps less with *The Handbook for Storytellers* than one might expect. Both works belong in any public or school library with an active storytime program (ideally, one circulating copy and another for the librarians' bookshelf). Further, any academic institution that teaches storytelling to future librarians, K-12 teachers, or performers would do well to acquire this book and its companion volume.—**Susan E. Searing**

C, P, S
245.   Freeman, Judy, and Caroline Feller Bauer. **Handbook for Storytime Programs.** Chicago, American Library Association, 2015. 616p. index. $65.00pa.; $58.50pa. (ALA members). ISBN 13: 978-0-8389-1265-2.

The late Caroline Feller Bauer's *Handbook for Storytellers* (1977) and its revision, *New Handbook for Storytellers* (1993), influenced generations of youth services librarians, including Judy Freeman. Freeman (a former school librarian, teacher of storytelling, and herself the author of several books on storytelling and children's literature) collaborated with Bauer before her death to thoroughly update and expand the handbook, which they split into two distinct books. This volume focuses on library storytime programming for children and is divided into two parts. Part one, "Interactive Storytelling," covers the use of pictures and objects, puppetry, creative drama, music, magic, and so-called "fillers," such as fingerplays, tongue twisters, riddles, and rhymes. In addition to annotated lists of books and Websites for each technique, Freeman includes many ready-to-use examples and instructions. Part two is organized by audience level: preschool and primary school children (birth to age 7); and upper elementary and middle school children (ages 8 to 14). For the younger group, Freeman provides some 130 ideas for programs, alphabetically arranged by theme. The themes include familiar things in children's lives (e.g., bicycles, bullies, houses, pets, weather), holidays, real and fictional creatures, and concepts (e.g., honesty, resourcefulness, time). For each topic Freeman recommends several books to read aloud or retell, describes an appropriate activity, and includes a short poem. She also supplies lists of "the funniest picture books ever," Spanish-language stories, and professional books that contain additional storytime suggestions. For older children, Freeman reprints full stories of several types: stories about mysterious objects; narrative jokes; "think stories" that require the listeners to solve a puzzle; stories of the supernatural; funny stories; reinvented fairy tales; love stories; and tales about death. These are followed by briefer descriptions of 35 thematic programs, ranging from poetry slams, book clubs, and library scavenger hunts to hands-on programs about ice cream, mummies, and gardening. Each idea is accompanied by suggested activities and annotated book lists. Altogether, this volume recommends stories in approximately a thousand current books; it will save story-hunters enormous time and effort. Because the companion volume, published simultaneously with the title *The Handbook for Storytellers,* provides several hundred more sources for stories, along with tips for publicizing and conducting storytimes, the pair of volumes belong in both the circulating collection and the professional collection of nearly all public and school libraries. Freeman's fluent, conversational prose makes them enjoyable to read as well as to consult for practical storytime programming ideas.—**Susan E. Searing**

P, S

246.   MacMillan, Kathy, and Christine Kirker. **More Storytime Magic.** Chicago, American Library Association, 2016. 190p. illus. index. $52.00pa.; $46.80pa. (ALA members). ISBN 13: 978-0-8389-1368-0.

MacMillan and Kirker continue their successful formula for helping librarians and others who plan stories and activities for children aged two and up. Their previous works, also published by ALA Editions, include *Storytime Magic* (2008), *Kindergarten Magic* (2011), *Multicultural Storytime Magic* (2012), and *Baby Storytime Magic* (see ARBA 2014, entry 380). *More Storytime Magic* opens with a short chapter that lists practical tips for engaging young participants, aligning story programs with the Common Core educational standards for kindergarten (which are included in an appendix), and assuring that storytimes are accessible to children with special needs. The remaining 16 chapters focus on themes for programs: all about me; animals; around the world; at home; bugs and insects; concepts (e.g., colors, opposites); fairy tales and castles; family and friends; food; holidays and celebrations; the natural world; people in my neighborhood; play; school and library; sing and dance; transportation. For every theme, the authors offer several songs and poems with accompanying movements, craft activities, and directions for flannel board stories and games, each keyed to one or more of the Common Core standards. Altogether there are 268 activities, ranging in complexity but all simple enough for a novice storyteller to undertake. Each chapter concludes with a brief unannotated list of recommended picture books related to the theme. The book includes hundreds of small black-and-white drawings that can be enlarged as patterns for flannel board stories and craft projects, but most readers will find it easier to download full-sized drawings from http://alaeditions.org/Webextras/. MacMillan and Kirker round out the volume with an appendix listing over 30 resource books for storytime planners (primarily collections of tales and activities) and an index of authors, titles, and subjects. Youth librarians are always looking for new ideas to enliven story hours for repeat attendees, so this book is a welcome addition for public and school library professional collections.—**Susan E. Searing**

C, P, S

247.   **Storyteller's Sampler: Tales from Tellers around the World.** Margaret Read Macdonald, ed. Santa Barbara, Calif., Libraries Unlimited/ABC-CLIO, 2015. 185p. illus. index. $45.00pa. ISBN 13: 978-1-4408-3527-8; 978-1-4408-3528-5 (e-book).

Margaret Read MacDonald is a highly respected folklorist, storyteller, and author of more than 65 books. She has inspired many storytellers, especially children's librarians, to bring a global perspective to their craft. Since the 1990s, Libraries Unlimited has been in the forefront of publishing folktale collections in its World Folklore Series, which now numbers 40 volumes, each focused on a country or a culture. For this delightful sampler, MacDonald selected 54 tales from 30 of the series' volumes. The contents are presented alphabetically by country (e.g., Australia, Brazil, Russia), ethnic/cultural group (e.g., Hmong, Kurdish), or, in single instances, by a region (Siberia) and a continent (South America). Each chapter offers one or two stories, none longer than three pages. A typical story is accompanied by a citation to the original publication in the series, a brief list of similar stories, one or more suggestions for "playing with the story" using crafts or activities, and a short biography of the storyteller. The book's index allows for searching by topic or motif. Some of the stories echo tales that American children have heard before. For example, "Mother Frog and her Twelve Children," a Haitian story, shares plot elements and a moral with the story of the Little Red Hen, while the wood goblin in a Croatian story bears a strong resemblance to Rumplestiltskin. Most of these traditional tales, however, will be unfamiliar to American readers, and their charm lies in part in the glimpses they provide into other cultures. Libraries that possess all of the original volumes in the series will rightly view this new book as redundant, but it is worth acquiring as a one-stop source for beginning storytellers. It is highly recommended for public and school libraries without comprehensive storytelling collections and for academic libraries that support education and/or LIS curricula.—**Susan E. Searing**

Technical Services

C, P, S

248.   Sandstrom, John, and Liz Miller. **Fundamentals of Technical Service.** Chicago, American Library Association, 2015. 213p. index. (ALA Fundamentals Series). $64.00pa.; $57.60pa. (ALA members). ISBN 13: 978-1-55570-966-2.

This new book in the ALA Fundamentals Series is a gem for anyone in need of an excellent briefing on Library Technical Services work. The basic functions of Technical Services are described clearly and understandably yet with enough detail to be useful. The book can be used as a textbook, for independent study, or as a reference tool.

Library Technical Services departments have seen many changes in recent years and like all areas of the library, they have been required to do more with less and do it faster. This book covers the changes, stressing the importance of communication and workflow at all levels. Each of the eight chapters is organized with: an introduction, "Before You Begin," "Specialized Terms," concise paragraphs for the body of the chapter, "Trends & Issues," "Final Thoughts," and a bibliography. Examples of helpful boxes include: "Care and Feeding of Vendors," "Approval Plans," and "Tips for Running an Efficient Meeting." Workflow charts and tables are found throughout. The book's appendix, glossary, and index are all exemplary.

This handy book on what goes on in Technical Services is written by experienced librarians who share their insights with helpful comments such as: "materials vendors can be your best friends, make sure you talk to your business office, licenses should be reviewed very carefully, and cataloging should always focus on the needs of the library users." Any library would benefit from this practical and well-written tool.—**Georgia Briscoe**

Publishing and Bookselling

C, P

249.   Woll, Thomas. **Publishing for Profit: Successful Bottom-Line Management for Book Publishers.** 5th ed. Chicago, Chicago Review Press, 2014. 370p. index. $26.95pa. ISBN 13: 978-1-61374-973-9.

This fifth edition updates a book considered to be essential for those venturing into or already in the world of publishing. Since the first edition in 1998, the industry has undergone rapid change, most obviously the shift to digital; the entire publishing industry also faces new challenges, due largely to the availability of electronic information. While still concentrating on the business aspects of the industry, this title also includes updated publishing statistics and figures, a new profit and loss form that reflects the need to view print sales and e-book sales separately, a focus on metadata, and a discussion of digital formats. This handbook is directed at a practicing publishing firm, but can be utilized by anyone interested in the publishing industry.

Publishing for Profit is divided into three parts: "The World of Publishing," "Managerial Organization: Strategy and Techniques," and "Functional Organization: Strategy and Techniques," with chapters on such topics as cash flow, creating a board of directors, cash and accounts receivable, editorial acquisition, contracts, production schedules, sales, subsidiary rights, publishing software, and electronic publishing and marketing. Valuably, this title also has a number of lists and forms, including a publishing timeline, an organization chart, a production checklist, a basic marketing plan worksheet, and a book club pricing template.—**ARBA Staff Reviewer**

12 Military Studies

General Works

Atlases

C, P, S
250.   Messenger, Charles. **The D-Day Atlas: Anatomy of the Normandy Campaign.** 2d ed. New York, Thames and Hudson, 2014. 176p. illus. maps. index. $24.95pa. ISBN 13: 978-0-500-29119-1.

The book is the second edition of the original published in 2004, and is now issued in paperback. The author, author of over 40 books on World War II, says in the preface that the volume is a straightforward account of what occurred rather than an in-depth study. But I would argue that it is the very best source that the interested lay person or a student could consult. The narrative is crisp and contains just the right amount of detail. However, the huge number of large color maps are what distinguish the volume. An abundance of photographs augment the narrative and maps. The volume is divided into five chapters—planning and preparation, fortress Europe, D-Day, the beachhead battles, and the post-invasion break out. The brief epilogue sums up the operation and its role in leading ultimately to V-E Day. Appendixes include code words connected with D-Day, diagrams of both the Allied High Command and the German High Command in June 1944, the divisions of all participants that fought in Normandy, a brief bibliography of some of the most useful studies of the event, and an index. At its very modest price for the high quality, glossy paperback, this is a book worthy of all libraries.—**Joe P. Dunn**

Dictionaries and Encyclopedias

P, S
251.   Tucker, Spencer C. **Wars That Changed History: 50 of the World's Greatest Conflicts.** Santa Barbara, Calif., ABC-CLIO, 2015. 609p. maps. index. $100.00. ISBN 13: 978-1-61069-785-9; 978-1-61069-786-6 (e-book).

As the author states in his preface "wars both fascinate and repel us." The esteemed encyclopedist Dr. Spencer Tucker gives his readers in *Wars that Changed History* everything a good encyclopedia should—the essential facts, clarity, and brevity. By using the selection criterion—that the included wars must have had "major impact on subsequent historical development, rather than being significant for costs, destruction, or new weapons" the reader is given a broad look at wars that traverse world geography from China to Mexico and time from 1479 B.C.E. to 2011.

For each war, Dr. Tucker goes over the causes, the course of the conflict, and the historical significance. A list of further reading accompanies each entry. Additionally, each war has a box with dates, locations, combatants, principal commanders, principal battles, and the outcome. Some even have maps.

The following are some of the many wars treated in this volume: The Peloponnesian Wars; The Punic Wars; The Qin Wars of Unification; Charlemagne's War; The Norman Conquest; The Thirty Years War; The War of Austrian Succession; The Napoleonic Wars; The Wars of Italian Unification; The American Civil War; The Russo-Japanese War; The Korean War; and the Iraq War.—**Scott R. DiMarco**

C, S
252.   **U.S. Conflicts in the 21st Century.** Spencer C. Tucker, ed. Santa Barbara, Calif., ABC-CLIO, 2016. 3v. illus. maps. index. $310.00/set. ISBN 13: 978-1-4408-3878-1; 978-1-4408-3879-8 (e-book).

Spencer C. Tucker, the master of military encyclopedias, offers another addition to his lengthy list of such volumes. Although it has a different name, in many ways this is an updated, leaner edition of Tucker's earlier five-volume *Encyclopedia of Middle Eastern Wars* (2010). Many of the entries are the same or updated from the previous publication. The difference is that the former encyclopedia was written while the wars were still in progress so the entries were interim reports. Also the earlier publication was more detailed with entries on all the countries and most of the military units involved. This latest encyclopedia has the advantage of addressing topics from the perspective of the supposed aftermath of the wars. Of course, none of the conflicts treated are really over in any substantive way.

No one does reference works better than ABC-Clio, and the military volumes employ a common model—lists of entries, documents, and maps; followed by preface, lengthy and valuable introduction essays, general maps, and the substantive essays themselves. As always, the entries are first-class. Appendixes include documents, chronology, glossary, bibliography, contributors, and an index.

These reference sources are excellent, expensive, and never-ending. Tucker's next volume, *The Roots and Consequences of 20th-Century Warfare: Conflicts That Shaped the Modern World,* which will overlap and duplicate some entries in the volumes discussed here, will be published later in 2016. Libraries have hard decisions concerning which of this array of encyclopedias to acquire.—**Joe P. Dunn**

Handbooks and Yearbooks

C, P
253.   Dixon, Jeffrey S., and Meredith Reid Sarkees. **A Guide to Intra-state Wars: An Examination of Civil, Regional, and Intercommunal Wars, 1816-2014.** Thousand Oaks, Calif., CQ Press / Sage, 2016. 801p. index. (Correlates of War Series). $175.00. ISBN 13: 978-0-8728-9775-5.

A Guide to Intra-State Wars: An Examination of Civil, Regional, and Intercommunal Wars, 1816-2014 is the latest volume in CQ Press' Correlates of War Series, which includes

Douglas Gibler's *International Military Alliances, 1648-2008* (see ARBA 2010, entry 629) and *Resort to War, 1816-2007* by Meredith Reid Sarkees and Frank Whelon Wayman (see ARBA 2011, entry 622). The authors of the respective volumes are all affiliated with the Correlates of War Project (COWP), which is dedicated to the study of warfare using quantitative data and scientific methodology.

The first two chapters introduce the reader to the methodology utilized in the work. The first, "The Correlates of War Project," details the nine different types of conflicts officially recognized by the COWP. The second chapter focuses specifically on the minutia of intra-state conflicts. Of particular importance are the distinctions that differentiate between civil, regional, and inter-communal wars. Also included is a breakdown and explanation of each component of an entry, which include: the assigned number of the conflict, the name(s) by which the war is known, participants, dates, battle-related deaths, initiator, outcome, war type, total system member military personnel, theater armed forces, antecedents, narrative, termination and outcome, coding decisions, and sources.

The heart of the work is found in the remaining six chapters, entitled "Intra-state Wars in North America," "Intra-state Wars in South America," "Intra-state Wars in Europe," "Intra-state Wars in the Middle East and North Africa," "Intra-state Wars in Asia and Oceania," and "Intra-state Wars in Sub-Saharan Africa." More than 400 conflicts are covered, beginning with the First Caucasus War of 1818 to 1822 to the ongoing Ukraine Separatists War that erupted in 2014. The work concludes with an appendix entitled "List of All Intra-state Wars in Chronological Order," an extensive bibliography, and an index. Since information about many of the conflicts included in this work is hard to locate, academic and large public libraries should definitely consider acquiring this work, especially if their constituencies include historians or political scientists.—**John R. Burch Jr.**

C, P, S

254.   Hughes-Wilson, John, and Nigel Steel. **The First World War in 100 Objects.** New York, Firefly Books, 2014. 448p. illus. maps. $39.95. ISBN 13: 978-1-77085-413-0.

Another entry in the "object analysis" genre of book launched by the 2011 Viking Press title, *A History of the World in 100 Objects,* by Neil MacGregor of the British Museum, Firefly's *The First World War in 100 Objects* stands out from similar titles with a compelling narrative organization and a strong selection of images. Suitable for high school, college undergraduates, and general readers, this collection consists of color images of 100 objects from the First World War accompanied by analysis of the specific object and the broader historical context associated with it. A photo of an aerial camera leads to a broader discussion about British intelligence during the war, for example. The connections drawn between the specific objects and bigger picture analysis of the war are fascinating, leading the reader to consider multiple aspects: social, political, economic, military, and more. A particular strength of the work is the chronological organization and narrative thread that runs through the entries. While some "objects" books tend toward thematic (or even more random) selections, this one's chronological structure tells the story of the war in a distinctive way. Most of the images are from the collections of the Imperial War Museums in the United Kingdom, and as a result, there is a definite U.K. emphasis here; more entries from France, Germany, and elsewhere would have provided a more diverse collection. The opening Contents pages list all of the objects with individual entry number, page number, and a phrase that indicates the broader theme that is connected to the object. Backmatter includes a collection of maps illustrating various phases and battles of the war, a list of further reading on the First World War, and an index.—**David Tipton**

C, P, S
255.   **Pearl Harbor: The Essential Reference Guide.** Spencer C. Tucker, ed. Santa Barbara, Calif., ABC-CLIO, 2015. 274p. index. $89.00. ISBN 13: 978-1-4408-3718-0; 978-1-4408-3719-7 (e-book).

Seventy-four years after the Pearl Harbor attack, this catastrophic event remains a focal point in U.S. diplomatic, military, and political history which has received renewed attention in light of the December 2, 2015, Islamist terrorist attack in San Bernardino, California. This reference guide provides detailed coverage of the personalities, weapons, and events resulting in the Japanese attack on Pearl Harbor and its consequences.

This work describes the December 7, 1941, attack and it features an alphabetically arranged list of entries on this attack covering such topics as the *USS Arizona* navy battleship and memorial, Cordell Hull, Japanese Americans, Husband Edward Kimmel, Japanese and U.S. Pacific Theater naval strengths, the Pearl Harbor Survivors Association, radar, Rainbow Plans, the United States' Two-Ocean Navy Program, and Isoroku Yamamato. A second section includes the transcripts of oral history interviews with attack survivors such as *USS Maryland* seaman Edmund R. Chappell; Nurse Corps Lieutenant Ruth Erickson from the Pearl Harbor Naval Hospital; and Honolulu Fire Department firefighter Frederick Kealoha.

A third section includes primary source documents from participating governments such as the March 27, 1933, Japanese announcement of their withdrawal from the League of Nations; President Roosevelt's October 5, 1937, quarantine speech in Chicago; notes from a September 19, 1940, Imperial Conference in Japan seeking to work with Germany to achieve greater U.S. and British concessions to Japan in East Asia; a December 6, 1941, letter from Roosevelt to Emperor Hirohito; a memorandum from the Japanese government to the United States breaking off diplomatic relations on the same day; and Roosevelt's December 8, 1941, address to a joint congressional session asking for a declaration of war.

A final section discusses the enduring political controversy and historiographical debate over whether Roosevelt and the U.S. government were responsible for the Pearl Harbor attack, citing relevant historical literature on this topic. This section also addresses what might have happened if there had been a second Japanese strike on Hawaii and whether the Axis Powers contributed to their defeat by failing to coordinate their objectives and cooperate against the United States and its allies. It concludes with a chronology of events starting with the 1921-1922 Washington Naval Conference and ending with the December 23, 1941, capture of Wake Island by Japanese forces.

This is a valuable work which will benefit users in all libraries desirous of understanding the causes and consequences of Pearl Harbor. Many of the factors contributing to this tragedy remain present today in the military and intelligence preparation of multiple nations against current and emerging national and international security threats. Highly recommended!—**Bert Chapman**

C, P, S
256.   **Understanding U.S. Miltary Conflicts through Primary Sources.** Arnold, James R. and Roberta Wiener, eds. Santa Barbara, Calif., ABC-CLIO, 2015. 4v. index. $415.00/ set. ISBN 13: 978-1-61069-933-4; 978-1-61069-934-1 (e-book).

Editors Arnold and Wiener (noted authors of several history and journal editors) provide the reader with a unique and special tool—the ability to examine in a collected and organized manner the primary documents from United States military conflicts. While this may sound like no big deal, it is in fact, a time-saving resource. This four-volume set is extraordinary in not only its detail, but chronological organization. Starting with the American Revolution and ending with the War in Iraq, each major American conflict is represented and has a brief introductory essay; a timeline; individual primary source documents; and a bibliography.

A typical example is the sixth document of the American Revolution in volume two— "George Washington: Instructions to General Sullivan, May 31, 1779." Over two pages the reader is given the context of the document; the actual words of the document; and analysis to inform the reader of the consequences of this order.

This resource is well-researched, easy to use, and affordable. Highly recommended.—**Scott R. DiMarco**

C, P, S

257. **Veterans History Project. http://www.loc.gov/vets/** [Website] Free. Date reviewed: 2016.

This project was started in 2000 by the United States Congress in order to help future generations understand the realities of war. The project aims to collect, preserve, and make accessible the personal accounts of American war veterans who participated in major wars and conflicts. In addition to veterans, U.S. civilians who were actively involved in supporting war efforts may be found in the project database, including industry workers, USO workers, flight instructors, and medical volunteers.

An Experiencing War tab at the top of the page provides firsthand accounts of war in the form of audio, video, photos, and text. The Database tab allows users to search for veterans by name, service, rank, or ID number. In addition, users can limit the search by conflict or era, branch of service, gender, and type of material. A few veterans have published memoirs relating to their war experiences, and these can be found under the View Digitized Collection tab after a search is conducted. This is an excellent resource for upper-grade students studying wars and conflicts who are in need of primary sources. The majority of the material on this Website is easy to read and informative. Students will benefit from reading memoirs and articles, and may even be able to locate friends and relatives previously in service. It is a recommended resource.—**ARBA Staff Reviewer**

Navy

C, P

258.   Smith, Myron J., Jr. **Civil War Biographies from the Western Waters.** Jefferson, N.C., McFarland, 2015. 329p. illus. maps. index. $75.00pa. ISBN 13: 978-0-7864-6967-3; 978-1-4766-1698-8 (e-book).

Myron J. Smith, Jr., Director of the Library and Professor at Tusculum College, has authored a number of books on how the Civil War was fought on the waters of the Cumberland, Mississippi, Ohio, and Tennessee Rivers, including *The Fight for the Yazoo, August 1862-July 1864: Swamps, Forts and Fleets on Vicksburg's Northern*

Flank (McFarland, 2012) and *Tinclads in the Civil War: Union Light-Draught Gunboat Operations on Western Waters, 1862-1865* (McFarland, 2010). His latest reference on that theater of conflict contains biographies of 956 individuals from both the Union and the Confederacy. The majority of the individuals profiled were military officers that held at least the rank of mate. The remaining entries focus on politicians, civilians that played a role in the war effort, Congressional Medal of Honor winners, or individuals who authored accounts of their experiences.

Most of the entries, which are alphabetically arranged, include the subject's date of birth and death, information about their lives before the outbreak of war, the name of the unit or boat on which they served, an account of their wartime experiences, and, if they survived, their postwar career. Some also include a portrait or photograph. The entries conclude with bibliographic information from sources such as *The War of the Rebellion: A Compilation of the Official Records of the Union and Confederate Armies* (Government Printing Office, 1880-1901) and *Official Records of the Union and Confederate Navies in the War of the Rebellion* (Government Printing Office, 1894-1922). The text is supplemented by three appendixes: "Individuals by Organization," "Campaigns, Battles, and Engagements," and "Ship Registers." The work concludes with a bibliography and index. This work fills an obvious gap in the historiography concerning the Civil War and should be acquired by libraries supporting research collections on United States history.—**John R. Burch Jr.**

Weapons and Equipment

C, P, S

259.   Levy, Joel. **Fifty Weapons That Changed the Course of History.** New York, Firefly Books, 2014. 224p. illus. index. $29.95. ISBN 13: 978-1-77085-426-0.

Weaponry, like fashion, has always fascinated history lovers as an iconic time-stamp of an era. The longbow may mark medieval times the same way the atomic bomb may mark the nuclear age. This well-designed book takes a respectful and efficient look at 50 important weapons produced throughout history and shows how even a relatively basic piece of technology can play a role in the greater historical narrative.

From stone axes to robots, the book chronologically presents the weapons via a descriptive essay preceded by an introductory page. This page contains an illustration of the weapon juxtaposed with a number of visually engaging reference points, which may include a contextual quote, the year of the weapon's peak usage, type of weapon, name of weapon inventor, and type of impact the weapon had upon its time (from a choice of social, political, technical, and tactical).

Descriptive essays touch on a weapon's evolution, statistics, significant moment(s) in history, and more. It is interesting to see how even minor changes to a basic weapon design (e.g., the sword), can have a major impact. It is also interesting to note the inclusion of some unexpected weapon choices (e.g., the stirrup) among the 50 covered. Evocative photographs and illustrations accompany the essays. Some illustrations may highlight a weapon's design, exposing its technical make up and abilities.

While certainly not meant to be comprehensive, the book succeeds in educating readers on this very select slice of history through its knowledgeable but concise narrative and visually intriguing style. The book also includes ideas for further research and an index that facilitates quick searches.—**ARBA Staff Reviewer**

C, P
260.   Tucker, Spencer C. **Instruments of War: Weapons and Technologies that Have Changed History.** Santa Barbara, Calif., ABC-CLIO, 2015. 428p. illus. index. $89.00. ISBN 13: 978-1-4408-3654-1; 978-1-4408-3655-8 (e-book).

Military conflicts throughout history have seen combatant nations and groups produce, refine, and modify weapons to meet desired military objectives. This compendium by a prominent and prolific historian seeks to introduce readers to many historically significant weapons and technologies.

It begins with a listing of chronologically arranged entries and an alphabetical listing of profiled weapons. An introduction describes the historical evolution of weapons while also mentioning that this work contains descriptions of 270 weapons systems and technologies and 25 sidebars documenting how these weapons have been used in military tactics.

Weapons systems and technologies covered in this compendium include dagger (knife), shields, trireme, land mines and mining, steam warship, Dahlgren guns, poison gas, Molotov cocktail, radar, hydrogen bomb, Ohio-class U.S. Navy submarines, and unmanned aerial vehicles. Entries for each of these works are succinctly written and feature bibliographic citations. Sidebars are presented for topics as varied as Attempt to Assassinate Napoleon I (1800), Torpedo Attack at Taranto (1940), First Successful Use of Poison Gas (1915), and the English ship *Mary Rose* (1509-1545).

The work concludes with detailed bibliographic references.

This work serves as a very helpful introduction to undergraduates and public library users interested in introductory information on the origins of world weapons systems. It could be strengthened further with coverage of directed energy weapons, cyber warfare, suicide bombers, missile defense systems such as the U.S.' Patriot and Israel's Iron Dome, and emerging military uses of space besides satellites.—**Bert Chapman**

13 Political Science

General Works

Dictionaries and Encyclopedias

C, P, S

261. **Encyclopedia of Modern Ethnic Conflicts.** 2d ed. Joseph R. Rudolph, Jr., ed. Santa Barbara, Calif., ABC-CLIO, 2015. 2v. index. $189.00/set. ISBN 13: 978-1-61069-552-7; 978-1-61069-553-4 (e-book).

The second edition of the *Encyclopedia of Modern Ethnic Conflicts* provides the college and university student with an up–to-date resource on late-twentieth- and early-twenty-first-century struggles between neighbors of differing identities. Indeed, 12 years have passed since the publication of the first edition and the revisions and additions to this new edition reflect how the world of ethnic conflict has changed over this period of time. The case studies for nations and regions that have changed borders and names have been updated, while other conflicts that have become more heated and global in scope have been added. For example, the Soviet Union is no longer a political entity in name, but its legacy can be read about in the case studies about Georgia and Armenia. Case studies added include conflicts pertaining to Guatemala, Kenya, and Christians in the Middle East to name a few. Generally the editor has attempted to include conflicts that have ongoing political importance in the twenty-first century. Given its ambitious scope—case studies cover conflicts in all continents with the exception of Australia—the encyclopedia cannot be comprehensive. Still, the articles reflect the variety of conflicts that derive from ethnonationalism and will provide the student with a solid understanding of the global ethnic conflicts that persist today.

The expanded room (from one to two volumes) allows for 44 case studies written by contributors of both genders from nine countries (Australia, Canada, England, Lebanon, Nigeria, Puerto Rico, Turkey, Wales, and the United States), all of whom are political scientists or have experience in military efforts and diplomacy in these areas. These case studies are alphabetically arranged, according to the country in which the given conflict takes place. For example, conflicts concerning Kurdish people are located in "Iraq: The Progress of the Kurdish movement in Iraq" and "The Middle East: The Kurds' Struggle for Kurdistan." The volumes no longer contain maps, but each one features the introduction, and there is an index at the end of the second.

Using the table of contents or index to locate a particular ethnic group as a topic for research, one first sees a timeline of events framing the conflict to be discussed in the case study. The case study then provides the following elements: a short introduction, which starts immediately after the timeline and does not have a heading; historical background; the conflict itself; the management of the conflict; and its significance. Most case studies also provide extensive end notes, suggested readings, and appendixes with primary source material. On the whole, this encyclopedia is recommended for colleges, universities, and other libraries supporting additional research of this kind.—**Amy Koehler**

C, P, S
262.   **Encyclopedia of Social Media and Politics.** Kerric Harvey, ed. Thousand Oaks, Calif., Sage, 2014. 3v. illus. index. $485.00/set. ISBN 13: 978-1-4522-4471-6.

This 1,500-page set explores the role, impact, and importance of social media in the realm of politics, both in the United States and the rest of the world. Entries such as Arab Spring, Middle East, China, and Latin America reflect the international scope of this work. Some of the entries will resonate more with younger readers of this work: Digg, Clicktivism, Vlogging, Ushahidi, etc. These articles, however, clearly present the importance of these "Web 2.0" sites and terms. Entries run from one to eight pages, with suggestions for further readings provided. Additional resources for users include a chronology, a glossary, a resource guide (bibliography) of books, journals, and Websites, a list of social media use by all 535 members of Congress, and an 80-page index.

Organized along the same clean lines as a number of other Sage encyclopedias published recently, the set (also available online) will be welcomed in public and academic libraries, as well as in many high school libraries, if they can afford it.—**Mark Schumacher**

Handbooks and Yearbooks

C
263.   **Global HIV/AIDS Politics, Policy, and Activism: Persistent Challenges and Emerging Issues.** Raymond A. Smith, ed. Santa Barbara, Calif., Praeger/ABC-CLIO, 2013. 3v. index. $194.00/set. ISBN 13: 978-0-313-39945-9; 978-0-313-39946-6 (e-book).

Emerging in the 1980s, AIDS and its parent virus HIV grabbed global headlines and sent fear through entire communities. Since then evolving awareness plus great strides in diagnoses and treatments have quieted the fear as well as the conversation and yet salient concerns remain. This comprehensive three-volume book contains contributions from an international network of thinkers working opposite the medical side of the HIV/AIDS conversation. Specifically, it presents 45 original essays covering the base politics, policies, and activism merging to drive the HIV/AIDS discussion forward.

Volume one–Politics and Government, discusses the politics of HIV prevention and treatment at international, national, and regional levels, and includes essays spotlighting several nations' successes (e.g., Brazil's "strategic internationalization") and failures (e.g., the infiltration of prejudice into crisis response), as well as the difficulties of creating national HIV prevention strategies.

Volume two–Policy and Policymaking, also addresses the range between international level and regional level policy debates, and includes topics concerning how policy shifts regarding Intellectual Property Rights can affect treatment costs and accessibility, how China tends to "exceptionalize" HIV/AIDS versus other communicable diseases in contrast to most other nations, and more.

Volume three–Activism and Community Mobilization, takes readers into the trenches of the HIV/AIDS discussion and includes pieces highlighting activism and its relationship to such issues as funding, education, and research. The volume notes the particular need for activists to pursue their agendas in countries such as Sudan where data is limited on program efficacy, and adapt to treatment program successes as part of a longer term public health movement, and much more.

The set shares solid biographical information about contributors, who range in expertise from university professor to advocate, and offers a truly eclectic mix of well-researched topics orbiting the HIV/AIDS sphere. Meticulously compiled, this set is an essential reference for anyone studying health epidemics, healthcare advocacy, policy-making, and more. Recommended for academic libraries.—**Laura Herrell**

C

264.   **InfoSci-Government Science and Technology. http://www.igi-global.com/e-resources/infosci-subject-databases/infosci-government/.** [Website] Hershey, Pa., Information Science Reference/IGI Global. Price negotiated by site. Date reviewed: 2016.

The *InfoSci-Government Science and Technology* database provides full-text access to over 100 e-books on government science and technology issues as they relate to and impact governmental issues around the world. This academic reference collection represents the scholarly research conducted on such topics as e-government, digital citizenship, law and policy, and social media uses and application—to name a few. Theoretical views (such as ethical considerations) as well as applied technical information (such as the engineering of structural control systems) are included.

The database provides three different research options including basic, advanced, and expert. The advanced search accommodates searches for full-text, keyword, title, author, DOI, and publication date. The "expert" search option allows search terms to be excluded, included, and/or weighted. While this is interesting, it may not be heavily used, especially in a collection of this size.

Each full e-book has an annotated table of contents to facilitate ease of use and browsability. The collection has also been indexed and is searchable at the chapter level. Each book and chapter has a search box to help drill down to an even more granular level. Book chapters are provided in XML and PDF format for easy download. The database also provides the tools for citing the books and book chapters.

Lawmakers, policy-makers, and anyone with technical service responsibilities at any level of government should know about this collection. Researchers in any of these fields as well as political and social scientists will find value in this collection. The titles are current, relevant, and timely. It is recommended as a source of authoritative and academic information the applications, implications, and impacts of technology and government.— **Kristin Kay Leeman**

P, S

265.   **The Politics Book: Big Ideas Simply Explained.** New York, DK Publishing, 2013. 352p. illus. index. $25.00; $9.99 (e-book). ISBN 13: 978-1-4654-0214-1; 978-1-4654-4107-2 (e-book).

"All men are created equal" wrote Thomas Jefferson in 1776. While sounding simple, these five words were both the culmination of a simmering resentment toward the British monarchy and a launching point towards proclaiming the universal rights of individuals. *The Politics Book: Big Ideas Simply Explained* is a wonderful collection of similarly challenging concepts that impacted contemporary and future societies around the world.

Seven sections, ranging from Ancient Political Thought to Postwar Politics highlight over one hundred "big ideas" and the thinkers behind them. Touching on philosophy ("What is a Woman?"), religion ("The objective of Islamic jihad is to eliminate the rule of an un-Islamic system"), militarism ("Political power grows out of the barrel of a gun"), and more, each idea receives a succinct yet robust explanation as well as historical background. The entries are conveyed chronologically, which helps readers trace idea development and influence. For example, the book clearly links the rise of communism to ideas germinating in 380 B.C.E. (Plato), sprouting throughout the nineteenth century (Hegel, Marx) and reaching full bloom in the twentieth (Lenin, Guevara, etc.). Shaded sidebars offer a timeline that puts each idea "In Context," reflecting its ideology, focus, and effects both before and after an idea's introduction to society. For example, in conveying Marsilius of Padua's medieval belief in secularism, we can refer to the crowning of Charlemagne as the Holy Roman Emperor five centuries prior as well as to Martin Luther's criticism of the Catholic Church 200 years after.

The design of the book is striking—large bold typeface demands that readers pay attention to each leading idea. Equally eye-catching graphics artistically render the essence of each concept, e.g., a silhouette of three climbers ascending a sharp black mountain peak via Friedrich Nietzsche's "will to power." The entries are cross-referenced and may include color illustrations, key works from notable thinkers, and clarifying diagrams of sometimes complex ideas.

The book includes a directory to provide additional information surrounding figures (George Washington, Adolf Hitler, etc.) who played a role in executing some of the "big ideas" but were not mentioned in their corresponding chapter. It also employs a generous glossary as well as section overviews, timelines, and an index. This dynamic book is a must read for any student of political science, history, philosophy and more. Highly recommended, especially given its price of $25.00 for a sturdy hardback title.—**Laura Herrell**

C

266.   **Research Handbook on Climate Governance.** Karen Bäckstrand and Eva Lövbrand, eds. Northampton, Mass., Edward Elgar, 2016. 640p. index. $335.00. ISBN 13: 978-1-78347-059-4.

This timely and readable compendium of research on global efforts to combat climate change was proposed at Edward Elgar in 2013 and completed just a few months before the Paris climate summit in December 2015. Climate governance became a research topic only in the 1990s, and since that time has proliferated in response to increasing efforts to find a solution to humankind's effect on the changing climate. Editors Karin Bäckstrand (Professor of Environmental Social Science, Stockholm University) and Eva Lövbrand (Centre for Climate Change and Policy Research, Linköping University) have assembled 50 articles from 77 contributors, chiefly from Europe and the United States, representing a broad range of expertise and opinion. The seven parts of the book cover the theories, processes, and sites of climate governance, the relationship to climate governance of the state and of nonstate agents and institutions, the technologies and normative ideals of climate governance, and the future of climate governance. Among the many topics discussed are climate leadership in China, the United States, the European Union, and Brazil, the North-South divide on climate change governance, low-carbon economies, carbon accounting, environmental democracy, and reform options. Every chapter comes to one or more conclusions and is followed by notes and a bibliography. The book also has a list of figures and tables and a comprehensive index. This volume will serve as a valuable resource for students, policy-makers, and citizens concerned about the environment; recommended.—**ARBA Staff Reviewer**

C, P, S

267.   Roth, Christopher F. **Let's Split: A Complete Guide to Separatist Movements and Aspirant Nations, from Abkhazia to Zanzibar.** Sacramento, Calif., Litwin Books, 2015. 626p. illus. maps. index. $75.00. ISBN 13: 978-1-936117-99-4.

Political change is ongoing throughout the world, constantly evolving over time and place. Groups want to remake countries, split into separate countries, areas want autonomy, states want borders changed, groups and individuals want sovereignty of local areas, or even social space on the Internet. All of these varying desires for a political rework of the current status are covered in this volume on separatist movements around the world. The author, who is a social-cultural and linguistic anthropologist, presents the material in a readable and enjoyable manner with a touch of humor thrown in for fun. Some users may question some of the implied humor depending on the user's place in the current political debate spectrum. This may say more to the user's apprehensions of objectivity than the author's political biases or neutrality in researching the volume.

Arranged by geographic region, starting in northern Europe and advancing eastward around the world, and subregion, if discussing a particular country or area, the work has a lengthy introduction to the region and country followed by the various political or organized groups desiring to split, the background and history to the movement, any territorial claims made in connection with the split, population affected by the split, images of flags associated with the group or movement, and prospects of current or future success. Maps for each section also help to explain the geopolitics discussed in the text. A selected bibliography grouped by region appears at the end. The work also has an extensive keyword index to round out the volume.

The volume will be useful in any academic, public, or high school library collection. Substantially bound, the work should withstand extended use by patrons. The information contained within will age faster than the binding itself. A planned update edition will be of importance to keep the information current with the fluid nature of political events around the globe.—**Gregory Curtis**

P, S

268.   **World Political Yearbook, 2016.** Hackensack, N.J., Salem Press, 2016. 900p. maps. $125.00. ISBN 13: 978-1-61925-952-2.

This first edition of the *World Political Yearbook* from Salem Press publishes information on 233 national entities, grouped by regions: Africa; The Americas; Asia (including Russia, Australia and New Zealand); Europe; and the Middle East. The publisher's note informs us that the book "profiles every nation and self-governing territory around the world with material from the critically acclaimed *Nations of the World: A Political, Economic, and Business Handbook* by Grey House Publishing." The cover, introduction, and format are copyrighted by Grey House. Political, economic, and ethnographic data are given for each country, with the emphasis on the power structure, security issues, and, especially, the economy. Each entry has a country map and a highlighted box of "Key Indicators" such as population, GDP, unemployment, exports, imports, and trade balance. Each also has a box of "Key Facts" (official name, head of state, head of government, ruling party, area, population, capital, official language, currency, exchange rate, and more) and concludes with a political and economic risk assessment; for Muslim nations, there is also a highlighted box giving the percentage of Sunni and Shi'a Muslim inhabitants. There is little to no information on the cultural heritage of any nation, but a great deal on its security situation and economic viability. At over 1,000 pages, this compendium could be of value to a wide range of readers, from students to businessmen, journalists and policy-makers. Salem Press offers free access to its online database with every print purchase of this book.—**ARBA Staff Reviewer**

Ideologies

Dictionaries and Encyclopedias

C, P, S
269.   Lamb, Peter. **Historical Dictionary of Socialism.** 3d ed. Lanham, Md., Rowman & Littlefield, 2016. 601p. (Historical Dictionaries of Religions, Philosophies, and Movements). $140.00; $139.99 (e-book). ISBN 13: 978-1-4422-5826-6; 978-1-4422-5827-3 (e-book).

This volume in the Historical Dictionaries of Religions, Philosophies, and Movements series provides foundational information on the particular topic of Socialism with the goal of acting as a catalyst for further, more in-depth research.

Over 500 compact entries document the various tenets, events, institutions, policies, people, and more associated with the Socialist movement. These entries are arranged alphabetically and are generously cross-referenced for ease of navigation. The paragraphs address big picture topics such as Marxism, Human Rights, or Religion, as well as precise, more obscure topics, such as Chartism, Bettino Craxi, or the Haymarket Affair. This third edition has been extensively updated with new entries, as well as expanded chronology, introduction, and bibliography sections. In particular, the extensive bibliography is highly organized, and the introduction section does well in defining Socialism as well as conveying its origins, development, and schisms that pushed it into the many-faceted force for social change it is regarded as today. The book also includes a helpful acronyms and abbreviations section, as well as a glossary.

While this resource offers limited context and detail within its entries, readers can absolutely benefit from the highly readable format and intelligent breakdown of its abundant material.—**Laura Herrell**

Politics and Government

Canada

C
270.   **Governments Canada, 2016 Winter/Spring Edition.** Amenia, N.Y., Grey House Publishing, 2016. 1276p. illus. index. $424.00pa. ISBN 13: 978-1-61925-965-2; 978-1-61925-968-3 (e-book).

This large publication is the well-organized contact information source for all levels of government in Canada. The book is published twice a year in order to provide the most up-to-date information, particularly in reference to departmental restructuring in light of recent elections at all levels.

Opening pages provide excellent foundational material and include a description of government structure, charts reflecting government statistics, and highlights of significant changes at all levels—for example, the report of a record number of women and aboriginals elected to parliament in 2015. A quick reference guide alphabetically lists general areas of interest (adoption, agriculture, etc.) with the appropriate agencies and contact information noted beneath.

The bulk of the book is devoted to all government listings beginning with federal offices and working down through provincial/territorial listings (for all 10 provinces and three territories), and municipal listings. Each regional section includes a table of contents and is tabbed for ease of reference. Federal listings are organized by office, beginning with the office of the Governor General and Commander-in-Chief of Canada and including myriad other offices ranging from the Pest Management Regulatory Agency to the Canadian Human Rights Tribunal and much more. Information accompanying each listing may include a brief description of the body, acts administered, executive staff, and all contact information. Provincial/territorial listings are arranged alphabetically by province/territory, and municipal listings are arranged alphabetically within province/territory and are further classified by type of municipality. Following the municipal listings is a new section including key contact information for both foreign embassies and consulates in Canada and Canadian embassies and consulates abroad.

This resource concludes with two notable indexes: one listing acronyms commonly used throughout the book, and one listing more than 25,000 key contacts, organized alphabetically by last name, of organizations referenced in the book.

Recommended.—**ARBA Staff Reviewer**

United States

Atlases

C

271.   **Atlas of the 2012 Elections.** J. Clark Archer and others. Lanham, Md., Rowman & Littlefield, 2014. 306p. illus. maps. index. $75.00; $74.99 (e-book). ISBN 13: 978-1-4422-2583-1; 978-1-4422-2584-8 (e-book).

The 2012 elections in the United States saw the reelection of Barak Obama as president, but the elections also highlighted the partisan divides that still confront the country. This atlas provides in-depth analyses of not only the presidential election, but also selected state and local elections, several referenda, and specific issues that affected the results. In addition to covering the presidential election specifically, chapters are dedicated to the Republican primary elections, focusing on Iowa, Florida, and Ohio, and the Republican and Democratic campaigns which examined topics such as individual contributions to the candidates, campaign expenditures, campaign stops, and newspaper endorsements. Other chapters provide penetrating analyses of the outcomes of the presidential vote by state and county levels, by metropolitan area, by counties, and by selected suburbs. Regional analyses (Northeast, Appalachia, Southeast, Midwest, Great Plains, Mountain West, and Pacific Region) are included as are special reports on Hispanic and Asian American voting and the impact of religion on voting. The roles of health care and foreign policy on the outcome are also examined. Several state elections are covered including key senate elections in Virginia, Indiana, Wisconsin, North Dakota, and Montana, as well as the governor races in Massachusetts and Wisconsin. Votes on legalizing same-sex marriage in Maine, Minnesota, Maryland, and Washington, and the legalization of marijuana use in Colorado and Washington are discussed. Thus, this atlas provides a wealth of information on electoral politics during this important election cycle that will benefit students of political science, public administration, and public policy for years to come. The maps themselves provide excellent data in a clear and meaningful way and are the true heart of the book. By closely examining the maps, the bifurcation of the country can easily be seen, although the divide is not only Democrat/Republican, but also rural/metropolitan, liberal/conservative, Christian/non-Christian, white/nonwhite, and young/old. This atlas can be recommended for all academic libraries and for larger public libraries.—**Gregory A. Crawford**

Biography

P, S

272.   **American Presidents.** 4th ed. Robert P. Watson, ed. Hackensack, N.J., Salem Press, 2015. 2v. illus. maps. index. $195.00/set. ISBN 13: 978-1-61925-940-9; 978-1-61925-941-6 (e-book).

A two-volume historical reference, *American Presidents* chronologically presents thorough biographies of all 43 U.S. presidents from George Washington to Barack Obama. This edition is the first to include the current president's biography, and has revised and updated entries for several recent presidents, the bibliography, and all appendixes. Many new photographs and illustrations enhance the publication and online access is newly available, as well.

Preceding the biographies are two excellent essays discussing the presidential office itself and touching on the general characteristics of its holders, as well as its origins, processes, duties, and evolution through modern times. Each biographical entry then offers rich information about the president's birth, education, political rise, election, time in office, postpresidency, and death. The particular administration's legacy is also assessed. Readers will find sufficient space given to a president's most remarkable moments, such as Lyndon B. Johnson's work with the Voting Rights Act of 1965, or Franklin Pierce's struggles with slavery and territorial expansion.

The book employs a number of tools which both organize and enhance the material. Shaded text boxes convey brief biographies of First Ladies and Vice Presidents, as well as important primary document excerpts such as Lincoln's Emancipation Proclamation. Each entry opens with listed administration information, such as years of term(s), birth and death dates and location, political party, and cabinet members. Essays conclude with updated, annotated bibliographies for further reference

The end of volume two offers a generous amount of supplementary information and include the U.S. Constitution and amendments, the Law of Presidential Succession, a timeline for each president, election returns, presidential libraries, a glossary, an index and much, much more.

This book works well as a companion to *American First Ladies,* third edition, published by Salem in 2015.—**ARBA Staff Reviewer**

Dictionaries and Encyclopedias

C, P, S

273.   **American Governance.** Stephen L. Schechter, ed. New York, Macmillan Reference USA/Gale Group, 2016. 5v. illus. index. $700.00/set. ISBN 13: 978-0-02-866249-7; 978-0-02-866255-8 (e-book).

This encyclopedic treatment of government in the United States covers the historical development and evolving characteristics of American political life, key institutions, recurring and major issues, and the implications of governing structures for citizens and civil society. The interdisciplinary approach draws on political science, law, history, economics, sociology, and economics. Significant events, individuals, concepts, texts, and events illustrate aspects of four major themes: the intellectual foundations of the system; the constitutional and legal framework; government and public policy; and the expression of these designs through citizenship and participation in public life. Representative articles range from "Voting Behavior" and the history of "State Constitutions" to "Civil Disobedience" and "Gender Discrimination," as well as important specifics such as *Roe v. Wade,* the Voting Rights Act and Magna Carta, plus concise biographies of selected presidents, jurists, and other leaders.

There are over 700 signed articles in alphabetical order, written by more than 400 contributors who are primarily American academics. The editor-in-chief is a widely published political scientist. The writing style is aimed at a college-level readership. Articles range in length from shorter definitions to longer essays on complex topics such as "Affirmative Action" or the stages of constitutional development. Historical coverage traces themes from classical Greece and medieval England to the present, with coverage as recent as the *Obergefell* v. *Hodges* court decision on gay marriage rights in June 2015. Most articles include citations for further reading, including scholarly books and articles published as recently as 2015. In print, this work consists of five volumes; it also is available in e-book format through the Gale Virtual Reference Library.

Ample additions support the text. An annotated Webliography identifies Websites for federal agencies, advocacy groups, think tanks, and collections of primary sources. Appendixes reprint the original Declaration of Independence, the Constitution, the Bill of Rights, and the later Amendments, as well as three issues of the *Federalist.* A case index covers court decisions and legal topics. A subject index deals with key politicians and statesmen, government entities and practices, ideology and concepts, legislation, advocacy groups, thinkers and writers, aspects of the Constitution, and topics in race, ethnicity, gender, and sexual orientation. Illustrations include maps, timelines, graphs, tables, and portraits based on engravings or photographs.

There are several comparable resources (sometimes with similar titles) that approach this general topic from different directions. *American Government* (see ARBA 2012, entry 724) is a database aimed at a high school audience, using primary and secondary sources to examine policies, leaders, and controversies. *Governing America: Major Decisions of Federal, State, and Local Governments from 1789 to the Present* (see ARBA 2012, entry 728) revolves around social, economic, and political policies and their impact. *Handbook to American Democracy* (see ARBA 2013, entry 631) consists of four volumes: an overview followed by separate volumes for each of the three branches of government, but these volumes are shorter than those of *American Governance.*—**Steven W. Sowards**

C, P, S
274.   **American Political Culture: An Encyclopedia.** Michael Shally-Jensen, ed.; Mark J. Rozell and Ted G. Jelen, advisory eds. Santa Barbara, Calif., ABC-CLIO, 2015. 3v. illus. index. $310.00/set. ISBN 13: 978-1-61069-377-6; 978-1-61069-378-3 (e-book).

This three-volume encyclopedia from ABC-CLIO provides a unique and comprehensive description of political culture (or, more appropriately, cultures) within the United States throughout its most recent history. The nearly 200 entries range from broad issues such as war and politics to more contemporary topics such as an entry describing the rise of the Tea Party. The narrative of each entry follows the same general format: an introduction that defines the topic, a contemporary historical analysis that provides appropriate context, an extended explanation of why the topic is significant within the overall milieu of American politics, often accompanied by a breakdown of specific issues concerning the topics, and a conclusion that summarizes key points. Text boxes are used effectively to highlight a specific issue within an entry. Entries are written primarily by faculty and doctoral students from institutions in the United States representing a variety of social sciences disciplines beyond just political science. Entries average about 3,500 words and are arranged alphabetically throughout the encyclopedia. They include *see also* references to related terms and a bibliography of books, articles from scholarly and nonscholarly sources, and Websites that provide further readings about the topics. Most entries include nontextual elements such as photographs, charts, or illustrations. Front matter includes a list of all entries and an introduction to the encyclopedia. Back matter includes a complete bibliography, a list of contributors, and an index to be used for finding topics that are not main entries. Although there are entries on state and local politics and states' rights, the encyclopedia focuses on national, and, where appropriate, international political cultures. This is an impressive work and highly recommended for beginning researchers; it would be of value in any public, high school, or undergraduate library.—**Robert V. Labaree**

C, P, S
275.   **The Central Intelligence Agency: An Encyclopedia of Covert Ops, Intelligence Gathering, and Spies.** Goldman, Jan, ed. Santa Barbara, Calif., ABC-CLIO, 2015. 2v. illus. index. $189.00/set. ISBN 13: 978-1-61069-091-1; 978-1-61069-092-8 (e-book).

This two-volume encyclopedia from ABC-CLIO, edited by intelligence expert Jan Goldman of Georgetown University, aims to give students real information, in capsule form, about the workings of the Central Intelligence Agency (CIA) and to provide them with tools for further research. Volume one has 216 entries, arranged alphabetically from Afghanistan to Zenith Technical Enterprises and dealing with individuals, countries, operations, topics, and organizations with which the CIA was involved. There is good coverage of the CIA's role in the recent wars in Iraq and Afghanistan, of government directives on how the CIA should work, and of how the agency has used front organizations in its covert operations. This reviewer would have liked to see more entries on the CIA's role in Vietnam, and there is one notable omission from the Cold War era: Adolf Tolkachev, a senior Soviet engineer who gave the CIA a treasure trove of information. (Tolkachev's story is told in David E. Hoffman's book *The Billion-Dollar Spy* (Doubleday, 2015). Volume two contains 98 documents arranged chronologically, most of which were classified secret or above when issued and many of which are redacted in this publication, dating from the 1940s to 2014. Jan Goldman writes in his introduction that all these documents have now been declassified by the U.S. government and that readers can use them in their own research. The documents selected open a window into U.S. intelligence-gathering activities and their outcomes. One is the debriefing in 1962 of Francis Gary Powers, the U-2 pilot who was shot down and captured by the Soviets and later exchanged for a Russian spy. Another intriguing, if unsettling, document is titled "A Review of CIA Guatemala Assassination Proposals during 1952-54." Each document is preceded by an introduction that tries to put it in context. Another feature of this encyclopedia is the "Timeline of Central Intelligence Agency and Intelligence Activities, 1939-2015." Although it mainly emphasizes events since 2001, this section will give the careful reader a fairly coherent idea of how the agency has developed over time. The bibliography lists many excellent books and a number of Websites, but appears to include only one book published after 2012. Overall, the encyclopedia lives up to its promise—it does not purport to be a history of the CIA, but rather a usable introduction to the work and world of the spy agency and is recommended for school, academic, and general libraries.—**Alice Chaffee**

C, P, S

276.   Conley, Richard S. **Historical Dictionary of the U.S. Presidency.** Lanham, Md., Rowman & Littlefield, 2016. 503p. (Historical Dictionaries of U.S. Politics and Political Eras). $130.00; $129.99. ISBN 13: 978-1-4422-5764-1; 978-1-4422-5765-8 (e-book).

This book, intended primarily for the general reader, provides an accessible and quite comprehensive outline of the presidencies of the 44 men who have held that office, from George Washington through Barack Obama. Author Richard S. Conley, associate professor of political science at the University of Florida, has written extensively on the presidency, including volumes on the Reagan-Bush, Clinton, and George W. Bush eras in the series of which this book is a part. Conley's introduction focuses on the evolution of executive power and its relationship to the other branches of government and the U.S. Constitution. The chronology which begins the book ranges from three lines for Zachary Taylor to nearly four pages for Franklin Roosevelt. The 200 plus entries in the dictionary section cover not only the presidents themselves but also their vice presidents, selected cabinet members, rivals, and other notable figures, as well as significant events. The bibliography has separate sections on each of the presidents and includes a list of presidential museum and library Websites. Perhaps the most notable feature of this volume is the series of 23 appendixes—over 120 pages—dealing with such matters as detailed election results, presidential approval data (beginning with President Truman), White House chiefs of staff, economic data, and much else. There is also a list of acronyms and abbreviations. The book contains essential information in a nutshell while also pointing the reader to more in-depth studies of the presidents and their times.—**ARBA Staff Reviewer**

C

277.   **Encyclopedia of U.S. Intelligence.** Gregory Moore, ed. Boca Raton, Fla., CRC Press, 2014. 2v. illus. index. $675.75/set. ISBN 13: 978-1-4200-8957-8.

The Encyclopedia of U.S. Intelligence is an in-depth reference work offering an accessible overview of the history and workings of U.S. Intelligence. The encyclopedia is well-organized: the entries are arranged alphabetically by topic and by subtopic.

The encyclopedia covers a wide range of subjects going beyond terrorism and well-known federal government agencies to include criminal intelligence and analysis, legislation, historical events and figures, and education and training.

Each full-text entry includes an abstract to further assist readers in finding truly relevant information. Some abstracts are in-depth and detailed while others are concise, one-sentence descriptions. Author affiliations for each entry are also provided. This is especially useful as the book represents the combined contributions of both scholars and former intelligence professionals at many levels from both the public and private sector.

The online version is updated quarterly to keep up with this quickly changing discipline.

The Encyclopedia of U.S. Intelligence is useful in two specific ways. First, its table of contents provides an easy-to-grasp view of the history, breadth, geography, major events, and major players in U.S. Intelligence. Second, the entries themselves are authored by scholars and practitioners offering insightful analysis of topics often experienced first-hand. The blend of the scholarly, professional, public, and private sector viewpoints is interesting and offers serious students many avenues for further analysis.

This work is recommended for collections in academic, government, and law enforcement collections. It would also be a useful addition for large public libraries.—**Kristin Kay Leeman**

C, S

278.   Vile, John R. **Encyclopedia of Constitutional Amendments, Proposed Amendments, and Amending Issues, 1789–2015.** 4th ed. Santa Barbara, Calif., ABC-CLIO, 2015. 2v. index. $189.00/set. ISBN 13: 978-1-61069-931-0; 978-1-61069-932-7 (e-book).

In the foreword to this fourth edition of a book previously published in 1996, 2003, and 2010 (see ARBA 1997, entry 596; ARBA 2004, entry 535; and ARBA 2011, entry 436), Sanford Levinson of the University of Texas Law School identifies the book's sole editor, John R. Vile, as the recognized national expert on the amendments and proposed amendments to the U.S. Constitution. Levinson convincingly argues that Vile's work is "an essential book for scholars, but it is written in such an accessible style that anyone interested in the United States Constitution can profit from picking it up and reading entries basically at random." (p. xvii) Vile, professor of political science and dean of the University Honors College at Middle Tennessee State University, aims to provide an "indispensable tool for those who are interested in constitutional amendments, proposed amendments, and amending issues." (p. xix) The 2015 edition, now in two volumes, contains revised entries, new entries, and additional cross-references. It covers almost 12,000 proposed amendments together with major constitutional reforms introduced outside Congress, "influential individuals," "influential organizations," Supreme Court decisions, unresolved issues, and "miscellaneous" related topics such as the Articles of Confederation and Critical Elections.

Vile suggests that readers ranging from high school students to "advanced researchers in law, political science, and history" (p. xxiv) may explore entries ranging from George Washington to Phyllis Schlafly and Confederate Debt to Polygamy. Volume one features the A to Z list of entries from A to M and explains the features of this new edition. Volume two, entries N-Z, also offers four appendixes that include the Constitution and its amendments, the number of amendments by decade, and other key data, as well as an updated, wide-ranging bibliography of more than 40 pages, a list of cases, and a revised, comprehensive index. This authoritative set is essential for college, university, and law libraries. Its relatively low cost, impressive content, and clear writing style distinguish it from the other published studies of constitutional amendments carefully cited by Vile and also make it an important purchase for many high school and most public libraries.—**Julienne L. Wood**

C, P

279.   **The War on Terror Encyclopedia: From the Rise of Al-Qaeda to 9/11 and Beyond.** Jan Goldman, ed. Santa Barbara, Calif., ABC-CLIO, 2014. 492p. index. $100.00. ISBN 13: 978-1-61069-510-7; 978-1-61069-511-4 (e-book).

The War on Terror Encyclopedia: From the Rise of Al-Qaeda to 9/11 and Beyond presents the history and course of modern terrorism from a U.S. perspective. The book's main concern is not terrorism in general; rather, it focuses on the people and policies involved on both sides of America's fight against different groups seeking to perpetrate violence and terror against the United States and its allies.

Its primary aim is to examine the U.S. war on terror from a policy perspective, rather than an academic perspective. Entries are drawn heavily from practitioners in the intelligence, defense, and security professions. The encyclopedia seeks to present a factual, neutral basis from which readers can formulate their own ideas and opinions.

The preface and introduction prepare the reader to understand an essential characteristic of the "war on terror"—namely that the enemy is not a nation-state (as in conventional warfare) and cannot be studied or understood in a conventional manner. As a result, the book is multidisciplinary: its entries touch upon policies, politics, doctrines, economics, sociology, warfare technologies, and individuals.

Entries are organized alphabetically and range from the Taliban to the Economic Impact of the September 11, 2001 Attacks and from the Bush Doctrine to Middle Eastern Television. There is a thorough index which also includes hyperlinked page numbers, making navigation to primary and related topics very easy. It would be ideal to have the *see also* options at the end of each entry similarly linked.

The entries are engagingly written and well presented. For example, entries on individuals (especially known terrorists) provide interesting biographical information, placing the individual in historical context, charting his activities, development, and connections in the terrorist world, as well as his current status today if he is still living. The author of each entry is included at the end of each entry along with *see also* entries and citations for suggested further reading.

Dr. Jan Goldman, editor, carries substantial credentials in this field. He has published several other well-received reference books about the CIA and the Intelligence Community The contributors are also listed with their respective affiliations.

This book is very strongly recommended for academic libraries and large public libraries. It should also find a place on the reading list for anyone in the defense, intelligence, and policy-making arenas (especially foreign and security policy). This is also a great read for anyone interested in a clearly presented, easy-to-digest history of recent events and topics that will continue to be very relevant for the foreseeable future. Anyone interested in strengthening their foundational knowledge in the study of terrorism will appreciate this book.—**Kristin Kay Leeman**

Directories

C, P
280.   **The Grey House Homeland Security Directory, 2015.** 11th ed. Amenia, N.Y., Grey House Publishing, 2015. 1141p. index. $195.00pa. ISBN 13: 978-1-61925-561-6.

With the growing interest in and concern with homeland security it is not unusual for patrons to go to their local public or college/university library to try to get contact information for federal and state employees working in this sector to express their concerns or to pursue research projects. However, finding this information can be a tricky feat since there are many federal and state agencies and subagencies that work in some way with issues related to homeland security and they may not be readily apparent to the librarian or the researcher. The 11th edition of *The Grey House Homeland Security Directory* helps fill this need in the reference collection for public and academic libraries. Information included in this comprehensive directory extends beyond governmental agencies and also includes entries for private sector companies which offer products and services related to homeland security issues and concerns, as well as a section for industry resources such as Websites, trade shows, publications, and other information resources.

This helpful directory is divided into five sections: Federal Agencies, State Agencies, Company Listings (provides information on companies that offer services and products to the consumer such as data security and emergency food and water rations), Industry Resources, and Indexes. In the first four sections, each of the 5,502 entries includes a brief description explaining how that entry relates to homeland security, contact information for the entry as a whole (department-level or company-level, for example), and the names and titles of important individuals (11,314 in total) and often their phone numbers and/or email addresses. A table of contents is useful for navigating this directory and section five is comprised of three indexes: entry name index, key personnel index, and products and services index to help the user find what they are looking for.

Length of entries and the level of information provided varies in section three: Company Listing. Shorter entries are often seen with smaller companies (less than 50 employees), but there are a few instances in which there is scant information provided on much larger companies. Despite the inconsistencies, this section is still very robust in the amount of information provided for the majority of companies profiled.

The most helpful section of this directory is section two: State Agencies. It can often be difficult to determine which state agencies play a role related to Homeland Security, and this directory clearly lists the applicable departments and includes a brief description in addition to contact information which is often buried on state Websites, if it is even listed at all.

Overall, the 11th edition of *The Grey House Homeland Security Directory* is very robust and a useful addition to public and academic libraries, especially those which are open to the public. It is a valuable reference tool, especially to libraries that have owned previous editions as contact information for many individuals has changed, more companies have been added to the Company Listing section, and Industry Resources have been updated and added.—**Julia Frankosky**

Handbooks and Yearbooks

C, P, S

281.   **The American Presidency Project.** http://www.presidency.ucsb.edu/index.php. [Website] Free. Date reviewed: 2016.

The American Presidency Project is an online resource collecting the messages and papers of the presidents, public papers, and other presidential documents. The site is run by the University of California, Santa Barbara, and is a strong resource for documents related to the presidency.

The site allows quick access to materials such as data, documents, election information, and other forms of media. The wealth of the material is found in the documents section. Features include original texts of State of the Union Addresses, Inaugural Addresses, public speeches and appearances, and more. Documents are efficiently organized by topics, such as news conferences, proclamations, and a unique feature of a president's term in office, such as the Fireside Chats by Franklin D. Roosevelt.

The data section provides information on a president's popularity and approval ratings, although this section is limited to the more recent presidents. Election information includes voter preferences, how specific events or speeches affected voter support, and more. The database also lists which candidates were running in each election.

Finding the material beyond the top navigation is very intuitive and can allow a user to directly access the documents they are looking for, even specific press briefs or executive orders. The basic search function is small and hidden in the top left corner of the site, which could make it difficult for a user to find, if they do not have specific needs in mind. For further research, the project also includes links to presidential libraries and museums.—**ARBA Staff Reviewer**

C, P, S

282.   **American President: A Reference Resource. http://millercenter.org/president.** [Website] Free. Date reviewed: 2016.

The *American President* Website is an information resource containing a wealth of material on each of the nation's 44 presidents. Maintained by the Miller Center of Public Affairs, a nonpartisan research affiliate of the University of Virginia that specializes in presidential scholarship and political history, the site is easy to navigate and attractively arranged. But it is the site's rich, deep, and authoritative content that gives it its distinctive value.

The *American President* home page features a standard search option, but many users will choose to explore the site's many treasures through its illustrated table of contents, which lists every president from Washington to Obama in chronological order. Each of these presidential links opens onto a home page for the president in question. On these home pages, users will find links to well-written and informative summaries of the president's personal background, his campaign and election experiences, his domestic and foreign triumphs and failures in the Oval Office, and his historical legacy.

In addition to these biographical essays, each presidential home page provides links to essays on key events of that president's administration, biographical profiles of the First Lady and key administration figures, transcripts of notable speeches and addresses, an image gallery, and Websites of historical sites and libraries devoted to the president in question. The site even includes video lectures from prominent historians on specific presidents of the nineteenth and early twentieth centuries.

The historical material available for every president is impressive, but students exploring the administrations of our more recent presidents will also have a terrific array of audiovisual materials at their disposal. These resources include Oval Office audio recordings from the Kennedy, Johnson, and Nixon administrations; audio recordings of important presidential speeches (beginning with Franklin D. Roosevelt); video recordings of important presidential speeches (beginning with John F. Kennedy); and an Oral Histories section where users can peruse the transcripts of interviews with leading officials and lawmakers from the Carter, Reagan, George H.W. Bush, Clinton, and George W. Bush administrations. The Oral History section for the Clinton presidency alone contains more than 60 interviews, including conversations with luminaries ranging from Secretary of State Madeleine Albright and Chief of Staff Leon Panetta to former Czech Republic president Vaclev Havel.

American President: A Reference Resource is a highly recommended site for high school, public, and academic libraries alike.—**ARBA Staff Reviewer**

C, P, S

283.   **Congress.gov. https://www.congress.gov/.** [Website] Free. Date reviewed: 2016.

Congress.gov is a presentation of the Library of Congress and is the official Website for U.S. federal legislative information. Its dignified look and abundance of useful links fits perfectly with its mission.

Not only is *Congress.gov* a great place to see what's actually happening in the House and Senate on any given day, it's a very useful Website for students—or others—who are interested in learning more about important issues like how a bill becomes law. The Website includes some simple informational videos, a search engine that helps users find information among more than one million records, access to the entirety of the Congressional Record, and quick access to all bills being considered in the House and Senate. A glossary provides brief explanations of legislative terms used throughout the Website. A link to the crowd-sourced "top-10 most-viewed bills" provides an easy entrée into the complicated world of reading legislation.

A list of Congressional committees links to the committee proceedings, recent activity, and Websites of each committee. Information about each member of Congress (current and former) is easy to find along with important details like their contact information, remarks in the *Congressional Record,* and committee assignments. Content on the site is constantly being updated; for instance, a new video series called "Two-Minute Tips" teaches users how to get the most out of the Website. A link to Law Library of Congress resources on Supreme Court Nominations ties into current news. Users can even stream live floor proceedings when the House and Senate are in session.

Because people interested in the U.S. Congress might be recent immigrants or even users from other countries, a significant detriment is the paucity of Spanish-language (and other-language) resources.

Overall, *Congress.gov* is an easy-to-navigate site that does a great job of making Congressional legislation available and comprehensible to the average citizen. It's also an excellent starting place for links to other important Websites like all those connected with the Library of Congress, information about visiting the Capitol, and a gallery of study resources about significant primary source documents from American history.—**ARBA Staff Reviewer**

C, P, S

284.   **Council of State Governments. http://www.csg.org/.** [Website] Free. Date reviewed: 2016.

The Council of State Governments (CSG), founded in 1933, serves all three branches of state government in the formation of state public policy; the CSG also supports state government in fostering regional, national, and international opportunities. The CSG site hosts a wealth of freely accessible data. From the home page, users can click on myriad links: Economics & Finance, Education, Energy & Environment, Federal Affairs, Health, International, Interstate Compacts, Public Safety & Justice, Transportation, and Workforce Development. All these links lead to other information treasure troves. A click on Interstate Compacts, for example, takes users to a database that allows searches across 1,500 statutes—searches can be conducted through basic or advanced search functions or via an interactive map. Additional links on the home page take users to events, leadership development, the *Capitol Ideas Magazine,* and the venerable *Book of the States* (BOS), which since 1935 has provided pertinent data for all 56 territories, commonwealths, and states of the United States. The 2015 edition has 152 in-depth tables, charts, and figures along with 29 articles by policy experts and state leaders. Archived editions of the BOS are freely available and easy to download. Designed for policy-makers, this Website is equally valuable to students and researchers.—**ARBA Staff Reviewer**

C, P, S

285.   LeMay, Michael C. **Illegal Immigration: A Reference Handbook.** 2d ed. Santa Barbara, Calif., ABC-CLIO, 2015. 382p. illus. index. (Contemporary World Issues). $60.00. ISBN 13: 978-1-4408-4012-8; 978-1-4408-4013-5 (e-book).

Author Michael LeMay, Ph.D., is a professor emeritus from California State University, San Bernardino, where he served as Director of the National Security Studies program as well as positions in the Department of Political Science and the College of Social and Behavioral Sciences. Le May has an extensive list of immigration writings, and also lectures on immigration history and policy.

Contemporary World Issues is a series well used as a starting point for studies on such contemporary issues as hate crimes, nuclear power, and immigration. This second edition of *Illegal Immigration: A Reference Handbook* explores the definition, history, and flow of unauthorized immigrants into the United States since 1970. This book, published in 2015, contains 400 pages starting with a concise table of contents. Like other books in this series, chapters are initiated with a black-and-white photograph. The glossary has a large list of terminology, which will be useful to those acquainting themselves with the immigration issue, and the index is comprehensive.

Chapters begin with an introduction, the topic text is followed by a conclusion or solution where warranted, and each chapter closes with references, both print and nonprint. The first chapter, "Background and History," describes how unauthorized immigration has come into being in the United States; the book comes full circle with the final chapter, "Chronology," providing an annotated timeline of important moments in immigration history. This book focuses on modern-day issues with immigration but historical information presents a contextual foundation.

Chapter three, "Perspectives," is a new addition to this second edition. Eight original essays give voice to all sides of the immigration issue. Groups who lobby for reform of polices or against those same policies are included here and will provide a strong springboard for discussion, debate, and further research. Chapter five, "Data and Documents," includes useful document resources for those looking for policy details and useable data. Tables like 5.4 "Unaccompanied Alien Children Encountered by Fiscal Year, Country of Origin 2014" (p. 222) will give definition to report writing, though the Gallup polls offer less in the way of concrete data.

Focusing on trends and policies since 2000, *Illegal Immigration* will give researchers a place to discover the current problems and controversies of immigration, border security, and human rights issues. Readers will learn the issue is one of many layers and continues to plague politicians, policy makers, and policy implementers. Key issues will be found by readers and will spark research in a specific area; those looking for an overview with find this text will be a catalyst for narrowing the scope of study and resources to assist in the research. For more finite information on immigration, another series The International Library of Studies on Migration will give researchers a more detailed background on immigration and its global implications. This book is recommended for high school and college students, policy-makers, and those looking to better understand immigration issues in the United States.

Recommended.—**Janis Minshull**

C, P, S

286.   Stanley, Harold W., and Richard G. Niemi. **Vital Statistics on American Politics 2015-2016.** Thousand Oaks, Calif., CQ Press / Sage, 2015. 448p. index. $135.00. ISBN 13: 978-1-4833-8031-5; 978-1-4833-8029-2 (e-book).

Vital Statistics on American Politics is a comprehensive compilation of statistics related to all areas of the federal government. The 2015-2016 edition is updated with the most current information available. As the title infers, this book covers statistics related to politics, such as voter turnout, election results, and campaign finance. However, it also goes beyond the obvious and provides information about the topics that surround and influence politicians in the areas of foreign, social, and economic policy.

More broadly, this book also provides statistics on how the American public gets its information and how we interact with American politics. Who reads newspapers? Who watches CNN or Fox News? How many people watch presidential debates? How has public opinion evolved on topics such as abortion, gay marriage, and gun control?

Students, researchers, historians, and everyday citizens will find useful information on the main subjects that surround politics and the entire political system.—**Lisa Schultz**

S

287.   **U*X*L Civics.** Rebecca Valentine, ed. Stamford, Conn., Gale/Cengage Learning, 2015. 3v. illus. index. $272.00/set. ISBN 13: 978-1-5730-2962-9; 978-1-5730-2966-7 (e-book).

Like other UXL sets, these volumes feature excellent supporting documentation and ancillary materials. Each volume contains the complete table of contents and index for the set, as well as appendixes with the full text of founding American documents and student guides to civic engagement.

The American Government volume includes extensive historical detail pertaining to the development of democracy and republican forms of government, as well as discussion of political philosophy. Although information about how the branches of the U.S. government work overlaps with information in the second volume on rights and liberties, the second volume focuses specifically on American history. The final volume considers extensive contemporary international issues, such as the current crisis in the Ukraine and the goals of Boko Haram in Nigeria. Ample color photographs and visual aids complement the material and add to reader interest. These are suitable for both in-class use and inclusion in reference libraries.—**Delilah R. Caldwell**

14 Psychology, Parapsychology, and Occultism

Psychology

Dictionaries and Encyclopedias

P, S

288.   **Abuse: An Encyclopedia of Causes, Consequences, and Treatments.** Rosemarie Skaine, ed. Santa Barbara, Calif., Greenwood Press/ABC-CLIO, 2015. 330p. illus. index. $89.00. ISBN 13: 978-1-61069-514-5; 978-1-61069-515-2 (e-book).

This encyclopedia helps define abuse and takes a hard but composed look at the varying reasons behind it, effects stemming from it, and ways to prevent and treat it. Over 150 alphabetized entries, ranging in length from several paragraphs to several pages, provide the latest information concerning such topics as child abandonment, hate speech, animal abuse, and rape. Entries are well-detailed, and some, like rape, are further analyzed through more specific subentries (statutory rape, date rape, etc.) reflecting a nuanced approach to conveying the topic's broader meaning. The book does well to include some of the current implications of the Internet era, such as the devastating issues of cyberbullying and cyberstalking.

Importantly, the book gives significant weight to society's expanding awareness of the devastation caused by abuse, and includes entries on legislation and systems arising from particularly notorious examples, like the 1998 murder of Matthew Shepard and the creation of the Hate Crimes Prevention Act of 2009, or of the encouraging success of the AMBER alert system.

Abuse is certainly a difficult topic with which to engage. This encyclopedia, however, successfully offers a straightforward approach to educating readers on the many facets of this troubling issue and providing helpful keys to unlocking strategies and solutions with which to confront it. It includes *see also* references, suggestions for further reading, helpful Websites, contact information for associated organizations, and a concluding subject index.—**Laura Herrell**

C, P

289.   **APA Dictionary of Psychology.** 2d ed. Gary R. VandenBos, ed. Washington, D.C., American Psychological Association, 2015. 1204p. $49.95. ISBN 13: 978-1-4338-1944-5.

Functionally, the new edition of the *APA Dictionary of Psychology* is very similar to its 2007 predecessor (see ARBA 2007, entry 649). The vast majority of the volume is dedicated to providing definitions of terms, arranged alphabetically. A brief "Guide to the Dictionary" provides basic information on how to use the source. Users familiar with other dictionaries will not need most of this content, but the section on "Hidden Entries" explains the protocol for locating related words–similar to cross-references–but these are terms in bold face in the text of the definitions and used in context. Entries also frequently include standard cross-references and brief etymological information as appropriate. A significant change is in the biographical information. In the 2007 edition, biographical entries were included in the text of the dictionary, with an index of biographical entries at the end of the volume. In the 2014 edition, these have been placed in a separate section at the end, but they have also been greatly shortened; the entry for Carl Rogers, for example, has gone from approximately 250 words to under 40. The preface notes, however, that this has enabled the editors to include far more biographies than in the previous edition. (p. vii) The remainder of the text has been updated to reflect current terminology and incorporate connections to the DSM-IV-TR and DSM-5. The volume concludes with lists of institutional entries, testing instrument entries, and techniques. Overall, this new edition is an excellent resource for students of all levels as well as practitioners. Recommended for high school, public, academic, and special libraries supporting researchers in mental health fields.—**Amanda Izenstark**

C, P
290.   Neukrug, Edward S. **The SAGE Encyclopedia of Theory in Counseling and Psychotherapy.** Thousand Oaks, Calif., Sage, 2015. 2v. index. $375/set. ISBN 13: 978-1-4522-7412-6.

The SAGE Encyclopedia of Theory in Counseling and Psychotherapy is a comprehensive resource that provides readers with in-depth knowledge of contemporary counseling and theories in psychotherapy. A team of international researchers and practitioners combined their knowledge of modern theories and theorists to create the cultural and historical context students require to apply psychotherapy and counseling effectively. An informative and easy-to-read introduction distinguishes psychotherapy from counseling and expounds on the important role of theory in the field today. With over 1200 pages, this two-volume source may be overwhelming for those new to the study of psychology, but will undoubtedly prove useful for students in graduate or undergraduate psychology courses and counseling education programs.

The encyclopedia includes both bibliography and resource guides that provide additional resources such as books, journals, and organizations for students looking for more specialized information. Also included is a chronology to help readers place each theory in a historical context; this is extremely useful for beginning professionals and students in their first years of study to assist in setting the backdrop for the evolution of psychotherapy theories. Under the reader's guide are a detailed index and cross-reference pages that allow users to search for specific information within the text for both print and electronic formats. This title is highly recommended.—**ARBA Staff Reviewer**

C, P
291.   **Salem Health: Psychology & Behavioral Health.** 4th ed. Paul Moglia, ed. Hackensack, N.J., Salem Press, 2015. 5v. illus. index. $495.00/set; $495.00 (e-book single user). ISBN 13: 978-1-61925-543-2; 978-1-61925-544-9 (e-book).

Whether you are just starting out in psychology or doing some quick fact checking, a good subject encyclopedia can be a great tool. There are many choices out there, and the fourth edition of *Salem Health: Psychology & Behavioral Health* is among the best. The college student will find that this five-volume set provides context for the many diverse areas of psychology, while offering structure and needed grounding when crafting a paper or assignment for class. There are 650 articles, nearly 100 are new and on current topics such as DSM-V controversies, Hoarding, and Exercise addiction. Culturally diverse material is a welcome inclusion with 18 articles listed under the multicultural category index. Scope is wide ranging, covering most areas of psychology and including historical, biographical, clinical, cognitive, forensic, and behavioral topics, to name just a few. Articles are written clearly and structured in a way that will be helpful to students, providing the type of psychology, an abstract, and key concepts. A bibliography completes each article and cross-referencing to other articles within the set will help with navigation. There are a number of useful and substantial appendixes (glossary, directories) and among them the Mediagraphy is an interesting feature. In this section are annotations of feature films and other mass media describing their relevance to psychology. *Psychology & Behavioral Health* would be an excellent addition for academic and public libraries.—**Lorraine Evans**

Handbooks and Yearbooks

P

292.   Bannink, Fredrike. **101 Solution-Focused Questions Series Set.** New York, W. W. Norton, 2015. 3v. $39.95pa./set. ISBN 13: 978-0-393-71125-7.

This set of three multicolored books is an attractive addition to a budding therapist's literary collection. Each book provides 101 questions for clients suffering from anxiety, depression, or trauma in order to provide healing. Solutions-focused and cognitive behavior therapy are both evidence-based practices, and this title provides the kind of applicable information that may be appropriate for professionals who have more experience in research and academia and less in conducting therapy. While not an academic resource, this title will undoubtedly be helpful for some.

Each book is divided into the same 10 chapters. Diagrams and exercises are provided to aid clients in mentally reframing their situations. A references section lists all individuals and studies used, and a brief Websites page provides links for additional information. An index helps readers locate subjects. This is an excellent title for students in psychology or those new to the practice of therapy, though seasoned therapists will likely be familiar with a solutions-focused approach and may find it repetitive.—**ARBA Staff Reviewer**

P

293.   Cohen, Lisa J., comp. **The Handy Psychology Answer Book.** 2d ed. Canton, Mich., Visible Ink Press, 2016. 544p. illus. index. $21.95pa. ISBN 13: 978-1-57859-600-3; 978-1-57859-599-0 (e-book).

This second edition book is a useful contrast to much of the dull and dense material written in the field of psychology. A blend of academic research and interesting facts will keep readers hooked regardless of their background in the study. It is structured in a basic question-and-answer format and includes approximately 1,300 questions that are answered concisely in one or two paragraphs, allowing for the reader to choose whether to read it from cover to cover or to simply skim over the content they find most interesting. Students of psychology will find the content refreshing and straightforward to read, and the concepts are uncomplicated enough to be read by those entirely new to the field. Revised to the newest edition of the DSM-5 (Diagnostic and Statistical Manual of Mental Disorders), this title is guaranteed to be relevant.

The book is divided into 11 sections that cover various subjects from history to mental health to forensics. The table of contents also lists page numbers directly next to the chapters as well as the content covered in them in addition to a thorough index, making subject search easy. A helpful introduction covers basic information contained in the book and a further reading section will be useful for readers who want additional information on any given topic.—**ARBA Staff Reviewer**

C

294. **Counseling and Therapy Online: Current Practices. https://www.alexanderstreet.com/discipline/counseling-therapy.** [Website] Alexandria, Va., Alexander Street Press. Price negotiated by site. Date reviewed: 2016.

Counseling and Therapy Online is an online multimedia collection of current resources designed to support the study and practice of counseling and therapy. The collection includes e-books, periodicals, real-life counseling session transcripts, and over 1500 hours of video (presentations, lectures, and instructional). Collection development and maintenance is guided by a scholarly editorial review board committed to delivering current information in all of these formats.

The main page offers a search box and promotes browsing by field-specific subject: Presenting Condition, Therapeutic Approach, Content Type, and Publisher. Selecting any one of these options then takes users to a screen with a wide array of options for narrowing the search such as therapist/psychologist, school of therapy, psychotherapy collection as well as standard criteria such as date, content type, and publisher. Users can also refine by format type (text, video).

The results list includes a thumbnail image (giving a nice visual aspect to navigation in general), a one-to-two sentence description, and links to save the result to a list, cite it, or share it via email or social media channels.

The really unique and useful feature of the collection is the recordings of actual client therapy sessions. These resources have application in both study and practice. These transcripts have loads of metadata for the researcher/student to mine such as age of therapist, therapeutic approach, specialized area of interest, counseling type, etc.

This thoughtful and powerful resource has obviously been built with both study and practice in mind. As a multimodal collection, it brings together a wealth of resources that address the real-life needs of practicing counselors and it appears to strive for currency with contemporary issues. It will be extremely valuable for students (both undergrad and graduate) and practitioners. It may also be a useful tool for large behavioral health centers as it provides not only case studies from real life counseling sessions, but it provides access to a lot of practical resources (tool boxes, handbooks, etc.)—**Kristin Kay Leeman**

C, P

295.   Korn, Leslie E. **Nutrition Essentials for Mental Health: A Complete Guide to the Food-Mood Connection.** New York, W. W. Norton, 2016. 464p. index. $42.50. ISBN 13: 978-0-393-70994-0.

Dr. Leslie Korn's comprehensive guide to food-mood connection is a much needed addition to the field of mental health. Few mental health professionals have training in nutrition, something that greatly affects behavior and emotions, and this guide will help them in a variety of ways. The title addresses why nutrition matters, nutritional culprits that wreak havoc on the body, assessment techniques for evaluating client nutritional needs, and more. Dr. Korn even discusses the effects of foods and nutrients on DSM-5 categories of illness, and addresses alternatives to medication through diet change.

The book is divided into nine highly detailed chapters. While there is some scientific language, all terminology is thoroughly explained and those already in the field will likely be familiar with most of it. Though the book is written by and for clinicians, clients and those interested in nutrition will also find this book accessible. Chapter three is particularly helpful for therapists, as it includes a clinician checklist, food journals, and sample dialogue with a client for those new to addressing nutrition in a clinical counseling session. This easy-to-read guide is an invaluable resource for mental health professionals and is highly recommended. The book includes appendixes, an index, and references for further reading.—**ARBA Staff Reviewer**

C

296.   **Oxford Clinical Psychology. http://www.oxfordclinicalpsych.com/.** [Website] New York, Oxford University Press. Price negotiated by site. Date reviewed: 2015.

This online database provides users access to more than 100 titles in Oxford University Press's global clinical psychology publishing program, which includes reference books, scholarly and research works, and therapist guides and workbooks from the Treatments That Work series. The database is designed for use by clinical psychologists in academic settings and in practice, for professors and instructors, and for students, interns, and trainees in clinical psychology. The regularly updated database will grow to include over 300 titles. The works are all written by accomplished, world-class authors and editors, giving users reassurance regarding the academic integrity of the information on the site.

In terms of navigation, the database is simple to use. Help tutorials and guidelines are provided, but most researchers will be able to skip these due to the intuitive design of the interface. From the main page, users can conduct a quick search from a simple search box, but searches can also be started by using one of three options. The first, Specialty, includes Geropsychology, Psychotherapy, School Psychology, and more. Disorders and Clinical Problems, the second option, allows users to choose from such topics as Anger Disorders, Hoarding Disorder, or Trauma. The third search option, Series, offers a choice of titles from Best Practices in Forensic Mental Health Assessments, Oxford Guides to Cognitive Behavioural Therapy, Programs That Work, Specialty Competencies in Professional Psychology, Treatments That Work, and Other. Searches can be narrowed further by using tools on the left-hand side of the page. For example, a quick search of hoarding will result in a list of 65 chapters and the three books in which they appear. From here, a click on the title of Gail Steketee and Randy O. Frost's book *Treatment for Hoarding Disorder: Therapist Guide* (2 ed.) produces an index card with an abstract, keywords, bibliographic information, and two brief biographies of the authors. Below this is a list of chapters in the book and a column on the left-hand side of the page with further links and information. Alternatively these same three books on hoarding could be found using the Hoarding Disorder link under Disorders and Clinical Problems. An added bonus is the Oxford Index Underbar, which allows users to search across all Oxford University Press journals and scholarly works. A toolbar at the top of the screen enables users to print, email, save and cite results. MLA, APA, AMA, and Chicago citations are offered; citations can be exported in a Word document, EndNote, ProCite, ReferenceManager, RefWorks, BibTeX, and Zotero (BibTeX). The database also features the ability to enlarge and download images; forms and checklists in the Treatments That Work series can be downloaded, edited, and saved for use in classroom and clinical settings.

Oxford Clinical Psychology provides a place for students (upper-level undergraduate and above), professors and teachers, and practitioners to conduct a thorough secondary search of clinical psychology journals and books available from Oxford University Press. More than a research vehicle, however, the database provides users with a reliable place to access images, forms, checklists, and lecture materials. Highly recommended for medical and academic libraries.—**ARBA Staff Reviewer**

Parapsychology

Dictionaries and Encyclopedias

C, P, S

297.   **Ghosts, Spirits, and Psychics: The Paranormal from Alchemy to Zombies.** Matt Cardin, ed. Santa Barbara, Calif., ABC-CLIO, 2015. 409p. index. $89.00. ISBN 13: 978-1-61069-683-8; 978-1-61069-684-5 (e-book).

Though many consider stories of the occult, the paranormal, or their related aspects such as psychics and ghosts to be remnants of a bygone, more superstitious era, one will often find that such phenomenon have had an important contribution to various cultures and creative traditions. This work seeks to serve as an introduction to such topics and to broaden the reader's perspectives on how they have influenced different sections of society. This includes not only popular culture but also art, literature, religion, and even the beginnings of science.

Through a selection of 120 articles each written by experts in their respective fields, this title provides a comprehensive overview of paranormal topics including psychics, spiritualism, alien phenomenon, and magic as well as detailing important individuals and organizations that have contributed to the study of these fields. Entries are listed alphabetically and the book includes a detailed index for quick reference. Topics vary from individual phenomenon, individuals, or concepts to larger schools of thought or societies. Each entry also possesses references to other topics in the text and a brief bibliography for further reading. Other features contained in the book include a master timeline of important historical events, sidebars within entries for additional information, and a more general bibliography at the end of the text.

One does question the editor's choice as to how certain entries should be listed and thereby which information is deserving of an individual entry. Examples of this would be the lack of entries for such individuals as Aleister Crowley and Madame Helena Blavatsky. While there is information on these individuals contained in the entries for Occultism and Theosophy, respectively, it is curious that they were not given their own entries while other persons of interest did receive such attention. Despite this they are mentioned in the index which overall proves to be a more than adequate reference for the entire work. On the whole this work is good introductory reference for general readers, high school students, or entry-level college students.—**W. Cole Williamson**

15 Recreation and Sports

General Works

Dictionaries and Encyclopedias

C, P

298.   Thompson, William N. **Gambling in America: An Encyclopedia of History, Issues, and Society.** 2d ed. Santa Barbara, Calif., ABC-CLIO, 2015. 505p. illus. index. $89.00. ISBN 13: 978-1-61069-979-2; 978-1-61069-980-8 (e-book).

Gambling in mainstream American life is a significant social and economic issue and *Gambling in America* is a concise encyclopedic look at what is a multimillion-dollar industry. This second edition (the first was published in 2001, see ARBA 2002, entry 824) presents 187 entries with nearly 100 covering nations, states, cities, and territories. Twenty-five feature individuals ranging from the well-known Howard Hughes to the lesser-known Moe Dalitz. Many entries are longer essays focusing on broader issues such as horse racing, sports betting, and lotteries. Entries are clearly written, avoid bias, and include reading references. There are generous illustrations, 10 tables, and an appendix with 13 major gambling legal cases. The comprehensive volume also includes a glossary, bibliography, and 20-page index—the last of which could be improved. Also of interest is a 17-page glossary of gambling events. Many individuals and events are embedded in larger entries such as the point shaving scandal at Boston College in college basketball and the many subsections in the entry on problem gambling. No one is more qualified than editor Thompson who has written widely on gambling in America for years. In all, this is a useful addition for reference collections on an often-overlooked social issue across the world.—**Boyd Childress**

C, P, S

299.   Williams, Victoria. **Weird Sports and Wacky Games around the World.** Santa Barbara, Calif., Greenwood Press/ABC-CLIO, 2015. 369p. illus. index. $89.00. ISBN 13: 978-1-61069-639-5; 978-1-61069-640-1 (e-book).

While it is not likely that many of the somewhat stranger pastimes will take over the popularity of, say, World Cup Soccer, it is definite that readers will find *Weird Sports and Wacky Games around the World* highly informative and engaging. While primarily designed as a research tool, the book nonetheless encompasses a fun topic that even general readers will enjoy.

Over 100 alphabetized entries showcase obscure yet beloved sports and games from around the world. Each entry provides general rules, in addition to any relevant history, folklore, literature, politics, and more surrounding the topic. Individual entries range in length from just under two pages to several pages and are followed by *see also* references and suggestions for future reading. We learn of broader sports that have been adapted geographically, like Elephant Sports (that is polo, soccer, and racing with pachyderms), and we learn of a simple pub game called Shove Ha'Penny which, though a mere board game for two, has nonetheless managed to hold an annual world championship. Readers certainly take away elements of fun and entertainment. Who wouldn't want to try a rousing game of Sepak Takraw, a Southeast Asian game which adapts elements of volleyball, soccer, gymnastics, and martial arts? But readers are also able to see how play remains a vital part of the human experience well into adulthood and throughout all cultures.

The book begins with an alphabetical list of entries, a geographic guide to entry origins by region, and a thematic guide to entries. It also includes a few black-and-white photographs, a selected bibliography, and an index. This highly recommended title is a handy place for students of all ages to begin a research project; though organized as an encyclopedia the fascinating subject matter makes this a good candidate for a cover-to-cover read for both students and the general public.—**Laura Herrell**

Directories

P

300.   **The Sports Market Place Directory, 2015.** Amenia, N.Y., Grey House Publishing, 2015. 1800p. index. $265.00pa. ISBN 13: 978-1-61925-562-3.

Need names and organizations for the sports business, then look no further. This massive (and expensive) volume lists over 14,000 contacts covering 100 sports in over 2,000 pages. There are nine specific categories covering specific sports, college sports, media information, facilities, and trade shows—and others. There are indexes for main entries, executives, and a geographic index. Two specific examples help explain—the section on college sports has over 1,700 listings including conferences and schools in the NCAA and NAIA. Each entry includes key personnel with contact information, Websites, e-mail addresses, fax and phone numbers, and a brief summary of sports the institution sponsors. There are outdated entries due to changes in coaches and administrations but the contact information is invaluable. The other example is 300 pages of media information including newspapers, magazines, and the electronic media. A typical listing includes contacts, phone and fax numbers, e-mail and Website information, and a brief description of coverage. Once again some names are out of date due to personnel changes. But overall the information is as accurate as reasonably possible. Grey House has been publishing this sports market directory for over 30 years and the volume has been a must for collections serving a sports business audience. Much of the information is now accessible on the Internet but the location of so much sports business in one source makes this a useful reference volume.—**Boyd Childress**

Handbooks and Yearbooks

C, P, S

301.   **Sports-Reference.com. http://www.sports-reference.com/.** [Website] Free. Date reviewed: 2016.

Sports-Reference.com provides users with freely accessible, complete sports statistics. The site that began as *Baseball-Reference.com* has expanded to include football, basketball, hockey, and the Olympics. Users will find player indexes, team histories, draft information, and much more by clicking on the appropriate tab at the top of the page. Statistics extend back to different dates depending on the sport. In the case of baseball, data is available as far back as 1871. Navigation within a sport is simple and intuitive. For someone wishing to see the trade history between two baseball franchises, for example, it only takes a couple of clicks to land on a baseball team's encyclopedia.

While the advertisements on the free site are not intrusive, a modest $20/year fee will allow ad-free browsing of the entire Sports-Reference family of sites.—**ARBA Staff Reviewer**

Baseball

P

302.   Gorman, Robert M., and David Weeks. **Death at the Ballpark: More Than 2,000 Game-Related Fatalities of Players, Other Personnel and Spectators in Amateur and Professional Baseball, 1862-2014.** 2d ed. Jefferson, N.C., McFarland, 2015. 344p. illus. index. $39.95pa. ISBN 13: 978-0-7864-7932-0; 978-1-4766-2258-3 (e-book).

Today's baseball fans likely would be surprised to discover that in 1930 the *New York Times* declared baseball the "most dangerous recreation." (p.5) That this unusual book detailing some 2,000 baseball-related deaths is now published in a second edition is clear tribute to baseball fans' fascination with statistics of all varieties and to the determination and diligence of its authors who have pursued their unusual subject for almost 15 years. As Gorman and Weeks graciously note, two other researchers, Ed Morton and Chuck McGill, also mined old newspapers and related sources and contributed greatly to the compilation of more than 1,000 additional baseball death reports not printed in the first edition. Interestingly, the authors note that the office of the Commissioner of Baseball does not track fan injuries and they recommend several practical safety measures to protect fans of sandlot games, high school and college contests, semi-pro, minor league, and major league contests.

Here Gorman and Weeks repeat their goal as given in the preface to the first edition, to provide "a comprehensive study of game-related baseball fatalities among players, field personnel, and fans at all levels of play in the United States." Each death is placed in the context of contributing factors and subsequent changes in the game of baseball including "style of play, the development of protective equipment, crowd control, stadium structure, and so forth." (p. 2) The authors provide specific and detailed definitions of game-related deaths and include all fan deaths if the deaths occurred "on the grounds," defined as the stadium, field, or parking lot. Section one of the book contains nine chapters tallying specific forms of death ranging from beaning to weather and violence. Section two offers two chapters on the deaths of field personnel. Section three presents four chapters on the deaths of fans. Appendix A covers unconfirmed fatalities based on plausible but possibly unreliable newspaper accounts. Appendix B yields a chronology of all fatalities by decades, from the 1860s through September 2014. Detailed chapter notes cite sources used and the bibliography includes books, journal and magazine articles, newspapers by state and city, other documents, and online indexes and databases. The index permits readers to locate death reports by name of person, location, league, and team. Reproductions of black-and-white photographs and drawings enhance the text. This book belongs in large public library and college or university baseball collections but its distinctive subject matter will be of interest to a wide range of baseball fans as well as many baseball players of all ages and to researchers interested in the sociology of sports.—**Julienne L. Wood**

Cricket

P
303.   **Cricker: http://cricker.com/.** [Website] Free. Date reviewed: 2015.

Cricker is a recently updated informational Web page that provides information about cricket games. A useful News section at the top of the homepage provides the latest information about recent cricket matches around the world and reroutes users to ESPN to read in-depth articles about game highlights. The Scores page shows scores of games currently taking place, and users can click on the game they would like to view to be rerouted to ecb.co.uk. Here, they can see who won the toss, find out the names of the umpires and officials, obtain player information, and eventually learn the end score of the game.

Though the Website includes some distracting advertisements, it has a simple format and is straightforward to use.

Cricker's extensive glossary may be the best feature of the site, as it includes over a hundred cricket vocabulary words. The terms can be searched at the top of the page alphabetically, and any additional questions can be sent to *Cricker* representatives in the feedback section located on the About page.

Overall, *Cricker* is a great tool for avid cricket fans and those looking to improve their basic knowledge of cricket terminology, and perhaps follow their favorite teams. While the site is simple and free to use, it is easy for all age groups to navigate and is a recommended resource for those involved with cricket in any capacity.—**ARBA Staff Reviewer**

Polo

P
304.   Laffaye, Horace A. **The Polo Encyclopedia. Second Edition.** Jefferson, N.C., McFarland, 2015. 411p. illus. $85.00pa. ISBN 13: 978-0-7864-9577-1; 978-1-4766-1956-9 (e-book).

This second edition of *The Polo Encyclopedia* updates the first edition in 2004 with the inclusion of approximately 8,000 more entries; previous entries were reviewed and corrected or deleted when necessary. The entries are cross-referenced and arranged alphabetically, providing a ready reference to more than 150 years of a game that is growing in popularity worldwide. The author, Horace A. Laffaye, has also written books on polo in Argentina, Britain, and the United States, as well as a book on how the sport has evolved. Users can find information on polo clubs worldwide, the rules of the game, individual riders, tournaments, technical polo terms, and more. The encyclopedia also has a generous sprinkling of black-and-white photographs, as well as several tables, like the one adjacent to the entry for the New Zealand Open that lists winners for the competition from 1977 to 2014. The cost of the book, $85.00 (paperback), and the breadth and quality of information makes this a good choice for libraries in need of information on this particular sport and for polo players and polo clubs everywhere.—**ARBA Staff Reviewer**

Soccer

P, S

305.   Dunmore, Tom. **Encyclopedia of the FIFA World Cup.** Lanham, Md., Rowman & Littlefield, 2015. 395p. index. $75.00; $74.99 (e-book). ISBN 13: 978-0-8108-8742-8; 978-0-8108-8743-5 (e-book).

Occurring every four years, the FIFA World Cup has come to be the world's largest staged sporting event, drawing soccer (or football) teams from over 200 eligible nations as well as hundreds of millions of television viewers. Producing many memorable moments from familiar players like Brazil's Pelé, England's Gary Lineker, or Germany's Thomas Müller, the competition continues to dazzle audiences and grow the sport. This encyclopedia is a necessary and thoroughly engaging companion to the sport that so many around the globe have come to adore.

Prefacing the alphabetical entries is an excellent and concise history of the tournament, beginning with the formation of the sport's governing body, FIFA (or the Fédération Internationale de Football Association), at the turn of the twentieth century. The preface touches on both moments of triumph, like the 1970 color television broadcast of Brazil's third tournament victory, and moments of controversy, such as the tournament's Eurocentric establishment or association with political propaganda. There is also a detailed tournament recap of each World Cup, including information such as host nation, number of matches, finalists, dates, and game highlights.

The entries themselves cover a wide range of players, countries, stadiums, coaches, awards, and other topics surrounding the tournament. Within the entries are fascinating facts and exciting moments from games worth reliving, such as American hero Landon Donovan's dramatic late goal against Algeria in the 2010 tournament, or French legend Zinedine Zidane's notorious red card received during the 2006 final. The book's encyclopedic format makes it easy for readers to track the ebbs and flows of a favorite player or home team. Including a number of appendixes to chart individual tournament award winners, the book offers entertaining, generous information about "the beautiful game" and its crowning tournament.—**Laura Herrell**

16 Sociology

General Works

Handbooks and Yearbooks

P, S

306. **The Sociology Book: Big Ideas Simply Explained.** New York, DK Publishing, 2015. 352p. illus. index. (Big Ideas Simply Explained). $25.00: $9.99 (e-book). ISBN 13: 978-1-4654-3650-4; 978-1-4654-4522-3 (e-book).

This survey starts with the founding fathers of sociology, like Auguste Comte, Karl Marx, and Emile Durkheim, and goes on to cover the broad spectrum of thought across the twentieth and into the twenty-first centuries. Essays encapsulate the key thoughts of a wide range of prominent sociologists with abundant graphics under the subject categories of Foundations of Sociology, Social Inequalities, Modern Living, Living in a Global World, Culture and Identity, Work and Consumerism, The Role of Institutions, and Families and Intimacies. Each section of essays starts with an introduction to set the context for the featured academicians. As a nice touch, each scholar's essay is cross-referenced to other relevant writers. A sociologist's work may be found in more than one category. For example, under the topic, Families and Intimacies, we learn about Michel Foucault's writings on how the advent of psychiatry melded with the longstanding Christian practice of confession to become a cultural obsession and means of therapy as seen in today's fixation on reality shows and social media. Foucault is then linked to Rousseau, Freud, and other thinkers. Foucault is also found in the category of Foundations of Sociology with his thoughts on power and in the category of The Role of Institutions with his comments on government. In addition to the featured sociologists, there is a directory with thumbnail sketches of additional scholars who have also contributed to the field. This episodic reference shows us an interesting cross-section of this field of study and helps us understand how our behavior is shaped and how changes come about in society.—**Adrienne Antink**

Family, Marriage, and Divorce

P

307. Bakst, Dina, Phoebe Taubman, and Elizabeth Gedmark. **Babygate: How to Survive Pregnancy & Parenting in the Workplace.** New York, Feminist Press, 2014. 343p. $18.95pa. ISBN 13: 978-1-55861-861-9.

The practical issues of welcoming a baby are many: spit-up, sleepless nights, and mountains of diapers among them. But today's expectant mothers face other challenges stemming from the fact that many are employed, and the climate in which they work may not be supportive of them. *Babygate* addresses those issues which specifically arise at the intersection of work and family life and aims to educate women about their legal rights.

Four chapters work along the timeline of informing employers of the happy news, managing the job as you plan for parental leave, returning to work after the baby's birth, and dealing with subtle but no less damaging issues of workplace stigma and prejudice. The book helps readers walk through the labyrinth of legislation which may or may not be relevant, such as the Family and Medical Leave Act of 1993 (applicable only to companies employing over 50 people, for example), the Americans with Disabilities Act (ADA), and the Pregnancy Discrimination Act, among others. Chapters take care to share real-life scenarios as they discuss issues like interviewing for a job while pregnant, breastfeeding on the job, initiating a flexible work schedule, and much more. The authors make generous use of personal stories, Q & A's, shaded sidebars, checklists, and other tools to make this important information truly accessible and easy to remember.

The book also provides thorough notes and numerous resources to address specific concerns from filing a claim with the Department of Labor, finding the most family-friendly companies, and understanding child and dependent care tax credits. It concludes with a very helpful state-by-state guide detailing the applicable legal mandates and methods of recourse. The state-by-state guide employs illustrative symbols for easy reference.

This book works as a true ally in educating family-minded women about their legal rights in the workplace.—**ARBA Staff Reviewer**

P

308.   **Domestic Violence Sourcebook.** 5th ed. Keith Jones, ed. Detroit, Omnigraphics, 2016. 620p. index. (Health Reference Series). $95.00. ISBN 13: 978-0-7808-1460-8; 978-0-7808-1459-2 (e-book).

This volume in the notable Health Reference Series is an invaluable reference regarding basic, comprehensible information about a wide range of issues connected to domestic violence. The book is designed to convey information to victims, their families, and others who have a personal interest in domestic abuse in a clear, straightforward manner. This fifth edition conveys the most up-to-date information on the many aspects of domestic abuse, including its definitions, risk factors, types, and much more.

The material is organized into six general parts which gather a profusion of specific topics: Facts about Domestic Violence; Stalking and Sexual Harassment; Intimate Partner Abuse; Abuse in Specific Populations; Preventing and Intervening in Domestic Violence; Emergency Management, Moving Out, and Moving On; and Additional Help and Information.

Each part is then broken down into manageable chapters housing well-defined topics. For example, part three—Abuse in Specific Populations—discusses child abuse, teen dating violence, digital dating abuse, elder abuse, workplace violence, and much more. Discussion of each topic is clear and concise, with a generous use of bullet points, Q & A's and short, well-demarcated paragraphs. Information conveyed for each topic is copious, but never overwhelming as this reference is targeted to the layperson.

Chapters in the last section include a glossary as well as hotlines, directories, and programs for easy access to proper assistance. An index rounds out the work.

This reference is not produced to replace professional counsel; however, it succeeds at providing intelligent, basic information about domestic abuse to consumers.

Recommended.—**ARBA Staff Reviewer**

Gay and Lesbian Studies

C, P

309.   **Archives of Human Sexuality and Identity.** [Website] Farmington Hills, Mich., Gale/Cengage Learning. Price negotiated by site. Date reviewed: 2016.

The *Archives of Human Sexuality and Identity* is a digital archive collection of LGBTQ history and culture since 1940. The collection provides access to material from hundreds of institutions and organizations representing/participating in LGBTQ history. The collection contains gay and lesbian newspapers; meeting minutes, and administrative records from LGBTQ organizations worldwide; private correspondence; government reports and memoranda, and photographs. The collection is able to shed light on: the response to the HIV/AIDS crises, LGBTQ activism in several countries including the United States, Canada, and Britain; development of women's rights activism; and political and social organizations founded by LGBTQ individuals.

Materials from major collections and libraries around the world are included such as the Mattachine Society and Daughters of Bilitis (the earliest gay and lesbian groups in the United States). Also represented are the Gay, Lesbian, Bisexual, and Transgender Historical Society; Canadian Lesbian and Gay Archives; National Organization for Women; the Albany Trust; and the Gay Activists Alliance, among others.

Due to its scope, the collection is able to also provide access to documents by and about organizations that no longer exists such as the Q Spirit forum and the Southern California Council on Religion and the Homophile.

The collection can be searched by keyword or browsed by collection. The homepage provides a simple search box and a link for an advanced search that allows keywords to be combined and filtered by such things as content type, illustrated works, and source library.

The Term Frequency tool allows a user to enter a search term and see the frequency of its use in the collection over time plotted on a chart. Users can then click on a point in the graph to see documents. Further, there is a Term Cluster tool to allow users to interact visually with the search results and see which words and subjects are found most often in the text of the search results. It is a fun way to reveal unexpected connections, and it is a powerful way to dig into a primary document collection.

Searches can be saved and tagged. Saved and tagged search results can be saved or used by individuals or groups. The group function is a nice option to support collaborative work.

This is a very unique resource and represents a major and meaningful effort to support the study of LBGTQ issues. It is highly recommended for academic and large public libraries. It is carefully and thoughtfully constructed and enhanced with advanced search tools. It is invaluable to have all of these major sources of information in one place, and the addition of the powerful search features make it even more valuable.—**Kristin Kay Leeman**

Philanthropy

C, P

310.   Philanthropy Roundtable. **Almanac of American Philanthropy.** Washington, D.C., Philanthropy Roundtable, 2016. 1317p. illus. index. $25.00. ISBN 13: 978-0-9861474-5-6.

In the almanac, Karl Zinsmeister, series editor of the Wise Giver's Guides, of the Philanthropy Roundtable in Washington, D.C., and head of publication of that organization, provides an extensive, introductory analysis of the cultural importance of philanthropy to the success of the United States of America. The creative prose of this introduction belies the ostensibly parochial title, and provides a compelling platform for the almanac as a "living document,"—a description coined by Adam Meyerson, current President of The Philanthropy Roundtable.

This unique resource features 11 sections detailing information about American philanthropy from the years 1636 to 2015. The aforementioned introduction is followed by a section profiling great men and women of American philanthropy: prominent living donors and 56 donors who brought about change in the United States and the world through their private giving. The third chapter outlines major achievements in several areas including medicine, education, arts, religion, and public policy reform, just to name a few. The fourth section focuses on an annotated list of essential books and articles about philanthropy, followed by sections on an original 2015 national poll, statistics on United States generosity, details on who gives the most, and an explanation of tax protection. A comprehensive index begins on page 1195, and an informative, 22-page foldout features a timeline of American philanthropy (1636-2015).

Readers and researchers of all stripes would gain perspective about the vital role philanthropy plays in our day-to-day lives through the stories and facts presented in this reference work. It is highly recommended for corporate, foundation, public, community college, and academic libraries.—**Laura J. Bender**

Social Work and Social Welfare

C

311.   **Encyclopedia of Social Work. http://socialwork.oxfordre.com/.** [Website] New York, Oxford University Press. Price negotiated by site. Date reviewed: 2015.

The *Encyclopedia of Social Work* (ESW) is an online product that builds on the print version of the encyclopedia. Under the direction of Editor-in-Chief Cynthia Frankel, an editorial board vets each of the hundreds of articles.

The main page offers a search by such subfields as Criminal Justice, Gender and Sexuality, Mental Behavioral Health, Poverty, and Social Justice and Human Rights. A click on Gender and Sexuality, for instance, takes searchers to 37 articles, alphabetized by title. The search can be narrowed through the use of tools located on the left-hand side of the page. Articles are easily accessed with one click, which connects users to the full text, starting with a content box that contains the publication date, a list of subjects, and a Direct Object Identifier, followed by an abstract, keywords, and the text. On the left-hand side of the screen are an outline of the article, a list of related articles in the ESW (all linked), and Other Resources (New & Featured and Forthcoming articles). A list of references with links to online sources, suggestions for further reading, and the author biography appear at the end of the article. An added bonus is the Oxford Index Underbar, which links the ESW with all of Oxford University Press's related online content. For example, in the case of the article "Mental Health Courts," the Oxford Index Underbar produces links to "Mental Health Act," from the *Oxford Handbook of Mental Health Nursing* and the book *Parenting by Men Who Batter.*

For librarians, the ESW provides a trusted source of information; content is timely, regularly updated, and easy to find. This site is highly recommended to academic libraries.—**ARBA Staff Reviewer**

Substance Abuse

P, S

312. **Drug Information for Teens.** 4th ed. Keith Jones, ed. Detroit, Omnigraphics, 2016. 339p. index. (Teen Health Series). $69.00. ISBN 13: 978-0-7808-1358-8.

This book is designed to convey basic, up-to-date information about drug addiction, abuse, and treatment in regards to a variety of different substances. Its information is clear and highly organized in direct targeting of the teen market. This book appreciates the need to continue to educate teenagers about the risks of drug abuse on their mental and physical health even as drug use amongst them continues to decline.

The book is separated into eight major parts which are, in turn, filled with short topical chapters for ease of reference. Parts include: General Information about Addiction and Substance Abuse; Alcohol; Tobacco, Nicotine, and E-Cigarettes; Marijuana; Abuse of Legally Available Substances; Abuse of Illegal Substances; Other Drug-Related Health Concerns; and Treatment for Addiction. A ninth, concluding part lists National Organizations for Drug Information, Substance Abuse Hotlines and Helplines, and a State-by-State List of Alcohol and Drug Referral Phone Numbers.

The book employs a variety of tools for ease of comprehension, including black-and-white illustrations, charts, bullet points, shaded text boxes, and more. Material is straightforward and is primarily conveyed via an appealing question-and-answer format. For example, the chapter on alcohol asks a series of such questions as what is underage drinking, why is underage drinking dangerous, and what is binge drinking. Answers are concise and stick to the question at hand. A particularly insightful chapter connects substance abuse with auxiliary issues such as teen pregnancy, mental illness, infectious disease, violence, and suicide. In addition, the book makes every effort to provide up-to-date information; pointing to the latest substances like bath salts, using street names alongside chemical names, discussing the most current treatments like Adolescent Community Reinforcement Approach (A-CRA), etc.

The reference is not produced to replace professional medical counsel; however, it succeeds at providing intelligent, basic information about many facets of this problem to patients, families, caregivers, and others. Recommended.—**ARBA Staff Reviewer**

17 Statistics, Demography, and Urban Studies

Statistics

United States

C, P

313. **America's Top-Rated Cities: A Statistical Handbook.** 22d ed. Amenia, N.Y., Grey House Publishing, 2015. 4v. maps. $295.00/set. ISBN 13: 978-1-61925-552-4; 978-1-61925-557-9 (e-book).

Now in its 22nd edition, this is a standard reference work in many libraries. With the addition of five cities (Palm Bay, FL; Roanoke, VA; Springfield, IL; Tyler, TX; and Winston-Salem, NC), the new edition covers 100 U.S. cities that have a population of at least 100,000. The entry for each city provides background information, rankings, and statistical tables. The background information summarizes the history of the area and touches upon the city's environment, politics, culture, and climate. For example, the entry on Boston includes its place in history, a survey of historic buildings, a listing of its major sports teams, and a discussion of the Boston Marathon. The rankings for each city are drawn from over 300 books, articles, and Internet sources that have been categorized into topics such as business/finance, dating/romance, education, environmental, health/fitness, and real estate. Specific rankings are as varied as most well-read, most wired, safest, most polite, most tax friendly, best for dogs, gayest, and most tattooed. The statistical tables are the heart of the entries and are divided into two broad categories: the business environment (such as city finances, demographics, economy, income, and employment) and the living environment (including cost of living, health, education, recreation, and climate). Each volume includes the same four appendixes: Comparative Statistics, Metropolitan Area Definitions, Government Type and County, Chambers of Commerce and Economic Development Organizations, and State Departments of Labor and Employment. The Comparative Statistics appendix includes 80 different charts which permit the user to compare the 100 cities on a wide variety of topics such as demographics, economy, income and poverty, employment and earnings, election results in the 2012 presidential election, housing, education, cost of living, health care, public safety, climate, and air quality. For most public libraries this set will be a well-used resource, especially for those examining business opportunities and for those who are considering relocating to other cities. For academic libraries, this set will be useful for many sociology and public policy courses.— **Gregory A. Crawford**

C, P

314.   **County and City Extra, 2014: Annual Metro, City, and County Data Book.** 22d ed. Deirdre A. Gaquin and Mary Meghan Ryan, eds. Lanham, Md., Bernan Press, 2014. 1404p. maps. (County and City Extra Series). $155.00; $154.99 (e-book). ISBN 13: 978-1-59888-719-8; 978-1-59888-720-4 (e-book).

County and City Extra 2014 is the fully updated, 22d annual edition of a guide to key demographic and economic data applied to various geographic subdivisions of the United States. Data has been grouped into five basic parts: States, States and Counties, Metropolitan Areas, Cities of 25,000 or more, and Congressional Districts of the 113th Congress.

Each part then presents copious data tables measuring information related to population, crime, income, housing, Social Security, agriculture, land area, employment, government finance, and much, much more. Each part opens with data "Highlights and Rankings" particular to that section, selecting points of comparison such as population, density, land area, and agricultural land value.

Preceding all the data tables is an overall introduction pointing to the newest sources of data—specifically the American Community Survey (replacing the census long form) and the 2010 census, as well as newly considered measurements such as "non-employer" (e.g., self-employed) businesses. The introduction also houses a subject summary, a colored map portfolio, and organizational information.

Appendixes provide excellent context for understanding the data in regards to Geographic Concepts and Codes, Metropolitan Statistical Areas (Divisions and Components), Core Based Statistical Areas (Divisions and Components), a Map of Congressional Districts and States, Cities by County and Source Notes, and Explanations.

This book is a greatly helpful resource for advanced students and professionals alike.—**Laura Herrell**

C, P

315.   **County and City Extra. Special Historical Edition, 1790-2010.** Deirdre A. Gaquin and Mary Meghan Ryan, eds. Lanham, Md., Bernan Press, 2015. 271p. $125.00. ISBN 13: 978-1-59888-804-1.

Using information from the U.S. Census, the Census Bureau's two-volume *Bicentennial Edition: Historical Statistics of the United States, Colonial Times to 1970,* and smaller bureau publications, this title supplies data from the earliest days of the republic into the early twenty-first century. Part A, United States, includes a short introduction, population statistics, life expectancy data, information on race, and more. It concludes with "Notes and Definitions," a section designed to help users understand and interpret the data, providing definitions for such things as housing unit, percent urban, and civilian labor force as well as explanations for how the measurement of urban areas or racial data have changed over time. States, part B, provides population data, percent change from previous censuses, percent Hispanic or Latino, personal income, farm income, etc., followed by "Notes and Definitions." Country population data is presented in part C, alphabetically by state and further by county. The "Notes and Definitions" after the data tables explain shifting boundaries, name changes, or other circumstances particular to each state. Part D, the final section, offers population data on the city level.

This handy reference compiles a wealth of data in one place; the graphs, tables, charts, and "Notes and Definitions" facilitate both use and comprehension.—**ARBA Staff Reviewer**

C, P

316.   **Patterns of Economic Change by State and Area: Income, Employment, & Gross Domestic Product.** 3d ed. Mary Meghan Ryan, ed. Lanham, Md., Bernan Press, 2015. 497p. $200.00pa.; $99.99 (e-book). ISBN 13: 978-1-59888-796-9; 978-1-59888-797-6 (e-book).

Patterns of Economic Change by State and Area, a special edition of *Business Statistics of the United States: Patterns of Economic Change,* is a complement to titles that include the *State and Metropolitan Area Data Book* and *County and City Extra. Patterns of Economic Change by State and Area* is arranged in three parts. Part A, Personal Income and Employment by Region, State and Metropolitan Area, includes annual data (some data going back to 1958) for farm and nonfarm earnings; payments to persons of dividends, interest, and rent; total personal income; population; per capita personal income and disposable income; and total number of jobs in state or area. Part A also includes a guide for researchers on "Notes and Definitions," as well income concepts. Tables are arranged by region (e.g., Far West, New England, Great Lakes); state, and metropolitan statistical areas (MSAs). Part B includes gross domestic product on a state-by-state basis. Part C includes the poverty rate by state (defined for a demographic group as the number of poor people in that group expressed as a percentage of the total number of people in the group). The appendix lists MSAs, metropolitan divisions, and components. Each MSA includes core-based statistical area number, state/county FIPS code, and a list of counties in the area. *Patterns of Economic Change by State and Area* fills a need for locating data on personal income, employment, and gross domestic product by region, state, and metropolitan statistical area. Recommended for larger public and academic libraries.— **Lucy Heckman**

C, P

317.   **Profiles of America: Facts, Figures, Statistics for Every Populated Place in the United States.** 3d ed. Amenia, N.Y., Grey House Publishing, 2015. 4v. maps. index. $795.00pa/set. ISBN 13: 978-1-61925-105-2.

This ready reference set of facts, figures, and statistics is thorough in its treatment of each place and comprehensive, including every populated place in the United States. Twelve data fields are new to this edition, including health insurance, median travel time to work, and median age. Each data field can be easily traced back to its source using the "Data Explanation and Sources" in the "User Guide" in every volume. Sources include the Census Bureau, other government agencies, and nongovernment sources. Places that the U.S. Census Bureau designates as Census Designated Places, Minor Civil Divisions, or unincorporated communities are included. The "Regional and Comparative Statistics" section of each volume takes 14 data fields and ranks them for the 100 largest cities in the region. "Regional Rankings" provide rankings for those same pieces of data. Information that may be a column in "Regional and Comparative Statistics" will be a page of data in the "Regional Rankings." To properly analyze the information and understand how these fit together, the "Data Explanation and Sources" in the user guide should be consulted. "Regional Rankings" assists individuals from a particular background to find communities that share that background.

The set has four regional volumes: Southern Region, Western Region, Central Region, and Eastern Region. Within each region, information is organized alphabetically by state, by county, and by place. Each state includes an index of the places in that state with their county and page number. In volume one, Southern Region, is the master index for all four volumes giving the volume, county, and page number.

Although the listings for each place are easy to use and understand by the general public and undergraduate students, other portions, such as the "Regional and Comparative Statistics" and the "Regional Rankings," require more expertise to properly interpret and analyze the data. Highly recommended for all academic and public libraries.—**Ladyjane Hickey**

C, P

318.   **State Profiles: The Population and Economy of Each U.S. State.** 6th ed. Shana Hertz Hattis, ed. Lanham, Md., Bernan Press, 2014. 554p. index. $165.00. ISBN 13: 978-1-59888-721-1; 978-1-59888-722-8 (e-book).

Finding statistics about states and the United States as a whole is not necessarily challenging for a librarian but it can be time-consuming and tedious to find answers to questions such as "which state uses the most energy?" Or, "how much money did the state of Arizona collect in taxes and what was the amount derived through property taxes?" At times it can also be tricky to remember which government agency would collect the information sought. The sixth edition of *State Profiles: The Population and Economy of Each U.S. State* does an excellent job of compiling basic economic and social statistics. From population counts through state government tax collection, this resource provides general statistics for each state and the District of Columbia in an easy to use volume.

Beginning with a textual summary about the United States, followed by statistical charts ranking each state based on a variety of topics (total population, median household income, and traffic fatalities, just to name a few examples), this volume is then organized alphabetically by state (including the District of Columbia). Each entry begins with a summary page, providing "Facts and Figures" such as location and size information; state motto, nickname, and song; date of statehood; and other basic facts. This page also includes a bulleted "At a Glance" section that highlights some key facts, such as rate of population growth, median household income, homeownership (actual bulleted points vary depending on the state), and the numerical ranking for the state for these factors. The rest of the entry consists of 16 tables, which are the same tables for every state and in the same order; a list of tables is provided following the contents page at the start of the book to enable users to easily see what information is provided for each state. In addition to tables, charts and graphs are provided for selected aspects.

A "Notes and Definitions" section at the end of the book provides information about each of the tables, such as the source of the data, definitions for the terminology used by the originating source, the source's methodology, and where to go for more information. One thing of note is the lack of citations for the statistics used for the United States Rankings in the first section of the volume. An index is included after the "Notes and Definitions" section, providing users with the specific page numbers for a particular state's statistical tables.

Statistical information was primarily collected from American FactFinder and other Census Bureau Websites. Additional sources include the Bureau of Labor Statistics (BLS), Bureau of Economic Analysis (BEA), U.S. Department of Education, and Uniform Crime Reports from the Federal Bureau of Investigation (FBI). For this 2014 edition, data is predominantly from 2012, with some tables using 2010, 2011, and some 2013 information as well. While the most recent data at the time of publication was included, some tables also include older data (often 2000 and 2010) to show users change over time.

While all of the data used to create the statistical tables that make up this resource are freely available, knowing where to look and how to use the various government Websites can be laborious for users. Because of this, this volume is an excellent ready reference source for a library of any type and size and its ease of use allows it to be accessible to library patrons of all levels of research experience.—**Julia Frankosky**

C, P

319. **State Rankings 2015: A Statistical View of America.** Kathleen O'Leary and Scott Morgan, eds. Thousand Oaks, Calif., CQ Press / Sage, 2015. 603p. index. (State FactFinder Series). $100.00. ISBN 13: 978-1-4833-8504-4.

State Rankings 2015 "provides an easily accessible collection of data in a broad range of quality of life factors in the United States" and "compares data from the fifty states and the District of Columbia in 566 tables." Tables are arranged within the categories of: agriculture; crime and law enforcement; defense; economy; education; employment and labor; energy and environment; geography; government finances: federal; government finances: state and local; health; households and housing; population; social welfare; and transportation. Sources for data were selected by the editors from various government and private sector sources. Subjects are designated as positive or negative (e.g., high state crime rates negatively affect a state's comparison ranking). In addition to the tables listed within the subject categories, this reference source contains 2015 state rankings; the date each state was admitted to statehood; state fast facts (e.g., state flower, name of capital); a list of names, addresses, phone numbers, and URLs; and an index. Each table's years of coverage vary, dates range from 2010 to 2015 (for instance, estimated new cancer cases is for 2014 and enrollment in institutions of higher education is from 2012). Each table includes title, national rates or totals, and states listed in alphabetical order. Sources are designated for each of the tables. Researchers can locate diverse data by state, such as: Internal Revenue Service gross collections in 2013; unemployment rate in 2014; population per square mile in 2014; employees in leisure and hospitality in 2014; cattle on farms in 2015; and percent of population enrolled in Medicare in 2012. *State Rankings 2015* is a valuable reference source that provides a wealth of data for researchers and also is a starting point for locating further information—the list of sources is especially helpful. Recommended for larger public libraries and academic library collections.—**Lucy Heckman**

C, P

320. **Statistical Abstract of the United States 2015: The National Data Book.** Lanham, Md., Bernan Press, 2015. 1024p. maps. index. $179.00. ISBN 13: 978-1-59888-729-7.

Ignoring the protests of many librarians and citizens, the Census Bureau recently decided to discontinue publication of this reference tool, the standard source for accurate, comprehensive U.S. statistical information since 1878. Issued in August 2011, the 2012 *Statistical Abstract of the United States* was the last edition published by the U.S. Census Bureau. Beginning in 2012 ProQuest and Bernan Press assumed responsibility for publishing "the most used statistical reference tool in U.S. libraries" (p. v). This 2015 edition, issued in December 2014 with more than 1,000 pages in a large 8.5 x 11-inch format, presents statistics current as of early September 2014. It contains 45 new tables listed on page xi and a deleted tables list on pages xii-xiii as well as updated tables from the 2012 Census of Agriculture and the 2012 Economic Census. New or infrequent users will appreciate the "Guide to Tabular Presentation," pp. xiv-xv and the third appendix, "Limitations of the Data," pp. 947-948. Source notes below each table in this volume guide readers to other statistical publications as does the first appendix, "Guide to Sources of Statistics, State Statistical Abstracts, and Foreign Statistical Abstracts." The extensive index yields references to table numbers rather than page numbers.

While Bernan Press produces the print version of the book, ProQuest offers an online version of this title. Updated monthly, the online edition yields additional back year's data, spreadsheets corresponding to each table in the print edition, and the option to refine and manipulate data. It can be purchased alone or as a part of the publisher's ProQuest *Statistical Insight* package that includes "The Tables Collection," over one million tables published since 1999 on the basis of U.S. and foreign statistical sources and "over 100,000 statistical reports in PDF," to enable users to locate a specific table or number easily.

This essential print resource belongs at or near the reference center and/or government documents service desk of all public and academic libraries as well as in many high school libraries. Larger libraries with substantial government documents collections and a research-oriented constituency or libraries with more expansive collection development budgets may prefer the online *Statistical Insight* package.—**Julienne L. Wood**

Urban Studies

C, P

321.   **Immigration and America's Cities.** Joaquin Jay Gonzalez, III and Roger L. Kemp, eds. Jefferson, N.C., McFarland, 2016. 300p. index. $39.95pa. ISBN 13: 978-0-7864-9633-4; 978-1-4766-2379-5 (e-book).

This book from McFarland offers a wealth of information on how American cities are dealing with immigrants. It is designed to serve as a handbook for the development of good services at the country and municipal level. Editors Joaquin Jay Gonzalez, III, and Roger L. Kemp, both professors at Golden Gate University—Kemp also spent 25 years as a city manager—have pulled together contributions from 45 scholars, journalists, and public servants (including a police chief and several city administrators) that delve into major immigration issues and how they are being handled by local governments across the country. Chapters cover the growth of the immigrant population over the past decades and specific topics such as immigrants and the law, safe havens, language access, driver's licensing, employment, public safety, education, and voting. The 10 appendixes include a 2014 letter to Congress from the U.S. Conference of Mayors, a list of sanctuary cities, and a national immigration resource directory. There is an index and a description of the contributors. The book will be of interest to general readers and could provide a valuable resource for those seeking solutions to immigration issues.—**Alice Chaffee**

C, P, S

322.   **New York City Water and Transit Infrastructure in Photographs http:// digitalcollections.nypl.org/collections/metropolis-new-york-city-water-and-transit-infrastructure-in-photographs#/?tab=about.** [Website] Free. Date reviewed: 2016.

This collection from the New York Public Library includes several archival collections of photographs in addition to supplemental published illustrated sources all relating to the transit and water infrastructure of New York City in the past 150 years.

The Web page is attractive and organized, and does offer a variety of reports and text documents related to the transit and water infrastructure. Students who are studying this specialized subject may find these items interesting, though many text documents are very dense and some are difficult to read due to the aging of the document. Each still image provides the user with the following information: type of resource, date issued, division, author, dates/origin, topics, notes, physical description, and citations (in MLA, APA, Chicago, and Wikipedia), as well as additional descriptive information. A timeline shows when the image was issued and digitized. Users can also download the images in a variety of sizes and resolutions. This highly specialized collection will be particularly useful for those interested in the history of New York City water and transit infrastructures.—**ARBA Staff Reviewer**

18 Women's Studies

Biography

P, S
323.   **American First Ladies.** 3d ed. Robert P. Watson, ed. Hackensack, N.J., Salem Press, 2015. 459p. illus. index. $165.00. ISBN 13: 978-1-61925-942-3; 978-1-61925-943-0 (e-book).

A companion to *American Presidents,* fourth edition, published by Salem in 2015, this well-conceived volume provides concise biographies of the 47 First Ladies who have served the nation from Martha Washington to Michelle Obama. Black-and-white portraits or photographs enhance these biographical offerings. This third edition is the first to include an entry on Mrs. Obama, and has also updated and revised entries for several recent first ladies, as well as the bibliography and appendixes.

Each essay presents clearly formatted and engaging information regarding the First Ladies' "Early Life," "Marriage and Family," "Presidency and First Ladyship," and "Legacy." Shaded textboxes offer biographical summaries of the president, along with interesting anecdotes from the subject's time as First Lady. For example, we learn of Nellie Taft's unprecedented accompaniment of her husband between his inaugural ceremony and the executive mansion.

Special to this volume is a series of topical essays adding further depth to readers' understanding of the role of the First Lady. Subjects include "First Ladies and Social Causes," "Family Life in the White House," and more. The book also includes supplemental information for further reference, including chronological lists of First Ladies and Presidents; a selection of appropriate libraries, museums, historic sites and Websites; an annotated bibliography; and an index.—**ARBA Staff Reviewer**

Dictionaries and Encyclopedias

P, S
324.   Hendricks, Nancy. **America's First Ladies: A Historical Encyclopedia and Primary Document Collection of the Remarkable Women of the White House.** Santa Barbara, Calif., ABC-CLIO, 2015. illus. index. $100.00. ISBN 13: 978-1-61069-882-5; 978-1-61069-883-2 (e-book).

This reference describes the lives of our First Ladies, from Martha Washington to Michelle Obama. Reading this survey, we see how the position of First Lady, a role that is unofficial and still undefined by any governmental directive, has evolved to a unique platform to do good and to make a lasting mark on our society. Each chapter gives the traditional biographic information as to family life, education, etc., but what makes this collection so engaging are the stories that bring to life the amazing women who in their own ways contributed to their husbands' presidencies. For example, we all know Dolley Madison saved George Washington's portrait and important cabinet papers when the White House was attacked by the British during the War of 1812. But she also saved her favorite red velvet drapes which she later used to make the ball gown she wore often and proudly as a reminder of the United States's victory over Britain. Elizabeth Monroe, while her husband was ambassador to France, rescued General Lafayette's wife from prison thus saving her from execution during the French Revolution. Louisa Catherine Adams and her young son accompanied her husband, John Quincy Adams, to Moscow when he served as ambassador to Russia for six years. Hurriedly called to Paris to negotiate the Treaty of Ghent, Adams left Louisa to close their affairs at the embassy and to get herself and her son from Moscow to Paris during the last year of the Napoleonic wars. Traveling alone and often through battle lines, she had only her son's toy sword as a weapon. Harriet Lane, niece of James Buchanan, served as First Lady for her uncle. Harriet accompanied Buchanan when he served as ambassador to Great Britain and became a favorite of Queen Victoria. It was rumored at the time, that Queen Victoria's government refrained from officially recognizing the Confederacy because of the Queen's friendship with Harriet, an action that changed the course of the Civil War. Clearly America's First Ladies are not just pretty faces but women of substance to be respected.—**Adrienne Antink**

C, P, S
325.   **Women's Rights in the United States: A Comprehensive Encyclopedia of Issues, events, and People.** Wayne, Tiffany K. and Lois Banner, eds. Santa Barbara, Calif., ABC-CLIO, 2015. 4v. illus. index. $415.00/set. ISBN 13: 978-1-61069-214-4; 978-1-61069-215-1 (e-book).

This encyclopedia is unique in its breadth of coverage of women's issues, describing events, controversies, and people from 1776 to 2014. In 2016 it won important awards from *Choice* and RUSA as an outstanding reference source. The editors have doctorates in history and are well-published. Wayne is the editor or author of three earlier works in women's history and Banner is a university professor and author of several important academic texts. As a resource it is nearly flawless: so well-organized, comprehensive, and readable, one may be tempted to read its four volumes from cover to cover.

The set includes 650 signed entries by about 300 contributors, as well as 127 primary documents. The editors' broad understanding of history is demonstrated in the selection of topics and organization of volumes. The interrelationship between the women's movement and contemporaneous struggles are made clear, and are highlighted in the subtitles of volumes: one, *Moral Reform and the Woman Question (1776-1870)*; two, *Suffrage and a New Wave of Women's Activism (1870-1950)*; three, *Civil Rights and Modern Feminism (1950-1990)*, and four, *Third-Wave and Global Feminisms (1990-Present)*.

Each volume begins with a specific introduction, alphabetical list of entries, list of primary documents, and list of entries by topic, and ends with the primary documents in full text. Volume one also contains a preface to volumes one-four and a chronology of women's rights in America from 1776 to 2014. Volume four also contains a general bibliography, information about the editors and writers, and an index.

The entries focus on individuals and subjects related to women's rights and gender equality, including significant events, organizations, all types of media, legislation, and court cases. They have *see also* references to other entries and primary documents in all volumes. Most include well-selected references for further reading, including books, articles, Websites, and videos, and some have black-and-white illustrations. Examples of entries are Coverture, Harriet Tubman, Women and World War II, Lesbian Feminism, Women and the Civil Rights Movement, Hillary Clinton, and Same-Sex Marriage. Primary documents include "Aren't I a Woman?" by Sojourner Truth (1851); "If Men Were Seeking the Franchise," by Jane Addams (1913); *Toward a Female Liberation Movement*, by Beverly Jones and Judith Brown (1968); and *Sexual Violence in the World of Online Gaming* by Anita Sarkeesian (2012). The variety and breadth of the content cannot be overestimated. It is an outstanding choice for all types of libraries, and readers from high school to college graduates.—**Madeleine Nash**

Handbooks and Yearbooks

C, P, S

326.   **Canadian Women's History. http://eco.canadiana.ca/?usrlang=en.** [Website] Free. Date reviewed: 2016.

Canadiana is an independent, not-for-profit charity established in 1978. Its goal is to preserve and share hundreds of documents through a "virtual library that holds the most complete set of full-text historical content about Canada." Its *Canadian Women's History* collection includes memoirs, diaries, collected letters, drama, political pamphlets, and more, with topics ranging from poetry to fashion to medicine. Those looking for early writings of Canadian female authors can find a multitude of resources here published from the eighteenth century to the twentieth century. One such document is the captivity narrative (published in London in 1760) of Elizabeth Hanson, taken into Canada in 1725 from her home in New England. While the majority of the items are written in English, there are a fair number written in French, as one would expect.

The collection is easy to navigate, offering users a simple search bar that filters titles, creator names, subjects, and texts. Users can also select a date range to find works published within specified years. This is a highly recommended resource for scholars studying Canada and Canadian culture. It will also prove beneficial for educators instructing students on how to find and appropriately implement primary sources into their academic work.—**ARBA Staff Reviewer**

C, P, S

327.   **Gifts of Speech: Women's Speeches from Around the World: http://www. giftsofspeech.org/.** [Website] Free: Date reviewed: 2016.

Gifts of Speech is a nonprofit project founded by Liz Kent León, Head of Digital Initiatives and Outreach at Sweet Briar College Library. This Website is dedicated to preserving and providing access to speeches given by influential and contemporary women across the world and is intended for secondary students and college undergraduates. Speeches are carefully researched in newspapers, magazines, Internet pages, reference works, news, documentaries, and educational media. All content on this Web page is used with permission. Most content has never been published in any paper-based format or speech index, and comes directly from the authors, though instructors should be aware that content is not vetted for accuracy and is not censored in any way, making some of the audio potentially inappropriate for younger users. Because online speeches can be difficult to find, this resource is excellent for students conducting research for projects and academia, especially debate.

Users can browse for content alphabetically by speaker name or by date under the browse tab; a How-to tab provides information on conducting searches on the site. The earliest speeches come from the 1848 Seneca Falls Convention and the most recent is from a 2009 by Huerta Muller, Nobel Prize winner in literature, entitled "Every Word Knows Something of a Vicious Circle." A Nobel Lectures page contains the Top 100 American Speeches of the 20th Century, as well a few dozen Nobel lectures by women laureates. A FAQ page should help to answer any questions. Overall, this is a very easy and helpful Website that is highly recommended.—**ARBA Staff Reviewer**

C, P, S

328.   **Women in World History. http://chnm.gmu.edu/wwh/.** [Website] Free. Date reviewed: 2016.

Women in World History is a Website created by George Mason University's Center for History and New Media to aid high school and college teachers in developing course content in women's history and gender studies. Recognizing the challenges of finding and effectively using classroom resources on these topics, the site provides primary resources and curriculum material emphasizing global history and cross-cultural connections, thus helping teachers and students keep up to date on the latest research approaches.

The site's main components are easily accessed through the homepage. The "Primary Sources" section, which can be searched by region, time period, or topic, includes letters, newspaper articles, photographs, and more. Primary sources are available for various regions of the world and for ancient through modern time periods; however, the site could benefit from a larger collection (there are about 200). Two other sections, "Analyzing Evidence" and "Modules," provide guidance, suggestions, and examples for using primary sources in the classroom. The "Analyzing Evidence" section includes explanations of how historians use primary sources (such as census data, art, and oral histories) in their research, while "Modules" presents clear strategies for creating document-based lessons. A potential drawback of the "Modules" section is the limited number (14) of lesson plans provided; however, even teachers unable to use the specific plans provided can still use them as models for their own lessons. Another section, "Teaching Case Studies," is a collection of accounts in which educators describe their experiences using historical case studies in their courses. Finally, reviews of other Websites on women's history will be very helpful to teachers looking for assistance in assessing online resources and their usefulness in the classroom.

It is unclear how frequently the site is updated: the "About" page refers to the project's upcoming completion in 2006, and the most recent archived discussion in the teachers' forum is dated March 2006. Nevertheless, the site's content is of high quality and is recommended as a resource for teachers wishing to incorporate primary source studies into their women's history courses.—**ARBA Staff Reviewer**

C, P, S

329.   **Women, War, and Violence: Topography, Resistance, and Hope.** Mariam M. Kurtz and Lester R. Kurtz, eds. Santa Barbara, Calif., Praeger/ABC-CLIO, 2015. 2v. index. (Praeger International Security). $184.00/set. ISBN 13: 978-1-4408-2880-5; 978-1-4408-2881-2 (e-book).

While we have learned a lot since gender studies was formalized as a discipline in the 1970s, there remains much to discover. This work takes a broader view of violence encompassing not only physical violence, but also psychological and emotional violence. The definition further extends to include structural and cultural violence (typically considered injustices). The introduction classifies violence as direct (perpetrated at the individual level), structural (perpetrated by the social system), cultural (perpetrated by the culture, and possibly endorsed by women themselves), and environmental (perpetrated towards the environment and adversely affecting women in particular). Gender is seen through the lens of a social construct (as in contemporary gender studies) rather than a biological construct. War is viewed more broadly as conflict, and is considered a manifestation of violence.

This two-volume work consists of 36 essays that explore the various facets of gender and violence. Most essays analyze sources of violence and possible solutions; some provide an overview. Essays on sex trafficking, violence towards immigrants, and the need to support legislation with other reforms summarize current scholarship. Other essays on the tools women use to function in highly violent environments, spouses of PTSD veterans, models used to resist gendered violence, and sexual assault on women in the armed forces, provide fresh perspective to current scholarship. Violence against LGBT women is not covered. A single chapter on women protecting the ecosystem outlines how women are affected by adverse environmental changes. However the analysis does not address gendered roles in impacting the environment.

The essays provide a broad perspective on gender and violence–albeit with some gaps in coverage. It is an excellent collection summarizing the intersection between gender and violence. Recommended as a starting point for those addressing issues of gender and violence.—**Muhammed Hassanali**

Part III
HUMANITIES

19 Humanities in General

General Works

Bibliography

C, P, S

330. Melton, J. Gordon and Alysa Hornick, comps. **The Vampire in Folklore, History, Literature, Film, and Television: A Comprehensive Bibliography.** Jefferson, N.C., McFarland, 2015. 380p. index. $45.00pa. ISBN 13: 978-0-7864-9936-6; 978-1-4766-2083-1 (e-book).

Prior to the age of zombies, vampires ruled the media landscape. A multitude of books and television series and movies, each featuring variations of the origins and abilities and vulnerabilities of those creatures of the night roamed the media landscape, hunted and feasted upon by fans whose hunger for vampire lore was never quenched. With the publication of *The Vampire in Folklore, History, Literature, Film and Television: A Comprehensive Bibliography,* even those who are merely peckish when it comes to vampire lore will appreciate the vampires' long reign and their supernatural ability to adapt their storyline to each new generation.

The bibliography, published in 2015 by McFarland and Company, Inc., was compiled by J. Gordon Melton and Alysa Hornick (with the assistance of six other bibliographers). The primary compiler, Melton, is a distinguished professor of American religious history at Baylor University in Waco, Texas, and wrote three previous books on the subject of vampires: *The Vampire Book: The Encyclopedia of the Undead* (originally published in 1994, revised in 1999 and 2010, reviewed by ARBA in 1995 and 2000 and 2011, see ARBA 2000, entry 1135 and ARBA 2011, entry 1037); Video Hound's *Vampires on Video,* 1997, (see ARBA 198, entry 1321); and *The Vampire Gallery: A Who's Who of the Undead,* 1998, (see ARBA 1999, entry 1214). The second compiler, Alysa Hornick, hosted *Whedonology: An Academic Whedon Studies Bibliography* online from 2005 to 2015 (as of June 2015, the Whedon Studies Association began hosting *Whedonology* on their official Website). The bibliography is divided into nine topic segments: Vampires and Vampirism: General Sources; Folklore and History; Literature; Vampires on Stage and Screen; Vampires on Television; Vampires in Music and Arts; The Metaphorical Vampire; The Contemporary Vampire Subculture; and Juvenilia. Each of the 6,018 citations listed are numbered for easier access when referring to the index. Taking the section Folklore and History as an example—that section is subdivided into the following sections: Folklore and Mythology;

Historical Perspective; Vlad Tepes; Elizabeth Bathory; and Vampire Slayers. Melton precedes each of these subsections with an introduction that offers an analytical summary of the section's topic. For example, with the first section, Folklore and Mythology, Melton provides a thoughtful overview of the vampire's evolution—from female blood-sucking, pitiless creatures such as the lamia that roamed Ancient Greece to the present-day depiction of humanoid vampires, male and female, afflicted with conscience, remorseful beings for whom readers and viewers feel empathy. The citations, as noted, are numbered. However, they are listed alphabetically, by author, in each section. The citations provide the following information: author; article, book, or journal title; journal information; date; publisher; and Web location (if applicable). The majority of citations provide only that information...but there are annotated exceptions such as when Melton points out that the work cited is a dissertation or if the cited work won an award or if the cited work has historic or cultural significance.

Melton describes the citation format in his very thorough introduction. In that introduction, Melton explains that in an effort to prevent the bibliography from burgeoning out of control, sources such as newspaper articles and movie reviews were not included. On the other hand, Melton and his co-compilers strove to infuse this bibliography with scholarly sources about vampires. Finally, Melton not only guides the reader through the many origins and versions of vampires in his introduction, he also devotes an off-shoot of the introduction to a brief overview of vampire studies, tracing those studies' origins from the 1700s to the first "Slayage Conference on Buffy the Vampire Slayer" in 2004.

The bibliography offers a vampire timeline with special references to literature, stage drama, the cinema, and television, 1800-2013. Three appendixes are included: top grossing vampire movies; vampire series on television; and Buffy the Vampire Slayer Conferences (2002 - 2014). The book also includes a thorough index arranged alphabetically by subject with reference (citation) numbers instead of page numbers.

Would Giles include this in the Library...if Sunnydale had not been destroyed? Should you? Whether your library is located in academic setting or public setting...or over a hellmouth...this bibliography would make an excellent addition to a library's collection.—**Brian T. Gallagher**

Dictionaries and Encyclopedias

C, P, S

331. **Creative Glossary. http://www.creativeglossary.com/.** [Website] Free. Date reviewed: 2016.

Creative Glossary is a free-to-use site that is easy to navigate and relatively unobstructed by advertising. From the home page, users can select from the drop-down menus of several tabs: Art, Craft, Culinary/Gardening, Design, Fashion, Performance Art, Story Art, and Trade. If one prefers to search alphabetically, there is a clickable A-Z list that takes users to hundreds of terms.

There is a wide range of subcategories. Under Art, for example, the glossary is divided into 15 such narrower sections as Business Art, Calligraphy, Jewelry, Print Making, and Sculpture. Blown Glass, Carpets/Rugs, Leather, Measures, Mosaics, Paper, Quilting, and Textiles are listed under Craft. Culinary/Gardening reveals three subcategories: Cooking,

Fermentation, and Gardening. Design is further subdivided into Architecture, Computer, Graphic Design, Interior Decorating, and Math. Fashion has one subcategory, while a click on Performance Art takes users to a glossary of terms for Dance. The drop-down menu for Story Art takes the curious to glossaries for Animation, Anime/Manga, and Film. Trade, the last tab, reveals further links to Carpentry, Cosmetology, Furniture, and Welding.

The Story Art tab provides a good example of the site's functionality. If one is interested in Anime/Manga, a click on this link will reveal the 56 associated terms. If Cosplay, for instance, is selected, users will see that it is a general Anime/Manga term meaning costume play that is rooted in the custom of anime watchers putting on the costumes of anime characters. Cosplay can also be found using the alphabetical links on the home page.—**ARBA Staff Reviewer**

Handbooks and Yearbooks

P, S

332.   **Essential Library of Cultural History.** Minneapolis, Minn., ABDO Publishing, 2015. multivolume. illus. index. 23.95/vol.

This six-volume set features ample illustrations and insets with specific information about topics and individuals. Written by different authors, each book consists of eight to nine chapters with the first chapter serving as an introduction and the remaining chapters arranged chronologically. Although the titles are general, the focus is on western art forms and specifically on finding space to explain the development of each medium within the United States. The art volume includes discussions of John James Audubon and Thomas Cole as American examples within the chapter describing innovations by Caravaggio and Bernini.

The content embraces the causal interactions between culture and art, explaining that works by female artists were often attributed to men and that television coverage of the Civil Rights movement helped convince Americans to support political change. The up-to-date series includes very recent examples in order to analyze the contemporary relevance of each art form, noting the use of Netflix and including still images from *The Game of Thrones* in the volumes on film and television, and explaining the recent use of transgender models.

Because the books target an 8th-grade reading level, they contain sophisticated sentence structures and end notes. Each volume provides a timeline and brief glossary specific to its content. The set provides a remarkably lucid general introduction to each of the six areas, managing to hit the highlights in the long history of art, music, fashion, and dance, and providing careful detail in the examination of the history of film and television.—**Delilah R. Caldwell**

20 Communication and Mass Media

General Works

Directories

C, P

333.   **Hudson's Washington News Media Contacts Directory.** 48th ed. Amenia, N.Y., Grey House Publishing, 2015. 262p. index. $289.00pa. ISBN 13: 978-1-61925-575-3.

It is the hub of our nation's government, and a significant source of the news affecting every American's life. In fact, Washington, D.C., maintains its long-held role as the home to the largest concentration of media in the world. This 48th edition of *Hudson's Washington Media Contacts Directory* is a highly valuable, one-stop resource for everyone from political consultants to public relations professionals and beyond who may be interested in and affected by the large and influential Washington, D.C., news network.

Over 3,000 news organizations (and their holdings) and over 4,000 major media contacts are distributed within seven general sections of the directory: News Services, Newspapers (DC Bureaus), Newspapers (DC Metro Area), Foreign News, Syndicates and Columnists, Radio and TV Stations, and Magazines and Periodicals. Within each section, listings are further subdivided as appropriate. For example, Magazines and Periodicals listings are subdivided by DC Bureau, Foreign, and DC Headquartered categories.

Listings may include such information as street address, fax, Website, social media accounts, and key contacts from publishers to staff writers and more. Large media companies will also list their holdings. For this edition, all listings have been updated with the most current contact information.

As found in prior editions, the directory includes a Geographic Index/Foreign Media which provides a home country and/or city guide to all D.C.-based foreign media. New to this edition are four other indexes: an Entry Name Index which alphabetically lists all main headings, a Personnel Index alphabetically (by last name) listing all key media contacts, a Magazine Subject Index which lists categories from Advertising to Urban Affairs, and an Assignment Locator Index which lists almost 100 topics with reference to specific correspondents.

The keen organization of the material, in addition to its comprehensive detail and unique focus, makes this book essential.—**ARBA Staff Reviewer**

Handbooks and Yearbooks

C, P, S

334.   **BBC Video Collection. http://alexanderstreet.com/products/bbc-video-collection.** [Website] Alexandria, Va., Alexander Street Press. Price negotiated by site. Date reviewed: 2016.

The BBC is well known and respected for their informative, entertaining, and timely documentaries The Alexander Street *BBC Video Collection* provides access to 700 of the most popular BBC documentary films. The collection also includes a small selection of performances (e.g., opera, dance, theatre, etc.) and covers a wide range of subjects including history, science, technology, art, religion, and politics. Documentaries range from an in-depth analysis of Hitler's rise to power to the design of the Coca Cola bottle.

All of the videos are provided in full-length version, and each video is fully transcribed. The transcript is interactive and synced with the video time code allowing users to click on any word or phrase in the transcript and jump to the corresponding place in the video. The transcripts also enable full-text searching of the videos. Each video has a visual table of contents to help users easily navigate the videos by memorable scene. Users are allowed to add their own bookmarks to the videos, and they can cite and share the videos, save favorites to a playlist, and generate a permalink embed code—an option very useful for teaching. Users are also able to make and save their own video clips allowing many different and useful applications for both teachers and students such as building an engaging lesson, presentation or report.

The video collection can be by browsed by title, discipline, people, and series. It can also be searched by keyword. Searches can also be narrowed by persons and places discussed and by content type (i.e., documentary, interview, performance, instructional material, etc.).

As an engaging and entertaining medium, video is also gaining ground for instructional use. This collection is highly recommended for school and public libraries. Teachers and students alike will enjoy using it. The layers of tools provided for using this video collection take it to the next level. Academic libraries will also find this collection beneficial for undergraduates in history, political science, business, and a range of humanities.—**Kristin Kay Leeman**

C

335.   **Media Violence and Children: A Complete Guide for Parents and Professionals.** 2d ed. Douglas A. Gentile, ed. Santa Barbara, Calif., Praeger/ABC-CLIO, 2014. 477p. index. $58.00. ISBN 13: 978-1-4408-3017-4; 978-1-4408-3018-1 (e-book).

In the 13 years since the publication of *Media Violence and Children,* edited by Douglass A. Gentile, not only has research in the field of violence and media evolved, but also our definition of media. Whereas the trends of the late 1990s and early 2000s focused on V Chips for censoring violence on television and presences of violence in video games, the dawn of social media and the new technology on which it became available has altered the focus of research. The interactive nature of the new media has created a host of new issues which made an update and reshaping of the original necessary.

Facebook, Instagram, smart phones, tablets, cyberbullying, and cyberstalking are all softwares, technologies, and issues that parents and researchers have faced in recent years. Gentile and his group of writers attempt to put these all new issues in perspective when understanding research in the field of media violence and children. In 15 essays the subject of media violence is explained both in historical terms ("Television Violence: Sixty Years of Research"), today's issues ("Cyberbullying"), and future approaches to the topic ("Media Violence and Public Policy").

Marketed as a complete guide for parents and professionals, this second edition would be an ideal companion to the first edition in academic and professional library collections. I am less convinced that parents would find this tool as useful. This is not a simple explanation of the issues involved with media violence and children—instead the essays are well researched and of a high academic standard.

I highly recommend purchasing for academic and professional collections.—**Rob Laurich**

Authorship

Style Manuals

C, P, S

336.   Mills, Elizabeth Shown. **Evidence Explained: Citing History Sources from Artifacts to Cyberspace.** 3d ed. Baltimore, Md., Genealogical Publishing, 2015. 892p. index. $59.95. ISBN 13: 978-0-8063-2017-5.

Evidence Explained: Citing History Sources from Artifacts to Cyberspace, now in its third edition, allows historians and other researchers to cite accurately almost every type of source, particularly those not covered in more traditional citation guides. The author encourages users of this hefty book to read the first two chapters, "Fundamentals of Evidence Analysis" and "Fundamentals of Citation" in their entirety and to reference individual types of works and citations as necessary. Each chapter begins with a list of "QuickCheck Models" followed by a list of "Guidelines & Examples" and source models. For instance, chapter 14 "Publications: Periodicals, Broadcasts & Web Miscellanea" delineates citation models for such sources as sound clips, podcasts, and blogs. Chapters are followed by a glossary, bibliography, index, and separate index for QuickCheck Models.

For libraries that already own a copy of the earlier editions (see ARBA 2007, entry 563 and ARBA 2009, entry 610), this may not be a necessary purchase. For other libraries, however, this source is an essential addition to the reference shelf, as it will quickly and easily allow users or librarians to find answers to tricky citation questions.—**ARBA Staff Reviewer**

C, P, S

337.   **MLA Handbook for Writers of Research Papers.** 8th ed. New York, Modern Language Association of America, 2016. 146p. index. $12.00pa. ISBN 13: 978-1-60329-262-7; 978-1-60329-265-8 (e-book).

This eighth edition of the Modern Language Association (MLA) handbook provides the updated guide to citing sources in scholarly writing. While seemingly simple in scope, the new edition offers valuable information that works well to adapt to the evolving landscape of research writing.

Since first experimented with in 1951, the MLA style sheet has undergone vast change. No longer does the manual need to remind writers to type their work; instead, the guide must deal with the proliferation of diverse sources and potentially complex rules. With mind to changes in literary studies, the needs of the modern student and certainly the advent of modern media, this eighth edition emphasizes a level of flexibility when creating the necessary source documentation.

The book is separated into two parts, dealing with Principles of MLA Style (covering such things as information gathering, organization, etc.) and Details of MLA Style (covering the nitty-gritty of quotations, numbering, abbreviations, punctuation, and much more). Information in this part is delivered in short, sectioned paragraphs with clear examples following. Aids such as highlighting, lists, cross-referencing, and a practice template help readers navigate the technical material.

The book is a must have for any student embarking on a path of academic writing and belongs in libraries of all sorts—public, middle and high school, academic, and personal.—**ARBA Staff Reviewer**

Journalism

C, P

338.   Roth, Mitchel P. **The Encyclopedia of War Journalism, 1807-2015.** 3d ed. Amenia, N.Y., Grey House Publishing, 2015. 673p. index. $165.00. ISBN 13: 978-1-61925-745-0; 978-1-61925-746-7 (e-book).

The original edition entitled the *Historical Dictionary of War Journalism* (see ARBA 98, entry 881) contained more than 900 entries and this retitled third edition has more than 200 additional entries. The volume is divided into two sections: the first part contains alphabetical entries on many topics including correspondents, illustrators, photographers, periodicals, news organizations, among many other subjects. Each entry includes a reference source; the article length varies from one to several paragraphs and the quality of the content ranges from sparse to good. The second section contains 56 primary documents including article and book excerpts and also photographs. The 29 appendixes are useful and contain much hard-to-find information: lists of many war correspondents (no comprehensive list is possible) from the Mexican-American War through the wars in Afghanistan and Iraq, films that portray war correspondents, journalism award winners, lists of photographers and camera people, and names of correspondents killed in several wars. The timeline notes significant incidents but unfortunately, only includes the year but not the specific date of the event.

Although other journalism reference works discuss war journalism, this title solely devoted to the topic provides unique and readily-accessible information compiled from numerous sources.—**Donald Altschiller**

C, P, S

339.   **Journalist's Resource. http://journalistsresource.org/.** [Website] Free. Date reviewed: 2016.

Journalist's Resource is a project of Carnegie-Knight Initiative of the Future of Journalism Education, and it is based at Harvard Kennedy School's Shorenstein Center. The team consists of Harvard faculty, staff members, researchers, and a developer, and is an open-access Website that curates scholarly studies and reports.

According to Tom Patterson, Acting Director at the Shorenstein Center, research and fact-based information are tools that today's journalists should use more frequently, and they form the basis for the articles on *Journalist's Resource*. This makes the site extremely beneficial for academics and educators who wish to avoid biased sources as well as anyone interested in or studying journalism. Though the information is often dense, this site will even be useful for younger students who need reputable sources for academic purposes. Many articles include bullet points that highlight important aspects of the piece, a feature that students can use to better understand the more advanced scholarly studies.—**ARBA Staff Reviewer**

Radio, Television, Audio, and Video

C, P

340.   Street, Seán. **Historical Dictionary of British Radio.** 2d ed. Lanham, Md., Rowman & Littlefield, 2015. 391p. (Historical Dictionaries of Literature and the Arts). $115.00; $109.99 (e-book). ISBN 13: 978-1-4422-4922-6; 978-1-4422-4923-3 (e-book).

While the history of British radio for the most part is dominated by the British Broadcasting Corporation (BBC), this historical dictionary also covers the early advent of radio in the United Kingdom as well as contemporary independent stations, podcasts, and digital audio downloads. British broadcasting began in the spring of 1922 and will soon celebrate its centenary in 2022. The BBC was pioneering in a number of areas including women news readers in August of 1933 and foreign language broadcasting, starting initially with Arabic language broadcasts in January of 1938. The work begins with an excellent historical essay that covers the period from the late nineteenth century up until the present. The BBC has been both a major national presence and an international one. The book is arranged topically and covers such things as: radio personalities, programming, and electronic technical topics. Entries are confined to short paragraphs on the topic. There are no illustrations in the book. The first edition was published in 2006 (see ARBA 2007, entry 783) and this second edition will serve as a reference tool for the centenary. Also included are a list of acronyms and abbreviations, a chronology, and a classed bibliography containing materials up until 2013. The book will be essential for collections on the history of radio, British life and literature, and world history.—**Ralph Lee Scott**

C, P

341.   **Complete Television, Radio & Cable Industry Directory.** 3d ed. Amenia, N.Y., Grey House Publishing, 2015. 1601p. $350.00pa. ISBN 13: 978-1-61925-287-5.

This is the third edition of the *Complete Television, Radio & Cable Industry Directory* published by Grey House. For nearly 75 years, R. R. Bowker published previous editions of this reference work under the title *Broadcasting & Cable Yearbook.* This information-packed book begins with a chronology of electronic media, information about the FCC and its regulatory authority, a glossary of terms, and a list of abbreviations. Following are 10 sections: Broadcast Television—United States; Broadcast Television—Canada; Radio—United States; Radio—Canada; Cable—United States; Cable—Canada; Programming; Equipment Manufacturers & Production Services; Professional Services; Associations, Events, Education & Awards; and Government. The table of contents makes it easy to find information about such topics as the top 100 television shows of 2014 in the United States or special programming on radio stations in Canada. For libraries serving users in the broadcasting industry or for anyone working in these fields, this is a valuable assemblage of a massive amount of information. The purchase of the print edition provides buyers with a year's access to the online database at http://gold.greyhouse.com. Highly recommended.—**ARBA Staff Reviewer**

C, P

342.   **60 Minutes: 1997-2014.** [Website] Alexandria, Va., Alexander Street Press. Price negotiated by site. Date reviewed: 2016.

60 Minutes: 1997-2014 contains 482 hours of videos, comprising 3,415 reports and editorials shown on the CBS network since the late 1990s. The material is, because of the show's stature in American popular culture and politics at the time, historically important on its own terms. The main page offers the ability to search by keywords or to browse by titles, subjects, reporters, people, organizations, places, and events. The most active reporters are also listed on the main page, as is a subheading for the most popular subjects. Each subject includes the number of shows about that subject. The "Advanced Search" feature provides tools for more targeted searches. Because "Terrorism (150)" is far and away the most frequently referenced subject in this collection—a "9/11" search generates 179 items. Adding the term "Clarke," however, as in Richard Clarke, the terrorist expert in the White House at the time of the attacks, generates only four hits, including a two-part interview just before Clarke's congressional testimony on the attacks, a rebuttal by National Security Advisor Condoleeza Rice the following week, and another episode that referenced these interviews. For any scholar working on natural security and foreign diplomacy in the late twentieth and early twenty first centuries, these shows are crucial material.

The collection is structured in a way to make research and educational use easy. Each video page includes full documentation of the show's production and broadcast. The transcripts are also available and searchable, making it a snap to quote and cite interviews or editorials accurately. The transcript search feature also automatically forwards the video to that segment. This is quite useful for using this material in lectures as long as the teacher realizes that they will need to queue up the video beforehand, since loading is dependent on bandwidth. The videos are not downloadable; they are also at a lower resolution, and the width of the image was compressed on my tablet screen. This means that projection will result in a grainy and distorted image. Thus while the material in this video collection is interesting and occasionally historically important, and the collection is useful for research and some teaching formats, users must be aware that the image quality degrades rapidly the larger is it projected.—**Joseph E. Taylor III**

21 Decorative Arts

Collecting

C, P, S

343. **Benjamin K. Miller Collection of United States Stamps: http://digitalcollections.nypl.org/collections/benjamin-k-miller-collection-of-united-states-stamps#/?tab=navigation.** [Website] Free. Date reviewed: 2016.

This collection of stamps and other materials was donated to The New York Public Library in 1925 by Milwaukee attorney Benjamin K. Miller. These items are revered for being the first complete collection of U.S. stamps ever assembled and were displayed at the library for more than 50 years until a 1977 theft robbed the collection of 153 of its rarest stamps. They are now available for viewing on this Website, though students who are not specifically studying Benjamin K. Miller may not get much out of this Website academically. Each item data includes the Title, Collection, Library Locations, Genres, and Type of Resource.

Overall, this page would be most useful for historians and those specializing in stamp collections in the early 1900s, as well as for individual collectors.—**ARBA Staff Reviewer**

Fashion and Costume

C, P

344. **Clothing and Fashion: American Fashion from Head to Toe.** Mary D. Doering, Patricia Hunt-Hurst, Heather Vaughan Lee, and José Blanco F., eds. Santa Barbara, Calif., ABC-CLIO, 2016. 4v. illus. index. $415.00/set. ISBN 13: 978-1-61069-309-7; 978-1-61069-310-3 (e-book).

This comprehensive look at the way Americans have dressed covers over 400 years of history, from bodices, footwear, and hairstyles of the seventeenth century to the latest styles of the twenty-first. Each volume has a timeline and a historical overview of the period (1600-1785, 1785-1899, 1900-1945, and 1945-present) as well as chronological and alphabetical indexes. The social and cultural breadth of this work is reflected in articles such as "Jazz," "African-American Clothing, 1715-1785," "Man Ray," and "Native American Influence." Attention to detail is seen in the division of a single subject, such as "Jewelry," into chronological slices within a single volume, each entry written by different scholar.

Each entry includes a "Further Reading" list, which, for the earlier eras, refers the reader to other books of use on the topic, only rarely citing journal literature. The last volume's reading lists include magazines, newspapers, and Websites. Each volume also includes a 16-page section of excellent color plates illustrating clothes and fashion from the era, a glossary, and a comprehensive bibliography gathering together the works cited throughout the volume. Any library with patrons interested in these topics will find this set a valuable set to have.—**Mark Schumacher**

C, P, S

345.	**Dress & Fashion: Design & Manufacture. http://digitalcollections.nypl.org/ collections/dress-fashion-design-manufacture#/?tab=about.** [Website] Free. Date reviewed: 2016.

This collection from the New York Public Library contains contemporary and practical works relating to apparel manufacturing, industry, design, and aesthetics in the early 1900s. It is intended to provide users a window into the daily practices and resources of a manufacturing industry that is still thriving in New York City today. The collection will continue to expand in the next few years.

The Web page is attractive and organized, but does not offer much apart from clickable images. Each still image provides the user with the following information: type of resource, genre, date issued, division, publisher, engraver, cartographer, dates/origin, topics, notes, and citations (in MLA, APA, Chicago, and Wikipedia), as well as additional descriptive information. A timeline shows the approximate date the image was issued and digitized. Users can also download the images in a variety of sizes and resolutions. This collection is highly recommended those interested in the history of manufacturing and design but will likely serve a variety of users.—**ARBA Staff Reviewer**

C

346.	English, Bonnie. **A Cultural History of Fashion in the 20th and 21st Centuries.** 2d ed. New York, Bloomsbury Academic, 2013. 255p. illus. index. $29.95pa. ISBN 13: 978-0-85785-135-2.

Bonnie English argues that haute couture, from its recognition in the nineteenth century as a system of social and status markings to the late twentieth century, underwent a process of democratization that now leaves that term of limited utility. She creates an interesting and engaging history that connects many of the major socioeconomic and artistic trends to ultra-high-end clothing designers and the complex reciprocal relationships among designer, ready-to-wear, and what she terms street fashion. English, Associate Professor of Art History and Theory at the Queensland College of Art, is most effective describing how clothing designs reflect modernity as she seeks to break down the boundary between so-called fine art and the applied art of fashion, including a discussion of the many groundbreaking female artists who were also successful designers in the early twentieth century. She is somewhat less effective with the dawning of postmodernism, in part because that trend is much more difficult to define and perhaps too recent for perspective, but she closes with a strong summary of the trends that are emerging in the twenty-first century. Though the impact of globalization and the Internet may seem obvious, she links these factors to specific changes at specific fashion houses, which makes her analysis more persuasive. With its strong narrative thread, *A Cultural History of Fashion in the*

20th and 21st Centuries is most likely intended as a textbook but, with its comprehensive bibliography and index, it will also serve as a useful reference. Black-and-white figures and color plates help the reader to see fashion change over the years although an interested reader is likely to seek many more examples. If there is a third edition (a little more copyediting could remove a few annoying errors and repetitions), it will be interesting to see how present ideas of fashion change in the future.—**R. K. Dickson**

Interior Design

C, P, S

347. **Empire and Regency: Decoration in the Age of Napoleon. http://digitalcollections.nypl.org/collections/empire-and-regency-decoration-in-the-age-of-napoleon#/?tab=navigation.** [Website] Free. Date reviewed: 2016.

This collection from the New York Public Library contains books and plates from the Astor and Lenox Library Collections as well as from the private library of the architect Thomas Hastings. The vast majority of this collection consists of still images of Empire and Regency style furniture and décor dating back to the early 1800s. The images may appeal to those who are studying fashion and design in this time period, as well as history buffs curious about the origins of fashion. These pieces are particularly interesting given their ties to Napoleon I, whose ambitious art and design program lasted until the end of his reign in 1815 and was highly influential.

The easily navigable Website offers a series of clickable images that provide the user with the following information: type of resource, date issued, division, author, artist, topics, identifiers, and citations (in MLA, APA, Chicago, and Wikipedia), as well as additional descriptive information. A timeline shows when the creator of the image was born and died, when the image was issued, and when it was digitized. Users can also download the images in a variety of sizes and resolutions. This collection will be useful for those curious about Empire and Regency design, specifically in furniture and décor.—**ARBA Staff Reviewer**

P

348. Jenkins, Alison. **300 Tips for Painting and Decorating: Tips, Techniques & Trade Secrets.** New York, Firefly Books, 2014. 176p. illus. index. $19.95pa. ISBN 13: 978-1-77085-452-9.

If you are looking for the impetus and inspiration to start that home improvement project you've been considering, look no further. *300 Tips for Painting and Decorating* is an easy-to-navigate source for many of your interior design and maintenance needs. The author has included 300 helpful tips aligning with particular home improvement tasks (e.g., sanding wooden floors) that are further organized into broader chapters.

The book gives plenty of space to the essential equipment, materials, planning, and preparation needed before beginning a project. It then delves into particular topics of décor and maintenance, from walls and floors to windows and doors, paying mind to practical concerns such as window security, as well as creative design approaches like marbleizing paint effects. The book also discusses overall maintenance issues pertaining to hardware, weather, and safety and points out when it may be worth it to hire a professional.

Within each chapter, readers will note the generous use of color photography and clear illustrations detailing toolbox must-haves, wall treatments, task demonstrations, and more. They will also find useful checklists, estimation and comparison charts, and "fix-it" and "try-it" panels revealing special tricks of the trade.

From the differences between grouts and sealants to painting do's and don'ts, *300 Tips* covers all the bases of a do-it-yourself approach to making a beautiful home. The book concludes with a glossary of useful terminology and an index. This would make a fine addition to the collection of a public library.—**Laura Herrell**

22 Fine Arts

General Works

Dictionaries and Encyclopedias

C

349. **The Bloomsbury Encyclopedia of Design.** Clive Edwards, ed. New York, Bloomsbury Academic, 2016. 3v. illus. index. $725.00/set. ISBN 13: 978-0-4725-2157-6.

This three-volume encyclopedia is a reference work for the general public, students, professionals, and scholars on the broad umbrella of design, which in a multidisciplinary world focuses on definitions, critiques, descriptions, and analyses of design culture, practices, and ideology for the last 150 years. There are over 1,800 entries written by 200 contributors and six editors, from simple definitions to short essays. Extensive cross-referencing is provided, along with a comprehensive index for each volume. Bibliographic references are included for each entry, as well as a bibliographic section for each volume. Black-and-white photos and pictures are included where appropriate. The introduction discusses some of the depth and breadth of the encyclopedia in terms of boundaries, history, people, concepts, ideologies, theories, practice, and geography. Overall, this work provides a basic knowledge on contemporary design worldwide, and would be an excellent addition to any reference collection.—**Bradford Lee Eden**

Architecture

C, P, S

350. **Archnet. http://archnet.org/.** [Website] Free. Date reviewed: 2016.

Archnet is the world's largest globally accessible online databank of Islamic architecture, art, and urbanism. Its mission is to provide access to visual and textual material that will help highlight the traditions and culture of Islam and assist students who lack resources for learning. It was developed in 2002 at the Massachusetts Institute of Technology (MIT) School of Architecture and Planning in partnership with the Aga Khan Trust for Culture.

This Website is highly aesthetic and organized and is free from advertisements. Interactive clickables allow users to explore timelines, a variety of archive collections, and a resources page that includes images, videos, drawings, publications, seminars, and academic articles. A course syllabi section allows users to access free material provided by faculty teachers about culture in the Muslim world. This is a perfect tool for students interested in Muslim studies who either do not have the resources to take formal upper-level courses, or those who want to try out the field without committing financially. The content of this site will best serve upper-level high school or college students as an academic resource, though the interactive pages will be fun for younger students to peruse as well.—**ARBA Staff Reviewer**

C

351. **Art and Architecture in Video. https://search.alexanderstreet.com/artv.** [Website] Alexandria, Va., Alexander Street Press. Price negotiated by site. Date reviewed: 2016.

An online media database, *Art and Architecture in Video* is a collection of 848 videos that provides information and opens doors to critical analysis of art forms. This assembly of videos contains over 500 hours from various visual media companies. Primarily the collection contains documentaries though there are also instructional videos, biographical videos, videos of interviews, and one book animation (*Hirsoshima no Pika* by Toshi Mauki).

The entire contents are easily accessible from a sidebar including: Browse, Subjects, and People. The advanced search box easily accesses your specific subject request and will include all videos that reference the selected subject matter. Having generated a subject list of videos, brief annotations help students determine which video is of interest. A simple click on the left photo brings you to the video. The Detail tab will provide more specifics on the video and this summary will give the strongest overview of the film. Where available, the Transcript tab shows the written text with narration highlighting. Options for e-mail, sharing, and saving are practical for collection of data for future review. The Cite link makes referencing the visual media easy as it includes necessary bibliographic data. Related Items links to other relevant videos.

Visual media can be a valuable tool for research, and in the area of art studies, visual media becomes a dynamic tool to understanding both theory and art forms. Art periods, styles, and critiques of work all contribute to art study via this video collection. Alexander Street Press has amassed a broad base of art, artists, architecture, and architects for an overview both historical and contemporary. The collection includes videos on well-known artists such as Auguste Renoir (*The Road to Impressionism: 19th Century France*) and less-well-known artists such as Man Ray.

Unfortunately, the quality of videos is not always consistent; *Louis Corinth-Self Portrait at his Easel 1914: Neve* has poor audio quality detracting from the video itself. Most videos are of a good quality and the information will be more useful to art students because of the visual aspect necessary for critical analysis of art.

Overall, *Art and Architecture in Video* is a collection of visual media that is a useful tool for undergraduate and graduate students researching a diverse array of art and architecture, historically or in the modern era. It will also be of use in multidisciplinary studies where researchers want to bring in an art/design/culture element.

Recommended.—**Janis Minshull**

C, P, S

352.   **Carnegie Survey of Architecture of the South.** [Website] Free. Date reviewed: 2016.

The *Carnegie Survey of the Architecture of the South,* a Library of Congress collection, is a systematic record of American buildings and gardens photographed by Frances Benjamin Johnston (1864-1952) primarily in the early 1930s. Users can browse more than 1,700 structures in this collection that focuses on rural and urban areas of Virginia, Maryland, North and South Carolina, Georgia, Alabama, Louisiana, Florida, Mississippi, and West Virginia. Johnston's photographs include grand mansions and public buildings as well as small houses and mills. Her initial work was funded privately; grants from the Carnegie Corporation funded the rest of the work based on the condition that the photographs be deposited in the Library of Congress. ARTstor digitized all the photographs in 2008.

This site contains a wealth of information about Johnston's history and photography methods, and the process of collecting and preserving her images. There are links to information about the background and scope of the collection, which includes listings of photographs by state. Users will also find a short bibliography and information about how the collection is organized. There are also links to related collections in the Library of Congress and other institutions. A subject index list will help users find specific information. The easy-to-use Website provides researchers in many disciplines with a trove of valuable information.—**ARBA Staff Reviewer**

C, P

353.   Radford, Anthony, Selen Morkoç, and Amit Srivastava. **The Elements of Modern Architecture: Understanding Contemporary Buildings.** New York, Thames and Hudson, 2014. 344p. illus. index. $50.00. ISBN 13: 978-0-500-34295-4.

Architects design buildings for the combination of order, space, form, and function, and interested readers can use this book to analyze how well they succeeded in particular instances. Fifty important buildings are covered here, from the Arab World Institute in Paris to the Menara UMNO in Penang, Malaysia. A wide variety of representative architecture is sampled here, with the earliest design being that of Frank Lloyd Wright's Guggenheim Museum in New York City (in this case, "contemporary" refers to the period after 1950). Some of these are quite striking, such as the Kunsthaus in Graz, Austria, while others are not quite so impressive on the outside. The exteriors might appear simple, but the interiors can be quite advanced. The photographs are all in black and white, so they are artistic statements in themselves as well as providing interesting views of the buildings.

The descriptions are brief, with most of the page space being taken up by over 2,500 illustrations. Floor plans, perspective views, landscape diagrams, and lots of drawings about the various structural details will prove attractive to architecture students. The book also discusses materials, lighting, and the various parts of each building, touching on the geographical context and public response (some of which had to be controversial). For each building there is also a map showing where on the globe and in a country the building is located.

At the end of the book is a bibliography divided up by building, with just a few important references for each structure. The endnote briefly discusses 15 common themes (e.g., ethics, identity, style, etc.) revealed by a study of these buildings. This reasonably priced book is suitable for the reference or circulating collections of public and academic libraries, as both experts and nonexperts can enjoy it. And it is attractive enough to sit on your coffee table as a conversation starter—**Daniel K. Blewett**

Painting

P

354.   Kloosterboer, Lorena. **Painting in Acrylics: The Indispensible Guide.** New York, Firefly Books, 2014. 320p. illus. index. $35.00. ISBN 13: 978-1-77085-408-6.

Painting in Acrylics is a beautiful book filled with ideas and expertise related to the creation and exhibition (whether personal or professional) of acrylic paintings. The author uses her vast experience as an award-winning artist and exhibitor to teach all aspects of acrylic painting in a visually appealing, easy-to-navigate, and encouraging manner.

Organized into six chapters, the book opens with the basics. Readers explore the qualities of different types of acrylic paint, common materials, and equipment available for acrylic painting and main principles of color theory, mixing, and more. Ensuing chapters focus on a large variety of acrylic painting techniques (washes, spattering, or glazing to name but a few), and explore acrylics in relation to different painting categories, such as still lifes, landscapes, and more. A final chapter offers more inspiration related to how best to care for and market the final acrylic product, and touches on framing, handling criticism, copyright issues, and other important topics.

Within each chapter are helpful tools such as tables, charts, a section navigator, technique swatches, text boxes, and more which make the experience of reading this book appropriately visual and very easy to follow. Many of the techniques are explained via step-by-step instructions, both verbal and pictorial. In fact, a generous selection of striking color photographs really tells the story of acrylic painting, and demonstrates, in addition to technique, a range of vibrant color, subject matter, and finished works with an eye toward fine detail and inspiration. The book also includes a helpful glossary of art terms (as associated with acrylic painting) and an important Color Index (C.I.) Pigment Chart, detailing standardized pigment codes, names, color examples, and opacity.

From mixing your first acrylic colors to signing your finished work, this book will guide both beginning and experienced artists along a satisfying creative journey.—**Laura Herrell**

Photography

P

355.   **Digital Photography Complete Course.** New York, DK Publishing, 2015. 360p. illus. index. $30.00. ISBN 13: 978-1-4654-3607-8.

This visual-centric book is designed to guide readers through a 20-week course on digital photography. The book uses a dynamic approach to convey its information, incorporating bright colors, assertive fonts, emphasized text, and, fittingly, an abundance of graphic images ranging from camera diagrams to stunning examples of photography.

Twenty chapters, or modules, are color coded for easy reference. Each presents a lesson overview, a visually engaging tutorial, and a module Q and A review to help readers mark progress. Modules cover such topics as getting the right exposure, using depth of field, how to compose, using natural light, black and white, and lenses. An introductory section explains the best way to use the book, a description of camera types, an explanation of how a camera works, and basic information on how to get started with a camera. A glossary and index complete the book.

The success of the book comes from the clear instruction juxtaposed with the wealth of visual aids; from varying samples of photography, to bulleted and boxed text, to technical diagrams and interactive "quizzes." Readers can easily find the appropriate information, work at their own speed, and track their progress. Even though the book is easy to use, its components are professional and appropriately technical. Whether the impetus is personal or professional, readers will find great value in the information and structure of this book.—**ARBA Staff Reviewer**

C, P, S

356. **Photographers' Identities Catalog. http://pic.nypl.org/.** [Website] Free. Date reviewed: 2016.

The Photographers' Identities Catalog (PIC) is an experimental interface from New York Public Library Labs. The catalog provides life dates; nationalities; dates and areas where the photographer, company, or studio was active; as well as links to museum and archival collections and further biographical information. The catalog currently (as of March 2016) contains information on 115,700 names related to the history of photography from 1687 to the present day.

The search feature allows the researcher to enter a name and/or to filter active dates or by such categories as nationality, country, format, process, or gender. A zoomable world map displays locations for birth, activity, business, and death for individuals, but moving from the map to finding the record associated with each dot on it is not easily accomplished, and the map was quite slow to load when zooming in on an area. That said, the catalog provides a starting point for a variety of research ranging from creating a list of female photographers who worked in a particular country or time period to dating a family photograph by finding when the photography studio was in business at the given address. This is a promising tool for photography researchers at various levels, though members of the public may be disappointed to find that it does not actually contain photographs but rather links to further information (including photographs) elsewhere online.—**ARBA Staff Reviewer**

23 Language and Linguistics

General Works

Handbooks and Yearbooks

C

357.   **Students' Right to Their Own Language: A Critical Sourcebook.** Staci Perryman-Clark, David E. Kirkland, and Austin Jackson, eds. New York, St. Martin's Press, 2015. 506p. index. $44.65pa. ISBN 13: 978-1-4576-4129-9.

The Students' Right to Their Own Language (SRTOL) resolution at the 1974 Conference on College Composition and Communication marked the beginning of an intense discussion about how to teach writing to diverse students. The need for self-expression and creativity seemed to clash with the need to learn standard English in order to fit in and find work. This collection of papers documents the SRTOL movement and the issues that it raised. The editors present articles covering all sides of several topics related to the resolution. The book has six sections. They cover the foundations of SRTOL, the politics of language and memory, African American language, pluralism, SRTOL in the teaching of writing, and questions that remain. The papers are dense and jargon-filled, but they raise important, relevant questions about the teaching of language in a world that is dealing with educational disparity and diverse populations. Libraries supporting programs in education, ethnic studies, and linguistics will want to consider it.—**Barbara M. Bibel**

English–Language Dictionaries

General Usage

C, P, S

358.   **Fowler's Dictionary of Modern English Usage.** 4th ed. Jeremy Butterfield, ed. New York, Oxford University Press, 2015. 928p. $39.95. ISBN 13: 978-0-19-966135-0.

Once described as the "most famous book about English usage ever written," the lexicographer Henry Watson Fowler first compiled this venerable work in 1926. This fourth edition edited by the lexicographer and Oxford University Press author Jeremy

Butterfield has added 250 new entries that have been coined or become more popular since the last edition (see ARBA 1997, entry 284; see ARBA 2010, entry 885). Among other discussions, these entries include how competing forms of a word can be used, e.g., "website" or "web site." The work relies heavily on the *Oxford English Corpus* which is based mainly on pages from the World Wide Web plus printed texts. It contains 2.5 billion words from twenty-first-century texts published since 2000. The introduction discusses the recurring debate among English usage scholars on prescriptive and descriptive language and this work skillfully navigates between those contentious linguistic poles. Unsurprisingly, this British work does not lack humor. An essential reference work which superbly complements the American usage manual *Garner's Modern American Usage: The Authority on Grammar, Usage, and Style* (see ARBA 2010, entry 843).—**Donald Altschiller**

Grammar

P, S

359.   Hult, Christine A. **The Handy English Grammar Answer Book.** Canton, Mich., Visible Ink Press, 2016. 419p. illus. index. $21.95pa. ISBN 13: 978-1-57859-520-4.

This clever volume offers an effective and engaging tool with which readers can explore the art of effective communication vis-à-vis the English language. It organizes its information into three major sections which migrate from a brief history of modern English, through a thorough examination of grammar basics, and ultimately into applying the best topic-targeted writing approach. Additionally, the author includes a generous appendix section with an excellent range of writing and common grammar examples. The book's readability is enhanced throughout by black-and-white illustrations, shaded text boxes, lists, intriguing anecdotes, and more.

Within each section are a number of chapters which hone in on more detailed matters such as sentence structure, punctuation, or business writing. If this seems a bit mundane at first glance, rest assured it is not! Each topic is presented as an answer to a question—a format both eye-catching and extremely readable. Further, the material is succinct and on point with topics moving smartly from one to another. One chapter deftly answers such questions as what is a noun, what is a pronoun, and what is a linking verb, as well as over 40 more queries relative to sentence structure alone.

Chapters also address matters of style like improving sentence variety and using action verbs. The author then puts all these pieces into place in the chapters regarding academic and business writing. Chapters discussing English as a second language and current electronic communication issues close out the book in advance of the appendix section and index.—**Laura Herrell**

Idioms, Colloquialisms, Special Usage

C, P, S

360.   **The Concise New Partridge Dictionary of Slang and Unconventional English.** 2d ed. Dalzell, Tom and Terry Victor, eds. New York, Routledge/Taylor & Francis Group, 2015. 864p. $88.95. ISBN 13: 978-0-415-52720-0; 978-1-315-75477-2 (e-book).

Every entry found in the new Partridge (an update of the 1984 edition) is included here, but without the original citations. The criteria for inclusion are words and expressions that lower the formality of language or express identity with a particular group and are used anywhere in the English speaking world after 1945. All senses of a word are combined in a single entry and some phrases that contain a similarity are combined under a shared concept (e.g., "roll the dice" and "roll on" are listed under "roll"). Entries are listed alphabetically and preceded with prefaces and an introductory essay, which describe the layout and intention of the entries and discuss the basic concept of unconventional English. Each entry is highlighted in bold print, as are any related terms. An indication of the part-of-speech (including if it is used as a nickname), brief definitions, an approximate date of first usage, a cultural or geographical place of origin, and any *see* references comprise the majority of each entry. The alphabetical listing is followed by a brief section of numeric slang. Many of the terms included are offensive, but offer a large cross-section of human expression. Not as thorough as previous editions, this version is a good source for quick reference or as a starting place for future research.—**Martha Lawler**

C, P

361.   Polashek, Timothy. **The Word Rhythm Dictionary: A Resource for Writers, Rappers, Poets, and Lyricists.** Lanham, Md., Rowman & Littlefield, 2014. 689p. index. $165.00; $164.99 (e-book). ISBN 13: 978-1-4422-3325-6; 978-1-4422-3326-3 (e-book).

"Embarrass" and "dilemma." "Napoleon" and "plutonium." "New York" and "outdoors." These are rhythm rhymes, or words and names with the same number of syllables and the same syllabic accents. The *Word Rhythm Dictionary,* a unique reference book by musician and music technologist Timothy Polashek, is designed for writers who want to add musicality to their prose, poetry, or lyrics.

Polashek delineates three methods for using this resource. The most obvious is to look up one's chosen word in the alphabetically arranged general index, which provides the page number(s) on which that word appears along with many others having the same rhythm. Alternatively, poets might turn to Appendix A, listing poetic feet such as iambs, dactyls, and anapests, to be directed to their rhythmic matches. In addition, lyricists might use Appendix B, listing music notations, to help them find terms that match musical rhythms. Words with more than one pronunciation, such as "progress," are followed by a plus sign.

The rhythm rhymes to which users are directed are organized first by number of syllables (from 1 to 14) and then by rhythm rhyme group number. For example, in the table of contents one can see that "7-Syllable Words" consists of 16 rhythm rhyme groups, each group being identified by syllabic emphasis, such as "u-S-u-P-u-S-u" for rhythm rhyme group 8 (u = unstressed, S = secondary stress, P = primary stress). Terms in each rhythm rhyme group are arranged by their sound—first by rhyming vowel, then by consonants—because, according to the author, "poets and lyricists often make use of similar sounding words, through the use of alliteration, assonance, and consonance."

Writers looking only for words that simply rhyme (black, back, stack, Jack) will also find them in this valuable resource—**Lori D. Kranz**

Thesauri

C

362. **A Thesaurus of English Word Roots.** Danner, Horace Gerald. Lanham, Md., Rowman & Littlefield, 2014. 990p. index. $165.00; $164.99 (e-book). ISBN 13: 978-1-4422-3325-6; 978-1-4422-3326-3 (e-book).

More than 1,200 word roots across a range of disciplines are included in this large thesaurus. Here one can expand one's knowledge of English word meanings by learning their roots, or combining forms. The sheer volume of information provided here is unmatched by other word root thesauri, as most are limited to a single discipline or offer few examples of terms containing these roots.

By way of example, consider the word "liberate." In the thesaurus, one finds the element "liber," listing the original source as Latin, meaning free, and the Indo-European base as "leudh-," meaning to grow up or rise. In the second column are numerous examples of words with "liber" and their meanings, under categories such as Simple Root ("liberal," "liberty" and their synonyms), Prefixed Root ("illiberal"), Leading Root Compound ("liberticide"), and Prefixed Disguised Root ("deliver," "deliverance," "delivery"); plus discipline-related examples like Academic (liberal arts), Geographic ("Liberia"), Historical ("Liberty Bell"), and Place-Name ("Liberal, Kansas or Missouri"); foreign-language terms (French "liberté"); Notes ("The Anglo-Saxon base of 'friend' is also 'free'"); and Cross-References to elements with the same or a similar meaning ("eleuthero, fran, lys, solv"). Additional categories for word roots are Trailing Root Compound (such as "androgen" and "anthropogenesis" for the root "gen," meaning race, birth, or kind); Doublets, or two words with different meanings and spellings that originally were one word ("gentle:genteel"); and Cognates (such as "gasp" under word root "gap"). If a word is used in more than one discipline, it is categorized as interdisciplinary and is presented in all-capital letters along with its meaning(s). If a word does not belong to a listed group (e.g., "labile" under word root "lab"), it is so noted.

At the end of the volume is an English to Roots Index, which lists major meanings of word roots and guides the user to the word roots themselves. It would have been useful to include all single word roots in alphabetical order with a *see* reference, as some entries contain more than one root. For instance, the author of the foreword suggests looking up the word "lexicographical" in the index, but it is not listed there; and if one looks for "lex" in the main section of the thesaurus, it is grouped under "lect" and "leg." This is a small caveat for what is otherwise a comprehensive and fascinating reference work.—**Lori D. Kranz**

24 Literature

General Works

Handbooks and Yearbooks

C

363.   Budick, Emily Miller. **The Subject of Holocaust Fiction.** Bloomington, Ind., Indiana University Press, 2015. 250p. index. $32.00pa. ISBN 13: 978-0-253-01630-0; 978-0-253-01632-4 (e-book).

The Holocaust is one of the most horrific events in modern history. Making sense of it is impossible. Fiction is one path to understanding it. The author, a professor at Hebrew University of Jerusalem, looks at the role of literature as a vehicle for understanding the Holocaust. She notes in her introduction that fiction provides a view of events through the eyes of the characters. This differs from a nonfiction historical account, but it is still an important vehicle for commemorating the events, mourning the victims, and considering the moral and ethical dilemmas presented. The book has three sections representing various aspects of Holocaust literature and approaches to writing about the events. She examines the work of many writers: Cynthia Ozick, Art Spiegelman, Aryeh Lev Stollman, Michael Chabon, and Aharon Appelfeld. She also looks at the work of non-Jewish authors such as William Styron and Bernhard Schlink. By examining the themes of mourning, memory, and love, and considering the relationship of the Holocaust to apartheid and animal slaughter, the author provides a framework for students of literature, history, religion, philosophy, and ethics. Academic libraries supporting programs in Jewish studies, Holocaust studies, and comparative literature will want to consider this volume.—**Barbara M. Bibel**

C, P, S

364.   **Literary Criticism Online. http://www.literaryhistory.com/.** [Website] Free. Date reviewed: 2016.

As its name implies, *Literary Criticism Online* is an aggregator of links to Websites that offer a wide variety of both mainstream and academic literary criticism. As such, the site can be a handy resource for librarians, students, and teachers who need to find literary critiques quickly and easily. The main page features clickable headlines for 20th-Century

Literary Criticism and 19th-Century Literary Criticism, which bring up alphabetical lists of author names. The left column of the main page begins with a topical commentary by the site's founder, Jan Pridmore (the February 1, 2016 entry is titled "The Anger Epidemic"), followed by a list of the most recent authors covered. Clicking on one of those authors—Wilkie Collins and Saul Bellow were at the top of the most recent edition—jumps to a full page divided into sections titled Introduction & Biography and Literary Criticism, pages whose content and format vary widely depending on the author. Some sections are focused on the author's titles (for Collins, for example, Literary Criticism *The Woman in White*), while other sections offer links to Websites and media. Links are displayed for sources as varied as *The New Yorker, The Guardian,* and academic journals. A major drawback, however, is that almost all the academic links merely connect to the JSTOR site, which requires registration and may be confusing to newer users. Otherwise, the site is easy to navigate. Pridmore launched the site in 1998, and has made little or no attempt to update its design to meet the standards of twenty-first-century Web design. In addition, the editorial inconsistency of the author pages themselves offers no illusions that the site is anything more than a simple aggregator. For example, the first subhead on the Wilkie Collins page reads Introduction & Biography, while the first subhead on the Saul Bellow page reads introduction and biography. The content of the author pages is very uneven, with some pages displaying long lists of links and some very short lists.—**ARBA Staff Reviewer**

C, P, S

365.   **Project Gutenberg: www.gutenberg.org/.** [Website] Free. Date reviewed: 2015.

Project Gutenberg is a volunteer effort to digitize cultural works and archive them on an accessible Website. It was founded in 1971 and is the oldest digital library today. The project contains over 50,000 full texts of public domain books that users can search and download easily. It is closely affiliated with an Internet-based proofreading community called Distributed Proofreaders comprised of volunteers committed to providing free literature to the public. Materials are added to the *Project Gutenberg* archive only if copyrights have expired or if it receives a copyright clearance, so as long as users download the literature within the United States, there is no danger of pirating information. Copyright laws outside the United States should be researched by users before downloading content.

The books on this Website are available in open formats that should be compatible with most computers. Users can download them in plain text as well as HTML, PDF, EPUB, MOBI, and Plucker. Though most titles are in English, users can use the search menu to locate books in German, French, Italian, and Portuguese, as well as a few other widely used languages. All the search tabs on the homepage are located either at the top or the left side, making navigation simple, though more links are included toward the bottom of the homepage for those who want additional information on digitized sheet music, free kindle books, offline catalogs, and much more. Search tabs allow for book searches by Popular, Latest, or Random, and a search bar in the top right corner makes it possible for users to search by title and/or author.

Project Gutenberg is a great resource for middle, high school, and college students who are studying the classics, such as Jane Austen's *Pride and Prejudice* or Dante's *Inferno*. Because this Website is easy to navigate, free to use, and provides access to some of the most popular literature read today, it is a highly recommended resource.—**ARBA Staff Reviewer**

Children's and Young Adult Literature

Bibliography

C, P, S

366.   Irwin, Marilyn, Annette Y. Goldsmith, and Rachel Applegate. **Autism in Young Adult Novels: An Annnotated Bibliography.** Lanham, Md., Rowman & Littlefield, 2015. 151p. index. $75.99; $74.99 (e-book). ISBN 13: 978-1-4422-5183-0; 978-1-4422-5184-7 (e-book).

This slim volume serves a vital need. As more diagnoses along the Autism Spectrum Disorder (ASD) are made, families, patients, and those in the medical community are looking for more ways to make sense of it. Literature is one of those ways. This book offers an academic analysis of the depiction of autism in young adult fiction with the goal of identifying accurate character portrayals and ultimately of finding the best fiction for use in autism education.

The first five chapters disseminate the authors' research about how the ASD is represented in young adult fiction. Using 100 young adult novels published between 1968 and 2013, the authors devised a series of questions regarding the characterization, schooling, and relationships of autistic figures (other parameters for the novel selection are explained in the book's introduction). For example, the authors asked which characters in the novels have ASD, if the autistic characters have friends, and with whom the autistic characters live. These short, academic chapters include a number of data tables to help visualize the analysis.

The second section of the book presents an annotated bibliography of the young adult fiction used in the authors' research. The listings are arranged alphabetically by author's last name, and include book title; publishing information; genre; plot synopsis and background; and a listing of criteria connected to the novel's handling of the autistic element/character: an Autism Content Scale, Autism Role in Story Scale, and a Literary Quality Scale. This is followed by a select bibliography of young adult novels where autism appears to be present but is never mentioned. As determined by the authors, the books are of very good or excellent literary quality. This bibliography is also alphabetical by author last name. Bibliographical information is followed by plot synopses.

Numerous appendixes classify the studied novels in a variety of ways: by the role of autism, by literary quality, by genre, by year of publication and by foreign press. The last appendix shares the coding sheets the authors used in their study. Recommended for school and public libraries, as well as personal libraries.—**ARBA Staff Reviewer**

Indexes

P, S

367.   **Children's Books in Print 2015.** 46th ed. Amenia, N.Y., Grey House Publishing, 2014. 2v. $605.00/set. ISBN 13: 978-1-61925-385-8.

This is the 46th edition of R.R. Bowker's *Children's Books in Print,* produced from the *Books in Print* database. This two-volume set begins with a usage guide, followed by publisher country codes, country sequence, language codes, and a list of abbreviations.

An alphabetical index of nearly 257,000 books published after 2003 from 16,583 U.S. publishers comprises the majority of volume one's 1,933 pages. Tens of thousands of these book listings have been added since the last edition. A shorter numeric title list completes the volume. In addition to standard publishing details, book entries include information about audience, grade level, and binding type. Publishers regularly review and correct (if necessary) book information, ensuring accuracy. Volume two contains author, illustrator, publisher, and wholesaler & distributor indexes. The author and illustrator indexes include references to the relevant pages numbers in volume one as well as *see* references. The publisher index indicates whether or not the publisher participates in the Cataloging in Publication Program of the Library of Congress and supplies ISBN prefixes, contact information, a Standard Address Number (SAN), and the names of distributors. Those publishers that also serve as distributors appear again in the wholesaler & distributor index where users can find ISBN prefixes, physical and Web addresses, SAN, and phone and fax information.

For those who want to search electronically, the entire *Books in Print* database is available online to customers. This venerable reference title is an important tool for librarians who work with children and young adults.—**ARBA Staff Reviewer**

P, S

368.   **Subject Guide to Children's Books in Print 2015.** 45th ed. Amenia, N.Y., Grey House Publishing, 2014. 2900p. $460.00. ISBN 13: 978-1-61925-388-9.

Used alongside the two-volume set *Children's Books in Print 2015* or as a stand-alone reference, the *Subject Guide to Children's Books in Print 2015* serves as an essential reference for librarians serving youth populations. Parents and teachers looking for books will also appreciate a source that groups titles by topic.

The title begins with a usage guide, publisher country codes, country sequence, language codes, and a list of abbreviations before presenting listings (hundreds of thousands) grouped into 9,610 subject headings from nearly 16,600 publishers. Tens of thousands of these book listings are new since the last edition. The subject headings adhere for the main part to Library of Congress Subject Headings. This, plus the use of guide words and *see* references, facilitates searches for books on subjects from aardvarks to Zulus and every imaginable topic in between.

The book concludes with a publisher name index followed by a wholesaler & distributor name index, both of which provide such information as ISBN prefixes, physical and Web addresses, and phone and fax numbers.—**ARBA Staff Reviewer**

National Literature

American Literature

Bibliography

C, P

369.   Gunn, Drewey Wayne. **Gay American Novels, 1870-1970.** Jefferson, N.C., McFarland, 2016. 192p. index. $39.95pa. ISBN 13: 978-0-7864-9905-2; 978-1-4766-2522-5 (e-book).

This book offers a survey of over 250 novels, novellas, and other literary works which feature gay or bisexual men as prominent characters. Entries are organized chronologically, for the most part. However, if one author is responsible for more than one work of this nature, all works are examined under the same entry (organized by earliest work). In addition, two or more authors may share the same entry if their works are considered similar.

Entries convey author's name, title(s) of work, and publication date, then go on to deconstruct the plot with particular emphasis on the gay character(s) arc. Entries also examine the work's gay themes in context with the times in which it was published and/or in relation to the writer's particular experience. For example, the entry covering Dashiell Hammett's *The Maltese Falcon* exposes his editor's request to change the homosexual subtexts (Hammett did not). Each entry also includes brief biographical information and a bibliography.

Readers will be quite satisfied with the appearance of many well-regarded authors such as Hammett, Gore Vidal, Truman Capote, Carson McCullers, James Baldwin, and more alongside pulp writers and lesser-known literary figures. In addition, this guide points to a wide range of genres encompassing the gay character and themes, ranging from murder mysteries to historical romances to westerns and beyond.

The book's introduction does an excellent job of detailing the history and parameters of the literature. A postscript tracks the further evolution of this literature in the decade following this book's range of discussion. The book also includes a general bibliography and index.—**ARBA Staff Reviewer**

Dictionaries and Encyclopedias

P, S

370. **Ethnic American Literature: An Encyclopedia for Students.** Emmanuel S. Nelson, ed. Santa Barbara, Calif., Greenwood Press/ABC-CLIO, 2015. 570p. illus. index. $100.00. ISBN 13: 978-1-61069-880-1; 978-1-61069-881-8 (e-book).

This diverse and important reference catalogs the major ethnic genres, figures, works, and themes emerging from the whole of the American literary tradition over the last two centuries.

Over 150 alphabetical entries by over 100 contributors are included and range from broader topics like Chinese American poetry to particular authors such as Sandra Cisneros, inspirations like the Civil Rights movement, works like *The Color Purple,* and themes like multiculturalism. While emphasizing four main ethnic groups (Native American, Asian American, African American, and Latino/a), the book pays clear attention to our America's rapidly changing demographics and allows a glimpse into newly emerging literary traditions such as Iranian American literature and its themes of exile, adjustment, and cultural pride.

The encyclopedia is directed at high school and community college students and teachers; its entries range in length from 750 words to 5,000 words and use clear language and an easy-to-follow A-Z arrangement. This is highly important when cataloguing topics as diverse as Hawaiian literature and jazz. Cross-referenced and with a plethora of ideas for further reading following each entry, this book is an excellent resource not only for students of American literature, but for lovers of history, writing, popular culture, and more. The title concludes with a selected bibliography, notes on contributors, and an index.—**Laura Herrell**

Handbooks and Yearbooks

C

371. **Critical Insights: American Writers in Exile.** Birkenstein, Jeff and Robert C. Hauhart, eds. Hackensack, N.J., Salem Press, 2015. 300p. index. $95.00. ISBN 13: 978-1-61925-517-3; 978-1-61925-518-0 (e-book).

This volume in the Critical Insights series focuses on the intriguing idea of American writers in exile. Contributions examine, of course, the literal acts of writers removing themselves from their home country to gain different perspectives. But pieces also delve into motivating factors behind their exile, figurative ideas of exile, questions of national identity, and much more. Essays touch on an array of such writers as W.H. Auden, Ernest Hemingway, Paul Bowles, Jamaica Kincaid, and Hart Crane.

An opening essay by the editors helps define the many aspects of exile; it is an "act of exclusion and banishment," "a scattering or dispersion" and can be political or personal, for example. The four-essay Critical Contexts section then offers broad-based foundational essays touching on the general need for writers to distance themselves. Jeff Birkenstein's essay "Paris Between the Wars: Gertrude Stein, Ernest Hemingway, Hunger and Language" uses the example of two renowned writers situated in the right place (post-World War I Paris) to observe the beginnings of a new age while removed from their more conservative, American origins. Joseph J. Cheatle then discusses the exile of two African American writers, James Baldwin and Richard Wright, who physically removed themselves from America's racial tensions but never really left them behind.

Critical Readings then presents 11 diverse essays examining the unique manifestations of writers abroad. Charlotte Anne Fiehn writes about Henry James, whom readers may consider the prime example of the American expatriate. Her essay looks at his contrasting views of nineteenth-century Americans and Europeans, and establishes James' influence on future exiled writers. Ashley E. Reis, in her essay "Edward Abbey's Ecological Exile," discusses how the author's exile came in the form of his scathing antidevelopment views, which were completely at odds with postwar America.

The volume concludes with a listing of other works by these American writers in exile, and a bibliography, and an index.—**ARBA Staff Reviewer**

C

372. **Critical Insights: Contemporary Immigrant Short Fiction.** Evans, Robert C., ed. Hackensack, N.J., Salem Press, 2015. 251p. index. $95.00. ISBN 13: 978-1-61925-832-7; 978-1-61925-833-4 (e-book).

Throughout American literature today, readers are hearing more diverse voices than ever before. This volume in the Critical Insights series devotes its pages to analysis of contemporary immigrant fiction, and showcases essays covering the works of such writers as Jhumpa Lahiri, Edwige Danticat, and Junot Diaz.

Emphasizing the short story form as key to the immigrant writer's literary aspirations, the volume's opening chapter "On Contemporary Immigrant Short Fiction" by Natalie Friedman provides an excellent foundation for understanding the origins and challenges of the genre.

The Critical Contexts section then presents historical contexts, critical surveys, and essays that emphasize the notion of the truly global nature of immigrant short fiction. In particular, Anupama Arora, in her essay "Forbidden Desires: Relationships in Chimamanda Ngozi Adichie and Jhumpa Lahiri's Short Fiction," compares the works of two successful immigrant short-fiction writers to show how they, of vastly different origins, can be concerned with similar issues (in this case, interracial relationships).The 10-essay Critical Readings section offers up insight naturally as diverse as this book's subject. Some highlights include King-Kok Cheung's "Somewhat Queer Triangles: Yiyun Li's 'The Princess of Nebraska' and Gold Boy, Emerald Girl," which exposes the added burdens placed on Chinese immigrant homosexuals so that their alienation is both sexual and ethnic, and Bridget Kevane's "Even the Dead Make Noises," which examines the need for the immigrant (in this case, the Puerto Rican of Spanish Harlem) to have his uniquely melded voice be heard.

The book also includes a chronological listing of recent contemporary immigrant short fiction as well as a bibliography and index.—**ARBA Staff Reviewer**

C

373. **Critical Insights: Harlem Renaissance.** Christopher Allen Varlack, ed. Hackensack, N.J., Salem Press, 2015. 335p. index. $95.00. ISBN 13: 978-1-61925-822-8; 978-1-61925-823-5 (e-book).

Thought to represent the most significant artistic period in African American history, the Harlem Renaissance gave voice to a unique culture. At the same time, the Harlem Renaissance challenged the assimilation (or the lack thereof) of this culture into greater society. This volume in the Critical Insights series serves this complex and long-studied artistic movement well by delving deeper into themes previously explored in the works of such icons as Zora Neale Hurston or Langston Hughes. The book also showcases more from lesser-known authors and critics to provide a truly fresh perspective.

The Critical Contexts section provides excellent foundational essays concerning a number of topics, including the multifaceted visions melding into the art of the Harlem Renaissance, the short-sighted "apathetic" criticism of the times, and, in Allyson Denise Marino's "Sugar Cane and Women's Identity in Selected Works of Zora Neale Hurston" the racial and economic oppression suffered by African American women during the 1920s.

Following this section are 14 essays making up the Critical Readings section. These essays are further subdivided into four sections covering the principal artistic and political sensibilities behind the Harlem Renaissance, racial passing, the rise of the new Negro woman in regards to both literary subject and author, and the more controversial or neglected works and/or approaches to them. Highlights of the Critical Readings sections include Tiffany Austin's essay "'Blue Smoke' and 'Stale Fried Fish': A Decadent View of Richard Bruce Nugent," which re-examines the more obscure, and only openly gay Harlem Renaissance artist, and Seretha D. Williams' "'The Bitter River': Langston Hughes and the Violent South" which points out how Hughes' poetry transcends the period of the Harlem Renaissance to capture the ongoing subjugation of blacks.

An extensive chronology, complete list of Harlem Renaissance works, a bibliography, and an index round out this intelligently conceived, thought-provoking essay collection.—**ARBA Staff Reviewer**

C

374.   **Critical Insights: LGBTQ Literature.** Robert C. Evans, ed. Hackensack, N.J., Salem Press, 2015. 347p. index. $95.00. ISBN 13: 978-1-61925-423-7; 978-1-61925-424-4 (e-book).

This volume in the Critical Insights series gathers a number of well-curated essays examining a genre of literature that has perhaps only been openly studied over the last half a century. With the crux of its focus on nineteenth- and twentieth-century American literature (although a few non-American works are considered), *Critical Insights: LGBTQ Literature* tracks the genre's challenges, dissemination, and evolution through this time.

The opening Critical Contexts section provides a necessary foundation for understanding the history of LGBTQ literature both from the perspective of its authors and critics. In two essays, Margaret Sönser Breen briefly catalogs the most well-known examples of LGBTQ work from the nineteenth century to the present, spotlighting such writers as Oscar Wilde, Frank O'Hara, and Patricia Highsmith. In doing so, she points out the ways these writers might have adapted to a potentially unwelcoming readership. For example, she notes that American author Ann Bannon managed to "affirm lesbian desire" in her pulp novels of the 1950s at a time when censorship defined lesbianism as "a deviant form of sexuality aligned with criminality and disease." Other essays in this section note helpful resources with which to pursue the thriving realm of LGBTQ scholarship, how "critical pluralism" may be an apt literary theory with which to approach LGBTQ literature, and how the marked sexual differences of two great writers, Gertrude Stein and Ernest Hemingway, affected their attitudes toward the devastating Great War.

Working chronologically from an analysis of James Fenimore Cooper's mid-nineteenth century work Jack Tier to more recent work by Sharon Dennis Wyeth, the essays in the Critical Readings section expose a number of compelling topics, including the use of cross-dressing, homo-erotic imagery, the advent of "openly" gay literature, the constraints of traditional gender roles, and more. For example, Lorna Raven Wheeler's essay entitled "The Fugitive Erotic in the Poetry of Mae V. Cowdery" adds another dimension to the study of the Harlem Renaissance via the cryptic but clearly sexual verse of this lesser-known poet.

The book finally presents a number of useful resources for further study of this burgeoning area of literature, including a listing of dramatic, fictional, and poetic works in the LGBTQ genre, a bibliography, and notes on contributors. As the world works towards better integration and understanding of its LGBTQ population, this book can be a discerning resource for further education at the public and academic level.—**Laura Herrell**

C, S

375.   De Roche, Linda. **The Jazz Age: A Historical Exploration of Literature.** Santa Barbara, Calif., Greenwood Press/ABC-CLIO, 2015. 237p. illus. index. (Historical Explorations of Literature). $61.00. ISBN 13: 978-1-61069-667-8; 978-1-61069-668-5 (e-book).

Linda De Roche's exploration of five 1920s novels—*Babbitt* by Sinclair Lewis, *The Great Gatsby* by F. Scott Fitzgerald, *Gentlemen Prefer Blondes* by Anita Loos, *The Sun Also Rises* by Ernest Hemingway, and *Passing* by Nella Larson—is an installment in a series aimed at students which views literature of important periods through a historical lens. Each work is summarized and accompanied by essays about its historical background, its author, its literary significance, and primary sources drawn mostly from contemporary periodicals which reflect the social and political themes relevant to each novel. The book also includes a high-level overview of the decade in question and a timeline of important events.

The selection of novels is a sound one. Hemingway and Fitzgerald are givens in any discussion of Jazz Age literature, but the others are just as essential to understanding this turbulent decade; even more so perhaps because they generally receive less exposure. The range of these works spans the entire decade and encompasses perspectives from different classes, races, genders, and geographic areas.

The historical themes highlighted and supported by primary resources are also apropos for an age when new music, new media, advancing technology, and the shadow of the Great War were overturning old mores: social unrest, race, gender, and class identity, capitalism, consumerism, and crime. The contextual background woven in tandem by the critical essays and historical documents permits a more nuanced appreciation of each individual work, as well as a broad grasp of this critical era in American history.

Other works in this series include *The Harlem Renaissance: A Historical Exploration of Literature* by Lynn Domina and *American Slavery: A Historical Exploration of Literature* by Robert Felgar.—**Autumn Faulkner**

British Literature

Individual Authors

P, S

376.   **The Shakespeare Book: Big Ideas Simply Explained.** New York, DK Publishing, 2015. 352p. illus. index. $25.00; $9.99 (e-book). ISBN 13: 978-1-4654-2987-2; 978-1-4654-3902-4 (e-book).

This informative and interesting book offers detailed analyses of each of Shakespeare's plays as well as his narrative poems and sonnets, presenting them using the chronology laid out in the *Complete Oxford Shakespeare.* Each entry is several pages in length and has a list of principal characters, a timeline of the action by act and scene, a full plot synopsis, and information about the ongoing reputation and impact of the work.

The treatment of *Othello,* for example, introduces the characters of Othello, Iago, Desdemona, Cassio, Emilia, Roderigo, Brabanizo, Monano, Bianca, Lodovico, Graziano, and the clown. This is followed by a plot discussion that explicates the themes and contextualizes the story. A sidebar lists the pertinent themes (jealousy, loyalty, betrayal, love), the setting, sources of inspiration for Shakespeare, and notable dates associated with the play. Another sidebar looks at the black American actor, Ira Aldridge, who in 1825 became the first black person to play Othello on the London stage.

For students unfamiliar with Shakespeare's works, these scholarly, yet accessible entries are an ideal starting point. The color photographs, images, and layout of the book will also hold the reader's interest. Highly recommended for school and public libraries.— **ARBA Staff Reviewer**

C, P, S

377.   **Shakespeare Online. http://www.shakespeare-online.com/.** [Website] Free. Date reviewed: 2016.

Shakespeare is central to the English literature curriculum at all levels, and this Website makes available a voluminous body of information related to his life and works.

The site includes the text of Shakespeare's plays along with explanatory notes, criticism, character analysis, and information about sources. The section for each play provides resources. Some of these are generic articles on how to read the plays, Shakespeare's reputation, and similar topics, while others are critical essays. For each scene of a play, study questions appear on the right and explanatory notes appear at the end of the scene. There are sections on the sonnets as well.

The site also includes reviews of a small number of books about Shakespeare and these reviews are generally a short paragraph without bibliographic information. There are also study guides for the major plays. Additional features include brief biographies of roughly 20 scholars active primarily during the late nineteenth and early twentieth centuries; excerpts from Shakespeare's sources; several timelines; information about Shakespeare's life; and an assortment of trivia questions.

Of special note is the attention the site gives to Shakespeare's language, with information about his words and imagery, a glossary, quotations in context, and a quotation of the day.

The Website would be most useful to students and general readers seeking an introduction to Shakespeare. Much of the material included was published in the early twentieth century or before then, including the texts of Shakespeare's works and the explanatory notes. While there is some critical material written expressly for the site, there do not seem to be excerpts from modern university press books and scholarly journal articles protected by copyright. The layout is attractive and engaging, but a serious drawback is that this free Website is littered with ads.—**ARBA Staff Reviewer**

Italian Literature

Handbooks and Yearbooks

C, P, S

378.   **Dartmouth Dante Project https://dante.dartmouth.edu.** [Website] Free. Date reviewed: 2016.

An ongoing endeavor of inestimable scholarly value, the *Dartmouth Dante Project* is a searchable database containing the text of more than 70 commentaries on Dante's *Divine Comedy* along with Giorgio Petrocchi's modern edition of the 1321 text of the poem. The commentaries are in their original languages and range from Jacopo Alighieri's 1322 commentary on the *Inferno* to a 2003-2015 commentary by Nicola Fosca. The commentaries typically offer line-by-line explications of the poem, with some providing more sustained narrative interpretations. Many of the commentaries are difficult to obtain, and some are protected by copyright.

Through the database, a user can conduct Boolean searches for words appearing in the commentaries or poem. Searches can be limited to particular commentaries, canticas, cantos, and lines, and the database provides clear instructions for initiating and refining queries.

Despite its utility, the database does have its drawbacks. While particularly strong in representing the Renaissance commentary tradition, it lacks, for example, the commentaries of Hermann Gmelin (1954), André Pézard (1965), and Robert Durling and Ronald Maritnez (1996). Since the database is a versatile concordance, it indexes keywords rather than concepts. Thus a reader searching for what the Italian commentators said about Dante's giants would need to look up "giganti" (812 results) rather than "giants" (87 results). It would also be helpful if the database included all of Dante's canon rather than just the *Divine Comedy.* Nonetheless, the database fulfills its objective.

While an essential tool for scholars, the database is less useful to undergraduates, high school students, and general readers, since the text of the poem is in Italian and many of the commentaries are in Italian and Latin. Users might also be interested in the *Dartmouth Dante Lab* http://dantelab.dartmouth.edu/, which builds on the *Dartmouth Dante Project* and allows users to compare commentaries; the *Princeton Dante Project* http://etcweb.princeton.edu/dante/index.html, which provides texts of Dante's works, critical material, and multimedia resources; and *The World of Dante* http://www.worldofdante.org/, a multimedia Website that includes texts, images, music, and teacher resources.—**ARBA Staff Reviewer**

Nonfiction

Handbooks and Yearbooks

C

379.   **Critical Insights: American Creative Nonfiction.** Jay Ellis, ed. Hackensack, N.J., Salem Press, 2015. 235p. index. $95.00. ISBN 13: 978-1-61925-417-6; 978-1-61925-418-3 (e-book).

This entry in the Critical Insights series provides an extensive overview of what editor Jay Ellis terms a "genre of genres" (p. vii)—American creative nonfiction. The volume opens with a detailed general summary of the book's contents followed by the editor's chapter outlining the history and challenges of studying a wide-ranging genre that encompasses several subgenres (memoir, captivity narratives, travel writing, nature writing, and illness narratives to name just a few). A Critical Contexts section presents four original essays reflecting on the background and critical reception of creative nonfiction as well as an in-depth consideration of Tim O'Brien's work in the genre. The Critical Readings section follows with 10 essays from scholars representing diverse educational interests. The essays build upon the material offered in the Critical Contexts section through their specific analyses of the creative nonfiction subgenres. Each essay in the volume concludes with endnotes and a works cited list. The volume concludes with a useful Resources section offering a general bibliography, a list of additional works of American creative nonfiction, entries on the professional credentials of the editor and contributors, and a subject index. The essays approach the genre from multiple critical perspectives (two notable examples include essays on African American autobiography as sociocultural criticism and the role of gender in nature writing) resulting in a well-rounded resource appropriate for an academic audience. Keeping in line with the aim of the Critical

Insights series, this volume provides comprehensive, authoritative scholarship suitable for both students and teachers. This volume is recommended for academic collections and large public libraries.—**Lisa Morgan**

Poetry

Handbooks and Yearbooks

C, P, S

380. **American Poets and Poetry: From the Colonial Era to the Present.** Jeffrey Gray, Mary McAleer Balkun, and James McCorkle, eds. Santa Barbara, Calif., Greenwood Press/ABC-CLIO, 2015. 2v. index. $189.00/set. ISBN 13: 978-1-61069-831-3; 978-1-61069-832-0 (e-book).

A modest two-volume set—though a single volume would not have been too thick—*American Poets and Poetry: From the Colonial Era to the Present* does just that, though it is by no means exhaustive. It provides a strong introduction or overview of key American poets and critical poetic concepts and movements—such as modernism and the Harlem Renaissance—in concise, critical entries. Biographical entries are anywhere from three to six pages in length and provide key biographical details relevant to the poet's life, development, and career; these entries also contain selected primary and secondary sources pertaining to the poet's work. Conceptual or movement-related entries contain critical events and figures and feature a listing for further reading. Some of these entries contain subheadings; many of these entries and some of the biographical entries would have benefitted from subheadings, given the density of the entries. The reader finds themselves facing walls of text when reading this title, unrelieved by graphics, illustrations, or photographs which would have contributed a great deal to an appreciation of both movements and individuals. In spite of this, the title is useful as an introductory critical title. It is highly recommended for secondary school libraries, public libraries, and undergraduate college/university libraries.—**Megan W. Lowe**

25 Music

General Works

Dictionaries and Encyclopedias

C, P

381.   Brown, Emily Freeman. **A Dictionary for the Modern Conductor.** Lanham, Md., Rowman & Littlefield, 2015. 421p. illus. (Dictionaries for the Modern Musician). $85.00; $84.99 (e-book). ISBN 13: 978-0-8108-8400-7; 978-0-8108-8401-4 (e-book).

Brown (director of orchestral activities and professor of conducting at Bowling Green State University) casts a very wide net, covering pretty much all aspects of music: orchestras, instruments, venues, festivals, and associations. Since most of these items can be found elsewhere in standard music sources (though perhaps not necessarily all under one cover), its true merit lies in the area most closely related to its purpose: conductors and conducting. A highlight is the keen insight into the legendary personalities of the world's most famous conductors, with which modern audiences may not be familiar. A sampling: Fritz Reiner "cultivated an intense stare bordering on the hypnotic"; Herbert van Karajan "sought total control over every element"; Leopold Stokowski "sought drama in performance whenever possible." Composers are included only if they were also conductors: Berlioz yes, Brahms no. In a field historically dominated by white males, Brown pays due homage to women (Marin Alsop, JoAnn Falletta), minorities (Henry Lewis, Isaiah Jackson) and both (Margaret Harris). On the conducting side, the dictionary provides illustrative notations of conducting technique, (e.g., the eleven dynamic signs) and multilingual entries in italics for French, German, Italian, and Spanish terms (though most without an English-language equivalent). For novice conductors, Brown includes Monteux's 5 "musts" and 12 "don'ts" for young conductors and Richard Strauss' 10 golden rules for a young conductor. All entries are listed in one straight alphabet with cross-references embedded within articles, even terms like conductor and orchestra. This extremely thorough and systematic system of cross-referencing often leads to overkill. For example, since the word "conductor" appears in every mention of the articles about conductors, when one turns to the definition for conductor, one finds simply "a person who conducts." A highly comprehensive thematic bibliography includes classics in the field as well as items published as recently as 2015. The dictionary concludes with several useful appendixes: six pieces that changed conducting, a two-page history of conducting, translations in French, German, Italian and Spanish of instruments and of pitch, interval

273

and rhythmic terms, and a sample recitative from Così fan tutte. Although one would expect that the professional conductor would be familiar with this material, this volume would prove useful to the music school or conservatory student; the public library user or college student would certainly find the information informative, if not entertaining, but the title might dissuade said users despite its wealth of potentially useful general music information.—**Lawrence Olszewski**

Handbooks and Yearbooks

C, P, S

382.   **Europeana   Music.   http://europeana.eu/portal/collections/music.** [Website] Free. Date reviewed: 2016.

Europeana is a wide-reaching digital library documenting books, paintings, films, objects, and audio recordings from museums, archives, and historical institutions across Europe. There are a variety of Europeana group projects: initiatives specializing in different disciplines. Europeana Sounds is behind the music collection housed on Europeana. From the site: "The Europeana Music Collections brings together a selection of the best music recordings, sheet music, and other music related collections from Europe's audio-visual archives, libraries, archives and museums. This month the spotlights have been carefully picked by the Danish Statsbiblioteket."

The site features an attractive, contemporary layout. The music collection also utilizes Soundcloud for curated listening lists as well as individual music pieces. The music collection boasts 184,698 images, 61,081 sound recordings, 19,995 texts, 11,318 videos, and five 3D objects. The site is arranged for both casual browsing and purposeful searching for professional, student, or recreational users.

The purpose of the collection is comprehensive historic documentation; therefore, it is most suited to vintage highlights rather than contemporary fads. For example, the above-mentioned Danish spotlight features sheet music from WWI, Irish Folk music, Jean Sibelius, Richard Strauss, Mongolian folk music recorded by a Danish explorer, and the early recordings of Robinson Crusoe. Also featured are exhibitions on musical instruments, and recording and playing machines.

Many of the sounds are downloadable, providing digitized primary sources directly to the user. Links to the institutional sources of the media are provided to explore more extensively if desired. This site is oriented toward researchers of primary documentation, so those seeking commentary, context, and explanation would need to refer to other resources.

The music collection on Europeana is a triumphant merger of contemporary technology with historic cultural preservation. Beautiful and informative, the site is rewarding and engaging for visitors. *Europeana Music* is a highly recommended immersive learning experience.—**ARBA Staff Reviewer**

C

383.   Holoman, D. Kern. **Writing about Music: A Style Sheet.** Oakland, Calif., University of California Press, 2014. 126p. illus. $29.95pa. ISBN 13: 978-0-520-28153-0; 8-0-520-95881- (e-book).

Scope mirrors the previous editions (1988, 2008) that outlined issues facing writers about music: title strategies, materials in multiple languages, formats, and access methods, plus the recording of terminology and notation in writings. The author concisely lists principles that writers need in the digital age, and the prime sources of information to create their narratives and citations. The author hopes to simplify citations of Internet locators, provides examples of World Music, addresses page layout in the paperless world, and notes the multiple platforms available for publication and dissemination.

The pattern resembles the *Chicago Manual of Style* (Chicago: University of Chicago Press, 2010), cited as *CMS*. Holoman provides guidance in musical terminology, and methods of constructing a narrative essay.

He begins with "Music Terminology," where he defines titles of works, distinctive and generic, liturgical works, movement titles, numbering of works, diacritical marks, thematic catalogs, pitch names, chords, and rehearsal marks. He clarifies the use of apostrophes in the citation of names. The thematic catalogs indexed are the basic ones for freshmen, but this list scratches the surface. The "Narrative Text" chapter details the use of diacritics, punctuation, and other details critical to writing about music. "Citations and Credits" proves very useful for those citing digital materials and recordings. The author presents further advice on the displays of musical examples, tables, and the textual layout of concert programs.

Although there is no index, the author provides a detailed table of contents. *Writing About Music* is simpler for musicians to use than is the *Chicago Manual of Style,* and addresses their specific issues. This volume should be on music reference shelves, near the *CMS* and Kate Turabian's *A Manual for Writers of Research Papers, Theses, and Dissertations* (Chicago: University of Chicago Press, 2013).—**Ralph Hartsock**

C

384.   Scott, Allen. **Sourcebook for Research in Music.** 3d ed. Bloomington, Ind., Indiana University Press, 2014. 497p. index. $35.00pa. ISBN 13: 978-0-253-01448-1.

Allen Scott takes a general approach similar to previous editions, to create an "introductory reference source…largely bibliographical, pertaining to research in the field of music." (p. xv) He concentrated on providing a selective representation rather than comprehensiveness. The editor expands and numerically systematizes many aspects of the previous editions' introduction, such as glossaries and classification systems. To the bibliographical terms in English, French, and German, Scott adds Italian terms. He then displays a summary of the Library of Congress classification for music and its literature. The Dewey classification guide for music is updated to show the 23d edition, followed by a guide to the 19th edition.

After this, the organization of the third edition departs from that used for the first and second. The editor created two large sections. Part one is literature about music, while part two cites specific sources to help users find the music itself.

The editor moves from general to specific in each chapter of part one: General Bibliographies, Dictionaries and Encyclopedias of Music, and Journals and Periodicals and Their Indexes. The meatiest portions in part one are the last two chapters. The fifth chapter covers musicology, ethnomusicology, music theory, education, music therapy, and music history. The next chapter presents sources relating to musical instruments, genres and forms, and repertory guides.

Part two begins with sources that describe early manuscripts, monuments, composers' complete works, and thematic catalogs. In this listing of monuments, the editor yields to George R. Hill's and Norris L. Stephens's mammoth volume, *Collected Editions, Historical Series & Sets & Monuments of Music: A Bibliography* (Berkeley, Calif: Fallen Leaf Press, 1997), for detailed descriptions. The second chapter of this part describes discographies.

Another departure from the second edition is the absence of miscellaneous sources, such as manuals of style, and general sources about the music industry. In this way, Scott focuses upon the sources for research in music, instead of processes. Those relevant to research are in the general bibliographies. The volume concludes with two indexes: one for persons, and the second for titles.

Those who desire fuller annotations of each title may still go to Vincent Duckles's and Ida Reed's *Music Reference and Research Materials,* 5th edition (Schirmer Books, 1997; see ARBA 98, entry 1189), up to that publication date. For major publications after 1997, Laurie Sampsel's *Music Research: A Handbook* (Oxford University Press, 2013) provides very useful annotations. Those who seek guidance in the processes of music research, citation of sources, and style manuals, should also consult Sampsel's volume and updated Website (http://global.oup.com/us/companion.websites/9780199797127/).

Scott did miss some significant titles about the blues: *Encyclopedia of the Blues,* by Gérard Herzhaft (Fayetteville: University of Arkansas Press, 1997; see ARBA 99, entry 1150); *The Big Book of Blues: A Biographical Encyclopedia,* by Robert Santelli (New York: Penguin Books, 2001; see ARBA 2002, entry 1167); and *Encyclopedia of the Blues,* edited by Edward Komara (New York: Routledge, 2006; see ARBA 2007, entry 1007). Readers will also find *100 Books Every Blues Fan Should Own,* by Edward Komara and Greg Johnson (Lanham, Maryland: Rowman & Littlefield, 2014; see ARBA 2015, entry 745) to be a useful source.

Nevertheless, Allen Scott has created a volume that is easy to use, which identifies titles important to the research of music. This is partially due to the numerical organization instituted by the compiler that resembles the organization of the *Chicago Manual of Style.* Libraries should keep a copy behind the desk for quick reference.—**Ralph Hartsock**

Instruments

Handbooks and Yearbooks

P, S

385.   Wilkinson, Philip. **The History of Music in Fifty Instruments.** New York, Firefly Books, 2014. 224p. illus. index. $29.95. ISBN 13: 978-1-77085-428-4.

This book is part of publisher Firefly's Fifty Things that Changed the World series that now includes volumes on machines, animals, plants, and foods. The author of this volume, Philip Wilkinson, is an English freelance writer of over 40 books with specialization in music, architecture, and history (e.g., *The British Monarchy for Dummies* from For Dummies Press in 2007). This volume traces the history of music-making through the production and evolution of 50 different musical instruments beginning in the 1300s with the creation of the lute and ending with the synthesizer in 1985, with stops along the way for 48 other creations. The length of the article depends on the importance of the instrument; for example, castanets (1845) and the harmonium (1842) get two pages each whereas the violin (1636), piano (1709), and baton (1812) have eight pages each. The text covers in lucid nontechnical prose such topics as the evolution and nature of the instrument, different types and their characteristics, the role and importance of the instrument in orchestral music, composers who wrote for this instrument, and famous art works in which the instrument is featured. Sidebars are used to give interesting tidbits of related material (e.g., the article on the English horn (1720) has a sidebar on how it got is name and the one on the violin features a list of great violin makers). Classical music is emphasized throughout although there are some references to jazz and folk music. The glory of this volume, however, is in its illustrations, mostly in color. They include diagrams of the instrument (often with labeled parts), other members of its family and their history, famous composers and instrumentalists associated with the instrument, and historical prints that feature the instrument. The book begins with an introduction that covers musical instruments and their families and ends with a bibliography for further reading, a list of important Websites, and a five-page index. This is an engaging, informative volume suitable for both reference and browsing.—**John T. Gillespie**

Musical Forms

Classical

C

386. **Classical Scores Library Package. http://alexanderstreet.com/products/ classical-scores-library-package.** [Website] Alexandria, Va., Alexander Street Press. Price negotiated by site. Date reviewed: 2016.

The Alexander Street *Classical Scores Library Package* provides access to approximately 51,000 in-copyright music scores for all major classical music genres from the "Middle Ages to the 21st century." All major composers (e.g., Bach, Mozart, Beethoven, etc.) are included as well as lesser-known contemporary composers. The complete collection is divided into four volumes that can be purchased separately or as a package.

The collection includes full, study, voice, and piano scores. It has been thoroughly indexed allowing it to be searched by keyword and browsed by title, genre, instrument, people, publisher, time period, and composer.

A high-quality image copy of the music score is provided with a wealth of accompanying metadata (composer, date, language, publisher, etc.). The in-score navigation feature allows users to jump between movements. The viewing interface allows users to create custom playlists, annotate the music, and share the score and their notes. Recommendations for related works are included. All scores and movements can be easily cited using any one of the major citation styles (powered by EasyBib).

The collection will certainly "enhance the study of music history, performance, composition and theory for a variety of scholars"; thus, it is highly recommended. The ability to access such a large scope of music collected from a wide range of publishers is a major benefit to musicians and researchers. Any academic or public library committed to serving serious music scholars should have this resource. The collection has over 1.3 million printable pages and claims the shelf space needed to house such a collection is over 200 meters. This kind of space-saving is valuable in itself, but the added search tools, enhancements, and the ability to access the collection online makes this an indispensable, go-to tool.—**Kristin Kay Leeman**

C, P

387. Murray, Lucy Miller. **Chamber Music: An Extensive Guide for Listeners.** Lanham, Md., Rowman & Littlefield, 2015. 427p. $85.00; $84.99 (e-book). ISBN 13: 978-1-4422-4342-2; 978-1-4422-4343-9 (e-book).

If music be the food of love, then chamber music is the food of angels who created that love. An excess of it would surely never whet any appetite for it for it is the breath of violets, the sweet odor of the beating, diaphanous wings. It is, in short, the language of God and hardly better understood than by Bach himself.

But it is, of course, more than Bach as these 600+ works attest. It is more far-reaching than Bach, too, since this collection covers the Classical through the Romantic and past the post-Modern. But that Bach is the only representative of chamber music in the Baroque period serves to validate the former assertions.

This current volume is a second edition of *Adams to Zemlinsky: A Friendly Guide* (Concert Artists Guild, 2006). This edition shakes off the alphabetic restrictions and focuses more on the wide expanse that is chamber music. The obvious in addition to Bach are here: Bartok, Beethoven, Brahms, Chopin, Debussy, and Mozart. But so are some that many general readers will never have heard of: Abramovic, Ades, Bridge, D'Rivera, Reger, and the modern composer Zorn. Each entry contains a survey of the composer's work, a note about the chosen piece (or pieces) of chamber music, and the author's personal assessment. Miller's personal viewpoints make the book since so much scholarly information is available online. Even she admits its quirkiness, as when she compares a moment in one of Beethoven's string quartets to a belly dance. But it is just this personalization that makes the book an interesting read and a must buy.

A detailed table of contents makes finding certain pieces simple and straight-forward. The book is laid out alphabetically, of course, for easy reference to the body of the chamber work by individual composers.—**Mark Y. Herring**

Orchestral

C, P

388. Daniels, David. **Daniels' Orchestral Music.** 5th ed. Lanham, Md., Rowman & Littlefield, 2015. 885p. index. $85.00. ISBN 13: 978-1-4422-4537-2.

The fifth edition of this staple of music libraries has increased by one third in its number of pages, entries, and updates from the fourth edition, but its purpose and format remain basically unchanged. The work is an alphabetical listing by composer and work that includes information to help orchestras schedule rehearsals and plan concerts. To save space due to its complex and detailed nature, instrumentation is indicated by a series of codes; for those not familiar with them, an explanation in the preface explains their interpretation. For orchestra staff responsible for programming notes, the work provides skeletal composer biography, date of composition, and approximate duration. As a collection tool, publication information indicates the availability of scores for music libraries that want to expand their collections, especially of lesser-known composers and works.

Even without the requisite omission of operatic works, any such source must needs be selective; nevertheless, the inclusion of over 8000 works in the repertoire by composers worldwide is indeed impressive, incorporating all the symphonies of Haydn and Mozart and Bach's cantatas, to name just three complete series of works by prolific composers.

A gem of this work has always been the appendixes. Where else can one find programmable works that are under five minutes? One appendix will assist planners of tie-ins to local ethnic programming events, another to celebrate the significant anniversaries of composers through 2026, and yet another of works intended for young audiences.

This resource is also available by annual subscription through Orchestralmusic.com with monthly updates.

Besides the obvious target audience of music librarians, conductors, and orchestra programmers, it will also be useful for critics, concertgoers, and music collectors. However, this edition may be the last overseen by octogenarian Daniels, now retired from conducting and from the faculty at Oakland University.—**Lawrence Olszewski**

26 Mythology, Folklore, and Popular Culture

Folklore

C, P, S

389.   Redfern, Nick. **The Bigfoot Book: The Encyclopedia of Sasquatch, Yeti, and Cryptid Primates.** Canton, Mich., Visible Ink Press, 2016. 381p. illus. index. $19.95pa. ISBN 13: 978-1-57859-561-7.

In much of the world there exist folk tales and legends of large humanoid creatures resembling great apes. Whether it is the Kikomba of the Congo, the Yeti of Tibet, or the Sasquatch of North America these creatures possess many similarities with one another that have inspired explorers of various backgrounds to search for conclusive evidence of their existence. The purpose of this reference is to gather together in one accessible volume the various accounts and legends of these creatures along with the fictional tales that they've inspired in film and other media.

With a collection of over 230 articles the author details various world legends of Bigfoot both ancient, such as Alexander the Great and the great hairy wild men, and more modern accounts, including Alabama's Ape man. The text also talks about notable hoax stories as well as entries for various adaptations of these legends in film and literature ranging from horror to comedic tales. The entire collection is arranged alphabetically with each entry listed in the contents. Many entries possess references to additional topics within the text and the book itself possesses a comprehensive index as well as a list for further study on the topic.

While the index is quite extensive it would be primarily useful to individuals with a previous working knowledge of the materials within. Despite this the individual entries are understandably written and engaging and thus this would serve as an adequate introduction to the subject for general enthusiasts, high school students, or early college students.—**W. Cole Williamson**

C

390.   **A Companion to Folklore.** Regina F. Bendix and Galit Hasan-Rokem, eds. Hoboken, N.J., Wiley-Blackwell, 2014. 660p. index. $54.95pa. ISBN 13: 878-1-118-86314-5.

A Companion to Folklore is a long-awaited, cohesive text on the study of folklore. With introductions to each chapter that bring together the topics of concepts and phenomena, location, reflection, and practice, this volume is an essential piece for folklore studies. Covering a wide scope and rich with information, editors Bendix and Hasan-Rokem have gathered thought-provoking and interdisciplinary scholars in a single volume.

References and notes follow each chapter, allowing for an even deeper understanding of the discussion by the author and further research. Anyone interested in the current trends and outlook of folklore studies needs look no further, at the moment, than this volume. Covering information across time periods and continents, this truly is a multicultural and multidisciplinary approach to folklore studies.—**Michelle Martinez**

C, P

391.   Elswit, Sharon Barcan. **The Latin American Story Finder.** Jefferson, N.C., McFarland, 2015. 318p. index. $45.00pa. ISBN 13: 978-0-7864-7895-8; 978-1-4766-2229-3 (e-book).

This is the third book published by this author related to ethnic stories, the other two on East Asian and Jewish tales. This guide provides access to stories from 21 countries and over 75 indigenous tribes in Latin America after the arrival of Spanish and Portuguese colonials in the sixteenth century. These tales from native cultures such as the Maya and Quechua tribes were mixed with those of Sephardic Jews and Catholic missionaries, sprinkled with ancient Inca and Amazonian cultures along with Anansi stories from African slaves. The author divides this "soup" of stories into a number of categories, from journeys to other realms to supernatural seducers, from winning and losing with the gods to tricksters and fools, among many. The real power in this book are the indexes and appendixes, which include a glossary and listing of indigenous peoples by country with alternate names, along with a story title and subject index. An extensive bibliography makes this a unique resource on over 470 Latin American tales.—**Bradford Lee Eden**

Mythology

C, P

392.   Aldhouse-Green, Miranda. **The Celtic Myths: A Guide to the Ancient Gods and Legends.** New York, Thames and Hudson, 2015. 207p. illus. index. $24.95. ISBN 13: 978-0-500-25209-3.

In recent history there has been a revival of interest in cultural traditions thought to originate with the Celtic peoples. Whether in the areas of music, the arts, or especially new age spiritual beliefs, many people are fascinated and drawn to this ancient culture both as a window into their own ancestry and as a rejection to many aspects of today's society. There is unfortunately a great disparity between what we sometimes ascribe to this civilization and what they actually thought and believed themselves. This is due in large part to a sizable dearth of information from their own point of view. Through painstaking archaeological and cultural research this guide seeks to piece together the actual legends and beliefs of this lost society.

In each chapter this book delves into various aspects of the Celtic traditions such as an examination of their surviving mythic tales, the cultural aspects of oral histories, legends of spirits, heroes, and enchanted lands, and finally how these tales evolved with the coming of Christianity. The chapters are divided in their focus with some homing in on individual locations such as Wales or Ireland, while others explore especially important practices in detail such as the celebration of significant events.

The arrangement of the text flows well and it includes an adequate if not exhaustive index. The real appeal in this work lies with its extensive use of beautiful photographs and highly informative charts strategically placed throughout the text. Special note may be given to a chart at the beginning that highlights pronunciation standards for proper names in the rest of the text that greatly aids the reader unfamiliar with linguistic intricacies. Overall this serves as an excellent guide to the richness of Celtic cultures for either the academic reader or general enthusiast.—**W. Cole Williamson**

Popular Culture

C, P, S

393.   **Holiday Symbols and Customs.** 5th ed. Detroit, Omnigraphics, 2015. 1437p. index. $133.00. ISBN 13: 978-0-7808-1364-9.

This large volume, a companion to *Holidays, Festivals, and Celebrations of the World Dictionary* (Omnigraphics, 2015) and an update to the fourth edition (see ARBA 2010, entry 1049), presents information about the activities and symbols of over 375 events of many sorts. Included, for example, are Christmas, the British Open (golf tournament), Tinkat (the Ethiopian celebration of Epiphany), Setsubun (a Japanese festival), and the Army-Navy Football Game. The symbols range from objects (crystals, masks, water lanterns, the moon) to activities within the celebration. Most entries include contact information and Websites, when available.

Besides the table of contents, other tools enhance access to the information herein: a list of entries by type of celebration, a list by symbols involved, listings of tourist information worldwide (including foreign chambers of commerce and consulates in the U.S.), and a 70-page general index. Libraries of all kinds would benefit from acquiring this volume, should budgets allow it.—**Mark Schumacher**

C, P, S

394.   **Holidays, Festivals, and Celebrations of the World Dictionary.** 5th ed. Detroit, Omnigraphics, 2015. 1500p. $177.00. ISBN 13: 978-0-7808-1362-5.

This massive volume provides information on over 3,300 events of all kinds, from the World Santa Claus Conference (held annually in Denmark) and the Pitra Visarjana Amavasya ceremony in India, to the Fourth of July and Festivus (inspired by the "Seinfeld" show). Details of the history of the event and its various activities are included. Websites and addresses for additional information are also available in many cases.

Appendixes and indexes provide numerous ways to explore the volume—legal holidays by state and by country, an index by date throughout the year, and a subject index (arts, religious, sporting, etc.). There are also discussions of world religions and calendar systems, tourism resources, a 25-page bibliography, and a 120-page general index. This work is recommended to all libraries whose users are seeking resources on these celebrations, from school and public libraries to academic institutions.—**Mark Schumacher**

C, P, S

395.   **Comic Book DB.com. http://comicbookdb.com/.** [Website] Free. Date reviewed: 2016.

Comic Book DB is a fairly comprehensive database of comic book issues, creators, artists, publishers, and characters. The site is mostly useful for anyone researching a popular character or creator.

The database allows users to browse by various categories from an alphabetical list of characters, creators, publishers, and more. The amount of information available is heavily in favor of the major publishers (DC Comics, Marvel, Image Comics, etc.), creators, and characters. Character searches such as "Superman" or "Captain America" include exhaustive lists of titles and various appearances by the characters over time. Moreover, such well-known creators Stan Lee and Jack Kirby are accompanied by significant biographies. Each creator is also paired with a very detailed chronological list of credited works and awards, making it easy for a user to jump from that creator into his or her works and accolades. Pages on creators without the legacy of Lee and Kirby contain less biographical information, but most creators still come with a strong list of credited works and awards.

The site does contain issues that limit the ability to search. For example, a search of "Lee, Stan" will not actually lead to results including the creator because the site lists him as "Lee, Stan 'The Man' – 'Stanley Martin Lieber'." Also, it appears the Website allows users to update information, much like Wikipedia. Nevertheless, the ability to search creators, their credited works, and some biographical information makes the database is a good starting point for students looking to research comic books and their creators or characters.—**ARBA Staff Reviewer**

P, S

396.   **Earth Calendar. http://www.earthcalendar.net//index.php.** [Website] Free. Date reviewed: 2016.

This fun, simple site allows users to find holidays and celebrations around the world by date. Holidays are defined as any day that recognizes a cultural event. The site's copyright dates are listed as 1998-2008, but holidays and celebrations are searchable until 2020. *Earth Calendar* is freely accessible and nonprofit, but there is no advertising on the site.

Navigation is simple. From the home page, users can click a today tab that produces the day's holidays. Holidays and celebrations linked to March 11, 2016, for instance, include Commonwealth Day in Tuvalu and the celebration for the Restoration of Lithuania's Statehood. From March 11, users can navigate to previous and following days. Other search options include Holidays by Date, Holidays by Country, or Holidays by Religion. For the more creative, there is a link to lunar phases. A country search using Bermuda and 2016 revealed in addition to New Year's Day on January 1, that Bermudans will celebrate Peppercorn Day on April 23, Bermuda Day on May 24, Dame Lois Browne-Evans Day on November 11, Christmas Day on December 25, and Boxing Day on December 26. Each country also has a basic map powered by Graphic Maps that shows its place in the world and its geographic outline. Those wishing to search for holidays by religion can choose from Baha'i, Buddhism, Celticism, Christianity, Hinduism, Jainism, Judaism, Muslim/Islamic, Paganism, Rastafarian, Shinto, Sikhism, Voudon, and Zoroastrian.—**ARBA Staff Reviewer**

C, P, S

397.   Nichols, Elizabeth Gackstetter, and Timothy R. Robbins. **Pop Culture in Latin America and the Caribbean.** Santa Barbara, Calif., Greenwood Press/ABC-CLIO, 2015. 402p. index. (Entertainment and Society around the World). $94.00. ISBN 13: 978-1-61069-753-8; 978-1-61069-754-5 (e-book).

Organized topically, this handbook is part of the ABC-CLIO "Entertainment and Society around the World" series, and covers music, literature, film, sports, television, fashion, and Internet and gaming culture in and Latin America and the Caribbean in the twentieth and twenty-first centuries.

Each chapter starts with an introductory essay that provides a broader historical and social context—a useful resource for beginning researchers—and a list of sources for further reading. The entries in each section highlight particular contemporary issues and people, with bibliographies citing reputable Websites as well as popular and trade publications. Many of the individuals and trends are easily recognizable, but the entries provide a greater context. For example, the entry for the Brazilian star Xuxa provides insight into her life prior to her rise to North American stardom, as well as what she has been producing in the years since her peak.

Its organization may be confusing to casual browsers, however. While the titles of the articles are clearly indicated at the tops of the pages, it would be useful to have chapter titles as well. The appendix includes a number of top 10 lists related to entertainment and culture, but they mostly focus on 2012-2014, which limits their usefulness for examining longer-term trends.

A more substantial bibliography at the end primarily refers to scholarly books that are excellent next steps for finding information. Written in a style accessible to high school and college-level researchers, this is a good introduction and suitable for most school, public, and academic libraries.—**Amanda Izenstark**

27 Performing Arts

Dance

Dictionaries and Encyclopedias

C, P

398. Snodgrass, Mary Ellen. **The Encyclopedia of World Ballet.** Lanham, Md., Rowman & Littlefield, 2015. 424p. illus. index. $95.00; $94.99 (e-book). ISBN 13: 978-1-4422-4525-9; 978-1-4422-4526-6 (e-book).

In 377 pages, the world surrounding the global emergence and growth of ballet historically and thematically is described through dense, informative entries. Immensely useful in both organization and structure, entries include choreographers, companies, dancers, and key terminology, among other things. These entries display not only the rich internal history of the dance world and ballet specifically, but also the role and impact this world has had on the larger social structure. This is echoed in the colorful timeline—noting, for example, the 23 years of censorship of the Iranian National Ballet between 1979 and 2002. This volume is both an encyclopedic look at the elements that comprise ballet, as well as the unfolding of the larger philosophy of movement and dance. Because we are presented with this wider scope in a compact volume, the listing of entries (and rationale for their inclusion or exclusion) might not be intuitive to the nonexpert. A companion volume would have ensured a more comprehensive sweep. The index does indicate which terms are found within as complete entries, and this makes cross-referencing easier. Useful for students and practitioners of dance; anyone with a broad interest in the historiography of the humanities will find this necessary as well.—**Stephen J. Shaw**

Film, Television, and Video

Dictionaries and Encyclopedias

P

399. Hischak, Thomas S. **The Encyclopedia of Film Composers.** Lanham, Md., Rowman & Littlefield, 2015. 819p. illus. index. $95.00; $94.99 (e-book). ISBN 13: 978-1-4422-4549-5; 978-1-4422-4550-1 (e-book).

Paying homage to those often-forgotten composers whose music serves as the backdrop of film, this encyclopedia focuses on 252 composers who have contributed significantly to movie music. Some entries feature artists who composed songs, but this is predominantly a collection of composers of film scores. Major film composers are covered, but this work attempts to give attention to Hollywood and foreign film composers often left out of other treatments on the subject. Entries provide biographical information, descriptions of the composer's career and musical style, and a complete list of film score credits. Only films in which the individual is listed as the primary composer or one of two composers are listed. For the common reader, the encyclopedia provides a few surprises such as an entry on Charlie Chaplin, who scored some of his own films decades after their release. Familiar names in jazz appear as entries as well. Featured in this work is more than a century of composers who have provided original music for silent films to contemporary movies.—**Brian J. Sherman**

C, P

400.   **The Routledge Encyclopedia of Films.** Sarah Barrow, Sabine Haenni, and John White, eds. New York, Routledge/Taylor & Francis Group, 2014. 665p. index. 205.00. ISBN 13: 978-0-415-68893-2; 978-7-315-77383-4 (e-book).

When applied to a book on a particular subject, the term "encyclopedia" usually means that it contains a comprehensive overview of that subject. This is not so with this volume although it deserves the attention of anyone interested in films because of its unique contents. The three editors with the help of almost 80 contributors (all film and media academics primarily in American and British institutions) have chosen almost 200 films that are considered among the most important, influential, trail-blazing, and also critically satisfying. Therefore, this is not the usual "best films" list (although some of the titles in this volume often appear on such lists). The films are arranged alphabetically by title and each entry is three double-columned pages in length. The coverage is truly international in scope—only about 50 (25% of the entries) are English-language films. These include such standards as *Citizen Kane* (1941), *On the Waterfront* (1954), and *Singin' in the Rain* (1952), as well as some questionable entries like those for *Mad Max* (1979) and *Moulin Rouge!* (2000). The remainder of the entries are for foreign-language films with particularly fine coverage for French, Italian, Spanish, and German films. Also included are films from such countries as Turkey, Senegal, and Burkina Faso. The most recent film included is *Milk of Sorrow* (2009) from Peru. Each entry is scholarly in tone and emphasizes material on why the film is important in cinematic history.

Entries begin with a listing of the cast and key production personnel and a brief plot synopsis. These are followed by an essay on the movie that includes a critical analysis of the film often with reference to particular scenes and performances and directorial techniques. Background material on social and political movements that affected the content of the film and its treatment are included. Sources of the script (novel, play, etc) and other influences on the film are covered as well as the material on the past (and future) of key personnel including the director and the stars. Each entry is signed and ends with a brief footnote-like section called "Notes." That is followed by a "Further Reading" bibliography that typically contains a list of four or five English-language sources. In addition to an excellent detailed index, the editors have provided lists of the films by both their English- and foreign-language titles and a chronology for films by their release dates (there are entries for 13 silent movies including *Birth of a Nation* (1915). This is a fascinating scholarly work that deserves a place in libraries needing quality material on movie history.—**John T. Gillespie**

Handbooks and Yearbooks

C, P

401.   Berumen, Frank Javier Garcia. **Latino Image Makers in Hollywood: Performers, Filmmakers and Films Since the 1960s.** Jefferson, N.C., McFarland, 2014. 335p. illus. index. $55.00pa. ISBN 13: 978-0-7864-7432-5; 978-1-4766-1411-3 (e-book).

The stated purpose of *Latino Image Makers in Hollywood* "is to document the history of Latino film images and icons in the Hollywood film industry from the 1960s to the present." Berumen begins with a chapter on the origins of Latino stereotypes followed by decade-by-decade chapters on Latinos in films from the 1960s to the 2000s and a postscript "Beyond the 2000s: Looking Back and Looking Forward." In addition to Latino performers and filmmakers, the author studies non-Latino performers in Latino roles (e.g., Natalie Wood as Maria in *West Side Story*). The author has viewed most of the films mentioned in the book and consulted reviews of films, interviews with Latino performers and filmmakers, and works on film history, biographies, and newspapers and magazines. Discussed are early film performers such as Ramon Novarro, Gilbert Roland, Lupita Tovar, and Dolores del Rio. It should be noted that Beruman's earlier work, *Brown Celluloid: Latino/a Film Icons and Images in the Hollywood Film Industry* (2003), documents the 1920s-1950s. Chapters profile and study key films and performers and analyze social and historical conditions of the times. For example, the 1960s focuses on major films such as *The Alamo, Che!, West Side Story,* and *The Wild Bunch* and profiles performers and filmmakers among which are Pedro Armendariz, Jr., Henry Darrow, Lalo Schifrin, and Raquel Welch. The following films are analyzed for subsequent decades: *State of Siege, La Bamba, Selena, Stand and Deliver, American Me, Frida,* and *Traffic.* Additionally, actors, actresses, and filmmakers profiled include Salma Hayek, Penelope Cruz, Javier Bardem, Carlos Avila, Jennifer Lopez, Benicio Del Toro, Antonio Banderas, Raul Julia, Jimmy Smits, Hector Elizondo, Luis Valdez, Mark Sanchez, Charlie Sheen, and Martin Sheen (Estevez). *Latino Image Makers in Hollywood* also contains copious illustrations, chapter notes, a bibliography, and an index. Highly recommended to public libraries and to college and university collections supporting programs in Latin American and Hispanic studies as well as motion picture history. It is recommended that libraries also purchase Brown's *Celluloid: Latino/a Film Icons and Images in the Hollywood Film Industry.*—**Lucy Heckman**

C

402.   **Film Scripts Online Series. http://search.alexanderstreet.com/afso.** [Website] Alexandria, Va., Alexander Street Press. Price negotiated by site. Date reviewed: 2016.

Alexander Street Press' *American Film Scripts Online* is an online resource of English-language film scripts. These are shooting scripts, which contain not only dialog but camera and setting direction. The materials are drawn primarily from the American film industry, but they also feature scripts from several British studios. In all there are more than 1,100 screenplays that, while not exhaustive, do offer access to many important directors and writers from across the twentieth century. Because these are shooting scripts, they also provide a more comprehensive textual analysis of direction, although researchers will still want to hunt down the original notes and diary entries when available. The Website also makes available 37 monographs from the British Film Institute's Film Classics Series. Each is a book-length critique of a major film from the twentieth and early twenty-first centuries. Suggestive of the range of this material are such films as *Nosferatu, Citizen Kane, Cléo de 5 à 7,* and *Pan's Labyrinth.*

Research can be done several ways. The site offers featured collections such as scripts by Billy Wilder or from the famed Ealing Studios, a powerhouse of British cinema in the 1940s and 1950s. Users may also browse by broad categories such People, Genre, and Awards. The browse function is usually a coarse sieve, but in this collection the People category is subdivided into director, producer, writer, and performer. For example, "Huston, John" brings up 20 items: 12 as director, 1 as producer, 17 as screen writer, and none as performer; "Streisand, Barbra" reveals 1 item as a performer and 1 as a producer. This is pretty nifty. The Genre and Awards browse functions are coarser in this respect, although the latter is useful for exploring minor film festival awards. The advanced function allows for much more targeted searches. One caveat for libraries is that this is the third script offering by Alexander Street Press. The company has previously released two other volumes titled *Film Scripts Online:* volume one released more than 1,000 screenplays, and volume two provided an additional 500 screenplays. The present site seems to present a subset of the two previous collections along with some additional material.—**Joseph E. Taylor III**

P, S

403.   **The Movie Book: Big Ideas Simply Explained.** New York, DK Publishing, 2016. 352p. illus. index. (Big Ideas Simply Explained). $25.00. ISBN 13: 978-1-4654-3799-0.

Part of DK's "Big Ideas Simply Explained" series, *The Movie Book* provides a nice overview of "the movies that best capture cinema," as it's put in the introduction. The book discusses 100 films, organized chronologically in six sections: Visionaries (1902-1931), A Golden Age in Black and White (1931-1949), Fear and Wonder (1950-1959), Rebel Rebel (1960-1974), Angels and Monsters (1975-1991), Small World (1992-Present). Each section includes a brief timeline and introduction. Each film entry begins with an "In Context" fact box with credits, noting related movies that preceded and followed the film, then discusses such topics as the inspiration for and origins of the film, production, and the wider impact of the film. Each film is also accompanied by a brief "What else to watch" list, and many have sidebars with director or actor profiles. Throughout the book are numerous photos (in color and black and white) and movie posters; infographics and quotes are also distributed evenly. *The Movie Book* includes a nice selection of widely recognized classics (*Casablanca,* 1942) along with some less obvious choices (*To Be or Not to Be,* 1942) that will benefit those without extensive knowledge of film history. As with any volume that seeks to single out key films in the history of cinema, film buffs might disagree with some of the choices (and omissions), but they may enjoy comparing their "essentials" to the authors'. Recommended for high school and public libraries.— **ARBA Staff Reviewer**

C, P

404.   Roots, James. **The 100 Greatest Silent Film Comedians.** Lanham, Md., Rowman & Littlefield, 2014. 432p. illus. index. $95.00; $94.99 (e-book). ISBN 13: 978-1-61069-832-0; 978-1-4422-3650-9 (e-book).

Ranking of the arts is always fraught with landmines. Here, author James Roots, a deaf man and disabilities advocate, takes on the challenge of ranking silent movie comedians in a bold manner.

Each entry includes the name of the comedian or comedy team, birth and death dates, a good sized black-and-white picture, and a rating which includes subscores for Funny, Creativity, Teamwork, Timelessness, Appeal, and Intangibles added up to a total score of 100 possible points. Charlie Chaplin and Buster Keaton tie at 99 points for first place. Cliff Bowes is at number 100 with 21 points. Then each article has a partial list of films for that act, an opinionated essay ranging from a couple of paragraphs to a several pages, and finally a list of films available on DVD at the time of printing. Many of these films are shorts and are included in compilation DVDs rather than as individual titles.

There is an appendix of also-rans, an annotated bibliography for both general books on the topic and for individual comedians, and an index. Websites are not included as they tend to change. An appendix of the available DVDs in one place and possibly ranked would have been nice and perhaps helpful in purchasing decisions.

Roots' deep knowledge of, and appreciation of, these films allows him to address many controversial topics and counter several generally received opinions about these artists, their contributions, and behind-the-scenes controversies. He is well read in the field and is not afraid of taking on well-known critics and their opinions and uses an entertaining writing style to make his points.

With the strongly subjective essays, this might be a better choice for a general circulating collection than reference. Recommended for all libraries with film studies collections or interest in the history of film.—**Robert M. Lindsey**

Theater

Dictionaries and Encyclopedias

C

405.   Fisher, James. **Historical Dictionary of American Theater: Beginnings.** Lanham, Md., Rowman & Littlefield, 2015. 525p. (Historical Dictionaries of Literature and the Arts). $135.00; $129.99 (e-book). ISBN 13: 978-0-8108-7832-7; 978-0-8108-7833-4 (e-book).

Historical Dictionary of American Theater: Beginnings is the first in a series of historical dictionaries of the theater in America. The series has been divided into three periods: Beginnings, defined as the first known historical mention of the performance of a play in 1538 to 1880, Modernism (1880-1930), and Contemporary (1930-present). *Beginnings* is the last published but the first chronologically and is a highly unique resource, which provides the basic historical context for early American theater and references many known but lost works. This volume is structured in four sections: a concisely written chronology (xv-xliv), an introduction (pp. 1-20), dictionary entries listed alphabetically (pp. 21-485), and an extensive bibliography (pp. 487-523). The chronology provides a timeline of important developments in theater and helps the reader trace influences and effects. The introduction surveys this period in sections with the following headings:

Beginnings to the American Revolution, Revolutionary Theater, The Drama of a New Nation, Finding a Voice, The Nation Divided, Broadway, and The Theater as a Profession. The introduction establishes for the reader how the progress of theater in America either halted or slowed during the Revolutionary and Civil Wars, providing examples of issues surrounding these conflicts being reflected through artistic expression. The researcher will also find a succinct explanation for how Broadway became the center of theater in the United States after the conclusion of the Civil War. The dictionary entries cover a range of topics, from individual practitioners and plays to major events and dramatic genres and issues. Entries are thoroughly cross-referenced, often to entries in one or both of the other volumes of the dictionary. The bibliography itself is an excellent resource as it has been carefully provided with its own introduction and table of contents. Researchers are provided with lists of bibliographies and general reference works, as well as historical and critical studies about a range of topics such as melodrama, minstrels, and Native Americans. This is followed by lists of biographies and memoirs of theater artists, plays and anthologies of plays, and theater practice, management, technology, and terminology. As most entries are cross-referenced with entries in the other two volumes, researchers will get the best use if they are additionally available. This historical dictionary would be an excellent resource for an academic collection supporting research in either American history or theater studies.—**Todd Simpson**

C

406.   **Theatre in Video. http://www.alexanderstreet.com/products/theatre-video-series.** [Website] Alexandria, Va., Alexander Street Press. Price negotiated by site. Date reviewed: 2016.

Theatre in Video is a collection of hundreds of hours of theater performances and documentaries of the world's most famous and important plays. Full-length performances of plays from Sophocles to Shakespeare and contemporary writers like Troy Mink and Jeff Nevers are included. The collection represents not only theater, but it is also a unique record of twentieth-century theater performance in the form of live broadcasts, classic works, experimental performances, and cinematic productions. Recently added volume two of the collection includes an additional 400 hours of video expanding the collection's focus to include more contemporary and international works and performances.

The video collection also includes interviews with actors and directors, and behind-the-scenes looks at dozens of performances. The documentaries bring another dimension to the study of theater telling the story behind the stage. There are also videos focusing on nearly every aspect of bringing a play to the stage from auditioning to costume and lighting design.

The collection provides both simple and advanced text searching as well as many ways to browse the collection by title, people, production company, discipline, publisher, genre, and content type. All of these categories can be combined to refine and create a very specific search.

Each video is fully transcribed, and the transcript is synced with the video time code. This allows users to click on any word or phrase in the transcript and jump to the corresponding place in the video. Each video has a visual table of contents to help users easily navigate the videos by memorable scene. Users are allowed to add their own bookmarks to the videos, and they can cite and share the videos, save favorites to a playlist, and generate a permalink embed code—an option very useful for teaching.

Users are also able to make and save their own video clips allowing many different and useful applications for both teachers and students such as building an engaging lesson, presentation, or report.

The scope, depth, and usefulness of the collection is very impressive. This is a highly recommended resource for theatre and performing art programs. Students at any level will find their study and enjoyment of theatre much increased by using this collection.—**Kristin Kay Leeman**

28 Philosophy and Religion

Philosophy

Dictionaries and Encyclopedias

C

407. Ariew, Roger and others. **Historical Dictionary of Descartes and Cartesian Philosophy.** 2d ed. Lanham, Md., Rowman & Littlefield, 2015. 388p. illus. (Historical Dictionaries of Religions, Philosophies, and Movements Series). $115.00; $109.99 (e-book). ISBN 13: 978-1-4422-4768-0; 978-1-4422-4769-7 (e-book).

Descartes is known as "the father of modern philosophy" and is a central figure in the study of rationalist philosophy in the pantheon including Spinoza, Leibnitz, and Kant. His philosophical and metaphysical works are part of the focus of philosophy study today overshadowing his many other considerable influences and accomplishments in mathematics, physics, and science (known then as "natural philosophy"). These were the major sources of his influence in European intellectual and religious circles of the seventeenth century.

The second edition of the *Historical Dictionary of Descartes and Cartesian Philosophy* builds upon the first (see ARBA 2005, entry 1228) by adding new material and expanding the first edition from 302 pages to 388 pages, covering over 300 entries. New material is primarily historic, detailing biographical and intellectual information about those historical persons who corresponded with Descartes on subjects of scientific or philosophical interest, including friends, supportive Cartesians, religious personages, or critics of Cartesianism. The expanding influence of Descartes and the Cartesianist movement is given a context in the historical milieu of church, science, intellectual debate, and conflict that opens philosophy and science to the modern era. New entries, for example, such as Anti-Cartesianism, Authority, Cartesianism, Catholicism, and Union of Mind and Body, have been added.

Enhancements include: an expanded chronology of events relevant to Descartes's life and the Cartesian movement; an introduction with subheadings and additional material on Descartes's place in modern philosophy; expanded biographical entries; footnotes at the end of each alphabetical section; bolded topics that point to separate entries; *see* and *see also* cross-references. The bibliography has been expanded from 40 to 49 pages. Subsections in the Bibliography with expanded entries are: Texts of Descartes, Texts and Editions, and Works on Descartes, and a new entry: Other Internet Resources.

These improvements to the second edition significantly enhance this valuable resource for the historical study of this essential modern philosopher.—**William Shakalis**

C

408.   Pasanek, Brad. **Metaphors of Mind: An Eighteenth-Century Dictionary.** Baltimore, Md., Johns Hopkins University Press, 2015. 372p. maps. index. $49.95. ISBN 13: 978-1-4214-1688-5; 978-1-4214-1689-2 (e-book).

Ever since the groundbreaking work of Auerbach's *Mimesis,* literary theorists have tried to improve upon that hallowed ground. Auerbach took two basic texts, Homer's *Odysseys* and the Bible's *Genesis,* to look at two ways in which authors view the reality of the world and how they go about that imitation. The book carried the day for a very long while, and still influences those who take the time to read it.

Pasanek has been involved in a similar but slightly different approach: how Enlightenment writers use various figures of speech to characterize the mind as it perceives reality, that part of philosophy that deals with both ontology and epistemology. Pasanek has one advantage over Auerbach by virtue of living in the twenty-first century: he has applied the vast ability of technology to distill the works in question to their discrete parts. Thus, from the gigantic database of the *Mind Is a Metaphor* (http://metaphorized.net) comes this volume on metaphorics.

Pasanek with his digital archive is able to bring to each chapter more than a smattering of quotations. He provides context and character of the works allowing readers insight not only on Enlightenment thinkers but also on today's digital natives. The book challenges assumptions about what Enlightenment thinkers meant by certain metaphors, as well as raises questions—if not hackles—about digital readers and their soi-distant "shallow" and/ or "surface" reading.

It takes some getting used to Pasanek's style: "This valedictory critical exercise further demonstrates how distant reading supports close interpretation by indicating the range of metaphors by which figure and ground may be defined." Or, "Because this dictionary arrays four-square superimpositions of mind and matter, metaphor and meaning, eighteenth-century thought and its social context, each becomes an excuse to say something about the other." While many of us will luxuriate in the style and panache, other readers may find it hard slogging. The conclusion is, however, worth the preamble.

The book has 11 chapters of metaphors broken down in broad terms such as animals, coinage, empire, fetters, metal, mirrors, room, writing, and so on. Within each chapter are various metaphors used by writers. For example, under animals we find man or beast, duck or rabbit, birds and flights of fancy, and so on. The conclusion, "The Mind Is a Metaphor" sums up Pasanek's findings and is worth the price of the book. While the book is not meant to be read as a monograph but as a dictionary, many well-versed readers will be tempted to do so anyway, so rich and lush are both language and litany.—**Mark Y. Herring**

Handbooks and Yearbooks

C

409.   **Electronic Enlightenment. http://www.e-enlightenment.com/.** [Website] New York, Oxford University Press. Price negotiated by site. Date reviewed: 2015.

Electronic Enlightenment (EE), a project of the Bodleian Libraries, University of Oxford, contains nearly 68,000 letters and documents in 11 languages from over 8,300 correspondents representing 52 nationalities across Europe, Asia, and the Americas. The project succeeds admirably in its aim to create a dynamic online network of Enlightenment correspondents and correspondence and is a boon to researchers.

Users can easily find letters with a simple word search or by utilizing a variety of fields (language, writer, recipient, location, etc.). A separate browse option allows users to search letters by decade or correspondents by surname, occupation, or nationality. Searchers can also access letters by locations or edition. "Locations" currently links over 32,000 letters to the corresponding source location. Letters themselves are titled and include a set of linked tabs underneath the letter heading—document (the default tab), enclosures, related, versions, and parent—that are enabled when applicable. On the left-hand side of every document page is a series of metadata that include editorial information, biographical information about the writer and recipient, and, when available, letter dates, location where the letter was written, location where the letter was sent, and information about the envelope. There is also information on instances (manuscript, digital, print) and annotations (authorial notes, textual notes, editorial notes, language notes, and remarks) of which there are over 300,000 in EE. A citation for the letters is available in the most common humanities styles—Chicago, MHRA, and MLA. Moreover, EE now participates in CrossRef so there is a Digital Object Identifier for all the EE letters, documents, and people.

The EE Coffee-House and EE Print-House add further value to this online resource. In the Coffee-House, users can find the EE classroom, which contains lesson plans and talking points; the EE Map Room, with such resources as EE's own atlas; and the Reading Room, with complimentary links to encyclopedias, dictionaries, biographies, and journals. In the Coffee-House, users can also find information about projects, such as EE's collaboration with leading graduate translation programs in North America and Europe. The Print-House has links to significant anniversaries, miscellany, the Fact-Sheet, and the Letterbook, which, among other things, will serve as a place for scholars to present their research findings in an informal setting.

Librarians receive free MARC21 records, quarterly updates, usage statistics, and technical support. Subscription and purchase prices depend on the size and type of institution. Personal and free trial subscriptions are also available. This online product offers upper-level undergraduates, graduate students, and scholars access to an unparalleled wealth of information. Highly recommended for academic libraries, large public libraries, and to individuals doing intensive research in the period.—**ARBA Staff Reviewer**

C

410. **The Routledge Companion to Phenomenology.** Sebastian Luft and Soren Overgaard, eds. New York, Routledge/Taylor & Francis Group, 2014. 716p. index. (Routledge Philosophy Companions). $68.95pa. ISBN 13: 978-0-415-85841-0; 978-0-203-81693-6 (e-book).

As one of the core ideas in modern philosophy, phenomenology and its discourse demands to be encapsulated for the contemporary student. *The Routledge Companion to Phenomenology* brings together over 50 chapters from leading contributors around the globe that expound upon this dynamic topic.

At its root, phenomenology addresses the role perception plays in comprehending and participating in the world around us. This sturdy companion highlights the many facets of phenomenology and examines such ideas as the self, the body, intentionality, subjectivity, being, and methods. Contributions are sorted into five sections that outline the most prominent thinkers in the movement, (Husserl, Derrida, and Merleau-Ponty, among others), focus on the most vital areas of discussion within the phenomenological movement, illustrate the ways in which phenomenology has worked within the greater philosophical realm, highlight areas where phenomenology intersects with other disciplines, and observe its study through a historical lens. In part three, for example, James Dodd writes how phenomenology can be the bridge to understanding the roots of political exchange, while in part four, Helen A. Fielding explains the mutual reliance phenomenology shares with feminism.

This generously referenced book emphasizes the importance of phenomenology to contemporary thought when applied over a vast array of ideas, from art and literary appreciation to logic and morals. It is simply a must-have for any student of contemporary philosophy.—**Laura Herrell**

Religion

General Works

C

411. **The Routledge Handbook of Research Methods in the Study of Religion.** Michael Stausberg and Steven Engler, eds. New York, Routledge/Taylor & Francis Group, 2014. 546p. index. $59.95pa. ISBN 13: 978-0-415-71844-8.

Since the literature on religion is so vast, it is difficult to fathom that there had been no comprehensive handbook to research methods for the study of religion in English until the publication of this title in hardback in 2011. Now, this handbook is available in paperback at a price that is accessible to most students. The goal of the work is to increase the importance of theoretical models as applied to the study of religion. As the editors say, "In the light of theories, methods construct, collect and/or generate the data for scholarly work" (p. 4). Thus, the contributors strive to provide information that has both practical and critical value to students, especially graduate students, and researchers. The first section provides general information related to methodology such as, epistemology, research design, and research ethics. The second section is the heart of the work and provides 22 chapters that detail specific research methods from content analysis and hermeneutics to semiotics and surveys. The final section includes five chapters that discuss materials such as auditory materials and visual culture. Although the structure of the chapters varies, of necessity, by the topics covered, each chapter provides a brief summary, helpful comments, references, and key concepts. Thus, although the work stands as a whole, each chapter can be used independently for background on specific methods. The index provides good access to the contents of the book. For academic and seminary libraries, this is a must purchase that will receive much use. Finally, there is an excellent sourcebook on methods for undertaking research in religion!—**Gregory A. Crawford**

C, P, S

412. **Spirit Possession around the World: Possession, Communion, and Demon Expulsion across Cultures.** Joseph P. Laycock, ed. Santa Barbara, Calif., ABC-CLIO, 2015. 414p. illus. index. $89.00. ISBN 13: 978-1-61069-589-3; 978-1-61069-590-9

(e-book).

In 2014, the Catholic Church increased the number of priests trained in the rite of exorcism due to a spike in public demand. As Joseph Laycock points out in his introduction, spirit possession is not an antiquated human response to the forces of nature; rather it is a diagnostic model for filtering culture. In this introductory primer, Laycock has brought together leading scholars to provide an overview of spirit possession across geographical, religious, and historical boundaries. More importantly, this encyclopedia intentionally underscores spirit possession in the twenty-first century to demonstrate its melding and adaptation into today's pervasive digital culture. Coupled with a chronology, a detailed and thorough introduction contextualizes spirit possession with a larger narrative of historical and cultural relevance. Entries are arranged alphabetically and span across countries, religious traditions, historical events, court cases, and persons of interest. Though varying in length and scope, each entry averages one to three pages and includes a small bibliography for further reading. Moreover, to facilitate searching, related entries are cross-referenced and indexed. Though representations of spirit possession in popular culture are mentioned in entries on television, film, and music, this facet of the subject is woven into larger entries where possible. Of particular interest are the original translations of several primary religious texts included throughout the encyclopedia. In addition to the smaller bibliographies included with each entry is a larger bibliography of works, delineated by religious and cultural tradition. Overall, this encyclopedia is a well-researched and expertly edited addition to the interdisciplinary subject of spirit possession. Coupled with Matt Cardin's *Ghosts, Spirits, and Psychics: The Paranormal from Alchemy to Zombies,* this encyclopedia is both a timely and necessary addition to any library's reference collection.—**Josh Eugene Finnell**

Buddhism

Handbooks and Yearbooks

C

413. **Digital Library of Northern Thai Manuscripts. http://lannamanuscripts.net/en.** [Website] Free. Date reviewed: 2016.

Presents more than 4,200 manuscripts from four collections. The Preservation of Northern Thai Manuscripts Project contains digitized microfilms with a focus on indigenous and secular traditions, including what are possibly the oldest Pali manuscripts in Southeast Asia. The Digital Library of Northern Thai Manuscripts features color images of manuscripts identified but not filmed during the aforementioned project and includes texts from eight temples. The Dokumentarische Erfassung literarischer Materialien in den Nordprovinzen Thailands (DELMN) collection contains digitized microfilm that was part of the first comprehensive survey of Lan Na manuscripts in the eight northernmost provinces of Thailand. The Harald Hundius Handwritten Collection contains color images of temple manuscripts copied by temple scribes during the DELMN project in the 1970s. Among the highlights, the digital library includes the entire library collection at Wat Sung Men, which became a center of Pali and Buddhist studies in the early nineteenth century. The digital library can be searched by simplified title, category, language, script, material, author, date, location, and other criteria. The manuscripts are primarily bilingual (Pali and Northern Thai) and written in Tham or Dhamma script, but additional vernacular languages and scripts are also represented. This collection will primarily be of interest to scholars studying the religious and secular literature of Northern Thailand from the fifteenth to the twentieth centuries.—**ARBA Staff Reviewer**

Christianity

Dictionaries and Encyclopedias

C, P, S

414. **The Concise Encyclopedia of Orthodox Christianity.** John Anthony McGuckin, ed. Hoboken, N.J., Wiley-Blackwell, 2014. 568p. $49.95pa. ISBN 13: 978-1-118-75933-2.

Here at last is an encyclopedia about Orthodoxy, written by scholars with expertise in both the academy and the contemporary Church! The one-volume *Concise Encyclopedia of Orthodox Christianity* does exactly what the title suggests: it provides succinct articles that cover a range of topics and are written in a way that is both readable and authoritative and scholarly. The list of contributors reveals a global network of scholars who write and teach about Orthodoxy every day. High school and college students as well as lay parishioners can easily pick up the text, navigate to an article and get immersed in its facts, and then continue their study by following the short References and Suggested Readings Bibliographies. Before doing so, however, it is worth the time to read through the artfully crafted Preface. This tells the intellectual history and impact of Orthodoxy with a passion directed not to cultivate sympathy, though it may, but an eagerness to appreciate its traditionalism and its relevance in the World today.

At the same time, readers will gain the most from the book if they come to it with a general understanding of the Orthodox tradition. There is no introduction to acquaint the novice with key terms or to justify why certain persons, places, and ideas are chosen while others are omitted by the editors. One misses an entry or cross-references for Orthodoxy itself, but does find distinct entries for Coptic Orthodoxy, Africa, Orthodoxy in, and the councils, all of which assume prior knowledge that the student may not hold. A simple introduction could, for example, instruct or perhaps remind the student of the Great Schism and then perhaps lead them by way of a historical timeline to the current complexities of Global Orthodoxy.

Still, the encyclopedia fills an important gap in the reference literature of the Orthodox Church. The features of the work enhance the content with beautiful illustrations, maps, a useful index, and list of entries. Finally, articles cross-reference and also provide short bibliographies for further reading.—**Amy Koehler**

C

415. **Encyclopedia of Ancient Christianity.** Angelo Di Berardino, Thomas C. Oden, Joel C. Elowsky, and James Hoover, eds. Downers Grove, Ill., InterVarsity Press, 2014. 3v. $360.00/set. ISBN 13: 978-0-8308-2943-9.

The *Dizionario patristico e di antichità cristiane* (DPAC) was published in 1983-1988 by Casa Editrice Marietti. In 1992, James Clarke & Co. in Great Britain and Oxford

University Press in the United States published an English translation as the *Encyclopedia of the Early Church (EEC)*. A second edition in Italian, the *Nuovo dizionario patristico e di antichità cristiane* (NDPAC), was published in 2006-2010. The EEC served as the standard source in English until the publication of the *Encyclopedia of Ancient Christianity* (EAC), an English translation of the NDPAC.

The EAC contains 3,200 articles by 266 contributors from 26 countries, an expansion of 35 percent from the original DPAC. The EAC offers a wide range of articles from the archaeological, philosophical, historical, geographical, and theological arenas; uses more work from art historians, linguistic experts, epigraphers, and papyrologists; provides better representation of Eastern European and Syriac traditions; and includes new entries from Arabic, Coptic, Armenian, and Gothic experts.

The work is grouped into three volumes, each of which contains notes on how to use the encyclopedia, a contributor list, a key to biblical and bibliographical abbreviations, and a complete list of articles. Coverage extends from the first century through the eighth century. Entries vary in length from a short paragraph to multiple pages. Contributors' names appear at the end of the entries, along with valuable bibliographical information. Cross-references, indicated by asterisks, enhance navigation throughout the three volumes. In the entry for Acesius, for example, an asterisk appears before Novatianist, Constantinople, Nicaea, Catholics, apostasy, and Constantine. While the editors did not choose to cross-reference the terms that one would expect in an encyclopedia of early Christianity, the complete list of articles included in each volume can assist searchers. People or places with the same name are distinguished. For example, the encyclopedia includes a Palladius of Helenopolis, Palladius of Ireland, Palladius of Saintes, Palladius of Suedin, and Palladius of Ratiaria. Guide words at the top of each page also facilitate navigation throughout this large work.

This encyclopedia is an unparalleled collection for anyone working in this period and is highly recommended for academic and larger public libraries.—**ARBA Staff Reviewer**

Islam

Dictionaries and Encyclopedias

C, P, S

416. **Encyclopedia of Islam and the Muslim World.** 2d ed. Richard Martin, ed. New York, Macmillan Reference USA/Gale Group, 2016. 2v. illus. maps. index. $489.00/set. ISBN 13: 978-0-0286-6272-5.

This encyclopedia of over 540 articles, prepared by over 350 scholars from around the world, explores the religious, social, political, and cultural realms of Islam over the last 14 centuries. There appears to be considerable "evolution" from the 2004 edition. For example, the articles "American Culture and Islam," "Americas, Islam in the," and numerous biographies are no longer present, while many new entries, such as "Australia and New Zealand," "Byzantines," "Damascus," "ISIS," and "Intifada" now appear. Broad articles exploring art, architecture, and literature exist alongside specialized topics of the Islamic faith and Muslim history.

Numerous maps and color photos enhance the work considerably, as do the bibliographies at the end of each article. Students and scholars of the Muslim world will find much useful information here. Academic and public libraries will benefit from having this set, as could high school libraries. Librarians might consider retaining the 2004 volumes as well.—**Mark Schumacher**

Handbooks and Yearbooks

C

417. **Oxford Islamic Studies Online. http://www.oxfordislamicstudies.com/.** [Website] Price negotiated by site. Date reviewed: 2015

   Oxford Islamic Studies Online (OISO), is under the direction of Editor-in-Chief John L. Esposito, Georgetown University, assisted by Deputy Editor, Natana J. DeLong-Bas, Boston College, senior editors, senior consultants, an editorial advisory board, and a library advisory board. Updated three to four times a year, OISO provides thousands of A-Z reference entries, approximately a thousand biographies, chapters from scholarly and introductory texts, Qur'anic materials, primary sources, images and maps, and timelines that can serve students, governments, community groups, librarians, scholars, and anyone interested in Islam.

   OISO content is discoverable in many ways. Users can conduct a quick search from the home page or utilize the five main headings also available on the main page—Advanced Search, Browse, Qur'anic Studies, Timelines, and Learning Resources. Advanced Search allows users to seek information by a Main Search, Biography Search, Image & Map Search, Primary Source Search, Bibliography Search, Qur'an Search, and Concordance Search. Under the Browse button, researchers can search content across the whole site or by subject entry, biographies, chapter works, primary sources, or images & maps. Three works are searchable under the Qur'anic Studies button: two Oxford classics, M.A.S. Abdel Haleem's *The Qur'an* and A.J. Arberry's *The Koran Interpreted,* and Hanna Kassis' *Concordance of the Qur'an.* Two timelines can be accessed via the eponymous button, one a timeline of world events and one a timeline of events in Islam. Both timelines are linked with related content throughout the OISO site. The Learning Resources button connects users to a wealth of information via the following sublinks: Thematic Guides, Teaching Islam, Internet Resources, Geography of the Islamic World, What Everyone Needs to Know about Islam, Glossary, Lesson Plans, Interviews, the Arab Sprint, Reference Works, and Further Reading. Once an entry is accessed, users can highlight and search within OISO for related terms. While reading an entry on Mu'ammar al-Qaddafi, for instance, you can highlight Qur'an, click "Look it Up" on the toolbar above the entry, and be taken to a new list of 41 entries on the Qur'an.

   OISO core content comes from *The Oxford Handbook of Islam and Politics, The Grove Encyclopedia of Islamic Art and Architecture, The Oxford Encyclopedia of the Islamic World, The Islamic World Past and Present, The Oxford Dictionary of Islam, The Oxford History of Islam, What Everyone Needs to Know about Islam, Teaching Islam, Makers of Contemporary Islam,* and the three Qur'anic texts mentioned above. Documents are drawn from the following Oxford collections: *Islam in Transition, Modern Islam,* and *Liberal Islam.* Primary sources have been carefully selected and all are contextualized by introductory editorial comments. *The Oxford Encyclopedia of the Modern Islamic World* is included in full on the site and archived articles can be excluded or included during the search process. Results are easily printed or emailed. Citations in Chicago and MLA are provided, and citations can be exported to EndNote, ProCite, ReferenceManager, or RefWorks.

OISO is available via annual subscriptions to institutions and individuals; individuals can also subscribe monthly. Librarians also have free access to downloadable MARC records. Given the importance of the subject matter, the features and functionality of the site, and the breadth and depth of the source material, OISO is highly recommended to large public libraries and academic libraries.—**ARBA Staff Reviewer**

Indexes

C

418. **Index Islamicus Online. http://bibliographies.brillonline.com/browse/index-islamicus.** [Website] Boston, Brill Academic, 2015. Price negotiated by site. Date reviewed: 2015.

Edited by Heather Bleaney, Pablo García Suárez, and Susan Sinclair at the editorial offices in the Library, School of Oriental and African Studies, University of London, and the Insituto de Lenguas y Culturas del Mediterráneo y Oriente Próximo in Madrid, the *Index Islamicus Online,* consisting of more than 475,000 records drawn from over 3,000 journals along with conference proceedings, monographs, and book reviews, continues to be the leading international classified bibliography of publications written in European languages on the Muslim world and Islam. Coverage areas include but are not limited to history, religion, law, literature, politics, economics, and archaeology. The classification scheme uses broad subject area headings such as education, Israel, and philosophy as well as subcategories. There are also indexes of names and subjects, searches on the article and author level, and article- and chapter-level indexing for journals and books. Users can also take advantage of personal tools for saving, alerting, sharing, and exporting. The *Index Islamicus Online* is updated quarterly. Libraries can choose to subscribe or to purchase the index outright. On the Brill site, potential purchasers can view a list of consulted periodicals as well as options for purchasing access for a day, a week, or a month. Proquest and Ebsco also host the *Index Islamicus Online;* purchasers can request trial subscription access through either of these providers.—**ARBA Staff Reviewer**

Judaism

Handbooks and Yearbooks

C, P

419. **The Jewish Year Book 2015: 5775-5776.** Elkan D. Levy and Derek Taylor, eds. Portland, Oreg., Vallentine Mitchell, 2015. 496p. index. $69.95. ISBN 13: 978-0-85303-978-5.

This venerable reference source for British Jewry begins with a preface that evaluates Jewish life and culture in the previous year called "2014: A Lose-Lose Situation." This is followed by seven essays: "Jews in Unexpected Places," "Women in Jewish Law,"

"UK/Israel Trade," "25 Years of Jewish Care," "The First World War Centenary," "The Jewish Film Festival," and "The Belfast Jewish Community." The majority of the book contains a wide range of information on Anglo-Jewish institutions and organizations, international and British; Jewish communities around the world, arranged alphabetically by country; historical information on British Jewry; a Who's Who; an abridged Jewish/British calendar for 2015; an index; and much more. Recommended for public libraries, as well as academic and institutional libraries.—**ARBA Staff Reviewer**

Shamanism

Dictionaries and Encyclopedias

C, P
420.   Harvey, Graham, and Robert J. Wallis. **Historical Dictionary of Shamanism.** 2d ed. Lanham, Md., Rowman & Littlefield, 2016. 366p. (Historical Dictionaries of Religions, Philosophies, and Movements). $100.00; $99.99 (e-book). ISBN 13: 978-1-4422-5797-9; 978-1-4422-5798-6 (e-book).

In 2016, Itzhak Beery will be the featured shaman in a new television show entitled, *Soul Search.* This newest representation of shamanism, coupled with characters in World of Warcraft and numerous Twitter accounts, in the popular culture canon further underscores the cultural impact of the shamanism in the twenty-first century. As Graham Harvey and Robert J. Wallis point out in the introduction, the appropriation of shamanism by western culture is both a challenge and an opportunity to demonstrate the diversity of shamans around the world. In this second edition of the dictionary, Harvey and Wallis continue to challenge a western-centric approach to both a global and localized historical movement. Unlike most dictionaries in the series, the chronology is not a Eurocentric, linear conception of time; rather, it is an overview of events and dates that help underscore the longevity of shamanism throughout history. Entries are arranged alphabetically and span countries, cultures, and individuals. Most entries are fairly concise. However, to facilitate searching, related entries are cross-referenced in bold—eliminating the need for an index. The brevity of each entry allows for a breadth of coverage, spanning continents, cultures, and history. Perhaps most impressive about this updated edition is the extensive bibliography, spanning nearly 100 pages in length, delineated by regions and themes. Intentionally, the one term lacking an entry in this dictionary is emblazoned across the front cover: shamanism. Always contextualized within a specific, culture, locale, and historical period, shamanism continues to be an evolving practice, identity, and experience that defies simple characterization. What Harvey and Wallis have accomplished in this updated edition is to show how that identity continues to transform and elude a reductionist characterization.—**Josh Eugene Finnell**

Part IV

SCIENCE AND TECHNOLOGY

29 Science and Technology in General

General Works

Dictionaries and Encyclopedias

P, S

421.   **U*X*L Doomed: The Science behind Disasters.** K. Lee Lerner and Brenda Wilmoth Lerner, eds. Farmington Hills, Mich., Gale/Cengage Learning, 2015. 3v. illus. maps. index. $272.00/set. ISBN 13: 978-1-4103-1774-2; 978-1-4103-1778-0 (e-book).

The three volumes in this excellent set cover 100 natural and man-made disasters occurring since 1900, beginning with a hurricane in Galveston and ending with faulty ignitions in General Motors vehicles. Each volume includes a complete chronology, glossary, table of contents, thematic table of contents, and detailed index. Alphabetically arranged entries within the volumes sometimes require consultation of the table of contents, chronology, or index to ascertain the title being used for a specific event. For example, the Challenger disaster is found under "Space Shuttle Challenger Explosion."

Some entries include primary source documents such as excerpts from government reports. Individual primary source documents are listed in the index, so readers can go directly to entries featuring such documentation if that is of especial interest. Most entries include both photographs and insets with information about related events or extended discussions of concepts causally involved in the disaster, such as building resonance.—**Delilah R. Caldwell**

P, S

422.   **U*X*L Encyclopedia of Science.** 3d ed. Amy Hackney Blackwell, ed. Farmington Hills, Mich., U*X*L/Gale, 2015. 10v. illus. $780.00/set. ISBN 13: 978-1-4144-3075-1; 978-1-4144-3086-7 (e-book).

In a world overflowing with information, finding good, concise research sources in clear language can be a difficult task. This is especially true with science. U*X*L has produced an encyclopedia set that helps the battle. In the Reader's Guide portion of the *U*X*L Encyclopedia of Science, Third Edition,* the editors perfectly state the objective of the work as "an alphabetically organized 10-volume set that opens up the entire world of science in clear nontechnical language" (ix). The set easily accomplishes this goal. Certainly no work is all inclusive, but the encyclopedias cover topics relevant to today from "physical, life and earth sciences, as well as health and medicine, mathematics, engineering, technology, and the environment" (ix). Each volume starts with an "Entries by Scientific Field" section with pertinent subtopics listed along with volume and page number. An example of a main entry is "Artificial Intelligence" with subheadings "Artificial Intelligence," "Automation," and "Robotics." This part of the set alone is useful for providing key words in subject areas a person might not know much about. The volume listings follow. Each volume contains the same "Where to Learn More" section at the end listing scientific books, periodicals, and Websites for further study. Volume 10 contains a cumulative general index for quick reference. Throughout each volume, entries are supplemented with colorful photographs, drawings, Words to Know sidebars, and cross-references. As a side note, the color choice for sidebars and headings is visually pleasing and makes navigation easier. The *U*X*L Encyclopedia of Science, Third Edition,* a good addition to any public or school library, would be useful for anybody just wanting general information and/or a place to start their research.—**Sue Ellen Knowlton**

Handbooks and Yearbooks

P, S

423.   **Science In Context. http://solutions.cengage.com/InContext/Science/.** [Website] Farmington Hills, Mich., Gale/Cengage Learning. Price negotiated by site. Date reviewed: 2016.

Science In Context is an online database that integrates science reference content with news, videos, academic journals, and more. The goal of the tool is to illustrate the connection between real-world life and science issues thus making science more appealing to students. This aim is illustrated by the layout of the homepage which is dominated by rotating images linking to recent and/or newsworthy scientific events.

The scope of the collection encompasses all the branches of science: natural, formal, social, and applied. A sampling of topics includes black holes, 3D printing, gene expression, cognitive behavioral therapy, etc. Information about these topics is collected from the spectrum of source types ranging from general reference to academic journals. Videos, images, audio files (e.g., NPR clips), magazine and news articles, and Websites are also included. All of these sources are presented together, curated on one page for a holistic view of the topic in question. This approach creates an information "command center" experience that is quite compelling.

The database can be searched by keyword or browsed by topic. There are so many topics to browse that a helpful filter for category (e.g., Chemistry, Health and Medicine, New and Updated, etc.) is also included. An advanced keyword search option allows users to combine keywords with article and/or publication title and limit their search to full-text or peer-reviewed journals, specify a desired document type (e.g., map, cover story, pamphlet, or video among many options), or content type (book, journal, experiments, Websites, etc.). Teachers will especially appreciate the ability to search by content level (beginner to advanced) and Lexile level. Educators will also appreciate the curriculum standards provided in the site. Curriculum standards for not only the United States (both national and state) are provided, but the standards for other English-speaking countries like Canada, Australia, New Zealand, Ireland, and the countries of Great Britain are included as well.

The database integrates with Google apps including Google Drive and Google Classroom making it easy for both students and teachers to save documents to their own Google Drive. The ability to save research to a central location is a very useful feature. Any highlights and notes made in the database can be retained when the document is saved to Google Drive. Teachers have the added ability to save a document to their Google Classroom as an announcement or an assignment.

This is a fantastic resource, and it is highly recommended for school and public libraries. It brings a fresh and engaging perspective to the study of science by powerfully illustrating its place at the heart of our day-to-day lives and by demonstrating this through engaging multimedia resources. Students and teachers alike will find this a "go-to" resource for anything science-related. By including the typical database tools (save and share search results, citation tools, etc.) this becomes a tool everyone will want to use. Rather than going to many different places to find this information, it is all now available in one powerful, user-friendly dashboard.—**Kristin Kay Leeman**

C, P, S

424.   **TryNano. http://trynano.org/.** [Website] Free. Date reviewed: 2016.

TryNano is a freely accessible, easy-to-navigate site sponsored by IEEE (the Institute of Electrical and Electronics Engineers), IBM, TryScience, and the New York Hall of Science. The information is aimed at students, parents, teachers, and guidance counselors.

From the top of the page, users can select from five main links. The first, Nanomaterials, provides a general explanation of the field and further links to specific nanomaterial types, including carbon nanotubes, graphene, inorganic nanowires, dendrimers, nanoparticles, and quantum dots; all of the explanations have helpful color illustrations. Applications, the second link, discusses ways that nanotechnology is already being used in information and communications, in materials and manufacturing, in the biomedical field, in transportation, in consumer goods, and in energy and engineering. Again, color illustrations enhance the material. The following link takes users to 36 interviews with nano experts from a variety of backgrounds. For those wanting more information on companies, universities, and government organizations, there are links to: Drexel University; IBM; Industrial Technology Research Institute (Taiwain), Johns Hopkins Institute of NanoBio Technology; Keithley Instruments, Inc.; Korea Institute of Science and Technology; Lockheed Martin; Nanofilm; Nano-Tex, Inc.; National Institute of Advanced Industrial Science and Technology (Japan), National Nanotechnology Center (NANOTEC) (Thailand); the National Nanotechnology Initiative; the Network for Computational Nanotechnology; POSTECH (Korea); Rice University; and Zyvex Instruments. The resources tab links to an image gallery, a glossary, nano games, worldwide universities with nano programs or coursework, nano standards and guidelines, and nanotechnology-related links. To top it off, teachers can find six lesson plans under the resources tab for students ages 8 to 18. Although not listed on the top of the page, there is a "what's new" tab on the left-hand side of the home page that reveals an impressive collection on newsworthy events in the nano world from 2009 to the present. The latest news feature from March 17, 2016, reports the findings of Washington University nano researchers on a nanoparticle that may help impact tumor growth.

Altogether *TryNano* is a multifaceted and very useful site.—**ARBA Staff Reviewer**

30 Agricultural Sciences

Food Sciences and Technology

Atlases

P
425.   Hoffman, James. **The World Atlas of Coffee: From Beans to Brewing—Coffees Explained, Explained and Enjoyed.** New York, Firefly Books, 2014. 256p. illus. maps. index. $35.00. ISBN 13: 978-1-77085-470-3.

Broken into three parts, *The World Atlas of Coffee* introduces the curious to worldwide varieties, production methods, and growing regions. The book focuses on specialty coffees rather than commodity coffee.

In part one, Introduction to Coffee, the author introduces readers to Arabica and robusta, types of coffee trees, various harvesting methods, the manner in which coffee is graded, shipped, and traded, and more. From Bean to Cup, part two, details the harvesting processes, professional tasting, tasting at home, purchasing and storing, grinding, and brewing. Part three, Coffee Origins, takes readers on a worldwide tour of coffee-producing countries. African countries covered include Burundi, Ethiopia, Kenya, Malawi, Rwanda, Tanzania, and Zambia. Asian countries include India, Indonesia, Papua New Guinea, Vietnam, and Yemen. Bolivia, Brazil, Colombia, Costa Rica, Cuba, the Dominican Republic, Ecuador, El Salvador, Guatemala, Hawaii, Honduras, Jamaica, Mexico, Nicaragua, Panama, Peru, and Venezuela represent the Americas. Each country gets its own brief introduction that provides details about such things as the history of coffee cultivation and a taste profile. Readers will also find out about growing regions as well as population and production statistics.

The book is packed with color maps and beautiful color illustration, which makes this a visually appealing read. The book concludes with a glossary and an index but does not have a bibliography, sources notes, or suggestions for further reading. Recommended for public libraries.—**ARBA Staff Reviewer**

Dictionaries and Encyclopedias

C, P, S

426. **Archaeology of Food: An Encyclopedia.** Karen Bescherer Metheny and Mary C. Beaudry, eds. Lanham, Md., Rowman & Littlefield, 2015. 2v. illus. maps. index. $195.00/set; $104.99 (e-book). ISBN 13: 978-0-7591-2364-9; 978-0-7591-2366-3 (e-book).

This two-volume set provides 284 articles on a wide range of information on topics "including eras, places, cultural groups, specific foodstuffs, landmark sites, analytical techniques, methodology, pioneers in the field, innovations, theories, issues, controversies, and more." (p. xxvii) Scholars from around the world explore the history of food over the last 40,000 years. Whether discussing sweet potatoes or rye, explaining the significance of a Mesolithic site in England, or describing the value of scanning electron microscopy, the entries provide a rich introduction to the archaeological history of food.

While some of the entries are somewhat technical, many are accessible to all readers. For students and faculty, or anyone interested in the history of our food, these volumes will provide useful, and often fascinating, information. One nice feature: the contents and index are included in both volumes.—**Mark Schumacher**

P

427. Cumo, Christopher. **Foods That Changed History: How Foods Shaped Civilization from the Ancient World to the Present.** Santa Barbara, Calif., ABC-CLIO, 2015. 451p. illus. index. $100.00. ISBN 13: 978-1-4408-3536-0; 978-1-4408-3537-7 (e-book).

This 7-by-10-inch, 451-page, hardbound book starts with an alphabetical list of 90 food entries, followed by lists of the same food items categorized according to their topics, a preface, and an extensive introduction. Next is a timeline that indicates when these food items became part of the diet. I have been in the food industry for over 60 years and was shocked as to how long these items had been utilized; the main portion of the book next goes through an alphabetical discussion of the individual foods. Most of these entries are several pages in length (in most books, these entries would be equivalent to chapters), often with highlighted areas that indicate notable facts. Often figures of the item and subchapters of the various factors that have influenced their usage are emphasized. This is followed by further reading recommendations. After the individual food items have been discussed, the book provides a lengthy bibliography and an extensive index. The binding is average and the font size is a little small but acceptable for short reading assignments. I would strongly recommend this book for most general libraries and particularly for individuals who are interested in history and/or foods.—**Herbert W. Ockerman**

P

428. Mariani, John F. **The Encyclopedia of American Food and Drink.** 5th ed. New York, Bloomsbury USA, 2013. index. $35.00; $24.99 (e-book). ISBN 13: 978-1-6204-0160-6; 978-1-6204-0161-3 (e-book).

This is the fifth edition of Mariani's *Encyclopedia of American Food and Drink,* a book that illuminates the origins, variety, creativity, and originality of food and drink in the United States. This review is based on the electronic version of the book, made available in 2014. The book's thoroughly informative introduction provides readers with a lively narrative of American food history that extends back to the colonial period and emphasizes how American fare, like food everywhere, has been shaped by a mix of cultural influences. Following the introduction, a guide discusses the goal the encyclopedia, which aims to demonstrate the array of American food and drink, how Americans speak about food and drink, how it is consumed, and how Americans have created a unique food and drink culture.

The main entries are arranged alphabetically and can contain other terms, types of food, or regional variations, so it is important to use the index. Words in boldface type within an entry have their own main entry. The list of food and drink is interesting, fun, and extensive. There are such foods as apple pie, baked Alaska, halibut, oysters Rockefeller, eggs Benedict, bonefish, the peanut, and Twinkies. Drinks include the fuzzy navel, the Alabama slammer, milk, sauvignon blanc, and pinot noir. There are also conceptual entries for topics like African American food, New American cuisine, tailgate party, and TV dinner. An added bonus is the new-to-this edition biography section with brief summaries of Julia Child, Charles Krug, James Beard, Clarence Birdseye, Martha Stewart, and many others.

In addition to the index, the book is rounded out by a bibliographic guide to what the author considers the most important and best resources—a great place for further research.—**ARBA Staff Reviewer**

C, P
429.   **The SAGE Encyclopedia of Food Issues.** Albala, Ken, ed. Thousand Oaks, Calif., Sage, 2015. 3v. index. $395.00/set; $316.00 (e-book). ISBN 13: 978-1-4522-4301-6; 978-1-5063-1730-4 (e-book).

This 8.5-by-11-inch, three-volume encyclopedia has 1506 pages. It contains 11,784 entries on food related history and facts, all under the editorship of Ken Albala, professor of history at the University of the Pacific and Director of the Food Studies MA in San Francisco. All of the more than 300 contributors are in positions of authority in the food area. The book's contents include an alphabetical list of entries, a reader's guide, information on the editor and contributors, an introduction, and an index. Most of the entries range from three-quarters of a page to more than a page in length. The encyclopedia treats the subject of food broadly across the social sciences. Users will find material on the environment, health, government, retail and shopping, hunger, and so much more. The entries themselves are interesting and informative and have cross-references and suggestions for further reading. The binding and paper are of average quality, and the font is small but adequate for short-term reading. I would recommend this book for all libraries and for anyone with a food interest.—**Herbert W. Ockerman**

Handbooks and Yearbooks

P
430.   Barnes-Svarney, Patricia, and Thomas E. Svarney. **The Handy Nutrition Answer Book.** Canton, Mich., Visible Ink Press, 2015. 374p. illus. index. $21.95pa. ISBN 13: 978-1-57859-484-9; 978-1-57859-553-2 (e-book).

This fact-filled and exhaustive work on nutrition contains the following chapters: "The Basics of Nutrition: Micronutrients," "The Basics of Nutrition: Macronutrients and Non-nutrients," "Food Chemistry and Nutrition," "Nutrition in Eating and Drinking Choices," "Food Preservation and Nutrition," "Nutrition and Allergies, Illnesses, and Diseases," "Nutrition Throughout the Centuries," "Modern Nutrition," "Controversies with Food, Beverages, and Nutrition," "Nutrition Throughout Life," and "Nutrition and You." Approximately 152 black-and-white pictures marvelously intrigue the reader. About 53 charts enhance the superb discussion. The text is a book a reader does not want to put down. The index is precise. Appendix one, "Food Safety Websites," discloses 12 Websites like FoodSafety.gov. Excellently, appendix two, "Nutrition Websites," shares 11 Websites such as Nutrition.gov. Outstandingly, appendix three, "Comparing Diets," exposes the advantages and disadvantages of diets presented in three sections. The further reading section points out 30 other fabulous texts on nutrition. The invaluable glossary defines 120 informative terms. Vital for academic, public, and school libraries, as well as people researching nutrition.—**Melinda F. Matthews**

C, P
431.   **Food in Time and Place: The American Historical Association Companion to Food History.** Paul Freedman, Joyce E. Chaplin, and Ken Albala, eds. Oakland, Calif., University of California Press, 2014. 395p. index. $49.95. ISBN 13: 978-0-520-28358-9; 978-0-520-95934-7 (e-book).

Interest in food and cooking is increasing rapidly. Cooking shows on television, magazines, and cookbooks covering a wide range of cuisines are everywhere. It is not surprising that food history is a growing academic discipline. The role of food in culture is important, so this interdisciplinary field calls on scholars from diverse areas. This volume edited by three academics includes essays by scholars, food writers, cookbook authors, and curators. The essays demonstrate different approaches to food history. Regional histories examine the food of a geographic area. There are chapters on premodern Europe, China, India, the Middle East, Africa, and America as well as a paper about migration and transnational cuisines. The section about cuisine is broader, covering topics such as restaurants, cookbooks as resources for social history, and the invention of modern cuisine by the French. The final part, Problems, looks at food and popular culture, postmodern food developments, and the search for artisanal and local foods rather than bland, mass-marketed brands. All of the papers have bibliographies for those seeking further information. This diverse collection will intrigue scholars working in the fields of history, anthropology, and culinary arts.—**Barbara M. Bibel**

C, P, S
432.   Newton, David E. **GMO Food: A Reference Handbook.** Santa Barbara, Calif., ABC-CLIO, 2014. 336p. index. (Contemporary World Issues). $58.00. ISBN 13: 978-1-61069-685-2; 978-1-61069-686-9 (e-book).

The multidimensional debate surrounding genetically modified organism crops (GMOs), is addressed in this volume of the Contemporary World Issues series.

Beginning with a comprehensive history of genetic science and its agricultural implications, the book then provides a balanced look at the issues surrounding genetically modified foods, such as how public opinion differs from Europe to America, how GMOs can benefit or harm human health, or whether or not to label GMO foods.

In addition, writers from fields as diverse as biology, pharmacology, law, and farming weigh in with strong research and varied personal opinions on multiple aspects of the subject. For example, organic farmer Tony Owen's essay defines the GMO debate as political rather than scientific. The book also profiles a number of leading figures and organizations on both sides of the debate, such as biologist and Genentech founder Herbert W. Boyer, environmental watchdog group Food and Water Watch, and the often newsworthy Monsanto. With ample access to data and documents such as court cases and government protocols, in addition to an annotated bibliography, helpful glossary, and a detailed timeline, this book is a go-to resource on the globally vital subject of GMOs.— **Laura Herrell**

C

433. **Routledge International Handbook of Food Studies.** Ken Albala, ed. New York, Routledge/Taylor & Francis Group, 2014. 408p. index. (Routledge International Handbooks). $65.95pa. ISBN 13: 978-1-138-01949-2; 978-1-203-81922-7 (e-book).

Interest in food and nutrition is growing rapidly. Cookbooks, diet books, and popular books on nutrition are best sellers. Academic studies in these areas are also very popular. Students and scholars are examining food in different cultures, eating habits, food history, as well as nutrition, health, and public health. Food studies, an interdisciplinary program, is emerging as an academic field. This new title in Routledge's International Handbooks series provides an introduction to food studies for students and professionals interested in pursuing careers in this area.

The editor, a professor of history at the University of the Pacific, has collected articles from more than 30 scholars working in various areas related to food. They are from all over the world. Chapters covering the social sciences, the humanities, interdisciplinary food studies, and special topics in food studies demonstrate the broad range of topics in this field: anthropology of food, food and communication, journalism, food and literature, food and American studies, food museums, culinary arts and food service management, food justice, and food and the senses. Each article contains a brief history of food research in the discipline, information about research methodologies, ideologies, and theories, resources for research, and a bibliography. Students will also find information about archives, grants, and fellowships. This is a very useful resource for academic libraries supporting any food-related programs.—**Barbara M. Bibel**

P

434. Thurston, Robert W., Jonathan Morris, and Shawn Steiman. **Coffee: A Comprehensive Guide to the Bean, the Beverage, and the Industry.** Lanham, Md., Rowman & Littlefield, 2013. 416p. illus. index. $61.00. $59.99 (e-book). ISBN 13: 978-1-4422-1440-8; 978-1-4422-1440-8 (e-book).

This could have been a glitzy (appropriately enough) coffee table book on the subject of coffee, but instead the editors have produced a comprehensive, scholarly (but not stuffy) volume on the subject that covers exhaustively all aspects of the product from its cultivation and marketing to its various manifestations and its world-wide consumption (there is even a concluding chapter, "How to Make a Great Cup of Coffee"). The book consists of 63 individually signed chapters of about five to eight pages each in length that are grouped into five different parts. The first and largest part (with 18 chapters) is called "The Coffee Business" and deals with general contemporary conditions, like the nature of the coffee plant, cultivation concerns, pickers, processing problems, and specialty coffees. The second part contains articles specifically on the contemporary coffee trade followed by profiles of seven major coffee-producing countries, including India, Vietnam, and Brazil, that stress the importance of coffee in each economy. This section ends with similar material on nine such countries as Russia, the United States, and France that are important consumers of coffee. Part three deals with a history of coffee and its effects on social life (e.g., the importance of coffee houses in English history). Part four contains nine chapters on the varieties and qualities of coffee and health concerns related to coffee. The last part contains five chapters on the future of coffee that covers topics like genetically modified coffees. The three editors also wrote many of the chapters (e.g., the editor-in-chief, Robert Thurston, wrote over a dozen). Their credentials and those of the other contributors are given in a separate appendix. Most are academics or people related directly to the coffee trade. Throughout each article important terms are given in bold type. Each of these terms is defined in a special glossary that is followed by a seven-page index. Although there is no general bibliography, each chapter concludes with a notes section that contains material on sources used. Scattered about the text are a few black-and-white photographs. This is an attractive, important, and fascinating sourcebook on one of the world's favorite beverages.—**John T. Gillespie**

Horticulture

Handbooks and Yearbooks

C, P, S

435. **The Gardener's Year.** New York, DK Publishing, 2015. 320p. illus. index. $24.95pa. ISBN 13: 978-1-4654-2457-0.

Lifelike DK photography and organization make this a worthy investment in horticultural reference. The drawings, instructions, and models explain seed and stock selection, planting, and harvesting of a broad range of flowers and edibles, including dwarf fruit trees. By arranging data and colorful landscapes by season, the work promotes variety, as with trees and shrubs that produce appealing, textured stems for winter viewing. Identification of flora by both common and botanical names increases likelihood of purchasing the same varieties shown in photos. The six-page index lists primary and secondary topics, as with bedding plants for summer and dwarf rootstock. A practical coffee table book for gifts to hobby gardeners and new homeowners and a reasonably priced resource for public, high school, and community college libraries. Highly recommended— **Mary Ellen Snodgrass**

31 Biological Sciences

Biology

Dictionaries and Encyclopedias

C, S

436. **The SAGE Encyclopedia of Stem Cell Research.** 2d ed. Eric E. Bouhassira, ed. Thousand Oaks, Calif., Sage, 2015. 3v. index. $475.00/set. ISBN 13: 978-1-4833-4768-4; 978-1-4833-4766-0 (e-book).

The SAGE Encyclopedia of Stem Cell Research (2d ed) is a three-volume reference source containing over 250 articles covering various topics related to stem cell science research as well as religious, ethical, legal, social, and political perspectives. The target audience for this source would include upper-level secondary students and undergraduate students seeking basic stem cell biology information, as well as information on clinical trial updates, legislative information, and information on the ethics of stem cell research.

Each volume contains a comprehensive alphabetical list of all articles. Volume one also contains a reader's guide (broad topics and their specific entry names), an introduction from the editor, a list of contributors, and a short chronology of key events. Articles continue in volumes two and three; volume three concludes with a resource guide, appendixes of key U.S. Presidential Executive Orders on stem cell research (2007 and 2009), a U.S. Senate Hearing report (2010), and a complete topic index to all volumes. There is a brief glossary.

Main entry narratives average two to four pages in length; some entries are divided into subcategory topics. Broad categories for articles include topics related to adult and nonadult stem cells, animal models, cancer stem cells, clinical trials in the United States and worldwide, industry and educational research institutions, methods to study stem sells, key organizations and people, stem cell applications, and stem cell legislation or information related to country or U.S. state. The tone and reading level for articles is academic, and not intended to be comprehensive. (The editor states in the Introduction that a fully comprehensive view of the subject was not possible). Articles conclude with *see also* cross-references to other articles and a further readings bibliography. Selective entries have medical images, charts, tables, or illustrations.

A minor criticism would be a lack of a comprehensive index at the end of volumes one and two for ease of use. *The SAGE Encyclopedia of Stem Cell Research* (2d ed) offers a basic introduction and overview to key topics related to stem cell science and research. Most appropriate for high school libraries and college libraries that have a need for academic material on the topics presented.—**Caroline L. Gilson**

Anatomy

Handbooks and Yearbooks

P, S

437.   Barnes-Svarney, Patricia, and Thomas E. Svarney. **The Handy Anatomy Answer Book.** 2d ed. Canton, Mich., Visible Ink Press, 2016. 370p. illus. index. $21.95pa. ISBN 13: 978-1-57859-542-6.

This volume in the Handy Answer series offers a close, system-by-system look at human anatomy. While focusing on descriptions and primary functions of each component of our body's system, the book shares other material readers may find helpful regarding the history, statistics, diseases, and more about human anatomy, physiology, and pathology. This second edition has been updated to reflect the most current science related to human anatomy.

Tabbed for easy reference, each chapter focuses on a particular body system, such as the skeletal system, with additional chapters discussing the history of anatomy, human growth and development, and helping human anatomy. A unique question-and-answer format makes the material extremely navigable and easy to comprehend. Questions are sensibly connected, for example, "what are the functions of platelets," "where are platelets produced," and "what happens if blood does not clot." The book houses over 1,200 of these questions and their concise, but scholarly answers.

The generous use of color illustrations, shaded text boxes, tables, and charts make the abundant material truly engaging. Supplementary material includes a list of books and Websites for further study, a glossary, and an index. The book is perfect for younger students in particular.—**ARBA Staff Reviewer**

Botany

Handbooks and Yearbooks

P

438.   Littlefield, Larry J., and Pearl M. Burns. **Wildflowers of the Northern and Central Mountains of New Mexico: Sangre de Cristo, Jemez, Sandia, and Manzano.** Albuquerque, N.Mex., University of New Mexico Press, 2015. 389p. illus. maps. index. $29.95pa. ISBN 13: 978-0-8263-5547-8; 978-0-8263-5548-5 (e-book).

Intended as a guide for anyone interested in the more common flora of the northern and central mountains of New Mexico, *Wildflowers of the Northern and Central Mountains of New Mexico* is the result of a collaborative effort by two well-respected experts. Pearl

Burns teaches wildflower identification courses and leads hikes for various groups, including the United States Forest Service. Larry Littlefield is professor emeritus of plant pathology and volunteers at the Sandia Mountain Natural History Center.

The introduction contains basic information on using the book and descriptions of the topography of the Sangre de Cristo, Jemez, Sandia, Manzano, San Pedro, Ortiz, and Manzanita Mountains. This is followed by entries on 350 wildflowers and flowering shrubs, arranged by color. Each entry includes several color photographs featuring the entire plant and close-ups of its flowers; family common name; scientific name; physical description; flowering period (selected); and habitat. The text ranges from approximately 150 to 180 words each. The work concludes with text and illustrated glossaries, references, and indexes of common names and scientific names.

Hikers, amateur botanists, or anyone interested in identifying wildflowers in their native habitats in the northern and central mountains of New Mexico will find this book useful, especially since there are not many books of its kind. Libraries in New Mexico and Colorado should purchase.—**January Adams**

Zoology

General Works

Handbooks and Yearbooks

C, P, S

439.   **Animal Ethics. http://animalethics.org.uk/.** [Website] Free. Date reviewed: 2015.

The *Animal Ethics* Website offers users basic information on animal rights issues. The Website provides access to a free online book that outlines the author's animal rights ideology and provides statistics in the form of illustrations to teach users about the extent of animal abuse that occurs worldwide.

The book is titled *How to do Animal Rights* and is separated by chapter on the home page. As the user scrolls down, he can access additional chapters and print illustrations that provide facts and information predominantly relating to factory farming. The author of this book is a self-proclaimed animal rights activist and has degrees in biology and psychology, as well as a doctorate in animal behavioral psychology. The writing is often pathetical, but informative as it includes a variety of statistics and facts.

The homepage is not complicated to navigate and there are many additional resource sites included on the left side of the page. There is no glossary to reference, but the author provides definitions within the online book for words that students may not immediately recognize.

Though this material may be useful for students and activists hoping to understand how to become an advocate for animal rights, it is not ideal for students who are not already interested in the subject matter. Overall, it is an adequate and well-priced resource.—**ARBA Staff Reviewer**

Birds

Handbooks and Yearbooks

C, P

440.   Baldassarre, Guy A. **Ducks, Geese, and Swans of North America.** Rev. ed ed. Baltimore, Md., Johns Hopkins University Press, 2014. 2v. illus. maps. index. $69.95/set; $69.95 (e-book). ISBN 13: 978-1-4214-0751-7; 978-1-4214-0808-8 (e-book).

The 2014 edition of *Ducks, Geese and Swans of North America* is the latest update of perhaps the most well-known and respected text on North American waterfowl. This series was first published in 1942 and has been updated several times since. This two-volume set covers all native species of waterfowl that breed in North America, as well the introduced Mute Swan. Volume one covers swans, geese, and dabbling ducks while volume two covers diving ducks and sea ducks.

Each chapter in the book covers one species and includes information on virtually every aspect of the species. The information is divided among 11 topics: Identification; Distribution; Migration Behavior; Habitat; Population Status; Breeding Biology; Rearing of Young; Recruitment and Survival; Food Habits and Feeding Ecology; Molts and Plumages; and Conservation and Management. The standardized format makes it very easy for the reader to find specific information. Each chapter has several color drawings and photographs plus maps of each species' breeding and wintering ranges. All of the information presented in the volumes is meticulously documented and referenced. Literature cited is included on a CD-ROM accompanying the books, apparently to reduce the size of the books, as the citations run to an impressive 104 additional pages of text!

The Ducks, Geese and Swans of North America series has long been one of the "gold standard" references to these species and this latest edition continues that tradition. It has been carefully updated with the latest information from the most recent studies and surveys up to about 2010. While waterfowl are generally well-studied and much information about them is fairly well-known, there is still a great deal of new information in this edition. I found it particularly interesting to read about the latest population trends among species, as waterfowl are carefully managed to try to protect their numbers.

The extensive information on a relatively limited topic may make this book more suitable for a college library or a scientific library with a similar focus. Certainly no library at a college with a wildlife management program or biology program should be without it. However, it would be an excellent addition to any library or the bookshelf of any individual interested in North American waterfowl.—**David Hawksworth**

P

441.   Eastman, John. **Birds Nearby: Getting to Know 45 Common Species of Eastern North America.** Mechanicsburg, Pa., Stackpole Books, 2015. 188p. illus. index. $24.95pa. ISBN 13: 978-0-8117-1484-6.

This highly enjoyable, regional guide elevates the stories of the ordinary, easily sighted birds residing in eastern North America through the use of gorgeous color photography and interesting facts. The author conveys his great appreciation for the natural world in compiling this guide, which showcases 45 common species of birds ranging from the ubiquitous American Crow to the ever noble Great Horned Owl. Simply organized as a bird-by-bird catalog, the author nonetheless provides ample information noting specific behavior, name origins, diet, breeding range, migratory habits, vocal characterizations, and much more. From details such as the favorite nesting sites of the American Goldfinch (dogwoods, shrub willows, and hawthorn thickets, if you please), we glean the author's tremendous respect for his subjects. Readers may also delight in the occasional obscure tidbit of birding lore, including, for example, how the writer Henry David Thoreau took joy in the "delicious sound" of crows in winter, or how a cofounder of American ornithology, the Scotsman Alexander Wilson, was inspired to compile descriptions of new world bird species immediately upon shooting a red-headed woodpecker the day he arrived in America.

Stunning and intimate photographs capture birds in their element, whether perching or taking to the air. This simple, yet lovely book can be enjoyed by avid birders or the casual nature lover alike.—**Laura Herrell**

P

442. Elphick, Jonathan. **The World of Birds.** New York, Firefly Books, 2014. 608p. illus. maps. index. $75.00. ISBN 13: 978-1-77085-304-1.

The World of Birds is a very informative introductory book on all aspects of birds and bird biology. Approximately the first half of the book is divided up into chapters covering various topics on birds such as anatomy, flight, breeding, migration, and bird habitats. One particularly eye-opening and rather startling chapter is entitled "Birds and Humans" and reveals many of the reasons why many bird species are declining due to the actions of people. On a more hopeful note, it also covers some of the ways people are trying to help save birds. All of these sections are richly illustrated with many fine color photographs and clear, easy-to-understand, drawings.

The second half of the book contains brief descriptions of all of the world's bird families. For each family, there is an information box with general information on the characteristics of the birds in that family such as number of species, size, range, nest type, number of eggs, preferred habitat and, typically, a listing of the species in the family that are threatened or endangered. The text for each family provides additional information for each of the families and highlights many of the more well-known or unusual species in each family. Obviously there are far too many bird species to go into great detail, but it does a very good job of describing what makes each bird family and its members unique. It details many unusual facts and characteristics about the various species. Every page of the bird family description section has one or more superb color photographs of species in that family.

The book also includes an index, a glossary, and an appendix describing The International Union for Conservation of Nature's criteria for rating the vulnerability of Threatened and Endangered Species. In addition, a list of suggested readings provides further information on each of the book's subjects and a list of organizations to contact for additional information on birds and bird conservation.

The book had only a few slight drawbacks. Some of the taxonomy is not up-to-date, but, of course, it's almost impossible for any book to be completely accurate with new research constantly revising the taxonomy of birds. The author is English, so the English bird names and English spelling of words may be unfamiliar to North American readers (although, in all cases, the scientific names of birds are also included).

However, these minor flaws don't begin to diminish the overall excellent quality of the book. I found it to be full of good information for people interested in learning about birds as well as many interesting facts about unusual species. The excellent photographs will be intriguing for any reader and I expect it will make them more interested to learn more about the birds depicted. I believe it would make an excellent addition to any general library and be an excellent resource to help people learn about birds and their many fascinating habits.—**David Hawksworth**

P

443.   Garrigues, Richard. **Photo Guide to Birds of Costa Rica.** Ithaca, N.Y., Cornell University Press, 2015. 256p. illus. maps. index. $24.95pa. ISBN 13: 978-1-5017-0025-5.

Casual travelers and bird-watchers will delight in this handy *Photo Guide to Birds of Costa Rica.* The book is designed as a small, portable guide that is easier to carry than larger, more verbose field guides. It is a companion guide to the more extensive *The Birds of Costa Rica,* but differs in its photographic focus and emphasis on the birds a traveler is most likely to see, or the rarer species one desires to see in the beautiful country of Costa Rica.

Opening pages do an excellent job of explaining the structure and information within the book. Readers will find birds demarcated by their family description. The species accounts then include the following: species name, measurements, field marks, habitat and behavior, voice, and status and distribution. In addition, each bird comes with a thumbnail map of Costa Rica which is color-coded in regard to a species' range.

The most wonderful feature of this book, of course, is the high-quality color photography. Some species may be accompanied by more than one photo if there are significant physical differences between male/female or adult/juvenile birds. The photographs do well to highlight the field marks of each species and are truly a pleasure to look at for experienced and novice bird watchers alike. It is also important to note that the order in which the birds are presented may slightly differ from the order in *The Birds of Costa Rica* due to design issues.

Additional material includes a two-page map of Costa Rica, an illustrated guide to a bird's anatomical features, a glossary, and a species index. In spite of the book's seemingly narrow focus, a variety of readers would find it interesting: travelers, photography buffs, and, of course, bird lovers.—**ARBA Staff Reviewer**

P

444.   West, George C. **North American Hummingbirds: An Identification Guide.** Albuquerque, N.Mex., University of New Mexico Press, 2015. 233p. illus. index. $24.95pa. ISBN 13: 978-0-8263-3767-2; 978-0-8263-4561-5 (e-book).

North American Hummingbirds is an attractive book with copious photographs and illustrations of the creatures that often appear to the uninitiated as tiny, colorful blurs. George C. West is professor emeritus of zoophysiology at the University of Alaska, Fairbanks, the author of numerous scientific papers, and the coauthor of various other books. His expertise on the physiology and ecology of birds shines through in this pocket guide.

The introduction contains basic information on identifying hummingbirds of North America using size; shape and proportions; gorget color and shape; body color; wing feather patterns; behavior; and voice. A helpful discussion of scientific names and species codes is also included. This is followed by four sections titled "large hummingbirds," "medium sized hummingbirds," "small hummingbirds," and "accidentals" (the eight species of hummingbirds rarely seen in North America). Each of these sections is divided by entries on specific birds. The information includes the common name; Latin name and its meaning; basic identification; descriptions of adults and juveniles; voice; similar species; distribution and migration; courtship and nesting; and nutrition and molt. Each entry is supplemented with eight colored illustrations and over ten photographs. The abundance of drawings and close-up photographs from different angles makes the work very user friendly. The text ranges from approximately 600 to 1,000 words each.

The book concludes with Measurements and Weights of Adult Hummingbirds, Diagrams and Glossary of Hummingbird Characteristics and Terms, References, and an index.

The work more than fulfills its intended purpose of helping birders and banders identify, age, and sex the 17 species of hummingbirds found in North America. Anyone interested in identifying hummingbirds will find this lovely book indispensable. As this book is probably most useful outside library walls, libraries may also wish to obtain a circulating copy.—**January Adams**

Mammals

Handbooks and Yearbooks

C

445. Feldhamer, George A. and others. **Mammalogy: Adaptation, Diversity, Ecology.** 4th ed. Baltimore, Md., Johns Hopkins University Press, 2015. 749p. illus. index. $110.00; $110.00 (e-book). ISBN 13: 978-1-4214-1588-8; 978-1-4214-1589-5 (e-book).

The fourth edition of *Mammalogy: Adaptation, Diversity, and Ecology* is a thorough introduction to the animals in the large and diverse Class Mammalia. Written by five leading mammalogists, along with contributions from numerous experts in the field, this text offers in-depth information on a very broad and rapidly changing field. Chapters are divided into five main parts: history of the field and current research, biological functions and physical structures, adaptations and diversity, behavior and ecology, and special topics including diseases, domestication, and conservation. New to the fourth edition are taxonomic revisions, newly discovered species, updated photos and figures, and citations to recent literature. The chapters on behavior and ecology especially have been updated to reflect recent advances in the field. This book offers a very comprehensive introduction to the study of mammals and should be required reading for students interested in the field.

This text is nicely laid out and while figures are somewhat lacking in color they are concise and nicely illustrate the topic at hand. A summary is provided at the end of each chapter, along with a short list of suggested readings and discussion questions. A much longer and detailed reference list is included at the end of the book. Although written as a textbook for a mammalogy course each chapter stands on its own and can be read independent of the others without a loss in understanding on the part of the reader. Written for an upper-level undergraduate or graduate audience, this book is best suited for the academic library.—**Andrea C Kepsel**

Reptiles and Amphibians

Handbooks and Yearbooks

C, P

446. **Amphibians and Reptiles of the US-Mexico Border States.** Julio A. Lemos-Espínal, ed. College Station, Tex., Texas A&M University Press, 2015. 1056p. illus. maps. index. (W.L. Moody Jr. Natural History Series). $90.00. ISBN 13: 978-1-62349-306-6; 978-1-62349-313-4 (e-book).

   In the first bilingual text on the herpetofauna of the 10 states bordering the U.S.-Mexico region, Julio A. Lemos-Espínal describes more than 600 species of frogs, toads, salamanders, sea turtles, alligators, lizards, and snakes. The 10 states making up this region include four in the United States—California, Arizona, New Mexico, and Texas—and six in Mexico—Baja California, Sonora, Chihuahua, Coahuila, Nuevo Leon, and Tamaulipas. Each chapter is dedicated to a specific state, with the first two providing an introduction to the book and justification for the nomenclature used, particularly when there have been disagreements in the literature about species names. The chapters begin with an introduction to the states that includes an overall description of species richness and broad geographical characteristics that influence species distribution. Next is a section covering previous herpetological studies, including an overview of major survey expeditions undertaken, the people and organizations responsible for the establishment of key herpetological collections, and significant publications. Finally, the bulk of each chapter is made up of the physiographic characteristics of the state and how this has influenced the distribution of the herpetofauna. This section provides an overview of the biotic communities, geography, hydrology, climate, and geological history that has shaped the present-day environment for amphibians and reptiles. Also, discussion includes the number of amphibian and reptile species present in each of the ecozones of the state, including those that are endemic and those that reside on both sides of the border. Six hundred colored plates of individual species are provided at the dividing point between the English and Spanish versions of the book. An appendix provides a checklist of all the species discussed in the book, followed by a 57-page list of references, organized by state, and approximately a 100-page index. Unlike other guides to reptiles and amphibians, this book does not provide biological or ecological information on individual species, but rather emphasizes how herpetofauna distribution is shaped by environment influences. Although written by a faculty member at the University of Mexico, the text is accessible to the common reader, and recommended for libraries in border states.—**Kevin McDonough**

P

447. **The Leatherback Turtle: Biology and Conservation.** James R. Spotila and Santidrián Pilar Tomillo, eds. Baltimore, Md., Johns Hopkins University Press, 2015. 219p. illus. maps. index. $45.00. ISBN 13: 978-1-4214-7108-0; 978-1-4214-1709-7 (e-book).

   This book comes at a crucial time, as this ancient and extraordinary animal—the largest reptile in the world, faces great challenges to its survival. The book expertly gathers contributions from an array of scientific disciplines (marine biology, environmental science, zoology, etc.) which provide readers with a multipronged understanding of the Leatherback and the issues it is facing. Writings thoroughly explore the animal's evolutionary biology, physiology, reproductive biology, geographical range, diving and nesting behavior and much more.

Experts offer exhaustive detail in terms of background, analysis, and conclusions regarding a particular topic with the goal of establishing the most comprehensive tool for understanding and protecting these unique creatures. For example, part two, Life History and Reproduction, relays extensive work on the turtle's reproductive biology and behavior. It examines such topics as male and female systems and cycles, nesting patterns, and egg and hatchling development. With the overarching threats of human encroachment on the turtle's nesting beaches and commercial fishing, each section further incorporates existing analysis of other potential threats to the Leatherbacks, such as climate variability, overfishing, egg harvesting, beach erosion, etc. In laying out these threats, the writers then work to create a conservation strategy with which to restore the turtles back to a significant population.

Detailed graphs and tables pinpoint meticulously gathered data. Color photographs highlight the magnificence of these sea creatures in regards to their size, their behavior, and their habitats. Despite the dire issues facing the Leatherback, the book shows tremendous respect for its subject and a genuine, educated commitment to save the remarkable Leatherback.—**Laura Herrell**

P

448.   Moore, Robin. **In Search of Lost Frogs: The Quest to Find the World's Rarest Amphibians.** New York, Firefly Books, 2014. 255p. illus. index. $35.00. ISBN 13: 978-1-77085-464-2.

This book creatively mixes the rigors of science with the excitement and mystery of an epic quest as it chronicles a series of international expeditions in search of lost frogs. The author, director of the Amphibian Program at Conservation International, has written an intelligent and very personal tome brimming with genuine wonder and admiration for the elusive creatures.

A key component of the book is the generous use of beautiful color photographs. Documenting various aspects of the many varieties of amphibian, as well as the surprisingly diverse landscapes the author traversed in his quests, the photos are a truly stunning gift to readers.

Three sections organize the material with the first—Unravelling a Mystery—providing foundational information about frogs, the author's developing interest in them, and the alarming disappearance of some of the more unusual specimens. The second and largest part—The Search—documents the origins and actions of the massive task of dispatching over 100 researchers on a quest to find these "missing" animals. Chapters here discuss organizational issues, share diary-like entries, and detail the successes and setbacks of the difficult challenge. Part three—A Journey's End—discusses some of the immediate and long-term concerns for the existence of the amphibians, but ends with a message of hope in the creatures' resilience. The book also lists the expeditions covered, organized by country, and has an index. Recommended.—**ARBA Staff Reviewer**

32 Engineering

General Works

Handbooks and Yearbooks

P, S

449. **Careers in Science & Engineering.** Michael Shally-Jensen, ed. Hackensack, N.J., Salem Press, 2015. 379p. illus. index. $95.00. ISBN 13: 978-1-61925-860-0.

This book provides a compact resource for examining the wide variety of careers in science and engineering. Readers will learn general information about this booming sector, as well as more targeted information regarding particular jobs.

Alphabetically arranged chapters guide readers through 25 different jobs, ranging from aerospace engineer to zoologist. Within each chapter, readers will find ample and varied information detailing specific work duties, the expected work environment, occupation specialties (e.g., an agricultural engineer may specialize in research, equipment or tech), educational requirements, earnings and advancement potential, and much more. The use of bullet points, shaded sidebars, tables, and an index make the material easy to navigate. Some special features include projected employment trends, "fun facts," a typical day in the life on the job, interviews with professionals, a "snapshot" of the job, and a listing of applicable organizations readers can consult for more information. The book also includes a list of selected schools which offer highly regarded programs in the particular field. An appendix explains the "Holland Code," which provides a useful tool to help potential job seekers match their personalities with career possibilities.

Compiled in a positive, straightforward manner, this book will appeal to those pursuing a science- or engineering-based university program, embarking on their first job search, or considering a shift into this dynamic job sector.—**ARBA Staff Reviewer**

P, S

450. **Engineer Girl. http://www.engineergirl.org/.** [Website] Free. Date reviewed: 2015

This freely accessible Website is made available through sponsorship and is a service of the National Academy of Engineering (NAE). The site grew out of the NAE Committee on Diversity of the Engineering Workforce and is overseen by the EngineerGirl Steering Committee.

The information on the site is easily navigated and organized under three main links. The first, Engineers, connects users to interviews with women engineers; information on a typical day of a woman engineer; short, alphabetically organized biographies; biographies of historical women engineers; and a place to ask an engineer a question. The second link, What They Do, takes users to fun facts; lets them "try on a career" by clicking on several categories like civil engineer or environmental engineer; and has Cool Links to other information. How To Get There, the third link, instructs users in how to apply for internships; hosts an essay contest; provides information about clubs and programs; offers links to quizzes and polls; and provides scholarship information. The site also includes further resources for teachers, parents, and students.—**ARBA Staff Reviewer**

C, P, S

451. **TryEngineering. http://tryengineering.org/.** [Website] Free. Date reviewed: 2016.

TryEngineering has something to offer parents, teachers, career counselors, and students K-12 and beyond. IBM, Career Cornerstone Center, the Institute of Electrical and Electronics Engineers (IEEE), and Teachers Try Science sponsor the site which is free to use and free of advertising.

From the main page, users can choose from four main search options: Become an Engineer, Find a University, Lesson Plans, and Play Games. For students getting ready to pick a school, the Find a University section links to over 3,500 universities in 75 countries; simple or advanced searches are available. The Lesson Plans link offers 126 PDF files of curriculum for students ages 4 to 18. The plans can be narrowed by topic and student age. A sample search of robotics lesson plans for students age 16 to 18 produced three plans as of the date of this review. The link for Games takes users to approximately 30 engineering games like Park World (build a thrill ride) and Build a Lifeboat. The information in the Become an Engineer section is the most extensive. Once the link is accessed, users can choose from different majors via a drop-down menu—options include chemical, civil, computer, electrical, mechanical, and more. Selecting mechanical engineering, for example, will take users to a page that has a description of mechanical engineering, career guidance suggestions, and information about the course of study for mechanical engineers. There are also links to camps, internships, scholarships, competitions, and projects related to mechanical engineering. Further links to profiles of practitioners and students of mechanical engineering add value because users can get first-hand insight into a career. A great resource for those interested in a STEM career.—**ARBA Staff Reviewer**

Environmental Engineering

C

452. Spellman, Frank R. **Handbook of Environmental Engineering.** Boca Raton, Fla., CRC Press, 2015. 726p. index. (Applied Ecology and Environmental Engineering). $186.98; $153.97 (e-book). ISBN 13: 978-1-4987-0861-6; 978-1-4987-0862-3 (e-book).

Scientific and technical handbooks are useful references readers can use to locate overviews of specific topics, reference materials, and data. *The Handbook of Environmental Engineering* (HEE) by Frank R. Spellman is an essential reference handbook on environmental engineering; engineering students and professionals in environmental engineering will find this book useful for their work. The book is published by CRC Press, a well-known publisher of scientific handbooks and references.

The HEE has 11 chapters and could be (but isn't) divided into two parts. Chapters one through six introduce and review the basics of environmental engineering (definition of pollution and its tie to technological advancement, causes of pollution, and more) and the fundamental engineering and quantitative skills (advanced algebra, statistics, model development, and the use of models, unit conversions, etc.) required. Chapters 7 through 11 provide a thorough, but not exhaustive, discussion of air, water, and soil pollution, the problem contaminants, and remediation techniques. Major environmental laws (e.g., Clean Water Act and Amendments, Clean Air Act, NEPA) and regulations are discussed when appropriate. Water pollution receives the most in-depth coverage of any topic, with over 200 pages devoted to surface waters, groundwater, and wastewater contaminants and treatment technologies. The chapter on industrial hygiene provides an informative discussion of the environmental problems in the work place, (airborne chemical and particulate contaminants, radiation, noise, and more) as well information on relevant government agencies and their requirements, workplace monitoring, and more.

Spellman, a retired professor of environmental engineering and author of over 100 books, has successfully written a handbook that is both accessible to environmental engineering students and informative for professionals and researchers in the field. Scientific and technical handbooks frequently tend to be dry reading. Spellman's conversational tone makes this a very readable text, especially for less-experienced readers in environmental engineering. Both the conversational tone of the book and the examples and anecdotes help to draw readers into a topic and to illustrate the author's points.

HEE provides readers with excellent access to content through its very detailed table of contents and index. The major sections of each chapter are listed in the table of contents, while the index provides a very detailed subject list of the content. In the index, contaminants are listed by name and include acronyms when applicable.

The book is illustrated with black-and-white line drawings and flow charts, and also includes data and unit reference tables and some graphs. One of the most eye-catching illustrations is a 3D rendering of an environment illustrating the origin and fate of a class of contaminants in that environment (p. 317). The book also includes a glossary of environmental engineering terms in an appendix. In addition, many of the chapters contain topical terminology lists that provide the definitions of more specialized terms. Both of these are especially valuable for students because, as Spellman points out, it is "... necessary to learn the core vocabulary..." (p.4).

In lieu of a bibliography at the end of the book, the author has included a list of "References and Recommended Reading" at the end of each chapter. It is very helpful for the references to be done this way since the citations are associated with the specific topic to which they apply. If the citations were collected into one long list at the end, readers would have a hard time finding pertinent items. The references used include documents from relevant government agencies, articles from research journals, books, and newspapers, and more.

The HEE is a welcome addition to the reference literature in this field. It is very timely, providing detailed information on both emerging (e.g., pharmaceuticals in drinking water) and established environmental topics. This book is recommended for academic and special libraries serving students, professionals, and researchers working in environmental engineering.—**Theresa Calcagno**

33 Health Sciences

General Works

Directories

P

453. **American Hospital Directory. https://www.ahd.com/.** [Website] Louisville, Ky., American Hospital Directory, Inc., 2016. Price negotiated by site. Date reviewed: 2016.

This subscription-based Website, created and maintained by the privately owned company, American Hospital Directory Inc., provides users with data on more than 6,000 national hospitals. Information is discoverable by using a quick search screen or a criteria-based search. There is also a link for state and national hospital statistics, so a user can find the number of hospitals, number of staffed beds, total discharges, patient days, and gross patient revenue for each state. A click on the name of the state provides specific information about the hospitals within that state. While some basic information is freely available, a subscription is necessary to access the full site. For example, the free profile for Santa Barbara Cottage Hospital provides such things as the address, patient satisfaction rating, total patient revenue, clinical services offered, and inpatient and outpatient utilization statistics. More detailed information about salaries or bed size, for example, requires a subscription. Data is drawn from a variety of sources, like Medicare cost data and private hospital reports. Included in the hospital profiles are data on accreditation, services provided, and more. An updates tab and sources tab provide copious details about both. For subscribers the site offers a variety of data services as well as advanced search tools, list creation, and detailed online reporting. Subscribers can also choose from a variety of apps, like a clinical cost analyzer and a market analysis app.—**ARBA Staff Reviewer**

P

454. **The Complete Directory for Pediatric Disorders, 2015-16.** 8th ed. Amenia, N.Y., Grey House Publishing, 2015. 1108p. index. $165.00pa. ISBN 13: 978-1-61925-551-7.

This award-winning reference is a smartly organized source for medical descriptions, resources, and support services covering 213 pediatric disorders. This eighth edition has been generously updated with the most current information, including contact data listing address, phone, fax, Website, email, and key executives. All listed disorders are clearly explained and report the most current diagnoses and treatments. Also included in the eighth edition is the new entry on Violence in Children and Teenagers, incidences of which have doubled over the past 30 years.

The bulk of this book's information falls into four sections. Section one alphabetically lists over 200 major disorders ranging from Achondroplasia to Wilson Disease. Entries begin with a detailed but comprehensible description of the disorder, including primary symptoms, potential cause, body system affected, and treatment. Entries then list a number of disorder-specific resources, such as federal and state agencies, support groups, associations, Websites, camps, and many others.

Section two includes over 1,000 entries regarding general resources such as government agencies, support groups, newsletters, and youth organizations. These listings may not be limited to a specific disorder, and some but not all entries may be familiar from the first section.

Essays in the third section detail components and functions of 14 body systems, such as the digestive system, or medical categories. This information offers a quick reference in regards to fully understanding a disorder's impact on a particular body system.

Section four provides three indexes for information accessibility: an entry Index, a geographic Index listing entries by state, and an alphabetical disorder and related term index.

Supplementary material rounds out this generous resource, and includes a glossary of medical terms and acronyms, a list of guidelines to follow when pursuing additional information, a list of disorders by biological system, and a timely essay on bullying and its impact on health. An index completes the work.—**ARBA Staff Reviewer**

P

455. **The Complete Directory for People with Chronic Illness, 2015/2016.** 12th ed. Amenia, N.Y., Grey House Publishing, 2015. 909p. index. $165.00. ISBN 13: 978-1-61925-548-7.

This book represents the 12th edition of the directory presenting a comprehensive look at 90 chronic illnesses, briefly describing the afflictions and offering many resources for support and education. This edition has been updated with a new entry on Post-Traumatic Stress Disorder.

Introductory pages convey helpful material for ease of reference and to promote greater understanding of the nature of chronic illness. These pages include a chart which matches the illness to the affected body system; a listing of body systems with applicable disorders categorized beneath them; an essay titled "Accepting and Coping with a Chronic Illness"; and a gentle but informative guide to moving on from a diagnosis, including questions to ask a doctor, how to seek out information and more.

The entries themselves run alphabetically, covering conditions such as Arthritis, Celiac Disease, Fibromyalgia Syndrome, Obesity, and Thyroid Disease. Some entries reflect general categories such as Mental Illness, Allergies, Growth Disorders, etc. Condition descriptions within each entry are very brief but offer a solid medical explanation of the affliction, its symptoms, and treatment. Following the description is a well-organized listing of national and state resources, support groups, hotlines, research centers, literature (including children's literature if applicable), and media such as audio, video, or Websites. State agencies and associations are listed alphabetically by state. Resource listings will generally include the name of the association, address, phone number, e-mail address, executive representatives, and a general mission statement. Note that each listing, including the condition description, is numbered continuously throughout the directory (for a total of over 10,000 listings). The numbering is of great assistance in organizing a directory of this size.

Closing sections include a listing of general resources (e.g., The American Academy of Pediatrics, The National Rehabilitation Information Center, etc.), a listing of wish foundations, and a listing of resources covering death and bereavement. Two indexes close out the book: an entry name index and a geographic index.

This well-organized and complete resource provides access to immediate information useful to patients, families, caregivers, and more.

Recommended.—**ARBA Staff Reviewer**

P

456.   **HMO/PPO Directory, 2016.** Amenia, N.Y., Grey House Publishing, 2015. 700p. index. $325.00pa. ISBN 13: 978-1-61925-754-2.

This softcover text is comprehensive, well-written, and timely. The publisher and editors have created a detailed and informative resource on the topics of Health Maintenance Organizations (HMO) and Preferred Provider Organizations (PPO). This text spans more than 500 pages.

The cover is professionally designed. It includes color graphics and images that are health care related. The text on the cover and the spine is easy to read; similarly, the text is laid out in a logical format that makes it easy to find information.

The text begins with an introduction and user guide. This provides the user with an overview of the guide including a description of how the HMO/PPO guide is formatted. Key features of the Affordable Care Act (By Years) is presented next. This includes topics such as new consumer protections, improving quality and lowering costs, and increasing access to affordable care. An overview of health insurance coverage in the United States (2014) is provided followed by state statistics and rankings. Throughout this text, tables are effectively used to summarize information. For example, the state statistics and rankings section includes an overview of public and private insurance coverage by state and age brackets, as well as managed care organizations by state, organization, and plan type.

HMO and PPO profiles by state are presented over the next 400 pages. Each state's HMO/PPO section begins with a single page that includes a table summarizing insurance coverage status and coverage by age. Next, detailed content is presented for the respective state with the HMO/PPO companies listed alphabetically. The myriad information includes insurer name, address, Website, subsidiary, year founded, ownership, health plan and services defined, coverage, payment plans offered, geographic areas served, report card publication status, key personnel, and specialty managed care partners.

The appendixes are presented next. Here users will find a glossary of terms and references to industry Websites. Additionally, a plan index directs readers to sources for dental, HMO, Medicare, multiple, PPO, and vision plans. This is followed by a list of providers and the organizations for which they work. Several indexes are included: membership enrollment, primary care physician, and referral/specialty physician. These sections include the organization's name, the number of members, and a useful reference to the organization's location in the text. Black-and-white tables and charts are present throughout this text.

This text will appeal to a wide variety of individuals who are interested in or involved with any aspect of HMO/PPOs. Similar to other health care texts, readers should consider this text as one of many resources that may be consulted. This text will likely complement professional libraries, with an emphasis on organizations that are involved in the delivery of health care including access to care, the delivery of care, and health care payment and reimbursement.—**Paul M. Murphy III**

Handbooks and Yearbooks

C, P, S

457.   **Centers for Disease Control and Prevention. http://www.cdc.gov/.** [Website] Free. Date reviewed: 2016.

The official Website of the Centers for Disease Control and Prevention (CDC), a government agency under the Department of Health and Human Services, is a comprehensive educational resource for a wide range of health topics.

The Website is organized by topics that fall under a series of broad categories, including "Diseases & Conditions," "Healthy Living," "Traveler's Health," and "Emergency Preparedness." Each topic leads to its own separate page that offers in-depth information. The main page for diabetes (under "Diseases & Conditions"), for example, provides articles that give a general overview of the condition as well as treatment strategies; studies published by the CDC; data and statistics; and multimedia resources. For teachers, each page offers fact sheets, pamphlets, diagrams, and educational videos that can be useful tools in the classroom.

The CDC's site also serves as a hub for health-related news, such as recent scientific findings and public announcements. For instance, the front page lists recent infectious outbreaks that are being investigated by the agency.

Although the subjects of health, disease, and nutrition can be complex, the site's material is generally accessible to a broad audience. Articles are written in such a way that scientific or medical terms are clearly explained. It should be noted, however, that some publications or studies that are hosted on the site are specifically targeted to scholars or health professionals.

Because the CDC offers such a wide breadth of information, navigating the Website and its many subsections may at first seem overwhelming. Fortunately, the Website offers various ways to search through its content. All topics are additionally organized in an alphabetical index that can be accessed on the front page, and there is also a search bar for users who want to look up a specific subject.

Overall, the official Website for the CDC is highly recommended for high school or college students, teachers, or individuals looking for reliable and up-to-date information on health and wellness.—**ARBA Staff Reviewer**

P

458.   **HealthCare.gov. https://www.healthcare.gov/.** [Website] Free. Date reviewed: 2016.

The health insurance exchange Website is a necessary page for those living in the 36 U.S. states that opted not to create their own exchange. While this is not an optimal source to gather academic information, it is helpful for those seeking to obtain health insurance and find answers for frequently asked questions relating to individual and family plans.

The exchange provides the most information on issues that users tend to face when applying for coverage, such as uploading documents, applying for Medicaid, open enrollment, and exemption qualification. Students may benefit from perusing the site to gain insight about the health care process and how complicated it can be. This site will not, however, be useful for students looking for educational information apart from a thorough glossary under the "Still Have Questions?" tab.

Consequently, this Website is recommended for those seeking to obtain health coverage for themselves and their families, but is not recommended as an academic resource for students, scholars, and researchers.—**ARBA Staff Reviewer**

C

459.   **InfoSci-Medical, Healthcare, and Life Science and Technology. http://www.igi-global.com/e-resources/infosci-subject-databases/infosci-medical/.** [Website] Hershey, Pa., Information Science Reference/IGI Global. Price negotiated by site. Date reviewed: 2016.

IGI's *InfoSci-Medical, Healthcare, and Life Science and Technology* collection provides full-text access to nearly 200 e-books of scholarly study and reference materials on a wide range of topics related to technology and the study, practice, and delivery of medicine. Titles in the collection address subjects ranging from the development of e-health services and telemedicine to tools for image analysis and mining technologies for improving health outcomes. Not all titles are exclusively focused on technology; some books are the result of research on new/shifting models of delivering care and tackling health-related issues.

The database provides a basic, advanced, and "expert" search option. The advanced search option allows users to combine keywords with author, title, and publication date parameters. The expert search option allows for search terms to be included, excluded, and weighted which allows users to rank the term within the search results. The expert search option also provides an "inflectional" search feature that includes a dictionary and thesaurus to provide all forms and tenses of the search term. This is a really interesting feature, and the especially direct or simply curious will enjoy it. Search results found using any of the three options can be refined by content type, copyright year, subject, or subject topics. The books are indexed and searchable at the chapter level further facilitating ease-of-access to the collection.

Each book has an annotated table of contents for easy access and browsability. A search box to search within the text is also provided for each book. Book chapters are provided in HTML and PDF formats for easy download. The database also provides tools for citing the books and book chapters.

This resource is highly recommended for health care practitioners, administrators, policy-makers, and students. This is an important collection for anyone with interest in the impact/potential impact of technology on the health care field. The electronic resource is especially recommended, as new titles are made available more quickly than the print copy.—**Kristin Kay Leeman**

P, S

460.   **KidsHealth. http://kidshealth.org/.** [Website] Free. Date reviewed: 2016.

KidsHealth is a group of Websites that provide accessible and easy-to-understand health resources for children, teenagers, parents, and teachers. The site is managed by the Nemours Center for Children's Health Media, a branch of the nonprofit health organization

The Nemours Foundation. All material featured on *KidsHealth* is reviewed by a board of medical professionals.

The front page of *KidsHealth* serves as a portal to four different Websites that each cater to a specific demographic (parents, kids, teens, or educators). With the exception of the site for educators, the *KidsHealth* Websites are structured similarly; the main page of each site features a sidebar that lists broad health topics, such as "Diseases and Conditions" or "Staying Safe." Clicking on one of these topics will lead to a new page in which articles, videos, and other educational resources are listed under further subcategories.

The Website for educators is distinct from the other sites in that it offers teacher guides, posters, worksheets, and quizzes that can be used in the classroom instead of educational articles. Teaching materials are organized by grade level (preschool to high school) and topic ("Human Body," Health Problems," and "Personal Health.").

Generally, all the *KidsHealth* Websites are designed to be approachable and are easy to navigate. Each site also features a search bar in which users can look up resources for specific topics.

For the Websites aimed at kids, teens, and parents, covered health topics are specified to its targeted demographic. For example, the site for parents offers articles on pregnancy and care for newborns, while the site for teens includes articles on such school issues as bullying or study habits. The articles are easy to understand, and technical or medical terms are clearly defined. Furthermore, the kids' Website includes an alphabetical dictionary of medical terms that can be accessed on the sidebar. Each site also features a special Q&A section for commonly asked health questions as well as a library of recipes catered to those with specific nutritional needs.

Overall, *KidsHealth* is an excellent and comprehensive online resource for parents and young students. In addition, *KidsHealth* can be a useful tool for health teachers.—**ARBA Staff Reviewer**

C

461. Sothern, Melinda S. **Safe and Effective Exercise for Overweight Youth.** Boca Raton, Fla., CRC Press, 2014. 374p. illus. index. $99.95; $69.97 (e-book). ISBN 13: 978-1-4398-7288-8; 978-1-4398-7289-5 (e-book).

Overweight and obese children and adolescents are part of a growing epidemic. There are numerous obstacles to kids getting appropriate and necessary levels of physical exercise despite evidence about the multiple benefits. Based on vast amounts of scientific research and the author's 24 years of clinical experience, this reference resource addresses this escalating problem and dispenses valuable guidance to health care providers, educators, public health personnel, and fitness professionals who work with youth populations. This guide is intended to complement the *Handbook of Pediatric Obesity: Clinical Management*(2006), coauthored by Sothern.

Chapters one through five review the scientific literature that supports tailored exercise for overweight and obese youth, providing illustrations, exercise instruction, and sample lesson plans. Chapters six through nine include such essential items as a 40-week exercise curriculum and discuss such fundamental matters as the importance of medical monitoring and self-monitoring, clinical and field protocols, realistic expectations for youth struggling with weight issues, and current recommendations for physical activity and fitness. Chapter 10 provides a summary of current studies, aiming to support future research.

Data is well-documented and topics are easily found within the text due to the book's organization and index. In addition to exercise curriculums, the title offers talking points, charts, tables, leveled activities, sample classes, and sidebars with key points and case studies. There are also handouts and forms, which are printable at http://publichealth. lsuhsc.edu. This portal additionally supplies users with further resources, including videos. As the incidence of obese and overweight youth increases, busy professional will need to consult a reliable reference. Thus, this book is highly recommended for academic and medical libraries.—**ARBA Staff Reviewer**

C, S

462. **Worldmark Global Health and Medicine Issues.** Brenda Wilmoth Lerner and K. Lee Lerner, eds. Farmington Hills, Mich., Gale/Cengage Learning, 2016. 2v. illus. maps. index. $310.00/set. ISBN 13: 978-1-4103-1752-0; 978-14103-1755-1 (e-book).

Worldmark Global Health and Medicine Issues is a two-volume reference source which offers 90 topical entries broadly addressing medical and public health issues within a global health context. Narrative entries address not only public health information but also the connections between health and social, economic, political, and ethical impacts. The target audience for this source would include high school and undergraduate students seeking an introduction to global health topics.

Entries are four to six pages in length and are arranged alphabetically. Each entry has six parts: Introduction, Historical Background, Impacts and Issues, Future Implications, a bibliography, and a sidebar which discusses a related topic such as a key organization or historical event. Some entries also contain an excerpt from a relevant historical text or contemporary article illustrating the entry topic. *See also* references to other entries are also given. Most entries have charts and graphs and/or color photos. Primary source material is also highlighted at the end of selected entries.

Also included are a glossary of terms and a chronology of events (at the beginning of both volumes), a list of selected organizations and advocacy groups, and a general resources bibliography of books, articles, and Websites (at the end of the second volume). The set concludes with a general index, referring readers to main entries or entries with primary source material.

Worldmark Global Health and Medicine Issues offers an introductory academic overview to global health and medical issues that broadly incorporates social, economic, political, and ethical issues as well. Most appropriate for school and academic libraries that field global health questions or teach global health courses.—**Caroline L. Gilson**

Medicine

General Works

Dictionaries and Encyclopedias

P, S

463. **The Gale Encyclopedia of Medicine.** 5th ed. Jacqueline L. Longe, ed. Farmington Hills, Mich., Gale/Cengage Learning, 2015. 9v. illus. $1,200.00/set. ISBN 13: 978-1-4103-1730-8; 978-1-4103-1739-1 (e-book).

The Gale Encyclopedia of Medicine, Fifth Edition is a nine-volume reference source with over 2,000 full-length articles covering common medical disorders, conditions, and diseases and tests, treatments, and drugs. The target audience for this source would include users seeking general health and treatment information. It is intended to be comprehensive, not definitive and to be a supplementary source to a consultation with a physician or health care provider.

Each volume begins with a comprehensive table of contents and an alphabetical list of all entries (which this reviewer very much appreciates for ease of use). Volumes one through eight contain main entry content. The ninth volume contains a brief chronology of major medical advances, events, and discoveries, a list of organizations listed in the Resources section of the main entries, a glossary, and a complete topic index to all volumes.

Main entries are arranged alphabetically and have been written by medical experts. Entries fall into one of three broad categories: Diseases & Conditions; Tests, Treatments, Therapies and Other Procedures; and Drugs, Herbs and Supplements. Entry lengths vary from 500 to 4,000 words. Some entries have accompanying color images, including photos, charts, tables, or illustrations. Within each entry, information is broken down into subcategories such as Definition, Precautions, Causes, and Symptoms, Treatment, Prognosis, and Prevention. Bolded terms within entries indicate they have their own main entry listing. Specific key vocabulary terms are defined within individual entries. Brief bibliographies and cross-references to related topics follow most entries. All entries are signed. Content is introductory and easy to read and offers a good overview to the topics addressed. In addition, the fifth edition offers articles covering alternative therapies and features specific Alternatives sections for diseases and conditions that may be helped by complementary therapies.

The Gale Encyclopedia of Medicine, Fifth Edition offers general medical information on diseases, disorders, and treatments in an accessible writing style that is not too technical for average readers. As with other medical reference sources, it should not be a substitute for professional medical care. Appropriate for school and public libraries.—**Caroline L. Gilson**

C, P, S

464. **The Gale Encyclopedia of Senior Health: A Guide for Seniors and Their Caregivers.** 2d ed. Farmington Hills, Mich., Gale/Cengage Learning, 2015. 5v. illus. index. $859.00/set. ISBN 13: 978-1-57302-746-5; 978-1-57302-752-6 (e-book).

The second edition of this four-color, five-volume set continues to be a highly readable, jargon-free, and beautifully illustrated reference on all aspects of senior health. Aimed at 9th grade to college senior readers, according to the publisher, these and other qualities make it a desirable addition to high school, college, and public libraries, as well as special libraries for seniors and health professionals. However, its high cost and continuing use of previously published material from other Gale encyclopedias also indicate it is probably not an essential purchase, at least not in its print edition and/or for holders of the first edition (see ARBA 2010, entry 1272).

Entries follow the format of other Gale health and medical encyclopedias. The scope of topics is wide and holistic, including diseases and conditions (about 50 percent of content); tests and procedures; drugs, herbs and vitamins; nutrition, exercise and diet; recovery and rehabilitation; professions; devices and tools, and other aging issues.

With 664 alphabetical entries, 73 are new and 229 updated. They are written and signed by medical writers and health care professionals. The publisher calls updates "classic entries," and notes they have updated bibliographies and statistics "so that every entry has at least some added value over the last edition." Many entries also duplicate or are very similar to entries in the Gale encyclopedias of medicine (see ARBA 2000, entry 1413; ARBA 2003, entry 1437; ARBA 2007, entry 1249; ARBA 2012, entry 1263) and nursing and allied health (see ARBA 2002, entry 1506; ARBA 2007, entry 1278, ARBA 2014, entry 1229). Positively, however, entries include *see also* references, and many have lists of resources (books, articles, Websites, and organizations) and/or boxes with key terms and questions to ask your doctor or pharmacist.

Additionally, there are 105 new color images and 179 new or updated tables, charts, and graphs. There is also a foreword and a list of entries grouped by 50 themes, ranging from addiction to women's health. These, as well as features from the first edition (introduction, alphabetical list of entries, and list of contributors) are included in each volume. The fifth volume also contains a list of organizations, a glossary of key terms, and an index. In summary, this is an attractive, comprehensive and easy to use reference that is highly desirable but a bit of a luxury.—**Madeleine Nash**

P

465.   **The Pregnancy Encyclopedia.** Chandrima Biswas and Paula Amato, eds. New York, DK Publishing, 2016. 351p. illus. index. $40.00. ISBN 13: 978-1-4654-4378-6.

This comprehensive encyclopedia is a welcome addition to the childbirth education canon. Uniquely conceived, its copious information is well-organized into 10 chapters which follow the major stages of pregnancy, delivery, and the postpartum period as well as the fundamental issues that accompany them. The distinct approach of addressing over 300 topics via question-and-answer segments is immensely readable and lends a personal appeal. Some examples from the Planning Your Care chapter include "What is a doula and how can they help with my labor and birth?," "Will I still need a doctor if I have a doula?," and "Can I have my older children present at my home birth?" Answers are concise but well-informed. Other topics range from breastfeeding concerns to pain relief to special needs and more.

To convey information, the book employs a dynamic visual style that includes many color photographs and illustrations, a variety of eye-catching typefaces, textboxes, scientific renderings, and charts. A notable highlight is the 14-page pregnancy timeline leading readers visually and textually from the moment of conception through to 40 weeks gestation. Thoughtfully crafted by leading experts in the field, this excellent reference also includes a glossary, an up-to-date listing of many useful resources, and an index.—**ARBA Staff Reviewer**

Alternative Medicine

Dictionaries and Encyclopedias

P

466.   **The Gale Encyclopedia of Alternative Medicine.** 4th ed. Laurie Fundukian, ed. Farmington Hills, Mich., Gale/Cengage Learning, 2014. 4v. illus. index. $714.00/set. ISBN 13: 978-1-57302-730-4.

The use of alternative medical therapies is increasing as people seek more holistic care. Many insurance providers now cover chiropractic and acupuncture. The fourth edition of *The Gale Encyclopedia of Alternative Medicine* reflects this with an article about the Patient Protection and Affordable Care Act (Obamacare) and how it will impact alternative care practitioners. This edition of the encyclopedia contains 800 signed, alphabetical entries. Fifty are new. All have resource lists and definitions of key terms in colored text boxes.

The entries cover therapies (acupuncture, chiropractic), herbs/remedies (milk thistle, vitamins), and diseases/conditions (breast cancer, osteoarthritis). Articles about therapies include their history, description, benefits, precautions, and side effects. Those about herbs and remedies include their general use, types of preparation, side effects, and interactions. Entries for diseases and conditions contain a definition, description, causes and symptoms, diagnosis and treatment, allopathic treatment, expected results, and prevention. The contributors provide evidence-based information about the effectiveness of the therapies. A list of organizations and a glossary help readers find further information.

The Gale Encyclopedia of Alternative Medicine is an excellent resource for health information collections in public and consumer health libraries.—**Barbara M. Bibel**

Handbooks and Yearbooks

P

467.   **Complementary and Alternative Medicine Sourcebook.** 5th ed. Keith Jones, ed. Detroit, Omnigraphics, 2015. 623p. index. (Health Reference Series). $95.00. ISBN 13: 978-0-7808-1378-6; 978-0-7808-1404-2 (e-book).

The numbers of people turning to nontraditional forms of health care is rapidly growing, whether due to such things as spiraling medical costs, drug scandals, or bureaucratic snags. A volume of the notable Health Reference Series published by Omnigraphics, this book is an invaluable reference offering basic, comprehensible information about a wide spectrum of topics related to complementary and alternative medical treatments. The reference is designed to assist nonmedical professionals, patients, caregivers, and others who are not schooled in these issues but may take a genuine, personal interest in alternative therapies whether for general well-being or targeted health concerns.

Six sections organize the essential topics, beginning with a generous overview of Complementary Alternative Medicine, or CAM. The overview defines CAM, highlights frequently asked questions, discusses CAM relative to children and adults, addresses CAM in relation to current insurance policy, and more. Following sections address current CAM systems (acupuncture, naturopathy, and others), current CAM therapies (vegetarianism, meditation, massage, etc.), dietary supplements (herbs, vitamins, minerals, etc.), and targeted afflictions (cancer, asthma, mental health disorders, etc.). A closing section provides a glossary of specialized terms and offers a useful directory of organizations that provide information and assistance regarding CAM.

As previously suggested, each section is further divided into detailed chapters addressing the particulars of its topic. Section two, for example, discusses acupuncture at length; defining it, applying it to various medical issues, and more. The vegetarianism chapter in section three discusses types, how to derive nutrients from a vegetarian diet, and more. All this information is presented clearly and concisely. Paragraphs make prolific use of headings, and with the addition of diagrams, Q & A's, shaded text boxes and bullet points, readers will find the format extremely navigable. Information is copious, but never overwhelming as this reference is clearly targeted to the layperson. What is notable about this volume is the care with which it reminds readers of the science, benefits, and risks of CAM, a relatively new and rapidly advancing realm of treatments.

This fifth edition conveys the most up-to-date information in regards to complementary and alternative medicine relative to the rapid advancements in research. The reference is not produced to replace professional medical counsel; however, it succeeds at providing intelligent, basic information about many facets of CAM to patients, families, caregivers, and others.—**Laura Herrell**

Specific Diseases and Conditions

Arthritis

P

468.   **Arthritis Sourcebook.** 4th ed. Amy L. Sutton, ed. Detroit, Omnigraphics, 2015. 704p. index. (Health Reference Series). $95.00. ISBN 13: 978-0-7808-1350-2; 978-0-7808-1401-1 (e-book).

A volume of the notable Health Reference Series published by Omnigraphics, this book is an invaluable reference regarding basic, comprehensible information about a wide spectrum of topics related to arthritis. The reference is designed to assist nonmedical professionals, patients, caregivers, and others who are not schooled in these issues but may take a genuine, personal interest in the issues of the all-too-common condition.

Six sections organize the essential topics, beginning with an overview of the joint disorder which points to statistics, risk factors, and affected joints. Following sections address types of arthritis and related rheumatic diseases, medical treatments, self-management strategies, and affiliated issues. A closing section provides a glossary of specialized terms and offers a useful directory of organizations working to assist those who suffer from this disease and their families.

Each section is further divided into detailed chapters addressing the particulars of its topic. Section two, for example, breaks down the great varieties of arthritis and related conditions, such as Rheumatoid Arthritis, Tendonitis, Bursitis, Carpal Tunnel Syndrome, Fibromyalgia, Lupus, and much more. Section three discusses drug therapies, joint surgeries, nonsurgical management, and more, while section four discusses diet, herbal supplements, and other complementary approaches. All this information is presented clearly and concisely. Paragraphs are mainly set up in a question-and-answer format (e.g., "Who provides care for people with Osteoarthritis?," etc.), and with the addition of diagrams, shaded text boxes, and bullet points, readers will find the format extremely navigable. Information is copious, but never overwhelming as this reference is clearly targeted to the layperson. Beyond basic topic information, chapters may include early signs, causes, risk factors, different forms of the disorder, prevention, associated conditions, diagnoses, treatment, latest research, and more. This particular volume is notable for its generous attention to arthritis treatment and pain management strategies.

This fourth edition conveys the most up-to-date information in regards to arthritis treatment, diagnosis, etc., relative to the rapid advancements in medical research. The reference is not produced to replace professional medical counsel; however, it succeeds at providing intelligent, basic information about many facets of this painful and all-too-common joint affliction to patients, families, caregivers, and others.—**Laura Herrell**

Brain disorders

C, P

469.   **The Brain, the Nervous System, and Their Diseases.** Jennifer L. Hellier, ed. Santa Barbara, Calif., Greenwood Press/ABC-CLIO, 2015. 3v. index. $294.00/set. ISBN 13: 978-1-61069-337-0; 978-1-61069-338-7 (e-book).

Neuroscience is a broad topic that includes research on how the brain and the nervous system work. *The Brain, the Nervous System, and their Diseases* includes a broad variety of topics, diseases, and issues within the complex field of neuroscience. This is a three-volume set, compiled by 73 authoritative experts including neuroscientists, family physicians, psychologists, and public health professionals who all work in this innovative and complex field. The books are easy to use as they are organized in the A-Z format. Entries range from popular issues such as Concussion and Alcoholism to more scientific topics such as Blood-Brain Barrier or Prions. The articles are written in a style that makes them useful to people working in the sciences, students working on research at colleges and universities, and the public. Each volume includes the alphabetical list of entries and the guide to related topics. Each entry includes *see also* references and includes citations for further reading on the topic. The third volume has a section at the end titled Experiments and Activities. This unique section includes hands-on activities and other experiments that could be completed in a classroom or school laboratory setting. Each experiment references the encyclopedia entry that is associated with the experiment. The experiments also include citations for further reading. Learning outcomes would augment the interactive educational component of this encyclopedia set. *The Brain, the Nervous System, and their Diseases* would enrich a university collection for undergraduates and graduates in the sciences, as well as the science collection in a public library.—**Amy B. Parsons**

C

470.   Petraglia, Anthony L., Julian E. Bailes, and Arthur L. Day. **Handbook of Neurological Sports Medicine.** Champaign, Ill., Human Kinetics, 2015. 401p. illus. index. $92.00; $49.00 (e-book). ISBN 13: 978-1-4504-4181-0; 978-1-4504-9697-1 (e-book).

Current medical research along with evidence-based practice has made significant advances in how trainers and medical staff treat sports-related injuries. This handbook focuses on the spectrum of neurological injuries in sports. Chapter one describes neurological injuries that are possible in 39 different sporting activities. American football, wrestling, and boxing are obvious violent sports that are discussed. Also included are less violent sports such as bowling, ballet, archery, cheerleading, and many more. There is a detailed discussion of the legal ramifications of closed head injuries and concussions in chapter two, including detailed cases of interest. Part two of the book consists of sports-related head injuries including pathophysiology descriptions, detailed medical definitions, frameworks, evaluations, symptom checklists, and syndromes. Part two also includes a chapter on natural neuroprotective remedies for concussions. The third part of the book focuses on the spine and peripheral nervous system. An important element in the field of sports medicine is "return to play" assessments. These are described and discussed in part three. Lastly, part four includes other sports-related neurological issues with a lengthy chapter on headaches and heat illnesses. All chapters have bibliographical references. Appendixes include sport concussion assessment tools for both adults and children, as well as the American Spinal Injury Association (ASIA) Standard classification of Spinal Cord injury. The *Handbook of Neurological Sports Medicine* would be a rich addition to any academic library collection that supports a health and sports sciences program, undergraduate or graduate level.—**Amy B. Parsons**

Cancer

C, P

471. **The Gale Encyclopedia of Cancer: A Guide to Cancer and Its Treatments.** 4th ed. Kristin Fust, ed. Farmington Hills, Mich., Gale/Cengage Learning, 2015. 3v. illus. index. $526.00/set. ISBN 13: 978-1-4103-1740-7; 978-1-4103-1744-5 (e-book).

This hardcover encyclopedia set is comprehensive and well written. The editor, advisory board, and contributing authors have created a useful and informative clinical resource. This set of three encyclopedias spans more than 2,000 pages.

The cover of each text is professionally designed. The layout is consistent among the three texts. The cover includes color graphics and images that are medical or scientific in nature. The text on the cover and spine of the book is easy to read.

This encyclopedia set consists of three volumes. Volume one includes "A-E," volume two includes "F-O," and volume three includes "P-Z." Each text begins with identical content. This includes listing the Advisory Board, Contents, Please Read-Important Information section, Foreword, Introduction, Alphabetical List of Entries, Contributors, and Illustrations of Body Systems.

The Please Read-Important Information section informs the reader that this encyclopedia set is intended to be one resource of many that may be used when researching or learning more about cancer. Similar to other medical conditions, it is often recommended that more than one resource be consulted or researched.

The content of each text is detailed and comprehensive. Volume one includes topics "Abarelix" through "Extragonadal germ cell tumors"; volume two includes "Familial cancer syndromes" through "Ovarian epithelial cancer"; volume three includes "Paget disease of the breast" through "Zolpidem".

The flow of the text is presented in a consistent manner throughout each text. For example, medical procedure information includes: Definition, Purpose, Description, Demographics, Preparation, Aftercare, Risks, Results, Morbidity and Mortality Rates, Alternatives, and Health Care Team Roles. Medical conditions include: Definition, Description, Demographics, Causes and Symptoms, Diagnosis, Treatment Team, Clinical Staging, Treatment, Prognosis, Coping with Cancer Treatment, Clinical Trials, Prevention, Special Concerns. Medication information includes: Definition, Purpose, Description, Recommended Dosage, Precautions, Side Effects, and Interactions. Following each topic resources are listed including Websites, references to specific books and periodicals, and related organizations. This format is very useful.

Text boxes, which are easy to read, are presented throughout the books. Examples include "Key Terms" and "Questions To Ask Your Doctor." Numerous colored illustrations and pictures are included throughout each of the texts.

The end of volume three includes detailed lists of organizations including "Organizations: National Cancer Institute–Designated Comprehensive Cancer Center" and "Organizations: Support Groups, Government Agencies, and Research Groups." Volume three also includes a detailed glossary and index.

This encyclopedia set is well written and detailed. It will likely appeal to a wide variety of individuals who are interested the topic of cancer. This text touches on numerous aspects of cancer, including assessments, treatment, and associated medical conditions. This encyclopedia set will likely complement personal or professional libraries, including those in academic and health care settings.—**Paul M. Murphy III**

Pharmacy and Pharmaceutical Sciences

P

472.   The Gale Encyclopedia of Prescription Drugs: A Comprehensive Guide to the Most Common Medications. Kristin Fust, ed. Farmington Hills, Mich., Gale/Cengage Learning, 2015. 2v. illus. index. $499.00/set. ISBN 13: 978-1-57302-742-7; 978-1-57302-745-8 (e-book).

Since there is so much information about medications available on the Internet for both consumers and health professionals, why bother with a print publication? The flip answer is because some consumers (dare I say older) still want it. This drug guide for the consumer is an excellent choice for public libraries to purchase.

The book includes entries on the top 300 drugs written by pharmacists, physicians, nurses, researchers, and other health care personnel. All articles are signed and give the author's credentials. The language is simple but does not talk down to the reader in the way consumer drug information books often do. Key terms such as bradycardia or triglycerides are defined clearly and the writers have accomplished their goal of providing an understandable yet comprehensive drug guide.

Unfortunately most users will skip the foreword, which provides a clear but concise explanation of the drug discovery process, clarifies the difference between adverse and side effects, and explains brand and generic drug equivalency. Drugs are listed alphabetically by generic name with an index of brand and alternative names. Entries include each drug's description, definition, and purpose including off label uses, dosage, precautions, side effects, and interactions. There are also a few sentences on the origins of the drug which provide a brief history in case anyone wants to know how long a product has been around. After each entry there is a list of resources that includes articles, Websites, and books. The books and articles are geared for the professional but the Web sites give consumers excellent sources of further information.

Four appendixes include a list of recommended questions for the pharmacist, the Institute of Safe Medicine Practices list of commonly confused drug names, a list of health organizations, and a glossary. This encyclopedia is a credible, easy to read place for the public to find basic drug information.—**Natalie Kupferberg**

34 Technology

General Works

Handbooks and Yearbooks

P, S

473.   Balaban, Naomi, and James Bobick. **The Handy Technology Answer Book.** Canton, Mich., Visible Ink Press, 2016. 431p. illus. index. $21.95pa. ISBN 13: 978-1-57859-563-1; 978-1-57859-595-2 (e-book).

This timely volume in the Handy Answer series offers an exploration of how different types of technology have affected and continue to affect so many aspects of the world in which we live. From the obvious example of computers to the things we take for granted like clocks and cars, the book does well to trace the many diverse ways technology impacts the ways people live today.

Thirteen sections address everything from the origins of technology through a wide variety of specific innovations, and ultimately to an assessment of technology's greater influence on a number of diverse fields.

Each section is further broken into chapters discussing narrower topics. What truly sets this publication apart is the unique question and answer format, which enables readers to quickly find their particular topic of interest, connect these topics to broader ideas, and pique their curiosity for more. In rapid succession, for example, we learn the answers to questions about which elements are metals and the importance of aluminum, along with much more relative to mining, minerals, and manufacturing. The book amasses nearly 1,200 of these incisive questions, covering such topics as computers, time, and energy.

Closing chapters highlight the impacts of technology on the environment, genetics, and medicine. The book, perfect for younger students, in particular, closes out with an index and many ideas for further reading on the fascinating subject of technology.—**Laura Herrell**

Computers

Handbooks and Yearbooks

P, S

474. **Code Academy. http://www.codeacademy.com.** [Website] Free. Date reviewed: 2015.

Code Academy is a free, interactive educational tool that allows users to practice coding. The company strives to create a beneficial online learning experience and operates under the knowledge that classroom learning has changed drastically over time and therefore teaching methods must shift accordingly. *Code Academy* offers a unique "net native education" and mimics the experiences of social media rather than a classroom in order to effectively teach students how to code.

The Website is minimalist and easy to navigate, providing links to coding tutorials at the bottom of the homepage. Here, users can choose to create their own interactive Websites based off the format of AirBnB. *Code Academy* offers tutorials on Javascript, AngularJS, HTML, CSS, and much more. Instead of lengthy text explanations, the tutorials begin with activities and are completely interactive from the start, guaranteeing that students will not fall asleep on the keyboard.

In addition to online instruction, users can read success stories from people around the world who have benefited from the site and have learned to code without prior knowledge of the subject material. Videos provide answers to frequently asked questions, such as "How can coding help you?"

This Website is a perfect tool for students who are easily distracted and would like minimal instruction before diving in to the coding process. Teachers will find this great educational tool to be helpful in the classroom as well. *Code Academy* is a highly recommended resource.—**ARBA Staff Reviewer**

P, S

475. **Code.org. http://code.org/.** [Website] Free. Date reviewed: 2015.

The makers behind *Code.org* believe that every student worldwide should be offered the opportunity to learn how to code. *Code.org* is a phenomenal nonprofit organization that seeks to provide computer science resources to women and students of color, both underrepresented groups in the computer science field. The Website offers an introduction to computer science through the Hour of Code, a free hour-long, self-guided introduction to subject basics that takes place during the second week of December.

Those interested in the Hour of Code can sign up on the Website and even organize an event at school to encourage more students to participate.

Code.org is partnered with Outlier Research & Evaluation at the University of Chicago. Together they work to find more effective ways to reach students and spark curiosity in technology as well as provide them with opportunities to explore their interests. The organization is funded through *Indiegogo.com* and raised over $5 million to reach 100 million students worldwide in 2014, making their campaign the most successful in *Indiegogo* history.

Both students and teachers can create accounts to access coding videos and tutorials appropriate for all ages, and users can even practice coding with *Frozen* characters Anna and Elsa. Other tutorials teach users to make apps or games, create Websites, and even provide access to university-level coding courses. Teachers can set up a free classroom coding course through available for their K-8 classes.

The courses are available in over 30 languages and are used in over 180 countries. *Code.org* is a top-notch resource for teachers and students alike.—**ARBA Staff Reviewer**

C

476. **InfoSci-Computer Science and Information Technology. http://www.igi-global. com/e-resources/infosci-subject-databases/infosci-computer-science/.** [Website] Hershey, Pa., Information Science Reference/IGI Global. Price negotiated by site. Date reviewed: 2016.

The InfoSci series is a comprehensive collection of academic databases incorporating the sciences and technology. A user profile will make it possible to access all tools for research. A user guide and help tab will provide instruction on using the databases and detail search options and features of the electronic resources. Found in a handy sidebar, search functions are: Basic, Advanced, Expert, and Classic. The larger sidebar provides options for further navigation forward or to return to a previous segment. Citing, favorites, and saved search tabs are essential for the researcher. Additionally, InfoSci offers this research feature—citings are found in MLA, ALA, and Chicago style.

The database *InfoSci-Computer Science and Information Technology* is a considerable collection of reference books available as e-books or hardcopy text. The format options are either HTML or PDF. Information is easily accessed by the series tools mentioned above, and further filtering may be necessary as there are 458 books in this grouping. Information on Web design, environmental impacts, big data, robotics, high performance and smart computing, artificial intelligence, and applications and systems are some of the areas covered in this database.

The 10-volume set of the *Encyclopedia of Informational Science and Technology* (3d edition) provides a full range of concepts, issues, methods, technologies, and trends and may be a good place for researchers to begin to define their focus of study. Other encyclopedia options are available. Some resources are practical like *Design Solutions for Improving Website Quality and Effectiveness.* Published in 2016, this covers analytics, metrics, usage, and security aspects of Web environments which may be useful for those involved in improving Web designs. There are several texts that describe expectations for trends in computer science and technology; *Emerging Innovations in Agile Software Development* provides research-based solutions for contemporary software development.

As with any technology-related data, the shelf life can be short. The four entries from 2000 will most likely be useful from a historical background only. Occasionally, older text is off-putting because of the age of it; *Information Technology Evaluation Methods and Management* (2001), Chapter 9 states "as information and communication technologies have rapidly developed in the 1990s, enormous changes have taken place everywhere," and unless looking for background on information technology, this will not be current enough for timely research or practical application.

InfoSci-Computer Science and Information Technology is strong in the range of technology subject areas and the tools will expedite the process of sifting through the content easily. Most book resources are current, offering information entrenched in practical and trending ideas on computer science and information technology. This database will be useful for high-level academic research, engineers, and others working in the IT industry. This database is relevant for any academic reference collection.

Recommended.—**Janis Minshull**

35 Physical Sciences and Mathematics

Physical Sciences

Chemistry

Handbooks and Yearbooks

C, P, S

477. **Chemistry Guide. http://www.chemistryguide.org/.** [Website] Free. Date reviewed: 2016.

This is a free-to-use aggregator of chemistry-related Websites. It is authored by Andry Frolov, who holds a Ph.D. in chemistry and has years of experience in organic synthetic chemistry. It is supported by the Moscow-based Exclusive Chemistry Ltd. and by Aurora Fine Chemicals, LLC. Its basic structure makes it easy to navigate.

A navigation bar includes tabs for Home, Top 10 Sites, Newly Added, Links to Us, About Us, Contact Us, and Privacy Policy. The heart of the data is found under the Home tab, which provides links to Websites grouped into 23 such subcategories as Analytical Chemistry, Chemical Dictionaries, General Chemistry, Green Chemistry, Organic Chemistry, Periodic Table of the Elements, and Polymer Chemistry. The Top 10 Sites link includes several related to chemistry jobs as well as an interactive periodic table, a site on analytical chemistry basics, and more. The newly added sites include three purporting to assist students in the writing of research papers, along with many others including a chemistry blog and an amino acids guide.—**ARBA Staff Reviewer**

C, P, S

478. **Dynamic Periodic Table. http://www.ptable.com/.** [Website] Free. Date reviewed: 2016.

Dynamic Periodic Table, created by Michael Dayah, is an interactive, user-friendly Website that provides reliable source data curated from primary sources on the elements. The home page opens to a periodic table which, when mousing over the elements, highlights whether the element is a nonmetal, metal, metalloid, noble gas, transition metal, etc. Tabs at the top of the home page take the user to a demo that walks one through the many options available and how to make the most of the site. There are also "properties," "orbitals," "isotopes," and "compounds" tabs and, as is the case with the homepage periodic table, mousing over the element brings up more information about that element.

This Website is an excellent source of information on the elements and will be of great use to teachers, students, and librarians.

Earth and Planetary Sciences

Astronomy and Space Sciences

C, P, S

479.   **Encyclopedia of the Solar System.** 3d ed. Tilman Spohn, Doris Breuer, and Torrence V. Johnson, eds. San Diego, Calif., Elsevier Science, 2014. 1336p. illus. $180.00. ISBN 13: 978-0-12-415845-0.

Edited by Tilman Spohn, director of the Institute of Planetary Research of the German Aerospace Center in Berlin and professor of planetology; Doris Breuer, head of the Department of Planetary Physics at the Institute of Planetary Research of the German Aerospace Center in Berlin and an associate professor; and Torrence V. Johnson, a specialist on icy satellites and a senior research scientist at Jet Propulsion Laboratory, the third edition of the *Encyclopedia of the Solar System,* contains 57 chapters by more than 75 eminent authors.

The book's 57 chapters are organized into nine sections: The Solar System; Fundamental Planetary Processes and Properties; The Sun; Earthlike Planets; Earth and Moon as Planets; Asteroids, Dust, and Comets; Giant Planets and Their Satellites; Beyond the Planets; and Exploring the Solar System. For the most part, the authors from the second edition updated their own work. Moreover there are important additions in this third edition. In light of the increased importance of geophysical tools for the exploration of planets and the increase in the theoretical knowledge of the inner workings of planets, there is a chapter on geophysical exploration tools in general and on exploration of the Moon and potential landing sites on Mars. There is also a new chapter on rotation of the planets and using its observation to constrain models of the interior of terrestrial planets. Chapters on the interiors of Mars and the Moon have been added along with theoretical chapters pertaining to the inner workings of terrestrial planets—the generation of their magnetic fields and the relation between the thermal evolution, convection in the interior, and their tectonics. There is also a new chapter on high resolution and stereoimaging tools of planetary exploration. Added to the suite of chapters on space exploration is a new chapter describing strategies that nations have jointly developed in the International Space Exploration Initiative.

There is also a glossary with *see* references and an extensive appendix, comprised of four tables: Selected Astronomical Constraints; Physical and Orbital Properties of the Sun, Planets, and Dwarf Planets; Physical and Orbital Properties of the Satellites of Planets and Dwarf Planets; and Solar System Exploration Missions. The latter table has data on missions to the sun, Mercury, Venus, the Moon, Marsh asteroids, Jupiter, Saturn, Uranus, Neptune, dwarf planets, comets, and the Kuiper Belt.

Tables, figures, and illustrations help readers understand the amazing amount of material in this highly recommended book.—**ARBA Staff Reviewer**

P, S

480.   **Exploring Space: http://www.pbs.org/exploringspace/mars/index.html.** [Website] Free. Date reviewed: 2015.

PBS's *Exploring Space: The Quest for Life* is a national public television show that explores space, recent discoveries, and the quest for life outside planet earth. To introduce this content to those who haven't seen the show, the Exploring Space Website is an exceptional tool that allows users to access information by reading articles, taking quizzes, and playing with games and interactive simulations.

This Website is best for students who may be studying space in the classroom and require additional sources or are looking to learn and play simultaneously. The sidebar on the homepage includes links for users to follow meteorites and stay updated on recent Mars discoveries. For those interested in alien life, the Designs of Alien Life page is a fun read for all ages.

An Essays page provides articles written by NASA scientists and researchers on the forefront of new discoveries in space. These short essays and opinions have the potential to be excellent nonfiction reading for student projects or papers.

Students can also simulate their own journeys to Mars. First, they create a schedule of events, then track their health based on the decisions they make in space while travelling thousands of miles per day. This creative simulation allows students to practice time management and understand the importance of balancing work with relaxation to stay in tip-top shape physically and mentally. It also highlights the challenges astronauts face in balancing their physiological and psychological needs in space. Additional activities include matching games and quizzes about Europa and Mars, complete with spectacular visuals.

The Web page has an attractive layout and is sure to hold the attention of younger readers as they play with the interactive tools and learn more about planets, moons, comets, and stars. A brief trailer of the PBS show on The Program page may even peak student interest and entice them to watch the show for even more information about the fascinating workings of space.—**ARBA Staff Reviewer**

Climatology and Meteorology

P, S

481.   **U*X*L Encyclopedia of Weather and Natural Disasters.** 2d ed. Amy Hackney Blackwell, ed. Farmington Hills, Mich., U*X*L/Gale, 2016. 5v. illus. maps. index. $436.00/set. ISBN 13: 978-1-4103-3290-5.

Outstanding ancillary materials complement the smart choices of entries in these five volumes to produce a first-rate encyclopedia set covering meteorology and the effects of weather on living systems. Although the emphasis on human death tolls and the destruction of cities by historic events such as volcanic eruptions, floods, and storms is evident from the title, the set includes an overview of such issues as mass extinctions in planetary history and the impact of tectonic movements and climate change on biological systems more generally. Topics range over both basic terms such as drought and cloud to less-known terms such as foehn and mesoscale convective complex.

Each volume includes a complete table of contents, list of entries according to scientific field, glossary, index, and practical guides to activities and further research. Individual entries contain microglossaries, and most include visual aids such as photographs and full-color diagrams of various cycles.—**Delilah R. Caldwell**

Geology

C, P, S
482.   Hinga, Bethany D. Rinard. **Ring of Fire: An Encyclopedia of the Pacific Rim's Earthquakes, Tsunamis, and Volcanoes.** Santa Barbara, Calif., ABC-CLIO, 2015. 402p. illus. maps. index. $89.00. ISBN 13: 978-1-61069-296-0; 978-1-61069-297-7 (e-book).

Framed within the context of plate tectonic activity in and around the Pacific Ocean, author Hinga provides encyclopedia entries describing the region's major volcanic eruptions, earthquakes, and tsunamis along with information about affected nations and influential geoscientists. Descriptions of related geologic terms are provided as well. To orient readers, two lists of entries are provided including an alphabetical listing and a listing by name of the related geologic event or natural disaster. Oddly, the listings do not include page numbers which would direct readers to the corresponding entries in the text. Following the listings are a brief preface, an informative introduction about the Pacific Rim's geographic and geologic settings, and a handy timeline of significant geologic events or natural disasters dating back to 1815. Each article entry is very well written using easy-to-understand language and some include black-and-white photographs. Regrettably, maps, which could help readers understand the location of a geologic event or disaster in relation to the Pacific Rim, were not included with the entries. All entries are cross-referenced to other relevant entries and are accompanied with a short list of suggested further reading. Finally, an extensive bibliography is located after the entries along with a comprehensive index. Overall, the value of the encyclopedia is in its treatment of the Pacific Rim's major geologic events or natural disasters, using nontechnical language, all within the context of plate tectonic theory.—**Jennifer Brooks Huffman**

General Works

Dictionaries and Encyclopedias

C, P, S
483.   Calaprice, Alice, Daniel Kennefick, and Robert Schulmann. **An Einstein Encyclopedia.** Princeton, N.J., Princeton University Press, 2015. 347p. illus. index. $39.95. ISBN 13: 978-0-691-14174-9.

Few scholarly reference works focused on the very famous can described as "delicious" reads, but that is the case here. Beautifully written and illustrated, this compact but rich single volume beautifully celebrates the 100th anniversary of Albert Einstein's general theory of relativity (and by chance is all the more timely, considering recent confirmation of Einstein's gravitational waves theory). Here one can explore his rich biography, and what influenced his life-long intellectual and personal interests. The authors chose wisely to avoid a rigid, alphabetic encyclopedia format. Instead, they address Einstein's life in three very accessible sections: the intimately personal and biographical; key scientific works and collaborations; and, last, the progression of his philosophical/political leanings and affiliations. So in addition to focusing on Einstein's work as a scientist, a different, intriguing portrait of the man is also revealed—painted in personal photos, snippets of poetry and letters, stories of his love of sailing, his family life, friendships, romantic interests, and so forth. These insights into Einstein's world view, via historical ephemera and anecdotes, bring the man to life. He is revealed as a whole human being, versus the quirky, enigmatic science genius of public perception. Among supplementary features are a chronology of Einstein's significant life events, and a deeply detailed index that follows three appendixes. The last of these offers a chronological, selective, annotated bibliography for those who wish to dig deeper into key lectures and seminal publications—since the goal this work was not to provide comprehensive coverage of Einstein's research in physics (impossible), here the authors have supplied additional resources for the scholarly reader to pursue. In summary, the authors have contributed to the literature a reverent, meaty, intriguing, and scholarly encyclopedia that is accessible to most readers. It truly honors the life and work of the world's most-renowned scientist. A much earlier reference book on Albert Einstein—*An Einstein Dictionary* (see ARBA 1997, entry 1409)— pales in comparison to this new title.

Highly recommended.—**Judith Matthews**

Handbooks and Yearbooks

C, P, S

484.   **Skeptical   Science.   http://www.skepticalscience.com/.**   [Website]   Free.   Date reviewed: 2016.

Skeptical Science is a combination blog-Website with the self-described mission of "get[ting] skeptical about global warming skepticism." It was created and continues to be maintained by John Cook, a Climate Communication Fellow for the Global Change Institute at the University of Queensland in Australia. Entirely funded by private donations, *Skeptical Science* asserts that it seeks to entirely remove political considerations and viewpoints from the issue of climate change and focus only on our evolving scientific understanding of the issue. The site has been endorsed by many influential researchers and journalists studying the issue of global warming, and in 2011 it received the Australian Museum's Eureka Prize in the category of Advancement of Climate Change Knowledge.

The most prominent element of *Skeptical Science's* home page is its blog, in which Cook and a team of contributors comment on news and developments in the global warming field. But the top of the home page also provides gateway tabs to a wide range of information on climate change, from updates on the latest scientific research related to global warming to refutations of various arguments and talking points that have been offered up by skeptics and denialists over the years. The heart of the Website's offerings, though, is "Arguments," which pairs more than 175 "climate myths" with summaries of "what the science says." These "what the science says" analyses, which distill the findings of studies published in peer-reviewed scientific literature, are offered in different versions tailored to basic, intermediate, and (sometimes) advanced reader levels.

Another tab on the home page, identified as "Resources," provides access to a broad array of additional information on climate science, including graphs and charts, a search engine to find the latest climate-related articles and papers published around the world, a glossary of terms, and a handbook authored by Cook called *The Scientific Guide to Global Warming Skepticism* (available in 19 languages).

Other Websites are more elegantly designed than *Skeptical Science.* Nonetheless, it contains a wealth of information on the true state of climate change research, and is thus a recommended resource for high school, public, and academic libraries.—**ARBA Staff Reviewer**

Mathematics

Handbooks and Yearbooks

C, P

485.   **The Best Writing on Mathematics 2015.** Mircea Pitici, ed. Princeton, N.J., Princeton University Press, 2016. 392p. illus. $24.95pa. ISBN 13: 978-0-69116-965-1.

This absorbing book is the sixth volume in a series of anthologies of mathematical essays for nonmathematicians. There are essays on particular problems, recreational mathematics, philosophy of mathematics, statistics and probability, math education, and applied mathematics. The introduction includes an overview of 2014 nonspecialist mathematical books, supplemented by a Website. The book concludes with a bibliography of 2014 articles not included in this book. The essays are accessible without advanced math education although real concentration is often required.

An attractive purchase for any public or academic library.—**Frederic F. Burchsted**

C

486.   **The Princeton Companion to Applied Mathematics.** Nicholas J. Higham, ed. Mark R. Dennis, Paul Glendinning, Paul A. Martin, Fadil Santosa, and Jared Tanner, associate eds. Princeton, N.J., Princeton University Press, 2015. 1032p. illus. index. $99.50. ISBN 13: 978-0-691-15039-0.

This very useful book supplements *The Princeton Companion to Mathematics* (2008) which covers pure mathematics. Applied mathematics includes the use of mathematical methods in a wide variety of areas, including physics, biology, medicine, finance, social science, computer science, and other fields. The book's over 180 articles are arranged in eight sections on concepts, major equations and laws, areas of applied mathematics, specific example problems, etc.

Applied mathematics is composed of numerous specialist topics, and it is impossible for one person to have thorough knowledge of, or keep up to date with, all of them. This book is designed to allow applied mathematicians to acquaint themselves with areas outside their specialties. It will also serve as an introduction to interested lay people or to scientists in other fields. Substantial mathematical education is required for full understanding of the articles, but most of the articles have sufficient verbal explanation to allow the nonmathematical to garner the basic ideas.

Essential for college/university libraries and a useful addition to large public libraries.—**Frederic F. Burchsted**

36 Resource Sciences

Environmental Science

Dictionaries and Encyclopedias

P, S

487.   Collin, Robert William. **Trash Talk: An Encyclopedia of Garbage and Recycling around the World.** Santa Barbara, Calif., ABC-CLIO, 2015. 484. illus. index. $100.00. ISBN 13: 978-1-61069-508-4; 978-1-61069-509-1 (e-book).

Based on his introduction, author Robert Collin intended this encyclopedia to serve as a review of waste management and recycling practices in countries from around the world. Written at a basic level, it serves as an entry-level resource for global information in these topical areas. Organizationally, the book contains a preface, a well-written introduction, eight "thematic essays," and articles on waste management processes for 173 countries. Articles include a brief narrative with supporting statistics; their lengths vary, but typically range from one to three pages. Each article sets the stage for a reader by very briefly describing each nation's population characteristics and geography followed by information on current waste management practices, emission sources and levels, and major waste issues. Each article also identifies suggested further readings. Black-and-white photographs accompany a few of the articles, as do some sidebar stories; but there is a noticeable lack of supporting tables, charts, or graphs. Finally, a basic glossary identifying key terms is provided, as is a bibliography and an index.

Overall, this encyclopedia should provide readers with a very basic understanding of waste management and recycling practices worldwide.—**Jennifer Brooks Huffman**

C

488.   **Encyclopedia of Natural Resources.** Yeqiao Wang, ed. Boca Raton, Fla., CRC Press, 2014. 2v. illus. maps. index. $1,560.00/set. ISBN 13: 978-1-4398-5258-3.

The earth's natural resources are crucial for maintaining life and the study of these topics reaches beyond a single discipline and requires input from across the scholarly spectrum. The two-volume *Encyclopedia of Natural Resources* provides the necessarily broad coverage of topics related to natural resources. The volumes are divided by subject, with volume one dedicated to topics related to land while volume two focuses on water and air. These volumes are well organized and feature both standard and topical tables of contents for efficient article locating. As stated in the preface, this reference work aims to deliver authoritative information across the multidisciplinary set of topics related to natural resources including science, technology, and societal impact. To that end, this encyclopedia is successful, offering informative articles on topics ranging from biodiversity and ecosystems, management and sustainability, hydrology, meteorology, and climate change written by subject experts in each field. Noticeably absent, however, is any discussion of energy. Considering the environmental and societal implications associated with coal and oil extraction or wind and solar energy, excluding the energy sector is a significant omission for a resource aiming for coverage in natural resources. Although expressly written to appeal to general readers, academics, and professionals alike, the writing in some articles is more appropriate for a scholarly audience and this encyclopedia is therefore recommended for academic and research libraries.—**Eric Tans**

P, S
489.   **U*X*L Sustainable Living.** Everett, Jason M., ed. Farmington Hills, Mich., U*X*L/Gale, 2016. 3v. illus. index. $272.00/set. ISBN 13: 978-1-4103-1783-4.

Although the title might imply a merely practical guide, this sophisticated encyclopedia also tackles concepts like the carbon cycle and intergenerational responsibility and concrete events such as the passage of the US Farm Bill and the UN Conference on Environment and Development. Each volume includes excellent ancillary materials such as a list of entries according to which component(s) of sustainability the topic represents (environmental, economic, or social), chronology of events, general glossary, list of relevant organizations, and thorough index. Individual entries include their own miniature glossaries and list resources, both Websites and books, for further study.

The encyclopedia does contain useful resources for readers interested in practical applications. Many sidebars provide information that can be used to research options. For example, the entry on Nongovernmental Organizations includes information about *The Charity Navigator* Website. Current events, such as the Fukushima disaster, are also covered in sidebars and referenced in the index.—**Delilah R. Caldwell**

Handbooks and Yearbooks

C
490.   **Ecological Forest Management Handbook.** Guy R. Larocque, ed. Boca Raton, Fla., CRC Press, 2015. 604p. illus. maps. index. (Applied Ecology and Environmental Management). $169.96; $139.97 (e-book). ISBN 13: 978-1-4822-4785-5; 978-1-4822-4786-2 (e-book).

From the potential benefits of mangrove forests and the threat root rot poses to the coveted clutch tree, this collection ties together rich and tantalizing lines of research. So wide is the expert reach of the multiple authors that the pluses and minuses of palm oil plantations, some of the philosophical debate over European beech forests (as in strive for diversity or not), and even John Haldane's canary are here. The product-yielding and cultural dimensions of forests both receive solid treatment. The complexity of managing forests benefits from models that provide guidance about how to manage; and authors from different geographical regions summarize the many existing models while fully describing some. The "wake effect" is a valuable concept that suggests when forests are managed well for wood production, other gains accrue, such as protection of watersheds and wildlife.

Each entry is supported by a robust list of references and there is an index. Because many authors are not writing in their native language, there are errors, such as leave for leaf and boarders for borders, and some verbosity and repetition. Quibbles aside, the most serious omission in the volume is a direct focus on the role of the human population, which has more than quadrupled since 1900. In fact, the world's population is not "an ecological indicator of stress on the world's forests" (page 365). The world's population actually puts direct pressure on forests. On the whole, coverage and content are good. The volume merits a place in a research library.—**Diane M. Calabrese**

P

491.   **The Environmental Resource Handbook, 2015-2016.** 8th ed. Amenia, N.Y., Grey House Publishing, 2015. 1000p. maps. index. $155.00pa. ISBN 13: 978-1-61925-560-9.

Largely a compilation that derives heavily (and verbatim) from information provided by such open sources as the U.S. Environmental Protection Agency and the Centers for Disease Control and Prevention, this volume also includes some original research by the editors. For example, there is a section on the recycling practices (voluntary or not, curbside or not, etc.) of 100 major U.S. cities. Fingertip access to a glossary of environmental terms and to acronyms and abbreviations will be useful in some work settings. So, too, will the index to all entries in the volume by name (group, association), the index to entries by state (and Canada), and the subject index. Financial resources, consultants, and green products catalogs are among the subheads for the section on resources. The resources include a wide range of entities ranging from the Chlorine Institute to Numi Organic Tea; the nugget description attached to each entry varies from none to a robust sentence or two. Statistics from agriculture, children's health and environment, air quality, energy, and more are presented via maps, graphs, and tabulations derived almost wholly (and without modification) from open sources of information at federal agencies. An online database, which is sold separately, allows searches of compiled information by keyword as well as ability to save and organize search results. Those immersed in environmental work of any kind will find the activity of reading entries on resources a way to both identify new links with kindred groups and to assess work that needs to be done.—**Diane M. Calabrese**

C

492.   **Handbook of Research Methods and Applications in Environmental Studies.** Ruth, Matthias, ed. Northampton, Mass., Edward Elgar, 2015. 534p. index. (Handbook of Research Methods and Applications). $290.00. ISBN 13: 978-1-78347-463-9.

Human life and well-being depend on the use of natural resources, while the utilization of those resources often results in environmental degradation. Environmental studies, as a discipline, exists as an examination of human interactions with the natural world and the tension between necessary use and damaging exploitation. Divided between sections on the social context and scientific modeling, the *Handbook of Research Methods and Applications in Environmental Studies* illustrates this tension while making clear that the very nature of environmental studies is interdisciplinary and multimodal. Each chapter introduces a research method concept or practice and then describes the practical application in the form of case studies. With an emphasis on mixed methods research, part one's social context section includes chapters on conducting cross-cultural research, constructing structured mental models, and fuzzy cognitive mapping, among other methods. The chapters in part two describe models for calculating, understanding, and predicting energy and water use, life cycle assessments, ecosystem dynamics, valuing ecosystem services, and gaming. Written for scholars and practitioners of environmental science research, this handbook succeeds in compiling not only the theoretical concepts behind interdisciplinary research methods in environmental studies, but also examples of practical applications of those same methods.

Recommended for research libraries.—**Eric Tans**

C

493.   **InfoSci-Environmental Science and Technology. http://www.igi-global.com/e-resources/infosci-subject-databases/infosci-environmental-science/.** [Website] Hershey, Pa., Information Science Reference/IGI Global. Price negotiated by site. Date reviewed: 2016.

The InfoSci series provides information for research studies relating to science and technology. Students attending schools that own these databases will want to create a profile to access full use of the tools. A user guide and help tab will provide instruction on using the databases and detail search options and features of the electronic resources. Search functionality options are: Basic, Advanced, Expert, and Classic. Classic search also offers a more traditional search using keywords and subjects. All of these are located on a high-left sidebar for ease of access. The main sidebar provides options for forward or backward navigation. Citing, favorites, and saved search tabs are essential for the researcher. InfoSci offers these features with scholarly options; citings are found in MLA, ALA, and Chicago style and choices include HTML or PDF for full-text format.

InfoSci-Environmental Science and Technology has 71 reference books. Each page can be sorted via titles or copyright dates. Date ranges of 2001 (1) through 2016 (14) will provide historical and contemporary studies on environmental science and technology. Subtopics are many and examples may include: climate change, energy harvesting, meat consumption, sustainability, and water pollution. E-book resources vary in geographical impact from the finite (*Impact of Climate Change on Food Security in Small Island Developing States*) to those with a broader scope (*Marine Technology and Sustainable Development: Green Innovations*). Most books contain introductions, acknowledgements, references, author and contributor information, and indexes. Because this database is a collection of independent resource texts, there is not uniformity in access. Case in point, *Impact of Meat Consumption on Heath and Environmental* appears to have no index.

Chapters are easily accessed by clicking on the chapter heading. As an environmental title is accessed, a search bar will allow further filtering for specifics within the clear listing of chapters. Because of the complexity of some studies, the search bar will be extremely useful for further filtering. Chapters are well documented, and tables, charts, and other data structures are followed immediately by sourcing. Information may be saved by chapter or the entire book.

InfoSci-Environmental Science and Technology provides detailed research for college students, researchers, engineers, scholars, government officials, and other practitioners seeking to understand and make a difference in the care and treatment of the environment.

Recommended.—**Janis Minshull**

C, P, S

494.   Newton, David E. **Fracking: A Reference Handbook.** 2d ed. Santa Barbara, Calif., ABC-CLIO, 2015. 362p. illus. index. (Contemporary World Issues). $58.00. ISBN 13: 978-1-61069-691-3; 978-1-61069-692-0 (e-book).

The Contemporary World Issues series features works on such topics as genetic engineering, GMO foods, and biodiversity. Author David E. Newton has written several of the titles in this series. In *Fracking: A Reference Handbook,* he investigates this newer process for attaining oil and gas for energy use.

Newton has a master's degree in education from the University of Michigan and an education doctorate in science education from Harvard University. As a professor, he taught sciences and mathematics. He has also authored more than 400 textbooks, encyclopedias, resource books, research manuals, laboratory manuals, trade books, and other educational materials.

Chapters begin with a black-and white-photograph. The text includes tables and lists where appropriate; tables such as Table 1.4 Petroleum Consumption (p. 36) provide clear data for researchers. Each chapter closes with a conclusion where warranted and a detailed list of print and nonprint resources that correlate to the preceding topic. A table of contents and index make it easy for users to navigate to a precise place in the book.

Starting with an overview of the subject of fracking, the text then moves into the first chapters which give background on the history and development of the gas and oil industries. Industry terminology is included in chapter one, yet would be more useful as an appendix to be easily referred to throughout the reading. By the second chapter, "Problems, Controversies and Solutions," the stage is set for the controversy that fracking has brought to the United States and other countries who use this process.

In the second half of the book, the reference aspect of this book expands with extensive resources for further research. There are biographical sketches and industry profiles, facts and data or documents, and authoritative essays which are all referenced. Charts and tables add to the informative text; specifics such as gas wells in the Marcellus Play in Pennsylvania establish facts with specific site data. Various drilling sites are included as part of this text. The plethora of hydraulic fracking and directional drilling concerns are presented, legislative remedies discussed, and the weight of independent energy sourcing versus deleterious effects on plants and animals represented.

Fracking is a complicated issue; *Fracking: A Reference Handbook* gathers a multitude of resources for further study whether on the social, political, environmental, economic, or health angle of this practice of expelling oil and gas from the ground. This is definitely a starting point for academic fracking research for high school and college students, scholars, and general readers such as legislators and activists who are seeking a collection of resources for further study. Recommended.—**Janis Minshull**

37 Transportation

General Works

C

495. **Handbook on Transport and Development.** Robin Hickman, Moshe Givoni, David Bonilla, and David Banister, eds. Northampton, Mass., Edward Elgar, 2015. 698p. index. $335.00. ISBN 13: 978-0-85793-725-4; 978-0-85793-726-1 (e-book).

This work contains 45 chapters, each devoted to analyzing current and emerging thinking among an international group of scholars about the relationships between transportation planning and development. Part one of the book is a brief introduction that reviews the topic of urban planning and travel and outlines the contents of the book. The remaining chapters are organized into four themes. Part two consists of chapters that focus on the built environment and movement of people, including the social, economic, spatial, cultural, demographic, and other variables that influence travel. For example, Xinyu (Jason) Cao uses a case study of Northern California to investigate attitude-related "self-selection" and travel behavior. Part three includes 16 chapters that examine the spatial dimensions of investments in transportation. Essays include analysis of freight distribution as an economic driver, high-speed trains as contributors to inter- and intraregional inequalities, and the impact of cargo and passenger air transport on global commerce. Many of the chapters in this section include important historical analysis that grounds their assumptions about the linkages among economies and the spatial distribution of modes of transportation. The 14 chapters in part four explore broader themes of analysis from a multidisciplinary social and cultural perspective, focusing on nonphysical dimensions of mobility and the influence of technology on travel. The book concludes with a summary chapter that reviews important advances in understanding transport and development and suggests new avenues of research. Chapters include notes, references, and a variety of nontextual elements. Considered collectively, this handbook provides a thorough, multidisciplinary examination of transport and development and is highly recommended for advanced students, scholars, and practitioner researchers who seek to understand these issues.—**Robert V. Labaree**

C, P, S

496. **Urban Transportation Innovations Worldwide.** Roger L. Kemp and Carl J. Stephani, eds. Jefferson, N.C., McFarland, 2015. 252p. index. $39.95pa. ISBN 13: 978-0-7864-7075-4; 978-1-4766-1827-2 (e-book).

Urban transportation planning has never been more exciting, and more important. As populations have swelled, planners are both embracing ideas from the past in developing more pedestrian and bicycle-friendly avenues and considering the future with advanced technologies, renewable resources, and alternative fuels and designs. This book presents an array of best practices from communities outside the United States which highlight the ability to meld the simplicity of the past with the promise of the future and ultimately devise the best transportation solutions for their citizens.

The book divides its information into three sections which focus on the general topic of urban transportation planning, specific case studies of successful planning from cities around the world, and the great potential of urban transportation planning as it faces a rapidly evolving future.

Chapters in International Transportation Planning point to many of the issues driving urban transportation planning today, e.g., restoring natural environments, reducing dependence on fossil fuels, reducing traffic congestion, and more. The second and largest section—The Best Practices—shares over 35 case studies from diverse global communities which creatively address many of the issues raised in the first section. For example, readers learn how Copenhagen, Denmark, employed a 10-step program to make its city center safer, cleaner, more pedestrian-friendly, and more aesthetically pleasing. Readers also learn how Nagano, Japan, applies the Intelligent Transportation Systems (ITS) technology to traffic management and trip planning. Many more examples, from the promotion of nonmotorized transportation in Bogota, Colombia, and Monrovia, Liberia, to the redesign of public spaces in London, England, are showcased.

The Future speaks more generally to the need to meet tomorrow's demands. Topics discussed include improving current transportation services, adapting roadways to new uses, finding funding, and understanding and implementing "New Urbanism."

Appendixes offer a good variety of supplemental information, including a periodicals bibliography, glossary, list of acronyms and abbreviations, and several resource directories.—**ARBA Staff Reviewer**

Author/Title Index

Reference is to entry number.

Subject Index

Reference is to entry number.

Practical strategies for academic lib
managers, 191

COMEDIANS
100 greatest silent film comedians, 404

COMIC BOOKS
Comic bk db [Website], 395

COMPUTER SCIENCE
InfoSci-computer sci & info tech
[Website], 476

CONDUCTING
Dictionary for the modern conductor, 381

**CONFEDERATE STATES OF
AMERICA. NAVY**
Civil War biogs from the western waters,
258

CONSTITUTIONAL LAW
Encyclopedia of constitutional
amendments, proposed amendments &
amending issues, 1789-2015, 4th ed,
278
US constitutional law [Website], 169

CONSTRUCTION INDUSTRY
Careers in building construction, 51

CONSUMER BEHAVIOR
Real-world decision making, 44

COSTA RICA
Photo gd to birds of Costa Rica, 443

COUNSELING
SAGE ency of theory in counseling &
psychotherapy, 290

CRICKET
Cricker [Website], 303

CRIME
Abuse, 288
Crime in the US 2015, 9th ed, 173
Hate crimes, 3d ed, 172
Research hndbk on intl financial crime,
182

CRIMINAL JUSTICE
Encyclopedia of criminal justice ethics,
171

Exploring & understanding careers in
criminal justice, 175

CUBAN MISSILE CRISIS, 1962
Defining moments: the Cuban Missile
Crisis, 130

CULTURAL STUDIES. *See also*
ETHNIC STUDIES
SAGE ency of African cultural heritage in
N America, 80

CULTURE CONFLICTS
Encyclopedia of modern ethnic conflicts,
2d ed, 261

CULTURES
Statesman's yrbk 2015, 20

DANTE ALIGHIERI, 1265-1321
Dartmouth Dante project [Website], 378

DEATH
Coffin hardware in 19th-century America,
78

DEMOGRAPHICS
County & city extra, 315
Patterns of economic change by state &
area, 3d ed, 316
Profiles of America, 3d ed, 317
State profiles, 6th ed, 318

DESCARTES, RENÉ, 1596-1650
Historical dict of Descartes & Cartesian
philosophy, 407

DESIGN
Bloomsbury ency of design, 349

DIGITAL PRESERVATION
Queers online, 217

DISASTERS
Great Chicago fire & the web of memory
[Website], 129
Technology disaster response & recovery,
224
U*X*L doomed, 421

DISEASES
Centers for disease control & prevention
[Website], 457

WHISTLE BLOWING - LAW AND LEGISLATION

WILD FLOWERS

WOMEN

WOMEN AND WAR

WOMEN NOBEL PRIZE WINNERS

WOMEN'S RIGHTS

WOMEN'S STUDIES

WORLD CUP (SOCCER)

WORLD HISTORY. *See also* **ANCIENT HISTORY; CIVILIZATION – ANCIENT; CIVILIZATION – CLASSICAL**